D1555550

FUJIMORI'S PERU

PITT LATIN AMERICAN SERIES

George Reid Andrews, General Editor

Catherine M. Conaghan and
Jorge I. Domínguez, Associate Editors

FUJIMORI'S PERU

Deception in the Public Sphere

Catherine M. Conaghan

UNIVERSITY OF PITTSBURGH PRESS

Published by the University of Pittsburgh Press, Pittsburgh, PA 15260

Copyright © 2005, University of Pittsburgh Press

Manufactured in the United States of America

Printed on acid-free paper

10 9 8 7 6 5 4 3 2 1

ISBN 0-8229-4259-3

Library of Congress Cataloging-in-Publication Data

Conaghan, Catherine M.
   Fujimori's Peru : deception in the public sphere / Catherine M. Conaghan
      p. cm. — (Pitt Latin American series)
   Includes bibliographical references and index.
   ISBN 0-8229-4259-3 (hardcover : alk. paper)
      1. Fujimori, Alberto. 2. Peru—Politics and government—1980– 3. Political
corruption—Peru—History—20th century. I. Title. II. Series.
   F3448.4.F85C66 2005
   985.06'4'092—dc22
                                                2005004967

To the memory of James F. Conaghan

CONTENTS

ACKNOWLEDGMENTS

The Fujimori era was never dull. I had the opportunity to witness firsthand many of the events described in this book. I was equally fortunate to draw on the expertise of a great community of scholars, journalists, and activists as I tried to understand those tumultuous times. My thanks go to all the wonderful scholars and writers cited in this book whose work made my own possible, especially to my fellow *fujimorólogos*. All of us greatly miss our friend and prolific writer, Pedro Planas.

The original inspiration for the book came in my conversations with Carlos Bustamante Baldeón, a veteran journalist who introduced to me to the complex, colorful world of the Peruvian media. Julio Carrión shared his scholarship on public opinion, his friendship, and his considerable talents in the art of translation. I was privileged to share editorial duties with Carlos and Julio in what was our labor of love, Peru Election 2000, a Web site supported by the Center for the Study of Democracy of Queen's University that tracked the saga of the 2000 *re-re-elección*. Paul Haslam was our very able and resourceful assistant editor.

One of the highlights of this research was the time I spent with Juan Gargurevich; he generously shared his encyclopedic knowledge of Peruvian journalism and his personal library with me. Edmundo Cruz of *La República* opened his voluminous newspaper files and told me fascinating stories of his search for the truth. Many other great journalists did the same. Thanks to Joseph Tulchin at the Woodrow Wilson Center, I had the great fortune of sharing an office and thinking out loud with one the most astute observers of the Peruvian political scene, Carlos Basombrío.

Cynthia McClintock, a valued colleague and great mentor to those of us who write on Peru, gave me great ideas on how to improve the book. Her sharp, meticulous scholarship sets the standard for us all. Phil Oxhorn offered insightful comments that helped me make the manuscript better. At different times and in different ways, Harold Mah, Marilyn Banting, Jorge Parodi, Isabel Bustamente, John Youle, and Helen Conaghan offered their wise counsel and support.

The book would not have been possible without the generous support of institutions: the Social Sciences and Humanities Research Council of Canada, the Woodrow Wilson International Center for Scholars, the Fulbright Program, the Instituto de Estudios Peruanos, the North-South Center of the University of Miami, and the Knapp Chair Program and the Department of Political Science and International Relations of the University of San Diego. The book draws on the Peru collection of the National Security Archive at George Washington University. Tamara Feinstein, the archive's director of the Peru Documentation Project, deserves great credit for her own scholarship and the contributions that she makes to the work of the rest of us.

I am grateful to Gerardo Barraza, the newspaper *Diario Oficial El Peruano*, and Thomas Crupi for the photographs used in the book and to Gregory Schmidt for lending a hand with the logistics of assembling them.

A final thanks goes to Reid Andrews and the outstanding editorial team at the University of Pittsburgh Press: Cynthia Miller, Nathan MacBrien, and Deborah Meade.

ABBREVIATIONS

AMPE	Asociación de Municipalidades del Perú
AP	Acción Popular
APRA	Alianza Popular Revolucionaria Americana
APRODEH	Asociación Pro Derechos Humanos
APRODEV	Asociación Pro Defensa de la Verdad
C90	Cambio 90
C90-NM	Cambio 90–Nueva Mayoría
CADE	Conferencia Anual de Ejecutivos
CAL	Colegio de Abogados de Lima
CCD	Congreso Constituyente Democrático
CCN	Cable Canal de Notícias
CGTP	Confederación General de Trabajadores del Perú
CNI	Central Nacional de Inteligencia
CNM	Consejo Nacional de la Magistratura
CODE	Coordinadora Democrática
COMACA	Comandantes, Mayores y Capitanes
CONFIEP	Confederación Nacional de Instituciones Empresariales
CPI	Compañía Peruana de Investigación
CPJ	Committee to Protect Journalists
CSJM	Consejo Supremo de Justicia Militar
CVR	Comisión de la Verdad y Reconciliación
DINTE	Dirección de Inteligencia de Ejército
DP	Defensoría del Pueblo
FARC	Fuerzas Armadas Revolucionarias de Colombia
FENPETROL	Federación Nacional de Trabajadores Petroleros y Afines del Perú

FIM	Frente Independiente Moralizador
FREDEMO	Frente Democrático
FRENATRACA	Frente Nacional de Trabajadores y Campesinos
JDEL	Jurado Departamental de Elecciones de Lima
JNE	Jurado Nacional de Elecciones
IDL	Instituto de Defensa Legal
IFHR	International Federation for Human Rights
IMF	International Monetary Fund
IS	Izquierda Socialista
IU	Izquierda Unida
MDI	Movimiento Democrático de Izquierda
ML	Movimiento Libertad
MOE	Misión de Observación Electoral
MRTA	Movimiento Revolucionario Tupac Amaru
NDI	National Democratic Institute
NM	Nueva Mayoría
OAS	Organization of American States
ONPE	Oficina Nacional de Procesos Electorales
POP	Peruana de Opinión Pública
PPC	Partido Popular Cristiano
PUM	Partido Unificado Mariateguista
RENIEC	Registro Nacional de Identificación y Estado Civil
SIN	Servicio de Inteligencia Nacional
SODE	Solidaridad y Democracia
TC	Tribunal Constitucional
UPP	Unión por el Perú

FUJIMORI'S PERU

THE PERMANENT COUP

THE president ran away.

Peruvians were about their usual weekend routines on Sunday morning when cabinet president Federico Salas called a press conference. With glum colleagues at his side, Salas made the awkward announcement: President Alberto Fujimori was forwarding his resignation as president of Peru from the swank New Otani Hotel in Tokyo. It was November 19, 2000.

Alberto Fujimori's long-distance resignation was the final act in a political crisis that started in September 2000 with the release of a videotape that showed Fujimori's longtime national intelligence advisor, Vladimiro Montesinos, bribing a congressman. The leak of the video set off a bizarre chain of events that starkly revealed the regime for what it was—corrupt, criminal, authoritarian. Montesinos fled Peru, leaving behind a cache of videotapes documenting the crimes that he and others had committed while in service to the president. Eventually, Fujimori followed suit, disguising his escape as a diplomatic trip abroad.

Ending his decade-long presidency from behind closed doors was a fitting conclusion for Fujimori. After all, he had run the government as a clandestine operation for years. In Fujimori's Peru, the most important decisions were always made out of public view and without regard for what Peruvians wanted. That Fujimori could not even face fellow Peruvians for a final farewell, a last hurrah, was equally telling. Fujimori once delighted in making public appearances and rubbing elbows with *el pueblo* (the people). He rode bicycles through dusty urban slums. He wrapped himself in ponchos in the sierra. No local headdress was too extravagant for the president to try on. The photo opportunities were endless.

In his last year as president, Fujimori's photographs were equally unforgettable, but for different reasons. Fujimori obsessively pursued an unprecedented third election, and it took a toll on his once-legendary popularity. On the last night of their 2000 campaign, President Fujimori and his daughter, First Lady Keiko Sofia, huddled behind plastic police shields as protesters hurled fruit and eggs—an image unimaginable five years earlier. In the months ahead, the pictures got worse. When cameras panned the scene of Fujimori's third inauguration, downtown Lima looked like a war zone, complete with clouds of tear gas and deadly fire.

Reengineering Peru

Back in 1995 there had been no flying fruit or tear gas and no reason to hide. On the evening of April 9, 1995, President Alberto Fujimori was in an expansive mood. He had just won 64 percent of the vote in his bid to serve a second term as Peru's chief executive. His political organization, Cambio 90-Nueva Mayoría (C90-NM), shared in the success. Fujimori could count on governing with an absolute majority in congress. The election victory was sweet, especially for a government that, three years earlier, had engineered a coup d'etat that obliterated the constitutional order.

Savoring the win, President Fujimori made his way through street celebrations and headed to the Hotel Crillon in downtown Lima, where the national and foreign press corps gathered. Pointing to the abysmal results of rival parties in the election, Fujimori declared that democracy based on parties was dead in Peru. He vowed never to govern with parties, including his own. Fujimori interpreted the day's election results as a sign that the public wanted an efficient, problem-solving democracy led by a president unencumbered by pesky legislators.[1] In an interview with the *Houston*

Chronicle, Fujimori offered his views on the future of democracy: "Democracy now should not include the participation of political parties. The people have learned a lot. They have said: Enough of this kind of democracy. We want democracy that is more efficient, that resolves our problems. Democracy is the will of the people—good administration, honesty, results. They don't want speeches, or to be deceived by images."[2]

Fujimori touted his vision as the "politics of anti-politics," and boasted that it was a new model for other countries where citizens were equally dissatisfied with traditional politicians. He called his government a *democracia con estilo* (democracy with style), an administration manned by selfless technocrats instead of self-serving politicians.

Alberto Fujimori's postelection ruminations may have sounded faintly familiar to Americans grown accustomed to Ross Perot and his antiparty diatribes.[3] Peruvians had heard the arguments before, too. On April 5, 1992, Fujimori had suspended the 1979 constitution, closed the national congress, and ordered a mass firing of judges and prosecutors. The military backed the measures and sent tanks cruising through the streets to show support.

The coup was the first salvo in Fujimori's effort to radically remake the political system. He justified his actions as a means to resolve Peru's economic problems and beat back violent communist guerrillas, and most Peruvians seemed to accept the rationale. In the days after the coup, the president called for a plebiscite to confirm public support. He planned to continue on as president until the next scheduled national election in 1995. Apparently, old-fashioned, one-man rule was Fujimori's idea of political reform. He pledged that the coup would not be used as a vehicle to arrange for his own reelection in 1995. It was a promise that would soon be broken.[4]

Fujimori's effort to represent his coup-based regime as new form of democracy did not go unchallenged. Rival politicians, intellectuals, and labor and community leaders believed that Fujimori was pushing Peru in the direction of authoritarianism, not democracy.[5] United States president George H. W. Bush told Fujimori that democracy had to be established or U.S. assistance would be in jeopardy. The Organization of American States (OAS) condemned the coup and threatened economic sanctions if representative democracy was not restored.

Fujimori reluctantly conceded and agreed to hold elections for a new congress that would write a new constitution. The OAS accepted the plan, which allowed Fujimori to direct his own, mostly unmonitored, political transition. The result was a new election for a constituent assembly and, subsequently, a new constitution that overturned the traditional ban on presidential reelection. In short, despite OAS and U.S. protestations, the coup had indeed opened the door for Fujimori to stay in power.

Fujimori's push to restore the appearance of political normalcy by holding elections and developing a constitution effectively quashed international criticism and removed the immediate threat of economic sanctions. But reconstructing the appearance of constitutional order did not mean that the president had changed his mind about how best to govern Peru. Fujimori's approach remained the same. He despised fellow politicians and made no bones about saying so. He liked to say that he was the "manager" of Peru, more like a Wall Street wizard beholden to no one than a mundane public official accountable to everyone.

This became the favored metaphor: Fujimori was "reengineering Peru" and his *oficialistas* (loyal officials) were managers.[6] Governing was to be a neat exercise in decision making and management, with little in the way of deliberation or consensus building. According to Fujimori, Peru's problems could be traced to the *palabrería* (excessive, useless talk) of the traditional political class and his administration would remedy that with action. The president's photo opportunities with the press were primed to produce action shots. Images showed the president handing out food, leading journalists through the jungle, and inspecting the gruesome cadavers of dead terrorists.

The disdain for *palabrería* was the central tenet of *Fujimorismo;* it permeated the culture of the administration from the cabinet to the congress. Talk did not just waste time; it was downright subversive. When opposition leaders demanded accountability from the government—explanations or investigations of conduct or policy—they ran up against a wall of silence. Government officials routinely refused to provide legislators and the press with information. They invoked national security considerations as a defense against discussing a whole range of unsettling issues, including the astronomical income of Peru's number-one appointed official, Vladimiro Montesinos.

The OAS may have forced Fujimori to remount the institutions of representative democracy, but what the OAS, the U.S. government, and other international onlookers either failed to grasp fully or blatantly chose to ignore was that leaders scornful of democratic institutions were being charged with their restoration.[7] The rebuilding of Peru's institutions was left to a president who was averse to the principles of democratic governance. Deliberation, oversight, and accountability never figured in Fujimori's agenda of reengineering Peru.

As Peruvians discovered, the aversion to talk only applied to the public speech of opponents. There was plenty of jawboning among *oficialistas*. That chatter went on in the offices of Vladimiro Montesinos, tucked behind the high walls of the national intelligence headquarters, the Servicio de Inteligencia Nacional (SIN). Under Montesinos's watch, the SIN became the regime's central command, where plots were hatched to subvert every institution for the purpose of keeping Fujimori, and by extension Montesinos, in power. Political power was not the only objective. For many insiders, especially Montesinos, unchecked political power equaled untold opportunities to amass vast personal fortunes through crime. In the Fujimori era, politics was a heady and lucrative endeavor.

A President Unleashed

One national television network promoted its coverage of Fujimori's second inauguration in 1995 by inviting viewers to witness the dawn of *democracia plena* (full democracy). The official line was that the 1995 election equaled democracy and an end to the era of coup-induced legal limbo. Fujimori's high job-approval ratings in public-opinion surveys and his success at the polls were cited as proof positive of the regime's democratic credentials.

Analysts at home and abroad were fascinated by Fujimori's apparent popularity. He was often cited as one of the new wave of leaders in Latin America that included President Fernando Collor de Mello of Brazil and President Carlos Menem of Argentina.[8] What all three leaders had in common were their neopopulist political styles and neoliberal economic programs.

Fujimori's high job-approval ratings diverted attention from one of the most important and persistent problems of his presidency. Fujimori was popular in general terms, but less so regarding the specifics of how he governed. Polls often showed widespread disapproval of many of the government's policies, especially in the realm of military, human rights, and constitutional or legal issues. Fujimori's much-touted popular support (at least as expressed in polls) frequently dissolved when it came to questions about the real political features of his regime and the conduct of government officials.

Public opinion was as troublesome as it was useful to the Fujimori government. By all accounts, Fujimori and Montesinos were obsessed, poring over surveys and focus-group studies at every opportunity. Their conundrum was one familiar to fellow politicians: figuring out how to simultaneously invoke public opinion (when it was favorable) and ignore it (when it was not). Fujimori made ample rhetorical use of public-opinion polls when they showed support for the 1992 coup or economic and counterinsurgency policies. But the same polls had to be discounted and rendered invisible when they ran counter to the administration's plans, especially on a fundamental issue like reelection. The Fujimori regime grappled permanently with the puzzle: it had to ensure that the Peruvian public (as represented in the polls) oscillated between "being and nonbeing." The public was, simultaneously, "of the utmost political importance and of no importance at all."[9]

Leaders of the political opposition were the subjects of similar prestidigitation. After the adverse international reaction to the coup, the government had to allow room for political opponents to operate because it helped to legitimate the regime. But at the same time, the administration demonized and stymied opposition leaders whenever they challenged the government.

Denial and deception became the defining features of public life in Fujimori's Peru, where contrary opinions were routinely dismissed and inconvenient facts were ignored. When all else failed, the government resorted to bald-faced lying. The C90-NM majority in congress, in both the legislatures of 1993–1995 and 1995–2000, played a critical role in mounting these elaborate games. Because civil liberties and the representative institutions stipulated by the OAS had to stay in place, *oficialistas* had to find ways to block opponents from using these tools to uncover the truth and disrupt the consolidation of the regime. Toward this end, rules and rule making in the legislature, judiciary, and other regulatory bodies had to be structured so the opposition could not use institutions as venues to debate, investigate, or lodge legal challenges to the regime.

Congress's C90-NM majority became the battering ram in what the opposition called the *"re-re-elección"*—the plan to grant President Fujimori a third consecutive term in office starting in 2000. Acting on instructions from Vladimiro Montesinos, the C90-NM legislators undertook a systematic assault on the entire system of checks and balances laid out in their own 1993 constitution. Politics became a "permanent coup"—a steady evisceration of the constitution and the rule of law.[10] No tanks were needed, thanks to the dutiful legislators of C90-NM, who readily hung a veil of legality over an inoperative constitution.

Congressman Carlos Ferrero began his career as an *oficialista,* a member of the C90-NM caucus. On election night in April 1995, an animated Ferrero joined in a televised roundtable analyzing the day's events. When asked to interpret Fujimori's stunning electoral victory that night, Ferrero breezily replied that the victory was a license for the president to *hacer lo que le da la gana* (do whatever he feels like). Ferrero's observation was far more prescient than he could have imagined that night. In fact, in the years ahead, Ferrero was shocked by Fujimori's willingness, and the willingness of those around him, to do whatever it took to pursue yet another reelection. Ferrero dissented and later abandoned the C90-NM caucus to become an acerbic opponent of Fujimori. Among *oficialistas,* Ferrero's rebellion was an aberration—but he was not alone. Many other Peruvians joined Ferrero in resisting the reelection, and by doing so, they played a critical role in the unmaking of the regime.

Authoritarianism Redux

Fujimori always liked to say that his government was unique while simultaneously insisting that it was a democracy. After the 1992 coup, Fujimori proclaimed that Peru was a "*sui generis* democracy." In the dark days following his 2000 reelection, Fujimori conceded that his country still was an "unconsolidated democracy." Whatever Peru was, Fujimori insisted that it was some kind of "democracy with adjectives," with the emphasis on "democracy."[11] Other analysts accentuated the less felicitous "adjectives." In a widely read 1997 essay in *Foreign Affairs,* Fareed Zakaria referred to Fujimori's regime together with other "illiberal" democracies—that is, governments founded in free and fair elections but faulty in the practices of constitutional liberalism.[12] Zakaria's description matched Guillermo O'Donnell's discussion about the rise of "delegative democracy" in Latin America. O'Donnell identified delegative democracy as a hyper-presidential system, characterized by few checks or balances to executive power and weak civil liberties.[13]

Where does the Fujimori regime belong in the annals of Latin American politics? In hindsight, conceding the word "democracy," even modified with adjectives, seems overly generous. Noted Peruvian analysts argued early on that the regime deserved to be regarded as authoritarian, notwithstanding the restoration of elections and institutions after the coup. As Romeo Grompone later noted, the apparent pluralism in the Fujimori regime was completely consistent with Juan Linz's classic definition of authoritarianism —no angst about the regime's "hybridity" was ever required.[14] North American author Cynthia McClintock strongly concurred. Drawing on the historical record of other civilian-led authoritarian regimes (e.g., Mexico under the PRI, the Dominican Republic under President Joaquín Balaguer), McClintock made a powerful case that the political competition and elections taking place in Peru under Fujimori should not be mistaken as proof of democracy.[15]

Fujimori undoubtedly earned his place on the list of Latin American presidents who set aside democracy and the rule of law for the purpose of staying in power. *Continuismo* (the practice by incumbents of keeping themselves in office) has a long history, and in so many ways, the Fujimori regime was dreadfully derivative. Hours after Peru's 1992 coup, neighboring Ecuadorians noted that their own populist president José María Velasco Ibarra had pioneered the *auto-golpe* (presidential-led coup) back in 1970 when he shut down the congress and governed by decree. In historical terms, Fujimori's successive reelections were hardly groundbreaking. Peruvians constantly compared Fujimori with President Augusto Leguía, the other Peruvian president who tried his hand at three terms in office from 1919 to 1930. Leguía insisted that he was creating a new political order, a *Patria Nueva* (New Country).

Fujimori's unchecked ambition was unoriginal, and so were his ideas about creating a new type of democracy rooted in technocratic values and public works. Since the nineteenth century, Latin American politicians had dreamed of a technocratic utopia. From Porfírio Díaz in Mexico to Juan Perón in Argentina, dictators hitched their wagons to public works and professed their love of technocracy.[16] The similarities between Fujimori and other dictators are hard to miss. For example, General Marcos Pérez Jiménez, the president-dictator of Venezuela from 1950 to 1958, was described this way by Fernando Coronil: "Pérez Jiménez derided politics and its language of deceit which only betrayed the people's interests. He offered instead material benefits. In return for which he asked for the acceptance of his authority as leader of the nation. Democracy was now to be judged by its deeds and practical accomplishments rather than by its origins or methods."[17]

Fujimori and the history of his regime readily evoke Latin America's past.[18] Analyzing the Fujimori regime solely through a lens of comparison with previous dictatorships, however, risks losing sight of today's particular mix of dilemmas in the region. Fujimori's regime evolved under internal and external conditions distinct from those that had prevailed in heyday of Latin America's tyrants during the 1950s and 1960s. When the 1952 election in Venezuela failed to produce a real victory for General Marcos Pérez Jiménez at the ballot boxes, the election was simply voided with a *golpecito* (little coup) that was tacitly approved by the U.S. ambassador.[19]

Fujimori executed the 1992 coup so that he could govern with complete dictatorial powers. But Fujimori's coup stopped short of morphing into Venezuela's *golpecito*. There was no automatic wink and nod from the U.S. ambassador. Instead, President George H. W. Bush telephoned to say, disapprovingly, that Peru had to return to the fold of democracy.[20] The OAS delivered the same message and urged Fujimori to restore representative democracy quickly.

The international reaction had a counterpart at home. While most Peruvians originally supported the coup, they also wanted new elections and a congress. Fujimori ceded to the demands to restore representative democracy, but the underlying antidemocratic values that inspired the coup remained. For the rest of the life of the regime, the objective was subterfuge: disguising authoritarianism as something else, something that could, at a minimum, be sold to Peruvians and the international community as a democracy. What emerged was not a democracy but a regime closer to the "competitive authoritarianism" described by Steven Levitsky and Lucan Way—that is, a regime that opened "arenas of contestation" to opposition forces, then structured ways to render them irrelevant.[21]

In the new international environment of the 1990s, the task of creating democratic forms devoid of substance was not always easy. Holding evidently rigged elections or holding elections while the opposition was in jail and the press was censored would not pass muster with international allies and would put Peru on a list of pariah nations. The situation was a far cry from the 1950s, when the United States unhesitatingly embraced dictators as long as they sported solid anticommunist credentials. With the Cold War over, dealing with the United States was complicated by new imperatives. Now relations were shaped by a new and often ill-defined "conditionality," which revolved around democracy, drugs, and neoliberal economic reforms. The U.S. government expected Latin American countries to be democracies, to join in a hemispheric war on narco-trafficking, and to implement neoliberal economic reforms.[22]

The Fujimori government manipulated these expectations for its own purposes. Fujimori never lost an opportunity to trumpet his government's achievements in economic reforms, counterterrorism, and counternarcotics policies—calculating that good behavior in those areas would tamp down criticism from the U.S. government. To a great extent, the calculation was correct, but the problem of Peru's political structure could not be cast aside completely. So Fujimori set about to restore representative democracy in order to win international acceptance, while preserving the powers he had usurped through the coup.

This type of restoration—one that could be marketed as credible by 1990s standards, but in essence was not—had two faces. First, the institutional side of democracy would have to be resurrected, and those institutions would have to be seen as meeting at least the minimum international standards for a democratic system. For example, Fujimori could not be elected president for life, since such a move would clearly have provoked condemnation both at home and abroad. There would have to be periodic elections, a legislature, a constitution laying out the framework of intergovernmental relations, and so on. Once these democratic institutions were established, however, subverting them, through practices that could be represented as normal politics, became the government's goal. Congress served as the linchpin of this strategy.

The other side of the restoration required creating the appearance of a public sphere normally associated with modern democracy while ensuring that it would not work properly. In other words, all the processes and institutions associated with public deliberation and the formation of public opinion, especially the media, had to look like they were functioning in standard democratic fashion. When opinions circulating in this sphere were useful for legitimating the regime, then they were welcome; when opinions ran against the regime, they had to be stripped of all significance. The challenging task of overseeing this oscillation—the being and nonbeing of the public sphere—ultimately fell to Fujimori's right-hand man, Vladimiro Montesinos.[23]

Disabling the Public Sphere

In contemporary democracy, political talk matters. Policy forums, radio call-in shows, opinion polls, town hall meetings, rallies, online chats, letters to the editor, and lobbying congress—all of these are part of the political communications that link society to the state in a democracy. The media play a central role in organizing and telling us about the political talk that goes on in a democracy. Broadly speaking, we can think of the public sphere as encompassing both the processes involved in political communication (deliberation on issues and expression of opinion) and the sites where those processes take place (the media, organizations in civil society, etc.).[24]

By definition, a democracy is a political system that allows political talk to take place in a relatively untrammeled way—that is, civil liberties provide people with the ability to express views that run contrary to majority opinion or the views of government incumbents. In the language of democratic theorist Robert Dahl, there is an expectation that the political preferences expressed in a democratic public sphere are "freely formed."

Political talk in a democracy is open and unpredictable, something more than propaganda or the recitation of a dominant ideology. This is not to argue that the modern public sphere comes close to approximating the ideal type of public sphere described by Jürgen Habermas in his classic book on the subject, *The Structural Transformation of the Public Sphere.*[25] In that work, Habermas located the origins of the liberal public sphere in eighteenth-century Europe—in the salons, coffeehouses, and clubs where members of the emergent "reading public" gathered to discuss the political news of the day. Habermas idealized the early public sphere as a realm of political communication marked by a deliberation among equals, where rational argument prevailed.

Historians have dedicated enormous time and energy to debating Habermas's interpretation of the early public sphere; these debates will not be reviewed here.[26] Whatever the problems in Habermas's interpretation of European history, his views on how the contemporary public sphere operates are much less sanguine. In contemporary democracies, political communication is dominated by the electronic mass media and shaped by corporate capitalism. In Habermas's words, the public sphere is always "power-infiltrated" and as such, constantly subject to distortion and elite manipulation.

Nonetheless, even relentless and sophisticated efforts to control the public sphere are never quite successful. People excluded from the public sphere find ways of being heard. Poor people, minorities, and dissidents of all sorts form their own communicative networks. They constitute "counter publics" and create counter-public spheres that push the boundaries of dominant political discourse, sometimes transforming the mainstream in the process.[27] Habermas refers to the communication that takes place in the media and in the organizations of civil society as an unregulated "wild complex," a periphery lying outside the administrative core of the state that supplies the opinions that become the raw materials for public policymaking.[28]

What makes the public sphere something more than a realm of idle talk is its relation to the state. In democratic systems, the opinions that emerge in this "wild complex" can and do, under certain circumstances, influence decision makers inside the state. The existence of civil society per se does not ensure that the public sphere is influential; what makes for an influential public sphere is the connection between political talk and institutional responses by the state.[29]

Legislatures play a crucial role in connecting the public sphere to the state. This is because legislatures are both deliberative and decision-making bodies. Legislators project themselves as representatives of the public and, in the course of making decisions in the public's name, they are obliged to debate and make their arguments about issues known. Parliamentary bodies are the "public sphere inside the state."[30] As such, a legislature is the entity most immediately attuned to the ebb and flow of ideas in the public sphere and its own agenda is shaped by that interaction. Since legislators speak and act primarily in public (in hearings or in debates on the floor, for example), they are natural targets for media attention and scrutiny.

As poll after poll indicated, Peruvians wanted all the normal features found in a modern democracy—elections, civil liberties, functioning institutions. The public's desire for democratic normalcy, however, clashed profoundly with what was required to reproduce the regime founded in the 1992 coup. For those in power, staying in power meant making institutions and the public sphere amenable to their project, no matter how this was accomplished.

Leaders in democratic systems routinely try to manipulate public opinion. The American political system is an example par excellence; politicians and lobbyists can conjure up public support using methods and techniques that are staggering in their sophistication and their cost.[31] The practices of the Fujimori government veered far from the accepted practices of spin found in contemporary democratic politics. Using the intelligence agency as his center for operations, Montesinos mounted an elaborate system to commandeer institutions and the public sphere through corruption. He paid off everyone who mattered—legislators, judges, bureaucrats, businessmen, executives, and entertainers. In doing so, he created a demimonde dedicated to doing whatever was necessary to reproduce the regime.

How and why so many people succumbed to Montesinos's temptations is one of the dark puzzles of the Fujimori era. But not everyone was prepared to conspire. The history of the Fujimori presidency is a chronicle of wrongdoing and complicity, but it is also a story about resistance and the limits of deception in modern politics. Because Peru's public sphere maintained some of its qualities as a "wild complex," the efforts to manipulate it eventually became more apparent and heavy-handed. The more government officials tampered with what was supposed to be the free flow of ideas and expressions, the more they inadvertently exposed the ills they were trying to cover up—and the more Peruvians got mad.

The Reelection Obsession

After the 1992 coup, the essential problem for Fujimori and his inner circle was this: how could the regime be maintained until 1995 (the original date for the end of Fujimori's term) and then beyond? There were no obvious candidates to succeed Fujimori in 1995 or 2000. No Eva Perón or Hector Trujillo waited in the wings; there was no pliable relative, no surrogate for Fujimori who was electable and who could be trusted to act as a guarantor of the regime. No matter what Fujimori's own personal wishes originally may have been on the subject, his reelection became the means to maintain the regime.

Securing reelection (in its 1995 and 2000 incarnations) was an ambitious political project. The idea of reelection had to be framed as a normal exercise in democratic politics rather than as a retrograde reversion to *continuismo*. For the 1995 race, reelection required a significant constitutional overhaul; for 2000, even more elaborate legal circumlocutions had to be mounted. In both cases, congress was the indispensable actor in laying the legal groundwork for reelection, thus special care had to be taken to ensure the legislature's reliability as a partner in the project.

Constructing the requisite legal cover was essential to the reelection project, and it had wide-ranging consequences. The drive for reelection shaped public policy, intergovernmental relations, political rhetoric, ethics, military affairs, and the conduct of the media. In terms of Peru's political development, the pursuit of the 2000 reelection was the political equivalent of a cluster bomb; its destructive effects spewed out across the entire landscape of state and society.

Fujimori and his administration officials reveled in representing what they were doing as a refreshing new departure, referred to as a *cambio de rumbo* (change of course, in the words of Finance Minister Carlos Boloña). Fujimori was changing history, but his changes did not take place on a tabula rasa. He was beholden to Peru's history in ways that he and his associates were always loath to acknowledge. The traditional practices that are part and parcel of the other "institutionalization" in Latin American politics—clientelism and corruption—were the keys to reproducing the regime.[32] The weaknesses in Peru's public sphere and the lack of government accountability were not invented during the Fujimori era. Peru's political development had long suffered from these problems. Fujimori and Montesinos were not the first to corrupt Peruvian politics, but they took the practice to a new level, unprecedented in its systemization and scope.

In the course of taking old ways to new extremes, Fujimori and Montesinos changed Peru's history for the worse, fusing criminality and authoritarianism in their own peculiar way. That symbiosis and the struggle against it are the subjects of this book.

2

FUJIMORI MEETS THE PRESS

WHEN Alberto Fujimori became president of Peru in 1990, it was great copy—the kind of story that journalists love. Fujimori was the son of Japanese immigrants, a man who seemingly came out of nowhere to up-stage and upset Peru's world-renowned writer, Mario Vargas Llosa, in his bid for the presidency. It was, as many observers noted, a tale worthy of a Vargas Llosa novel.

Alberto Fujimori reveled in his newfound celebrity. But like most politi-cians, he had a love-hate relationship with the media. Fujimori was happi-est when surrounded by friendly, female television correspondents. Derided as geishas by their colleagues, the women journalists were later discovered to have received money in exchange for their bootlicking.[1] Fujimori had little use for the more hard-nosed reporters in the press corps, preferring to keep them at arm's length.

In his first two years as president, Fujimori navigated the channels of Peru's public sphere in a style reminiscent of Peru's previous presidents. All of them had, in their own way, used a carrot-and-stick approach in their dealings with the press, and Fujimori was no different at first. Fujimori charmed and selectively co-opted some reporters and their bosses, while others were conspicuously left out of the loop, even barred from the presidential aircraft. When backslapping and blackballing failed, other sorts of informal pressures and threats of legal action could be brought to bear.

Throughout its long and complicated history, the Peruvian press had never functioned as a consistent and effective watchdog on government, despite the efforts of some scrappy reporters and hard-nosed editors to make it so.[2] More often than not, the press was regarded as a partisan player or as a pawn in the service of powerful interests. Like previous governments, the new Fujimori administration readily exploited the media's existing weaknesses; as time went on, many members of the media establishment embraced the president and reaped the rewards.

Man from Nowhere

It took some time for the media to take notice of Alberto Fujimori. Until his surprising surge in the polls just a month before the first round of the presidential election in April 1990, Fujimori was a nonentity. The media darling of the 1990 race was Mario Vargas Llosa, the urbane, internationally acclaimed author. His long list of works includes such novels as *Conversations in the Cathedral, Aunt Julia and the Scriptwriter,* and *War at the End of the World.* Vargas Llosa's meteoric rise to political stardom was a story all its own, one that began when he led mass protests to block President Alan Garciá's ill-advised plan for a state takeover of banks in 1987.

In comparison to the pack of veteran politicians ready to take on Vargas Llosa in 1990, Fujimori was a neophyte. He had never run for office before. After earning a master's degree in mathematics from the University of Wisconsin at Milwaukee, Fujimori became a professor and then the rector of Universidad Nacional Agraria La Molina in Lima, an agricultural school. In 1987 he was elected to head the organization of university rectors, Asamblea Nacional de Rectores.[3]

At first glance, Fujimori appeared to be a classic political outsider, the "man from nowhere" as the *Economist* called him. Others referred to Fujimori's amazing political debut as a tsunami. But Fujimori's career ascent was more complicated, and it was by no means a vault from total obscurity. Fujimori had spent years cultivating his connections with the ruling party, Alianza Revolucionaria Popular Americana (APRA), and President Alan

García. That relationship prompted García to offer Fujimori a job as host on a weekly public affairs program on state-run television in 1988. The show was called *Concertando* (Getting Together). Fujimori was a low-key host and his ratings in Lima were disappointing but, because the show ran on the state-owned network, Fujimori garnered a nationwide audience.[4]

Fujimori launched his 1990 presidential bid in conjunction with his campaign for a senate seat. At the time, Peru's election law permitted candidates to run for both offices simultaneously. Running for president was generally thought to boost a candidate's notoriety, thus making it easier to win the congressional seat. Spending moderately on political advertising in the first round, Fujimori used grassroots networks, especially evangelical religious groups and his university contacts from La Molina, to build an organization. Fifty of the 240 congressional candidates fielded by Fujimori's organization Cambio 90 (C90) were evangelical church members.[5] One of his two vice-presidential running mates, Carlos García, was an evangelical minister.

Fujimori's campaign was short on specifics, but chock-full of symbols and slogans. In contrast to Mario Vargas Llosa, who boldly called on Peruvians to embrace austerity and neoliberal economic reforms, Fujimori promised "honor, jobs, and technology." At campaign appearances, he drove a tractor (dubbed the Fuji-mobile) to show his commitment to developing agriculture and improving the plight of the rural poor. Fujimori called himself *El Chino* and exhorted voters to elect "A President Like You."[6] The slogan was an obvious reference to the fact that Fujimori was, like the majority of his countrymen, not a member of Peru's white upper class. He artfully played on his Japanese ancestry, tapping into the traditional stereotype of the Japanese as hardworking and efficient and the hopes that his presidency would attract significant foreign aid and new investment from Japan.[7] On the campaign trail, the differences between Fujimori and Vargas Llosa were plain to see. Fujimori was at ease in his role as "man of the people"— riding a bicycle, wearing a poncho, speaking his folksy and ungrammatical Spanish. In contrast, Vargas Llosa looked like an envoy from the upper class. He arrived at events in an armor-plated Volvo, surrounded by bodyguards, and appeared to suffer through the long programs of speeches and folklore.[8]

Fujimori's appeal was understandable. He offered simple, direct, and optimistic messages to a nation in need of hope. Peru in 1990 was a country teetering on the verge of breakdown. The economy was reeling from the failed heterodox policies of President Alan García and international debt. In the years 1989 and 1990, annual inflation rates topped 3,000 percent and 7,000 percent, respectively.[9] Consumer purchasing power plummeted, unemployment soared, and government revenues plunged.

As bad as it was, the economy was not the only source of Peru's woes. Equally stunning was the failure of two successive civilian governments to win the war against the Marxist-Leninist guerrilla movement, Sendero Luminoso. After nearly ten years of conflict, Sendero had not been beaten back by security forces. On the contrary, Sendero was on the move, plunging Peru into a nationwide war and terrifying residents of the nation's capital with daily acts of violence. By the end of the 1980s, 40 percent of Peru's territory had been declared to be "emergency zones" under the administrative control of the armed forces. Between 1980 and 1990, the number of people dead or missing in the conflict totaled more than fourteen thousand. Economic losses were estimated in the billions.[10]

Facing war and economic collapse, Peruvian voters were desperate for a change. As Fujimori's campaign gathered steam, other candidates faltered. Vargas Llosa's center-right coalition alienated voters with lavish spending and saturation advertising. The APRA candidate, Luis Alva Castro, suffered by virtue of his association with outgoing President Alan García. On the left, voters were divided as the Izquierda Unida (IU) coalition split into separate wings, further damaging the prospects for a win by its principal leader, Alfonso Barrantes, who ran a sluggish campaign.[11]

Desperate to defeat Vargas Llosa, a man who had caused him so much grief in 1987, President García looked for an alternative. He found one in the man whom he had put on public television. Fujimori was inching up in the polls and García decided to help him along. He arranged some clandestine support for the Fujimori campaign. Fujimori got access to the government's own tracking polls done at the SIN and began showing up on television programs in the weeks just prior to the first round.[12]

No longer an unknown, Fujimori won 24.6 percent of the vote in the first round of the presidential election, less than three percentage points behind Vargas Llosa, who took 27.6 percent of the vote. The APRA candidate, Luis Alva Castro, trailed with 19 percent. Fujimori's affinity with lower-class voters was evident in the results; he won strong pluralities in Lima's shantytowns and in working-class neighborhoods. In contrast, Vargas Llosa's strongest showings were in voting districts where the upper and middle classes resided. Fujimori's strong second place not only assured him a spot in the second-round runoff, it turned him into the presumptive winner. Vargas Llosa, unambiguously positioned on the center-right of the political spectrum, was unlikely to attract voters from APRA and the left in the second round.

Even with Fujimori poised to win, the second round was a bitter slugfest. Both sides traded fierce personal insults. Fujimori feared that the muckraking might turn up something damaging. Rumors surfaced about his possible involvement in tax fraud, irregularities in a land deal, sexual harassment cases at his university, and even falsification of his birth records.[13] It was at this point that Fujimori began his long, fateful association with Vladimiro Montesinos, an attorney known for his shadowy connections to Peru's underworld, the SIN, and the CIA. Montesinos's checkered career, including his dishonorable expulsion from the military, was public knowledge; it was the subject of a 1983 exposé in *Caretas* magazine.[14] It didn't seem to matter, since Montesinos's particular kind of expertise was exactly what Fujimori needed. Montesinos quickly became Fujimori's "fixer" and principal campaign strategist. He made sure that there was no paper trail connecting Fujimori to anything unsavory.

Media owners unabashedly joined in the fray of the second round. They openly endorsed either Fujimori or Vargas Llosa and gave journalists the green light to tilt their coverage on behalf of the favored candidate. Openly allied with Fujimori were the APRA-controlled newspapers *Pagina Libre* and *La Crónica* and the left-leaning *La República*. Television station Channel 5 (Panamericana Televisión), under the control of Hector Delgado Parker, a longtime friend of Alan García, was also in the Fujimori camp.

Siding with Vargas Llosa were the newspapers *Expreso, El Comercio,* and *Ojo* along with the magazine *Oiga*. Channel 4 (América Televisión), controlled by a group of bankers, was a staunch ally. Jaime Bayly and César Hidelbrandt, the journalist-commentator stars of Channel 4, weighed in heavily for Vargas Llosa. Both hosted current affairs programs. In his memoir, Vargas Llosa recalled how César Hidelbrandt turned his show *En Persona* into a weekly attack on Fujimori: ". . . Hidelbrandt took it upon himself as a moral duty to do whatever was in his power to prevent what he called 'the leap into the dark,' for it seemed to him that a victory at the polls by someone who combined improvisation with cunning, plus a lack of scruples, could be like the final, fatal kick for a country which the politics of the last few years had left in ruins and more divided and violent than ever before in its history. Each Sunday 'En Persona' presented both more and more attestations and the most severe denunciations concerning Fujimori's personal business deals—whether open and aboveboard or suspect —together with his hidden ties to Alan García and his authoritarian and manipulative character, of which he had shown signs during his term in office as rector of the National Agrarian University of La Molina."[15]

Despite the negative campaign, there was no stopping Fujimori. He trounced Vargas Llosa in the second round, winning 62.5 percent of the vote to Vargas Llosa's 37.5 percent. Dispirited after his defeat, Vargas Llosa headed for Spain to resume his life as a writer. Preparing for his first term, Fujimori sought counsel from Montesinos and began laying the foundations of a hermetic presidency, intent on keeping pundits and snoopy reporters at bay.

The Press and Its Public

Peru's journalists openly acknowledged that their coverage of the 1990 election was biased and politicized and carried out with the blessings of media owners.[16] Some journalists regretted their partisan reporting, but many others did not. Among the unrepentant was César Hidelbrandt. He believed that his responsibilities as a citizen far outweighed concerns about journalistic neutrality. In his view, Peru was on the brink of disaster and electing Vargas Llosa was perhaps the last, best chance to restore order and build democracy. Hidelbrandt thought Fujimori to be an untested and unpredictable "tornado," tied to President Alan García.[17]

In the annals of Peruvian journalism, the highly charged 1990 coverage was extreme, but the tradition of mixing opinion and reporting was nothing new. The paradigm of impartiality and neutrality, so pivotal to the development of North American journalism, was never fully embraced in the Peruvian media. "Opinion" journalism, rooted in the Spanish intellectual tradition, remained an important, competing current in the Peruvian press.[18]

Throughout the twentieth century, the opinions expressed in Peruvian journalism served an array of ideological and class interests. Newspapers were sometimes founded as a soapbox for political groups, like APRA's *La*

Tribuna of the 1930s or the Izquierda Unida–leaning *Diario de la Marka* of the early 1980s. By the 1950s and 1960s, the pillars of Peru's newspaper establishment (*El Comercio, La Prensa, La Crónica, Correo,* and *Expreso*) were in the hands of elite families or cliques that used them to champion their political views and economic interests.[19] When the leftist military regime of General Juan Velasco came to power through a coup in 1968, the unambiguous identification of the media with the country's dominant economic groups made the industry an obvious target for reformers. One by one, the government took over newspapers and mandated a forced transfer of stocks in radio and television stations to the state.[20] Peru's newsmagazines, *Caretas* and *Oiga,* escaped confiscation, but *Caretas* editor Enrique Zileri was deported.[21]

The quality of journalism was damaged immeasurably during the military interregnum as most of the media were forced to toe the official line. The end of military rule in 1980 and the return of civilian government set the stage for a revival in Peruvian media. President Fernando Belaúnde immediately revoked government control over the media and returned the confiscated outlets to their original owners. For the newspaper industry, market conditions had improved. Rapid urbanization and rising literacy rates enlarged the pool of potential consumers, especially in Lima. In the early 1980s, the leftist *Marka* enjoyed daily circulation in excess of one hundred thousand copies. Relying heavily on crime reporting and sensational photographs, the legendary journalist and editor Guillermo Thorndike turned the tabloid *La República* into a sales leader in the second half of the 1980s.[22]

The boom in print journalism was, however, relatively short-lived. Throughout the 1980s, television and radio audiences expanded rapidly, and entrepreneurs and advertisers took notice. Most Peruvians were turning to the broadcast media, not newspapers, for news and entertainment.[23] By the end of the decade, Lima television viewers could choose from six privately owned television stations and the state-run Radio Televisión Peruana.

As television eroded interest in the print media, a severe economic crisis depressed consumer purchasing power. Newspapers felt the impact as circulation dramatically declined at the end of the 1980s and in the early 1990s. *El Comercio,* the newspaper that enjoyed a broader readership, nationwide distribution, and a near-stranglehold over the classified advertising market, weathered the storm. So did *La República* and *Expreso,* but other newspapers went bankrupt, most notably *La Prensa.*[24]

In search of customers, publishers tried new products and marketing strategies. A new generation of cheap, sensationalist tabloids, the so-called *prensa chicha,* made their way onto newsstands.[25] Offering abundant coverage of sports, crime, and the latest gossip about popular showgirls (and their nude photos), the tabloids typically featured little political coverage. When politics was mentioned, the focus was usually on corruption cases and the personal woes of politicians. Taking a cue from the tabloids, the mainstream press intensified its promotional schemes and turned to prize drawings, games, and special weekly "collectibles," which ranged from maps to recipe files to sex education manuals. Publishers also turned their sights on smaller audiences with specialized interests. The newspaper *Gestión,* marketed as a Peruvian-style *Wall Street Journal,* became a staple in corporate and government circles even though its general circulation was limited.

Despite innovations in marketing, the newspaper and magazine business in Peru still struggled with limited readership and stagnating sales in the 1990s. Not surprisingly, consumption patterns were skewed according to income. In a 1994 survey, less than one-third of low-income people reported reading newspapers, while close to 50 percent of the middle class and more than 60 percent of the upper class did.[26] Low-income readers almost exclusively constituted the market for the cheap and lurid *prensa chicha,* while middle- and upper-class readers gravitated to the mainstream papers and were the major purchasers of pricey magazines.

For the most part, Peru's print media mirrored the country's social fragmentation, class distinctions, and political divides. A majority of Peruvians, by virtue of being impoverished or ill-educated or both, had almost no relationship to the world of print. Among those who did, understandings of the world varied greatly. Readers on the left viewed politics through the lens of *La República,* while businessmen turned to the sober, more conservative *Gestión.* The blunt association between particular outlets and political or economic groups always made it easier for politicians to avoid being held accountable. They readily dismissed newspapers and magazines as partisan and self-interested when they reported negative stories, and took comfort in the fact that most Peruvians would never actually read the publications.

Still, the relatively small size of the reading public did not mean that news generated in print was blocked from mass consumption. As the sway of broadcast media grew, so did the synergy between print and broadcast journalism. By the 1990s, all of the major newspapers were morning editions, so their coverage influenced the topics and discussions on popular morning television programs like *Buenos Días Perú* and the highly rated news and interview shows on the popular radio station Radio Programas.

Peru's print and broadcast outlets played a critical role in transforming how politicians and the public viewed themselves. The media turned public-opinion polls into a fixture in political life. Starting during the transition from military rule in 1978, *El Comercio* and *Caretas* were among the first news organizations to feature polls as a regular feature in their political coverage. Television stations quickly followed their lead and also began commissioning political polls. A small collection of privately owned firms, originally specializing in commercial market research, became the primary providers of polls.[27] At the beginning, political polls focused mostly on predicting election outcomes, although *Caretas* did add presidential approval ratings to its reporting on President Fernando Belaúnde. By the 1990s, presidential approval ratings were a staple in political discussions, and no one was more interested in the topic than President Fujimori.

Fear and Loathing, Continued

Presidents and the press in Peru share a long history of antagonism and anxiety. As one historian observed, "Governments fear the press and the press fear governments and the authorities."[28] Throughout the twentieth century, governments acted on that fear, deporting editors and shutting down offending outlets. Every Peruvian constitution nominally guaranteed freedom of the press, and virtually every government in the twentieth century enacted legal statutes aimed at circumscribing that freedom.

While the end of the military government's control over the media in 1980 offered hope for a new era in journalism, those prospects were quickly dashed by the country's bloody war against guerrilla insurgents. The war profoundly shaped every aspect of state-society relations in the 1980s and well into the 1990s. Like so many other groups in Peruvian society, journalists and media outlets were caught up in the violence of both the guerrillas and government forces. Guerrilla actions included kidnappings, the occupation of media offices, the forced broadcasting of guerrilla communications, office bombings, threats of physical violence against journalists, and assassinations.

In their efforts to report on the war, journalists ran the risk of running afoul of antiterrorist laws and were subject to the military's accusations that they were aiding and abetting subversives. Inside newsrooms, editors wrestled with questions about exactly how to cover the war and whether to report violent incidents as crime stories (and thus minimize their importance) or as part of the national news. Whatever the editorial choices, however, one thing was clear: both civilian and military officials were hostile to any reporting that focused on human rights violations by government security forces.[29] When horrific cases did come to light, they were usually covered up or remanded to the military justice system and quickly dismissed. The lack of accountability was all too apparent. In the conduct of the war, impunity reigned.

By the time Fujimori was sworn in as president, Peru was in the midst of a serious human rights crisis. Like his predecessors, Fujimori wanted to have a free hand in directing the conduct of the war, which implied keeping a lid on war reporting. In December 1990, a presidential decree forbade the publication of the names of military and police officers serving in Peru's "emergency zones." The law was a response to a *Caretas* report that named the military officers allegedly linked to the 1987 execution of one of its own reporters, Hugo Bustios.[30] In 1991, congress passed a law that mandated a five- to ten-year prison sentence for anyone who revealed "secret information" having to do with national defense. News organizations criticized the law because it included no definition as to what constituted secret information. Nonetheless, Fujimori signed it into law, along with another decree that obliged all public- and private-sector organizations to provide any and all information requested by the SIN.[31] In an effort to quash reporting on the SIN and his growing influence inside the organization, Vladimiro Montesinos filed and won a defamation suit against Enrique Zileri, the editor of *Caretas,* in 1991.[32]

The fixation on secrecy became a key feature of the Fujimori administration. The president's own personal style set the tone for how his administration would deal with demands for information and accountability. A first glimpse came during the 1990 campaign, when Fujimori was a no-show at a much-anticipated news conference where he was to unveil his economic program. Instead, he sent his wife Susana Higuchi de Fujimori to tell skeptical reporters that Fujimori was suffering from food poisoning brought on by a bad piece of codfish. The fish story quickly became part of journalistic lore, emblematic of Fujimori's disregard for the press and his use of surrogates to deal with the pesky questions that he preferred to dodge.

Such disregard began even before Fujimori first took office. In 1990, right after the June runoff, president-elect Fujimori took up residence in an exclusive military facility on the advice of Montesinos. His stay at the Círculo Militar facility served several purposes. First, it signaled Fujimori's desire for a close alliance with the armed forces. The stay also gave high-ranking military officials a chance to make their views known to the new president. Among the views circulating in Peru's military was the so-called Plan Verde, referring to secret contingency plans developed in the 1980s that advocated a permanent military takeover of the government and an all-out assault against guerrillas.[33] Only after the 1992 coup, when the newsmagazine *Oiga* broke the story, did Peruvians become aware of such plans. The unusual stay at Círculo Militar was important in another way. Vladimiro Montesinos reestablished his own standing with his former colleagues and showed that he was Fujimori's right-hand man, a principal gatekeeper. He was now *"El Doctor,"* a person to be respected and taken seriously.[34]

The high walls of the military residence kept the curious press at a distance and also warded off job seekers from Fujimori's own C90 party. No longer needing their help, Fujimori brushed off his fellow C90 members, refusing to see them or even take their phone calls. Instead, he plotted out policy with a new set of advisors who were intent on doing what Vargas Llosa had promised—implementing neoliberal economic reforms.[35] Behind the walls of the Círculo Militar, a new administration, far different that the one that voters imagined when they cast their ballots for the tractor-riding *El Chino,* had taken shape.

For journalists hungry for leaks and insider information, the Fujimori administration was a dry well. In previous governments, dissidents inside the president's own party were often the best sources for reporters. But the C90 populists and evangelicals rapidly were purged or marginalized. Dissenters in Fujimori's first and only "unity" cabinet met the same fate. Leftist economist Carlos Amat y León lasted just two months before resigning, and Fujimori's first agriculture minister and welfare minister, Gloria Helfer, quickly followed suit. In early 1991, Finance Minister Juan Carlos Hurtado

Miller resigned, followed by Industry Minister Guido Pennano. From then on, cabinet ministers were low-key and loyal. Fujimori's designated president of the cabinet of ministers (sometimes referred to by Peruvians as the prime minister or premier) and the minister of finance were usually the most visible spokespersons for the administration. If there were disagreements among cabinet members, they rarely played out in public.

Like his predecessors, Fujimori handled the palace press corps in an informal, often improvisational manner. There was no tradition of holding regular formal press conferences, nor did the palace provide daily briefings. Reporters tagged along with the president at public events, but their role was usually confined to recording the president's remarks. When the president wanted more coverage, he offered exclusive interviews to genial journalists and sympathetic media outlets.

Fujimori's innermost circle eschewed the limelight and shunned reporters. Vladimiro Montesinos gave no interviews and studiously avoided having his picture taken. Santiago Fujimori, the president's brother who served as a principal advisor on personnel matters, did the same. Other members of the Fujimori family, especially those who became involved in the operation of charitable foundations, also stayed away from the press. It was an administration so closed-mouthed that even the president's press secretary Carlos Orellana won a reputation for avoiding reporters.

No Peruvian president had ever championed the principle of the public's "right to know." The country's politicians and bureaucrats had long regarded information as either government property or as a personal possession to sell or trade. It was not something that journalists and citizens had a right to claim, especially if the information was damaging to the military or high-ranking officials. Fujimori was not about to change that ethos. In fact, his plans were moving in the direction of providing less information and accountability, not more.

3

DISSOLVING PERU

IT started as a classic *golpe de estado,* staged on a late Sunday evening as Peruvians settled in for the night. Television viewers had just seen an interview with Fujimori's cabinet president, Alfonso de los Heros. He spoke of a new political deal to end the conflict between President Fujimori and his opponents in congress. Neither viewers nor the newspaper editors wrapping up the morning editions were expecting anything more that night. No one anticipated that President Fujimori was about to appear on television to tell Peruvians that he had assumed dictatorial powers. Summoned to the presidential palace just an hour before the event, Fujimori's own cabinet ministers were taken by surprise. So were television station owners who were ordered to broadcast the president's videotaped statement at 10:30 p.m.

Around ten o'clock that evening, troops and tanks from the army's armored division made their way to strategic locations around Lima. Soldiers encircled the principal government buildings, including the Palacio Legislativo. Congress's top-ranking officials, Roberto Ramírez del Villar and Felipe Osterling, were placed under house arrest. They were not, however, the primary targets for security forces. If there was going to be any trouble that night, Fujimori expected it to come from his former patron, ex-president Alan García, and his political party APRA.

The roundup of APRA leaders began. Agustin Mantilla, former interior minister under García, was meeting with fellow party members over dessert at his home in the Pueblo Libre section of Lima. Suddenly, troops in black ski masks surrounded the house and instructed Mantilla to come out with his hands up. He did and was whisked off to jail. Across town in the upscale neighborhood of Chacarillas, the same scene was unfolding at the home of Alan García. But García didn't come out with his hands up. Eluding his captors in the dark, García made his way to the Colombian embassy and eventually to an exile in Paris. Other APRA leaders and political notables did not escape the sweep and were picked up.[1] Troops cordoned off APRA party headquarters along with those of the Partido Popular Cristiano and Acción Popular.

Army officers and guards occupied newspaper offices, printing presses, and radio and television stations. The officers told the news directors of *Expreso, El Comercio, La República, Ojo,* and *El Nacional* that news reports about the coup would be subject to review. Under military surveillance, the evening pressrun went ahead as scheduled. *La República* and *El Nacional* ran blank pages in their morning editions as a show of the military censorship. Radio Atena 1 was forced off the air as it attempted to broadcast interviews with APRA party officials. Journalists from Atena 1, Radio Red, and the tabloid newspaper *Super Idolo* were taken into custody. A total of twenty-two journalists were detained. Among them was Gustavo Gorriti, a feature writer for the magazine *Caretas* known for his work on Sendero Luminoso and national security issues. Gorriti was spirited off to SIN headquarters.[2]

The first few hours of the coup of April 5, 1992, were no different from military takeovers in the past. By the next day, however, the coup had taken on a different, less menacing tone. Unlike previous coups, this one would be polled. On April 6, polling firms sent their teams out across Lima to take "flash" polls. The polling firm Peruana de Opinión Pública (POP) claimed to find substantial support for the coup, and its survey was published in the government newspaper *El Peruano* on the morning of April 7. The speedy POP poll and its publication seemed suspicious at first, but doubts about the results faded when every other major polling firm came to the same conclusions over the next days and weeks.

Peruvians did not take to the streets to oppose the coup, so there was no need for repression. By Tuesday, April 7, the military guards in the media offices and the printing presses were gone. Gustavo Gorriti was released. Except for Mantilla, who was charged with illegally possessing firearms, APRA leaders were released by the end of the week.

Newspapers began publishing statements by parties and groups opposed to the coup. With the obvious exception of Fujimori's own C90, every major party denounced the coup as unconstitutional. So did trade unions, universities, and the national bar association.

Free speech, breached during the coup, was quickly restored. Alan García's clandestine calls for an insurrection could be broadcast because they were irrelevant. With no congress or judiciary, citizens who spoke out against the coup had nowhere to go with their complaints. Without functioning institutions, the public sphere housed idle critics who posed no threat at all. In fact, this situation was a boon to the coup, as Fujimori quickly discovered how useful freedom of speech sans institutions could be in his public-relations offensive.

The Polls as Prelude

Speaking to the nation on the night of April 5, Fujimori announced his decision to *disolver* (dissolve) the congress. He stopped briefly, then looked into the camera again and forcefully repeated *"disolver,"* as if to make sure that there was no mistaking what he had just said. Closing congress was part of a package that included a "reorganization" of the entire judicial branch and the comptroller's office. It translated into a mass firing of judges that shut down the supreme court and the Tribunal de Garantías Constitucionales. Newly created regional legislatures were also disbanded.[3]

Fujimori laid out the official case for the coup, justifying the need for a new "government of emergency and national reconstruction." Fujimori characterized Peru's democracy as a formal, dysfunctional shell—an arrangement that benefited a self-serving political class and left the rest of Peru submerged in terrorism, narco-trafficking, and poverty. Peru's politicians were immoral and obstructionist, and only decisive action could rescue the country from the acute crisis of governability. From the start, Fujimori framed the coup as a democratic exercise; the coup was "not a negation of real democracy, but on the contrary, it is the initiation of the search for an authentic transformation to assure a legitimate and effective democracy."[4]

Skepticism about parties and democracy was not a new trend in Peruvian public life. Previous twentieth-century dictators, from Augusto Leguía in the 1920s to Manuel Odría in the 1950s, played on the same themes. During the Velasco military regime of the 1970s, the "no-party" model proposed by the intellectual Carlos Delgado shaped the thinking of government officials and influenced their attempt to mobilize popular support through vehicles other than political parties. As for liberal democracy, parties on the left had long questioned its authenticity and effectiveness. Fujimori's rhetoric fit comfortably in a political culture steeped in cynicism and disappointment with traditional politics.

There was plenty of evidence—in opinion polls and in Fujimori's surprising victory in 1990—that the public approved of the "anti-politics" rhetoric. In his first hundred days in office, Fujimori blasted congressmen as "unproductive charlatans" and judges as "jackals."[5] In his first speech as president to the prestigious 1990 Conferencia Anual de Ejecutivos (CADE) meeting of business leaders, Fujimori rendered his dark view of the political system: "Are we really a democracy? And the democracy . . . is it a government of the people, by the people and for the people or a government of the majority? I find it difficult to say yes. We are a country that in truth has always been governed by powerful minorities, oligopolies, cliques, lobbies, rings, families, sects that sometime confront each other to the death, but always come together to obstruct progress when their interests are threatened."[6] At the next CADE meeting in 1991, Fujimori depicted congress as dominated by "mean spirited partisan interests" obstructing the efforts at economic reform and pacification. Fujimori proposed holding a plebiscite to reform congress and queried businessmen if they would support a reorganization of the judiciary. The audience applauded.[7]

Fujimori's approval ratings improved as his attacks on congress intensified. After the heated public exchanges and threats between Fujimori and congressional leaders in December 1991, Fujimori reached an approval rating of 65 percent—his best rating since his inauguration. As Fujimori's personal approval ratings improved, those of the congress crashed. By March 1992, less than 20 percent of the public expressed confidence in congress as an institution.

In the days immediately after the coup, Fujimori argued that the country had been on the verge of a congress-led coup attempt. Fujimori said that his own actions were an "anti-coup." Coup supporters Carlos Torres y Torres Lara and Enrique Chirinos Soto characterized the coup as a preemptive "counter-coup."[8] They maintained that opposition legislators were planning to remove Fujimori from office and would use Article 206 of the constitution to do so. That article allowed congress to remove the president based on "moral incapacity." In December 1991, the senate passed a "moral" censure of the president after Fujimori made an incendiary speech accusing some legislators of having ties to narco-trafficking. The chamber of deputies, however, backed away from the senate's provocative measure and the motion died.[9]

It will forever remain a matter of speculation whether a congressional majority could have been mustered in 1992 to remove Fujimori from office. Another unknown is whether the executive-legislative conflict could have been settled in a compromise. In the days just prior to April 5, congressional leaders negotiated agreements with cabinet president Alfonso de los Heros to resolve various policy disagreements about pacification and judicial issues. Still, fractious issues were in play. One was the prospective congressional investigation into an accusation made by First Lady Susana Higuchi de Fujimori. Speaking out against her husband's administration, she charged that relatives of the president were profiteering from the sales of clothing from Japan that were supposed to be charitable donations to the poor.

While Alfonso de los Heros negotiated with congressional leaders, President Fujimori was planning the coup with the head of the Comando Conjunto of the Armed Forces, General Nicolás de Bari Hermoza Ríos, and national security advisor, Vladimiro Montesinos. Montesinos later said that the coup was a response to congress's derogation of a series of counterterrorism and counternarcotics measures decreed by Fujimori in November 1991. Hermoza testified that his involvement in the coup meetings began in early February after congress passed Law 25379, a measure aimed at reducing the president's ability to use decree laws to govern. Fujimori confirmed that he began thinking about a possible coup months prior to its execution.[10]

As Fujimori pondered the prospective coup, polling data gave him every reason to believe that the public would accept it. In addition to the overall improvement in Fujimori's own personal approval ratings, polls indicated that most people had lost confidence in the congress and the judiciary and agreed with Fujimori that institutions be "reorganized." After his December 1991 speech to CADE, a major poll reported that a little more than 70 percent of the public approved of the president's criticisms of the congress and the judiciary. Popular support for Fujimori's tough talk went hand in hand with the popular belief that institutions were failing to act in the public interest. A supreme court decision of February 1992 that dismissed the corruption charges against former president Alan García was opposed by 60 percent of those polled; a subsequent poll indicated that 69 percent of the public believed that APRA was influencing the judicial branch through the numerous García-era appointees still on the bench. Making the credibility crisis of the judiciary even worse was a series of unpopular judicial decisions that released convicted and suspected terrorists from jail, and a ruling that found insufficient evidence to support a slew of criminal charges against Abimael Guzmán, the leader of Sendero Luminoso, who remained at large.[11]

Crumbling confidence in government institutions was matched by a near-complete alienation from political parties. In a poll taken just prior to the coup, 84 percent of the public declared themselves to be "political independents" rather than supporters of any political party. Among government institutions, only the executive branch and the armed forces scored approval ratings above 50 percent.

As pollster Alfredo Torres observed, most of the polls done prior to April 5 showed that "conditions were extant" for a coup: in all likelihood the public would accept a coup done in the name of reform. Historically, military coups in Peru have never been met with massive popular protest at their outset, and the polls gave Fujimori no reason to believe that it would be different this time.[12]

The Spin Begins

For most people in Lima, the Monday morning after the coup was the start of a workday like any other. There were tanks parked in front of public offices and a few party headquarters. But other than the small band of journalists gathered around the homes of the congressional leaders under house arrest, there was nothing much to see. The atmosphere on the street was resoundingly normal.

The rush to take the public's temperature began. On April 6, all of the major commercial polling firms swung into action, taking the first "flash" polls. The three leading polling firms—Apoyo, Datum, and Compañía Peruana de Investigación (CPI)—confirmed public support of the measures that Fujimori announced. Apoyo, Datum, and CPI reported approval ratings for the closure of congress at 71 percent, 84 percent, and 87 percent, respectively. The reorganization of the judiciary was even more popular; Apoyo reported an approval rating of 89 percent, while CPI and Datum recorded approval ratings for this measure of 94 percent and 95 percent, respectively.[13]

Fujimori and his cabinet ministers swiftly incorporated the poll results into their explanations and justifications of the coup. With favorable poll results in hand, they could argue that the coup was a democratic exercise. In his first formal speech after the coup, Fujimori underscored the extensive popular support for the coup to a crowd of businessmen and journalists gathered at the Asociación de Exportadores.[14] In subsequent interviews and speeches, Fujimori continued to talk about the legitimacy conferred on the coup by the polls. In an interview with the Mexican media, Fujimori likened the coup to a "popular uprising."[15] Fujimori reasoned that democracy was constituted by "respect for public opinion." And in his view, respect for public opinion in this instance entailed sticking to the measures announced on April 5 since they had proved to be so popular.

Talking about the coup's popularity became the key component in the rhetorical strategy aimed at redefining the coup as something other than an unconstitutional use of force by the executive. Fujimori admitted that military occupation of media outlets and the arrests on April 5 made it appear, at least initially, that he had staged a "traditional military coup." Fujimori enlisted Foreign Minister Augusto Blacker Miller and his new cabinet president Oscar de la Puente to help in constructing a benign interpretation of the event.[16]

All three men steered clear of using the word *golpe* (coup), to refer to the events. Fujimori initially tried out the term *anti-golpe* (anti-coup)— suggesting that he had saved the republic from a treasonous opposition. The bland term *las medidas* (the measures) was also used to project an image of April 5 as a low-key exercise in technocratic governance. Blacker Miller experimented with a variety of terms. He referred to the government as a *regimen de necesidad* (regime of necessity). He insisted that it was a "civilian government" operating in a "special and provisional" situation.[17] In a more extreme attempt to downplay the breakdown in constitutionalism, de la Puente depicted events as a "temporary interruption of institutionalization."[18] Finance Minister Carlos Boloña insisted on referring to the events of April 5 as an "institutional reform." By May, Fujimori was telling reporters that, thanks to April 5, Peru was a "*sui generis* democracy."[19]

The official discourse portraying the coup as an essentially democratic measure was bolstered by the quick restoration of press freedom in the days after the coup. Thirty-nine hours after taking up their posts at media outlets, all military personnel were withdrawn.[20] Along with the release of those detained on April 5, lifting the press censorship lent credibility to Fujimori's claim that the coup had not installed a traditional dictatorship. However, the military's occupation of media offices, although brief, shaped the parameters of press coverage on the first day of the coup and, thus, the public's initial view of the events. All of the major newspapers, including *La República,* refrained from using the word *golpe* to describe the events of April 5. In the first two days following the coup, headlines were full of references to the official terminology being employed by the government. The words "reorganization," "restructuring," and "reconstruction" dominated the coverage. Only after the military withdrew did newspapers start publishing the statements of opposition parties that used the words *golpe de estado* and *dictadura militar* to describe what had happened.[21]

The pro-coup polls gained credibility because they were published by a free press. For the administration, it was important that the numbers be taken seriously, both at home and abroad. Fujimori urged journalists to go out on their own and confirm popular support for the coup. The international press corps joined the local press in reporting the pro-coup poll stories.[22] Fujimori's defense of the poll results was unequivocal: ". . . the unanimous results, and the fact that these come from the broadest spectrum of polling agencies or companies, grant the polls their credibility. No one has dared to reject the results, given their outright evidence. I repeat that polls cannot replace institutional and legal forms of popular expression; that is not the question. But the fact that these polls reflect the belief and sentiment of the Peruvian people is not the question either. These results are objective, and one must respect popular opinion. In my opinion, the essence of the true democratic attitude lies in respect and consideration of popular will."[23]

Leaders opposing the coup did, at first, question the veracity of the polls. Mario Vargas Llosa virulently denounced what he characterized as a *golpe de estado* and dismissed the poll results.[24] Máximo San Román, Fujimori's dissident vice president who refused to recognize the unconstitutional seizure of power, argued that the polls were manipulated by the SIN.[25] Enrique Bernales, the left-wing social scientist who lost his senate seat on April 5, took aim at the polls, asserting that findings could be structured by the types of questions posed in surveys.

The critical press also questioned the polls. *La República* and *Caretas* published methodological challenges referring to the classic problems affecting poll results—the high refusal rate in polling, the possibility of "interviewer" effects, and the chance that the initial polls might have induced a "spiral of silence" effect among those opposed to the coup.[26]

Opposition efforts to question the polls fell flat. The intellectual counterattack on the polls was scattershot; there was no uniform interpretation regarding the problem with the polls. The criticisms fell all over the spectrum, including accusations of simple conspiracy (e.g., San Román's reference to SIN manipulation) to emphasis on sophisticated methodological problems that were not easily understood by the public. The media that opposed the coup (*La República, Caretas*) had neither the expertise nor the interest to spearhead a national debate about the uses and abuses of polls. Polls had become a staple in the political reporting of both print and broadcast media outlets, so discrediting them was problematic. Progovernment newspapers—*Expreso, Ojo,* and *El Peruano*—had no interest in challenging the polls, nor did the television stations that had lined up to support the coup.

Like the press, opposition political parties lacked the capability and the will to attack the polls. As longtime consumers of polls themselves, many politicians were accustomed to taking the numbers at face value. Predictably, Peruvian pollsters were quick to defend the accuracy of their findings. Among pollsters, Alfredo Torres of Apoyo was outspoken in his personal opposition to the coup, but he always insisted on the accuracy of his polling.[27]

The polls would not allow opponents to argue that the coup was unpopular; nor did critics make headway in defining the regime as a dictatorship in the public mind. The idea that the government was a *dictadura* (dictatorship) did not catch on, nor did the opposition's subsequent use of *gobierno de facto* (de facto government) to describe the post–April 5 regime.[28] An April poll by Apoyo showed that slightly more than half of the public viewed the government as "democratic" while only 30 percent called the government "dictatorial." The public's willingness to accept Fujimori's characterization of the regime as democratic was closely connected to how the public viewed the essential characteristics of democracy. In a May poll, Apoyo surveyed the public on what criteria were most important to defining democracy. Freedom of the press, respect for human rights, and having a freely elected president were identified as the most important characteristics of democracy for more than 50 percent of the respondents. Other features, such as respect for the constitution, division of powers, and judicial independence, were identified as important by less than 50 percent of those surveyed.

With an elected civilian president still in power and press freedom restored, most Peruvians went along with Fujimori's claim that the government was democratic, albeit with some qualifications attached. But Fujimori did not win the battle for public opinion completely. Polls also revealed that the public, while supporting the coup, viewed it as a temporary corrective action. Most Peruvians favored a return to "representative" democracy. So did the U.S. government and OAS.

No Going Back

The rest of the world did not approve of the coup, at least not at first. Neighboring Latin American governments condemned the coup and called for a restoration of constitutionalism. President Carlos Andrés Pérez of Venezuela issued the toughest rebuke, suspending diplomatic relations between his nation and Peru. Spain recalled its ambassador in Lima. In the United States, President George H. W. Bush characterized the coup as "unjustifiable" and "unacceptable." The *New York Times* joined in the calls to punish Peru with economic sanctions.[29] The Permanent Council of the

OAS issued a statement on April 6 deploring the events and calling for an immediate reestablishment of democratic institutions; a meeting of OAS foreign ministers was scheduled to discuss what the OAS course of action would be vis-à-vis Peru.[30]

Fujimori later confessed to having underestimated the international backlash to the coup and its impact on the government's efforts to reestablish Peru's standing with international financial institutions. Foreign Minister Augusto Blacker Miller was dispatched to the OAS meeting of April 13 to argue against the proposals by Canada and the United States to impose economic sanctions on Peru. Blacker Miller's address to the OAS played heavily on the notion that the coup was legitimate because of its 90 percent approval rating in the polls. He repeated Fujimori's arguments about the inefficiency and corruption of Peruvian institutions; the official view was that the coup overturned the "formal legality" of dysfunctional institutions and replaced it with a "real legality." At the end of the speech, Blacker Miller reiterated the equation of poll results with government legitimacy: "the popular support on which we rely and is made clear in the results of polls carried out on a near daily basis confers on us [the Fujimori government] the status of being the legitimate bearers of the sovereign will [of the people]."[31]

Blacker Miller was successful, at least in staving off any immediate OAS action. Instead, the OAS dispatched a fact-finding mission to Lima that included OAS secretary-general João Baena Soares and Uruguayan foreign minister Héctor Gros Espiell. The mission was charged with promoting a dialogue between the government and opposition forces for the purpose of "re-establishing a democratic political order." But the mission's mandate made no mention of restoring the 1979 constitution. Fujimori insisted that there was "no going back" to the pre-coup political system.

The OAS mission in Lima almost immediately conceded to the idea of "no going back." Even before the mission arrived, the idea of forcing the restoration of pre-coup institutions was losing ground inside the OAS. The governments of Brazil, Uruguay, and Argentina were plotting out a moderate position that "permanent but not excessive pressure" be applied to Peru.[32] On the basis of initial meetings between the OAS and various groups, Gros Espiell concluded that the armed forces solidly backed Fujimori and that the public was alienated from the traditional political class.[33] Restoring the

1979 constitution meant that Fujimori would have to back down and re-open congress, or that Fujimori would have to be forced into a resignation and replaced by first vice president, Máximo San Román.

Gros Espiell concluded that neither option was feasible. San Román had failed to inspire confidence as a potential successor. He was out of the country on April 5 and remained conspicuously silent until April 10, when he came out against the coup. In the meantime, the dissident rump of the deposed congress went through the motions of swearing in the second vice president, Carlos García, as constitutional president. San Román made a belated return to Peru on April 18. He was subsequently sworn in on April 21 as constitutional president by what was left of the deposed congress. But the opposition's attachment to San Román was purely symbolic. His appeals for support to the armed forces and to the public fell flat. The U.S. government's decision on April 23 to continue recognizing Fujimori, rather than San Román, as Peru's president effectively ended the opposition's effort to establish a parallel government. Notwithstanding its tough talk after the coup, the Bush administration effectively had given Fujimori a pass.

With no international pressure to reinstate the 1979 constitution, opposition leaders had little choice but to move toward what Gros Espiell later referred to as "unavoidable realism." Namely, opposition party leaders had to come to grips with the fact that the coup was irreversible and that the only option was to try to negotiate a swift resumption of competitive electoral politics.

Polling data provided ample evidence that Peruvians wanted elections. In an April poll by Apoyo, 80 percent of the respondents in a national survey voiced support for holding the 1992 municipal elections as scheduled. In the same poll, 58 percent of the sample favored holding an election for a new legislature before 1995. The public's desire for a return to normal democratic politics was undeniable. When people were queried about a scenario in which Fujimori failed to return the country to constitutional rule, 69 percent voiced disapproval. An overwhelming majority, 87 percent, said that they would not approve of the Fujimori government in the event that it restricted freedom of the press.

Speaking on behalf of opposition parties, Máximo San Román offered a blueprint for political transition on April 28. He proposed that a constituent assembly be elected and installed in July. Once installed, the constituent assembly would accept the resignations of Fujimori, San Román, and the deposed congress and then elect an interim government. That interim government would subsequently stage new elections in 1993.

San Román's formula ran directly counter to Fujimori's plan. In a speech on April 21, Fujimori announced his plan to hold a referendum on July 5 to allow the public to express its opinion regarding the "conceptual basis of April 5." A panel of experts selected by the government would write a new constitution, which would be subject to a referendum. New elections for congress would be slated for February 1993, and a new congress would be installed by April. Fujimori's proposal also included a plan for a "National Dialogue" to sponsor public discussion about constitutional reform.

Given the state of public opinion right after the coup, Fujimori had everything to gain by holding a quick plebiscite. Victory would seal the coup as legitimate and would also allow Fujimori to interpret it as a mandate for subsequent measures, including postponing any elections. San Román's constituent assembly formula was a considerable risk for the government. If pro-Fujimori forces failed to win a majority in the constituent assembly, the entire process of political restructuring could slip out of government control altogether. Given the disarray in Peru's party system and the ephemeral state of Fujimori's own C90 party, the outcome of a constituent assembly election was anyone's guess.

The OAS representatives and opponents recognized how easy it would be for Fujimori to stage a successful plebiscite. In early May, Gros Espiell returned to Lima on a second OAS mission with a clear message that Fujimori's proposed transition via plebiscite was unacceptable. But Fujimori refused to budge. The plebiscite was the most democratic option, he argued. Once again, Fujimori invoked public-opinion polls as evidence. An Apoyo poll indicated that 68 percent of the public backed Fujimori's transition formula. Fujimori said that other polls showed more than 90 percent of the public favoring a referendum. "Public opinion must be respected," he asserted.[34] In a television interview, he made an impassioned plea for direct democracy: ". . . the people have adopted a clear stance. The people want direct participation. The people want more democracy. They want a democracy like they see in other countries, for example, Switzerland. In Switzerland they hold plebiscites, the people are consulted. Why can't the Peruvian people have this direct participation? That is precisely what we are suggesting, more democracy. We are suggesting that the measures be adopted and constitutional precepts not be agreed on in negotiations among various groups that meet behind closed doors."[35]

Fujimori remained intransigent on the issue of the referendum, and opposition leaders refused to cede on the constituent assembly. The OAS mission made no headway in bringing the two sides to the bargaining table. Gros Espiell concluded that the mission was a failure, citing Fujimori's position as the major stumbling block. On the heels of Gros Espiell's declaration, reports surfaced that Uruguay and other countries were considering taking a harder line on Peru in the upcoming OAS meeting of foreign ministers in the Bahamas.

Fujimori's advisors realized that clinging to the plebiscite might provoke the OAS to levy economic sanctions and seriously complicate Peru's already uncertain status in international financial circles. Carlos Boloña, the Oxford-trained economist who served as Fujimori's finance minister, had already been advised during his first post-coup trip to Washington in mid-April that international financial institutions would cut off all financial flows to Peru if no progress were made on restoring democratic institutions. Hernando de Soto, an economist and close advisor to Fujimori, sided with Boloña. De Soto, who was well connected with Washington circles, knew that they needed to change their political strategy.[36]

Just before the OAS Bahamas meeting, Fujimori agreed to a partial concession. In a final meeting with Gros Espiell in Lima, Fujimori agreed to hold elections for a constituent assembly in the calendar year. However, the understanding meant that the government would control the political restructuring. Contrary to the opposition plan that involved joint resignations by Fujimori and the deposed congress and the formation of an interim government, Fujimori made it clear that he would not step down any time prior to the scheduled end of his term in July 1995. Moreover, Fujimori stipulated that the new constituent assembly would be a small body of no more than eighty members. Gros Espiell communicated Fujimori's revised position to leaders of the twelve opposition parties. They rejected it. Nonetheless, Gros Espiell concluded his visit with an approving report that cited Fujimori's revised plan as a prospective "basis for dialogue."[37]

Fujimori flew to the Bahamas to deliver his plan to the meeting of the OAS foreign ministers in person. His speech included a long tirade against political parties in Peru.[38] He pledged that his government would create channels for popular participation to replace the "traditional elitist dialogue" among party cliques. Details were sketchy regarding the actual conduct of the elections for the combined legislature and constituent assembly, the Congreso Constituyente Democrático (CCD), but Fujimori made it clear that he would accept OAS observation of the voting.

By ceding to the demand for a legislative election, Fujimori averted the possibility of economic sanctions. The Bahamas meeting concluded with a resolution recognizing Fujimori's commitment to reestablish a representative democracy in a timely way by scheduling the constituent assembly election. The resolution included a call for democratization within a "framework of dialogue" among the respective political forces in Peru.[39] Yet there were no specifics regarding the ground rules for the dialogue, nor did the OAS provide mechanisms to handle disputes between the government and the opposition or to monitor government behavior during the transition period. The OAS had forced Fujimori to blink, but no matter. The essentials of the coup were on their way to being institutionalized.

Government by Decree

In the interim between the coup of April 1992 and the swearing in of the new congress in December 1992, the executive branch issued hundreds of decrees recasting government institutions and their operating procedures.[40] There were new rules governing public administration, the economy, and the legal system. Virtually all the changes concentrated more powers and control in the executive branch. In the absence of a congress, none of the decrees were subject to open debate or review. Many of the decrees, especially those authorizing budgetary transfers and expenditures, were never even made public. In retrospect, it is easy to understand the secrecy. Millions of dollars were being siphoned from ministries and deposited in slush funds in the SIN. As Montesinos later confessed, the slush funds were often used for political purposes, especially for the president's reelection campaigns. One official estimate put the total of monies clandestinely rerouted to the SIN at approximately US$50.5 million in the period 1992–2000.[41]

In the days immediately after the coup, scores of government buildings remained closed and under the exclusive control of the armed forces and police. In the interregnum, SIN agents were free to comb through court files, police records, and other confidential documents for information on friends and foes of the new government.[42] How much information was gathered or "disappeared" is not known since so many of the civilian employees never returned to their offices. Executive decrees were used to legalize the mass firings in the public sector. Of the first seventy-two decrees issued after the coup, forty-seven decrees were devoted to the firing of officials in the judiciary, the public ministry, the central reserve bank, and the comptroller's office.[43] One of the decrees prohibited fired judges and prosecutors from appealing their dismissals. Instead, a selective rehiring took place, which ensured that the entire justice system was firmly under appointees directly beholden to the president for their jobs. Santiago Fujimori, the president's brother and one of this closest advisors at the time, played a critical role in vetting all high-ranking appointments until his departure from government in 1996.

The sweep of the executive's control over the state apparatus was not confined to the national level of government. Another coup decree eliminated newly created regional assemblies. It also gave the executive the power to appoint regional prefects, effectively creating a loyal corps of provincial officials beholden to the president. This proved to be an enormous advantage in election campaigns, especially since C90 had no real party organization.

Another decision laid the basis for a bureaucratic-based clientelism. Fujimori created the Ministerio de la Presidencia in May 1992. The ministry, established by executive decree, administered international aid donations and built public works, including housing. With one stroke of the pen, Fujimori created a superministry with a budget that would be wielded indiscriminately for electoral purposes.

Other decrees greatly enhanced the government's repressive powers.[44] New legal provisions stiffened the penalties for crimes classified as terrorism to include mandatory life sentences and routed these cases to military courts, where the rights of defendants were circumscribed. Another key reform revamped the country's intelligence system, elevating it to a cabinet ministry reporting directly to the president. Other reforms followed that altered promotion rules, making it possible for military officers working in intelligence to move into the highest service ranks. Through the reforms, the SIN acquired a new weight in the executive branch, as did Vladimiro Montesinos, who manipulated the promotion system to insure that his cronies rapidly ascended to the top ranks of the military and intelligence systems. With money pouring into the SIN, Montesinos expanded the facilities. In 1993, he inaugurated a new electronic surveillance operation that was used to spy on political opponents and government employees as well as traditional targets such as terrorists or criminals.[45] As the regime developed, its powers to harass opponents steadily expanded. From 1994 onward, Peru's internal revenue service and its customs agency were used to hound opponents and create a climate of fear, especially in the business community.[46]

In the institutional vacuum that followed the coup, the contours of a new regime emerged. On the surface, Fujimori embraced elections and civil liberties. Behind the scenes, Fujimori and Montesinos were at work on a labyrinthine construct—a political apparatus that would assure them unchecked powers and untold opportunities.

4

FORMALIZING THE COUP

Whatever their mistakes and miscalculations, Fujimori's opponents always had a keen sense of what they were up against. Well in advance of the coup, critics warned of the impending authoritarian turn. When Fujimori mused in late 1991 that Peru might be in need of an emperor, the remark sounded more like a threat than a lame joke.[1]

When the coup came, it confirmed what many critics had feared—that Fujimori, Montesinos, and the military were joined in an unholy alliance. Vice President Máximo San Román was blunt in his assessment of where the regime was headed. San Román believed that Fujimori planned to establish a dictatorship that would keep him in power for decades. And San Román warned that Fujimori's right-hand man, Vladimiro Montesinos, had ties to drug trafficking.[2]

Fujimori's opponents united in their gloom after the coup, but they remained divided on how to organize against what they saw as a dictatorship under construction. Their fractiousness proved useful to the president. Fujimori later acknowledged that the coup was effectively "formalized" in the political processes that took place during 1992–1993: elections for the constituent assembly, the CCD; the development of the new constitution; and a subsequent referendum on that constitution. Bowing to the pressures to restore electoral politics, Fujimori and his inner circle fashioned a political system designed to look democratic, but function otherwise. Allowing opponents to vent, but keeping them out of kilter and far removed from institutional sources of power, was central to how the new political system worked.

Muting the National Dialogue

Opponents had little to celebrate in the months after the coup. For scores of career politicians, the coup was a stiff, dislocating blow. It meant hundreds of lost jobs, lost paychecks, and lost pride. Veteran politicians were mortified by the jeers that greeted them in Lima's cafes and restaurants from patrons who scorned them as *políticos tradicionales* undone by the auto-coup. Ousted politicians privately acknowledged that people were fed up and that Fujimori had played artfully on the public's sour mood.

Deposed congressional deputies and senators constituted the core of the opposition in the period immediately following the coup. They hailed from a wide range of organizations and ideological persuasions. On the right to center-right side of the spectrum was Frente Democrático (FREDEMO), the organizational vehicle behind Mario Vargas Llosa's failed 1990 presidential bid. The principal partners in FREDEMO were Vargas Llosa's original vehicle, Movimiento Libertad (ML); the social Christian party, Partido Popular Cristiano (PPC); Fernando Belaúnde's Acción Popular (AP); and the small party of technocrats, Solidaridad y Democracia (SODE). On the other side of the spectrum were the populist party APRA and the leftist Izquierda Unida (IU) and Izquierda Socialista (IS). Among the small independent parties were Frente Independiente Moralizador (FIM) and the Frente Nacional de Trabajadores y Campesinos (FRENATRACA).

All of these groups and their leaders were long-standing rivals with little in common. But suddenly, the coup gave the leaders of these disparate political groups something that they could agree upon, at least for the present time. They all wanted electoral politics reestablished quickly.

Fujimori had reluctantly accepted the idea of a constituent assembly, but that concession came along with the message that he would not step down at any point before 1995. Opposition leaders declared the Bahamas meeting a "defeat" for the president, but they knew that Fujimori retained the upper hand and that the government would do everything possible to interpret the vague parameters laid out by the OAS to its advantage. The opposition's task, in turn, was to try to extract sufficient concessions to ensure fair elections and a reasonable constitution, or to delegitimize the government by demonstrating that it was failing to live up to even the vague parameters set out by the OAS.

The OAS required that the government start a "dialogue" with the opposition to plan the political transition, but it never stipulated how the dialogue would be structured. Even before Fujimori's trip to the Bahamas meeting, the government began crafting the means to control any future negotiations with domestic groups. On April 24, 1992, the office of the National Dialogue for Peace and Development was created. Headed by cabinet minister Oscar de la Puente, the office had a vague mandate to seek "alternatives to solve the country's problems." Only delegates from organizations accredited by the National Dialogue office would be eligible to participate.[3]

By early June, one report estimated that as many as ten thousand people had signed up to participate in the National Dialogue; other reports placed the number of potential participants between three and four thousand.[4] Whatever the exact figure, the unwieldy number of potential participants led opponents to conclude that the National Dialogue was a ruse—that it was created to give the appearance of public consultation, confuse the debate over the transition, and diminish the role of rival political leaders.

Meanwhile, Fujimori continued his furious attacks on traditional parties and the political class. In a nationally televised speech, Fujimori accused the opposition of mounting an "anti-national campaign to damage the project of the Peruvian government." He referred to the previous congress as a "large, heavy, thick-skinned pachyderm" and reiterated the idea that there was no "going back" to pre-coup political practices.[5]

Opposition leaders reacted, announcing that they would not participate in the National Dialogue meeting of June 30 unless it included separate meetings with party leaders to address issues related to the restoration of democracy.[6] In their eyes, the government sent another signal of its ill will when it announced that the scheduled CCD election would be pushed back from October to November, and that municipal elections would be postponed until early 1993. The official reasons for postponing the municipal elections seemed hazy. Fujimori said that he wanted to encourage more participation and that "independents" needed more time to organize.

As the government geared up for the National Dialogue at the end of June, opposition leaders called for a separate dialogue with parties, to be mediated by the Roman Catholic Church, but Fujimori rejected the idea. In a complaint to OAS secretary-general João Baena Soares, Máximo San Román accused the government of not complying with the Bahamas agreement because it had not issued formal invitations to parties to participate in the National Dialogue.[7] Soares issued a public call for party leaders to be included, and cabinet president Oscar de la Puente subsequently issued formal invitations to party leaders, asking them to participate in exclusive one-on-one meetings with him.[8]

The National Dialogue got off to a raucous start when opening ceremonies attracted an unruly crowd of more than four thousand people at Lima's Civic Center. Meanwhile, de la Puente's invitations to parties succeeded in splitting the opposition, dividing those who decided to accept the invitation from those who did not. On June 30, de la Puente held his first meetings. FIM leaders Fernando Olivera and Enrique Gamarra became the first to participate officially in the talks. On the same day, Enrique Bernales of IS, Roger Cáceres of FRENATRACA, Antero Flores Araoz of the PPC, and Fausto Alvarado of SODE delivered a document to de la Puente's office detailing opposition views on the dialogue.[9]

On the following day, de la Puente met with SODE's Alvarado, and later with Antero Flores Araoz and Lourdes Flores of the PPC. Movimiento Libertad did not send representatives to the talks, but ML dissidents Beatriz Merino, Luis Delgado Aparicio, and Raúl Ferrero did meet with de la Puente.[10] No substantive agreements were struck, but just the sight of opponents arriving at de la Puente's Civic Center office prompted *La República*'s columnist Mirko Lauer to conclude that some politicians were "throwing in the democratic towel in an oblique and subtle way."[11] Leaders of APRA and AP said that they would participate only if the municipal elections were held as originally scheduled.

De la Puente insisted that he wanted the major parties, APRA and AP, on board, but Fujimori signaled otherwise. In an interview for Chilean television, Fujimori undercut the importance of the dialogue process, stating that the elections would be held no matter what happened: "The elections must be held. They already have been set. They will be held independently of the results of the dialogue. If the dialogue is not successful, it will not be the government's fault."[12]

In mid-July, de la Puente announced meetings with representatives of the Roman Catholic Church, trade unions, and the national business federation Confederación Nacional de Instituciones Empresariales (CONFIEP). But the president showed his disdain of the entire process in his annual Independence Day speech to congress on July 28. Vigorously defending the coup, Fujimori insisted that he had not gone to the OAS meeting in the Bahamas to "repent." His contempt for the dialogue was clear: "I am not in the government palace to manage Peru's overall crisis the best I can. I am not there to carry out the kind of public relations work that people call national agreement, which is really just an agreement to bury certain matters. . . . The people put me in the government to break the mold, not to solemnly warm up a seat for five years. That is not my style, and I will not do it." Fujimori concluded with a bold announcement: the election for a unicameral CCD of no more than eighty members would take place on November 22, 1992, to be followed by municipal elections in February 1993.[13] In short, Fujimori had already decided on how the transition would proceed even before de la Puente had concluded the National Dialogue.

Opposition party leaders were furious. They called on Fujimori to retract the decision and announced that they would not attend a final meeting proposed by de la Puente.[14] But the division opening up inside the opposition was now apparent. Five groups agreed to meet again with de la Puente on August 5. Fernando Olivera of FIM; Manuel Moreyra, Fausto Alvarado, and Javier Silva Ruete of SODE; Edmundo Murrugarra of Convergencia Socialista; and Edgar Terán and Wilfredo Alvarez of the tiny independent group Coordinadora Independiente attended the meeting. Manuel Moreyra emerged from the meeting and told reporters that de la Puente had assured them that Fujimori was simply outlining proposals in his July 28 speech and not imposing them. De la Puente suggested a final meeting with all parties on August 7.[15] The boycotting parties responded with a call for a parallel dialogue. They wanted a meeting of all sides that would include outside observers, to be held somewhere other than de la Puente's office.[16]

The call fell on deaf ears. De la Puente had managed to cobble together an agreement that included four party organizations along with the government's own C90. The accord settled on the CCD as a unicameral body, elected with deputies selected in a single, national electoral district using a double-preferential voting system. Olivera, Moreyra, Murrugarra, Alvarez, and Andres Reggiardo of C90 signed the accord.[17]

The accord was an enormous blow to the rest of the opposition. Even though the four parties reeled in by de la Puente were tiny organizations with scant electoral support, their official involvement was sufficient to create the appearance that the government had complied with the OAS demand to consult with the opposition.[18]

The president's cabinet, the council of ministers, brought the controversial dialogue to an official close on August 18. In its final pronouncement, the cabinet concluded that it had fully complied with paragraph 6 of OAS Resolution No. 01-92 and that many political parties had opted for "self-exclusion" from the process. The legal decree authorizing the CCD election was attached, with a few surprises included. The law provided that the CCD would stay in operation until July 28, 1995, thus ruling out the prospect of advancing a new set of elections. The decree also mandated a reregistration of all political parties for the CCD election, subjecting even established parties like APRA and AP to the onerous process of collecting one hundred thousand signatures on registration petitions in short order. The reregistration requirement allowed the government leeway to block the participation of some parties or to flood the contest by allowing scores of "independent" movements to register. Another provision barred representatives elected to the CCD from being candidates in the next legislative election in 1995. The term limits provision was an obvious disincentive for top opposition leaders to contemplate a run for the CCD.

Even more alarming were three provisions in the decree that restricted the autonomy of the CCD. One provision established that bills presented by the executive branch were to be assigned "priority" status in the congress, and that such bills could be signed into law by the president if they were not passed within thirty days of being submitted. Another provision stated that if a future constitution was rejected twice in referendums it could, nonetheless, be amended and enacted by the president. Finally, the CCD could not annul the coup and post-coup measures taken by the government.[19]

The CCD decree was proof of how irrelevant the dialogue had actually been in shaping the government's thinking. Opposition leaders condemned the decree, arguing that it effectively created a legislature subordinated to the executive branch.

The OAS scheduled another meeting to assess the situation in Peru on August 28. Former senator Alberto Borea of the PPC announced that he and former IU senator Javier Diez Canseco would take the opposition's case to the meeting. Less than forty-eight hours after the original CCD decree, the cabinet reconvened to amend it. It struck all of the controversial provisions concerning the reregistration of existing parties, the presidential power to promulgate a constitution rejected by referendums, and the thirty-day term for congressional approval of bills presented by the executive.[20]

Dumping the controversial measures just before the OAS meeting buttressed the government's claims to flexibility. Both OAS secretary-general João Baena Soares and mission chief Héctor Gros Espiell offered positive evaluations of the transition plan. Speaking for the opposition, Borea called the dialogue a "farce" and urged the OAS to boycott the CCD election by withholding observers, but he was clearly at odds with OAS officials. The meeting ended with a vote that unanimously endorsed the Gros Espiell mission and authorized an OAS mission to observe the CCD elections.[21] It gave a green light to the Fujimori administration, a clear sign that neither the OAS nor the American government were prepared to be exacting monitors of the transition.

Fujimori wasted no time in interpreting the outcome as a resounding endorsement of his government: "At an international level, there is already an understanding of how Peru is handling this entire electoral process. I believe the OAS and the countries that have played a leading role in this event support the process we are implementing. The process, of course, will not be stopped."[22]

The CCD Election

Once it was clear that elections would proceed on Fujimori's terms, opposition leaders had to decide whether or not to participate. Participation was risky because it would likely be interpreted as legitimating the coup. But in the minds of many political activists, boycotting the election did not seem like a smart move. Boycotting meant ceding, in the words of opponents, all the "political space" to Fujimori. Without seats in the legislature, the opposition's access to the media, already spotty, was likely to disappear altogether.

Again, opposition leaders divided on how to proceed. Prompted by former president Fernando Belaúnde, who led his party in abstaining from the 1978 constituent assembly election mandated by the military government, AP opted to sit out the CCD election. Other parties were less sure-footed. APRA initially floated the idea of participating in the CCD election as part of a united opposition front.[23] The proposal died immediately because none of the other mainstream parties were interested in associating themselves with APRA, an organization discredited by the poor performance of the government of Alan García. From exile in Colombia, Alan García called on his party to abstain and the party hierarchy heeded the call, with one exception. Former APRA senator José Barba Caballero had split from the party to form his own group of independents, the Coordinadora Democrática (CODE), to run for the CCD.

Heated debates over whether to run or stay out of the CCD election raged on the left and the right. Former members of IS, Henry Pease García and Gloria Helfer, created a new organization called Movimiento Democrático de Izquierda (MDI). Edmundo Murrugarra, also formerly affiliated with IS, created a new vehicle Convergencia. Favoring abstention, former senator Javier Diez Canseco led the Partido Unificado Mariateguista (PUM), previously affiliated with Izquierda Unida, in a boycott of the election.

On the right, Alberto Borea split from the PPC, denouncing his colleagues as "camp followers of the dictatorship" when they voted to participate. Pro-participation advocates in the PPC argued that the CCD election was an opportunity analogous to the 1988 referendum in Chile—an opening that was used by the opposition to discredit the dictatorship. Borea disagreed with the Chile comparison and believed that the CCD was just a vehicle for legitimating Fujimori's autocratic regime.[24]

The PPC's decision to enter the race was decisive, prompting other parties to get on the bandwagon. SODE, the tiny party of technocrats, also opted to run. SODE leader Manuel Moreyra said that his organization sought seats in the CCD in order to "unequivocally reject the dictatorship and its actions" and to draw attention to ongoing corruption in the government.[25] Moreyra later admitted that he had doubted the wisdom of his party's decision to participate at the time, and ultimately admitted that it was a mistake.[26]

Movimiento Libertad, floundering since Vargas Llosa's 1990 defeat, finally disintegrated. Vargas Llosa was a furious critic of the coup, but he no longer lived in Peru. ML officials Luis Bustamante and Miguel Vega Alvear, along with other party notables such as former business leader Ricardo Vega Llona, were staunch advocates of electoral abstention. But other ML activists—Rafael Rey, Beatriz Merino, and Luis Delgado Aparicio—favored participation. Rafael Rey resigned and organized a new movement, Renovación, to stand for election to the CCD.

The participation of some groups and the abstention of others produced the worst possible outcome for the opposition as a whole. With the largest organizations (APRA and AP) out of the race and the left and right wings split apart, it was unlikely that opposing forces could win enough seats to control the CCD. Opposition leaders on both sides of the CCD issue were painfully aware that the divides among them played to Fujimori's advantage, but were at a loss to overcome them.

With the opposition flummoxed, Fujimori began the campaign to elect a docile majority to the CCD. To do so, he needed to remount his own political organization. Fujimori's famous disdain for political parties and personal domination had eviscerated his own original organization, C90. Fujimori forced out many of his old allies and organizers early on, then purged the C90 legislative caucus of dissidents. After the coup put an end to the congress, C90 was effectively nonexistent.

To recreate his political organization, Fujimori recruited professionals with proven loyalties to him. In early September, the minister of energy, Jaime Yoshiyama, left his post, and cabinet minister Oscar de la Puente announced that Yoshiyama would head an "independent list of sympathizers and supporters of the government." De la Puente counseled former C90 activists to "adjust" to Yoshiyama and the new organization since the two organizations would field a single list of candidates for the CCD.[27]

In the merger with C90, the new organizational wing named itself Nueva Mayoría (NM).[28] Yoshiyama, an engineer, headed the list of eighty CCD candidates, and he took an active role in recruiting the other candidates. Yoshiyama tapped Carlos Torres y Torres Lara, former law school dean of the Universidad de Lima. Torres y Torres Lara had served as minister of labor and foreign relations in Fujimori's cabinet. Also joining the ticket was Víctor Joy Way, another engineer, who had held the post of minister of industry in 1991–1992. Other recruits included Martha Chávez, a hard-driving, ambitious attorney who had served as secretary of the cabinet of ministers. Luz Salgado, former journalist and campaign organizer for C90, was one of the few holdovers from 1990 and was given the second slot on the ballot.

The new NM elite understood that their organization was created to serve immediate political purposes and that it would never become a real political party. According to Joy Way, NM "embodied principles," but it was not, nor would it become, a card-carrying political party.[29] Torres y Torres Lara offered the official reasoning behind the decision not to form a political party: "Our problem is that, if we create a political party, we would have to 'institutionalize favors,' since many people think that is the function of a political party. There is the belief that by belonging to a political party that one receives things in exchange. Especially here in Peru, jobs are like gold dust. . . . That's why Nueva Mayoría is a professional structure and not a mass-based party. It is necessary to create a consciousness with regard to participation and national development. The invitation [to join NM] is extended to the political class."[30] Equating parties with corruption provided an official rationale for turning the new organization into an exclusive club, rather than an inclusive political party.

In almost every aspect, the 1992 campaign and the CCD election foreshadowed the abuses that plagued every subsequent election under Fujimori. Questions about the integrity of election officials, the fairness of election rules, unchecked government spending, inequitable access to the media, and the role of the military were all at play in the CCD election, just as they would be 1993, 1995, and 2000.

The Jurado Nacional de Elecciones (JNE), the institution charged with overseeing elections, was a cipher from the start. Using the unchecked decree powers made possible by the coup, the government dismissed the two members of the JNE who were appointed by the supreme court, including the president of the JNE, Carlos Castañeda La Fontaine.[31] The same decree authorized that replacements be chosen by the Sala Plena of the supreme court, a body stocked with new appointees after the coup. In similar fashion, the Jurados Departamentales de Elecciones, or department-level election boards, were reconfigured in the hiring and firing following the coup.[32]

Opposition leaders questioned the neutrality of the new JNE president César Pollack, but to no avail. Pollack kept his job.

Effectively serving at the pleasure of the president, none of the recently appointed judges, prosecutors, or election officials were likely to rock the boat. Throughout the campaign, Jaime Yoshiyama batted away the press's questions about finances. He maintained that private contributors were covering campaign expenses. But Yoshiyama's constant campaign appearances alongside Fujimori and his travel on the presidential jet suggested that public resources were being used to promote the C90-NM ticket in an obvious violation of election law. At those appearances, crowds were treated to the standard handouts of food, clothing, and other items that accompanied a presidential visit.

There was no skimping on media spending either. Toward the end of the campaign, the government treated television viewers to a miniseries entitled, *Tres años que cambiaron la historia* (Three Years That Changed History). The series aired in prime time over five nights on all the major television stations, and its host was Jaime Yoshiyama. Framed as a documentary, the miniseries depicted opposition politicians as the source of all of Peru's ills, from hyperinflation to political violence. In contrast to those who had wreaked chaos, Fujimori and his technocrats were portrayed as modernizing saviors.[33]

Despite the obvious questions about where all the campaign money was coming from, neither Fujimori nor Yoshiyama offered any detailed accounting. Nor was there any investigation of charges made by opposition candidates that the military was proselytizing on behalf of the government.

Questions about the conduct of the election were sidelined, however, by a news story that dwarfed all others: the stunning capture of Abimael Guzmán. Guzmán, the notorious leader of Sendero Luminoso, was a near-mythic figure, having eluded arrest for more than a decade. The chase came to an end on September 12, 1992, when police intelligence agents found Guzmán in a safe house in Lima. Coming after months of high-profile terrorist attacks in Lima, Peruvians gleefully celebrated Guzmán's capture. The media provided extensive coverage of the event, including Guzman's post-arrest appearance. In an obvious attempt to humiliate the once-invincible guerrilla leader, authorities treated the press corps to a look at Guzmán, jailed in a cage and wearing a classic black-and-white-striped prison jumpsuit. The public relations value of the capture was enormous and Fujimori's approval ratings, which had begun to sag, recovered.[34]

Another dramatic event that preyed on the public's fear of political instability also worked in the government's favor. On the night of November 13, General Jaime Salinas and other dissident officers were arrested on charges of plotting to overthrow the Fujimori government. Amid the evening's confused events, Fujimori headed to the Japanese embassy for protection. He later asserted that the plot included a plan to assassinate him, thus minimizing his potentially embarrassing run for cover that evening.[35]

General Salinas's version of events, smuggled out of jail to the magazine *Oiga,* differed substantially from that of Fujimori. Salinas acknowledged his involvement in the failed coup plot, but he maintained that there was never any plan to kill Fujimori. Salinas said that the objective was to remove Fujimori from office and turn him over for trial for violating Peru's constitution. Moreover, Salinas said that he acted in order to stop the ongoing electoral fraud. He charged that a JNE employee had been ordered to surrender a copy of the vote-counting computer software to the armed forces, and that military access to the software would allow them to tamper with results. Salinas also claimed that armed forces personnel had been forced to sign registration petitions on behalf of NM and that those who refused were punished.[36] But with Salinas and his supporters behind bars in a military prison, the allegations went uninvestigated.

The CCD election was set for November 22. Eighteen political organizations made it onto the CCD ballot. Most of the groups were new and unknown to voters. In a departure from the traditional format of ballots in Peru, the JNE designed a ballot that listed the organizations in three separate categories: parties, independent groups, and alliances. As the only official "alliance," C90-NM Alianza ended up as a highly visible entry at the bottom of the ballot, separated out from the unrecognizable names that preceded it.[37]

When the votes were counted, the government alliance got its expected majority, but it was not a stunning victory. C90-NM won 38 percent of the valid vote and forty-four of the eighty seats. Voter abstention, which accounted for 27.8 percent of the electorate, was the highest registered in any contemporary election. Taking abstention into account, the results meant that the government majority had been voted into power by just 27.7 percent of all eligible voters. Taken together, all the other parties accounted for 38.6 percent of the valid vote, but there was little hope that a solid anti-government majority could emerge from so many disparate groups, especially since the government was ready to reach out and co-opt many of the new, self-proclaimed "independent" legislators.

Heading an election mission with two hundred observers, OAS secretary-general João Baena Soares baptized the CCD election as free and fair, despite the profound discord between the government and the opposition on the transition plan and election conditions.[38] The OAS approval of the election set the stage for a resolution declaring that the special meeting of OAS foreign ministers, which had been convoked in response to the April coup, was to be officially closed—in other words, the OAS now considered Peru to be back on a democratic track. Luigi Einaudi, American ambassador to the OAS, said that the CCD was an "important first step" but cautioned that Peru needed to work on developing an "independent congress" and "strong, representative institutions."[39]

Fujimori and Yoshiyama readily claimed victory. Fujimori called the CCD election "the birth of a new system, a new national political panorama . . . the beginning of a new era with a new system and a new style. What we have really achieved is a formalization—in soft terms—of the 5 April process."[40] Fujimori was right in depicting the CCD as a departure. But he made it clear that the kind of a legislature he had in mind might not exactly be the "independent congress" that Einaudi had called for. In a speech to business executives, Fujimori offered his view of how the CCD would work: "We want people who like to work and not just speak. We need to do things and make decisions. We need to produce and not to waste time. We want opinions and disagreements to be discussed but we reject everlasting debates. The country wants to build, and we should march to the same rhythm."[41]

The CCD in Action

The CCD held its inaugural session on December 29, 1992. Elected as CCD president, Jaime Yoshiyama acted swiftly to insure that all the coup-era laws were ratified. The government majority legalized all the decrees issued by the executive branch on and after April 5 and also ratified Alberto Fujimori as the "constitutional head of state." The CCD voted to reinstate the 1979 constitution (suspended in the coup), except for the government's decree laws, which took precedence over the constitution.[42] Yoshiyama took his job as leader of the C90-NM majority seriously; he called regular meetings to instruct legislators on how to vote and equipped them with beepers so that they were always within his reach.

The CCD began work on its major project: writing a new constitution to be ratified in a nationwide referendum. The task of coordinating C90-NM's efforts fell to Carlos Torres y Torres Lara, the law professor handpicked to head the constitutional commission charged with drafting the text.

Even before the constitutional commission convened, the issue of presidential reelection was on the agenda. Like many other Latin American countries, Peru's constitutions barred immediate presidential reelection. In the days immediately after the coup, Fujimori denied that he wanted to stay in power beyond the single term prescribed by the 1979 constitution, but the rhetoric soon began to shift. Fujimori ruminated that presidential reelection was something to be decided by "the people" in a referendum on the constitution, thus signaling that the CCD would consider the issue of reelection rather than stick with the traditional ban on it. At the same time, Fujimori frequently denied that he harbored any ambitions to stay in office.[43]

Despite Fujimori's disavowal of interest in reelection, C90-NM legislators wasted no time in taking up the cause. Martha Chávez was among the first to step up, beginning a combative legislative career in which she would become known as *más fujimorista que Fujimori* (more of a Fujimori loyalist than Fujimori).[44] In early February 1993, Chávez announced that C90-NM would propose a clause in the new constitution that would allow for immediate presidential reelection and might also include abolishment of any term limits.[45] The constitutional commission did consider the proposal for unlimited terms, but only Martha Chávez and Víctor Joy Way voted in its favor. Other C90-NM members of the commission voted to limit reelection to one term. In the view of commission president Carlos Torres y Torres Lara, limiting presidential reelection was more in step with international standards than unlimited terms.[46]

Reelection was not the only provision aimed at enhancing presidential powers. In a break with previous practice, C90-NM members of the commission backed a provision giving the executive complete control over promotions in the armed forces, thus eliminating any congressional oversight of the process. In the years ahead, this provision effectively allowed Vladimiro

Montesinos to completely control the top echelon of the armed forces by promoting only those loyal to him.

In another controversial provision, the president was given the power to dissolve congress once during his term and call new legislative elections. But as in the case of unlimited presidential reelection, questions about how the provision would be viewed by the international community came into play. Signals from one U.S. official that the measure provided for excessive presidential power and opened the door for a repeat of the auto-coup led to rethinking.[47] Eventually, the provision was reformulated to allow the president to dissolve the congress only in the event that congress voted to censure two cabinet ministers in a row, thus making dissolution unlikely.

As the backtracking on the dissolution provision showed, the writing process was hasty and improvised. The administration wanted a quick constitutional fix and believed that the new document would put a definitive end to the international pressures to democratize. The constitutional commission labored under great pressure to get the text completed quickly, egged on publicly and privately by Fujimori. To accelerate the pace of the commission's work, Torres y Torres Lara tried to limit the debate time allotted to opposition members. When opposition members walked out of a meeting on June 28, Torres y Torres Lara took advantage of their absence to strip a number of provisions out of the draft text and have it unanimously passed by C90-NM members.

The blatant disregard for the opposition and the lack of deliberation that characterized the commission's conduct prompted editorial criticism from Peru's most respected newspaper, *El Comercio*. In the editorial view of *El Comercio,* the final, hastily produced text effectively established "a political system in which an excessive and dangerous concentration of executive power" would prevail.[48] The new constitution and the rules of procedure empowered the executive branch by making other institutions more pliable, more prone to manipulation by the executive. The text established a unicameral legislature, with rules of procedure designed to make it easier to limit debate and rapidly push through measures.

The floor vote on the constitution was a foregone conclusion. Opposition members used the final debate on the reelection provision to reiterate their views on the dangerous, authoritarian proclivities of the regime. Opposition members argued that the reelection provision was framed exclusively with Fujimori in mind. Fernando Olivera of FIM launched a broad attack on reelection, arguing that Fujimori would use all the resources available to him to fix the election result and that an "electoral fraud" was already in motion. He concluded with an attack on Montesinos, alleging that he had ties with narco-traffickers and that the government was complicit in his wrongdoing.

Opposition fears about Fujimori's appetite for power fueled suspicions about how the reelection provision might be applied in the future. Congressman Manuel Moreyra of SODE predicted that the government might attempt to use the reelection provision to extend Fujimori's mandate beyond 2000. He anticipated that they would argue that the ban on more than two terms in the presidency could not be applied retroactively to the 1993 constitution: "Basically, what has been approved is the principle of unlimited re-election, an expression of Mr. Fujimori's desire to remain in office as long as he can, using whatever method he can (legal or illegal, violent or nonviolent, moral or immoral). . . . This casts a terrible shadow over the future."[49]

During the August 4 debate on the floor, Torres y Torres Lara was pressed to clarify whether the president's election in 1990 would count as one of his two consecutive terms, or whether his possible reelection in 1995 could be interpreted as his first term under the 1993 constitution. Torres y Torres Lara insisted that C90-NM had rejected the idea of unlimited re-election and stated his interpretation of the new provision: "If President Fujimori participates in the electoral process, he can be president only one more time (1995–2000) because the current term (1990–1995) counts as such. I do not think that I can be any clearer."[50]

Torres y Torres Lara's clarity may have been genuine at the time, but he was later forced to reinterpret his own interpretation in the service of a president whose appetite for power was as insatiable as Manuel Moreyra predicted.

Yes or No

While the constitution was being written in the period from January to August 1993, it was never clear whether the promised referendum would take the form of a vote on the constitution in its entirety, or as separate votes to accept or reject specific articles of the constitution. Nothing in the OAS resolutions stipulated how the referendum was supposed to proceed.

In an April interview, Torres y Torres Lara confided that formulas for proceeding with the referendum were diverse and could even include the enactment of the new constitution, with a referendum on specific articles to follow after the fact.[51] Initially, opposition leaders believed that the government was preparing a partial referendum focusing on the issues that voters were most likely to understand and endorse at the moment—namely, the reelection provision and the death penalty for crimes classified as treason or terrorism. Fujimori frequently spoke about the two issues, arguing that the public should pronounce on both.

Suspecting that the government would slant the referendum questions in order to set up a huge victory for itself, opposition leaders agreed to push for a referendum on the constitution in its entirety. A diverse group of leaders —intellectuals, journalists, party officials, mayors, and trade unionists— kicked off the campaign for a No vote on the constitution with a meeting in July 1993 and the publication of a statement demanding a referendum on the full text.[52] Also stirring up the debate on Peru's political future was the new, multipartisan Foro Democrático. Founded in April 1993 by a diverse group of political and cultural notables, Foro described its mission as the "diffusion and promotion of democratic values, the strengthening and preservation of democratic institutions and the rejection of any authoritarian project."[53]

But viewed from the presidential palace, the most troubling opposition lay elsewhere, outside of Lima. In July, the national congress of the mayors' association, Asociación de Municipalidades del Perú (AMPE), elected Arturo Castillo Chirinos as its president and José Murgia as its vice president. Castillo Chirinos was the popular AP mayor of Chiclayo, and Murgia was the APRA mayor of Trujillo. Angry with the government's stand against decentralization and the president's control over public spending in the provinces, the mayors passed a declaration characterizing the CCD as "lacking autonomy and independence" and pledging the organization's "rejection of the authoritarian and anti-democratic constitutional project." They also demanded a referendum on the entire text of the constitution.[54]

Fujimori unleashed his fury at the dissident mayors, calling them a *mazamorra negra* (black pudding), a vile collection of corrupt officials. Dismissing their demands for more control over municipal finances, Fujimori was blunt about how he planned to deal with the mayors: "So they have declared war against El Chino. . . . So to all of them, to that municipal black pudding, I will stop you and we will bury you. . . . My response to this declaration of war is clear: I will be the one in charge of public works."[55]

Fujimori's tough response showed how sensitive he was to the potential clout of provincially based opposition. C90-NM did not field mayoral candidates across the country in the 1993 municipal elections. It was a sign of its organizational disarray and the government's willingness to gamble that "independents" could be co-opted. That left the field open to traditional parties like APRA and AP and an array of new independent vehicles. In Lima, Mayor Ricardo Belmont, the maverick television personality turned politician, rejected the opportunity to run for reelection as an *oficialista* candidate, but he received the personal endorsement of Fujimori after the C90-NM mayoral candidate withdrew. Belmont ran a strong race with his independent Movimiento Obras, winning 45 percent of the vote in his own reelection bid while his movement took twenty-one of the forty-two district-level mayoralties in metropolitan Lima.[56] But the Belmont-Fujimori alliance was short-lived. By mid-1993, Belmont was touted as a potential rival to Fujimori in the 1995 presidential election, and AMPE looked like it could become an organizational center of resistance to the regime.

In a surprise move, the C90-NM congressional majority voted on August 31, 1993, to accept the opposition's call for a referendum on the entire constitution. Voters would be given the opportunity to cast a Yes or No on the complete text. Torres y Torres Lara said the decision demonstrated C90-NM's flexibility toward the opposition and its willingness to listen to public opinion.[57]

The logic of the government's strategy was immediately apparent. Indeed, some political strategists argued that the opposition had fallen into a government trap. By agreeing to hold the referendum on the whole constitution, the government would take advantage of the high job-approval ratings that Fujimori still enjoyed. Fujimori quickly spelled out what he thought the referendum was all about: "I am going to be very frank. What is involved, in short, is approving or disapproving of Fujimori."[58]

The No campaign began in earnest with the formation of the Comité Cívico por el No (Civic Committee for No) in early September. The Comité attracted politicians, intellectuals, grassroots leaders, and labor leaders, but the participants emphasized that they were joining the movement as individuals, not as party leaders.[59] Legislators in the CCD opted to form their own Comando Unitario to campaign for the No vote. The Comando included Fernando Olivera (FIM), Manuel Moreyra (SODE), Henry Pease (MDI), Roger Cáceres (FRENATRACA), and Luis Bedoya (PPC). Still at the helm of AP, Fernando Belaúnde contemplated pushing his party to abstain (as it had in the CCD election), but he finally came out in favor of the No position. Belaúnde warned that the new constitution would end up being amended to allow Fujimori additional terms in office.[60]

The leaders of the PPC also opted for the No position, but PPC secretary-general Lourdes Flores announced that her organization would conduct its own separate campaign. So while a broad range of political organizations were prepared to campaign for the No vote, there was no single, unified organization leading the charge, largely due to the aversion that some groups had for working in any official capacity with APRA. Instead, the No campaign unfolded as a grassroots effort that joined popular organizations and party activists and Peru's major trade unions.

Fujimori's view of the opposition was simple. Fujimori described the No side as the resort of traditional politicians, the enemies defeated by his coup. He was as merciless as he had been on the AMPE mayors. "How awful," he remarked, "now they want to resuscitate the old politicians of APRA-communism not just to form a *mazamorra negra,* but the funeral procession for the No." Branding opposition politicians as the "living dead," Fujimori accused them of trying to destabilize the country and provoke a military intervention.[61]

Scare tactics were an important element in the Yes campaign. Fujimori and Yoshiyama sent C90-NM legislators to campaign across the country with the message that economic instability and terrorism would return if the constitution was rejected. Stumping for the Yes vote in the provinces, Congressman Víctor Joy Way said that victory for the No vote would constitute a victory for the jailed Sendero leader Abimael Guzmán, and that it would imply a return to insecurity and terrorism.[62] On the eve of the referendum, Fujimori threatened to resign if he lost since it would mean a return to the pre-coup political system.[63]

But the Yes campaign was not exclusively negative in its appeals. Jaime Yoshiyama pronounced that the economy was "the heart" of the new constitution because it would bring new business, industry, and jobs.[64] Argentine publicist Daniel Borobio masterminded the Yes campaign and projected optimism in its slogans: "To Modern Peru, Say Yes"; "To the Peru with a Future, Say Yes"; "To the Peru You Want, Say Yes."[65]

Rather than focus attention on Fujimori, the No campaign zeroed in on the unpopular provisions in the constitution. The strongest issues for the No side were the lack of plans for decentralization and the provision in the new constitution that abolished across-the-board free tuition for public universities and established a means test to determine eligibility for free tuition. The No campaign argued that, by abolishing free university tuition, the government was laying the groundwork for the privatization of education.

As in the CCD election, the government's resources dramatically exceeded what was available to the opposition. The No side pieced together its media campaign with support from sympathetic radio stations and Gustavo Mohme's newspaper *La República*. In contrast to the austere No campaign, the Yes campaign mounted a blitz of television ads.

From the start of the campaign, opposition leaders charged that Fujimori and other officials were using public monies and other resources. Fujimori scoffed at the allegations, saying that the inauguration of public works was an essential part of his job as president. He dared the opposition to prove the charges that he was misusing funds in a court of law.[66] But given the state of the judiciary and the JNE, Fujimori knew that no effective legal recourse existed. The OAS electoral mission acknowledged instances of inappropriate conduct by public officials, but the mission remained conspicuously silent on the question of whether the president's conduct was appropriate and had nothing to say about campaign finance.

Seeking to remind voters at home and international observers of the government's successes in the war against terrorism and its spectacular capture of Abimael Guzmán, Fujimori made a stunning announcement during a speech to the United Nations in early October 1993. He revealed that Guzmán had written a letter from jail advocating a peace accord between Sendero and the Peruvian state. Fujimori argued that the defeat of the guerrilla insurgency in Peru was a direct result of the measures taken in conjunction with the coup, and thus the coup was fully justified.[67]

A second, even more remarkable letter appeared several weeks later. In that letter, Guzmán described the coup as a necessary measure for the Peruvian state and acknowledged the accomplishments of the Fujimori government. Seasoned journalists had predicted that the government would try to stage an event involving Guzmán during the campaign. In early August, *Sí* magazine reported that Montesinos and Guzmán were meeting in secret to discuss an official "surrender" by Sendero.[68] As an electoral ploy, the Guzmán revelations fell flat. Skeptical Peruvians interpreted the letters as a politically motivated stunt. An Apoyo poll reported that 56 percent of the public disapproved of the release of the Guzmán letters just prior to the referendum.[69]

By mid-October, the grassroots No campaign was chipping away at the huge margin that the government had enjoyed. In late August, an Imasen poll registered public support for the Yes vote at 59 percent, with the No vote trailing behind at 20 percent.[70] Fujimori predicted that the Yes vote would garner 70 percent of the vote. But as the campaign wore on, the race tightened. A week before the election, Apoyo pollsters projected that the Yes vote would win by just 8 percent of the vote or perhaps less.[71]

When the polls closed on October 31, pollsters delivered projections that gave the Yes vote a victory by a ten-point margin of 55 percent to 45 percent of the valid vote. Both Fujimori and CCD president Jaime Yoshiyama quickly claimed victory, and tried to put the best face on the results that had clearly fallen below their own expectations. Fujimori conceded that his own personal popularity had failed to translate into an equivalent level of support for the government both in the CCD elections and in the referendum. Nonetheless, he claimed that 55 percent was a solid endorsement because it was a majority.[72]

By the following day, Fujimori's majority was being whittled away as new projections narrowed the margin further. The Apoyo polling firm readjusted its projection, giving 52.9 percent to the Yes vote and 47.1 percent to the No vote; a subsequent readjustment took the percentages down to 51.6 percent and 48.4 percent, respectively.[73] The contest had become, in the view of opposition leaders, a "virtual tie."

As the wait for the official results went on, the magnitude of the government's defeat outside of Lima became clear. Ten of Peru's sixteen departments opted for the No vote. Of the six departments voting Yes, two were Lima and Callao. The concentration of the Yes vote in the metropolitan Lima area made opposition leaders suspicious of the ongoing vote-counting in Lima by the Jurado Departamental de Elecciones de Lima (JDEL). Opposition leaders charged that unsecured election returns were being delivered to the board and that the circumstances surrounding the delivery were suspicious. The JDEL's decision to count *actas* (documents recording the votes cast at each polling place) that were signed by only two polling officials (rather than the obligatory three) was interpreted by the opposition as a way of ensuring a government victory in the tight race.[74] The opposition lodged legal challenges to 3,200 *actas* in Lima, but unsurprisingly JDEL rejected the challenges.

The OAS election mission paid little attention to the opposition's complaints about the Lima vote count. The mission noted the tardiness in the delivery of the *actas* to department election boards, which affected the first two days of the count, but the mission attributed the delay to "weather difficulties and logistics."[75] The OAS mission offered no observations about why the JNE waited until December 17 to confirm the final results of the referendum, nor did it directly address the fraud accusations made by the one dissenting member of the JNE, Juan Chávez Molina. Molina refused to ratify the final referendum results, arguing that the election conditions had not been fair because of the executive's use of public resources to swing votes and Fujimori's inappropriate threats about resigning during the campaign.[76]

Absent any serious criticisms from the OAS mission, opposition leaders glumly concluded that there was little hope of challenging the results. Still, the narrow margin of victory reduced the utility of the new constitution as a means to relegitimize the regime. Taking absenteeism and voided votes into account, only one-third of eligible voters had approved the new constitution. In light of the near fifty-fifty split in the electorate and the obvious rejection by voters in the provinces, opposition leaders argued that the results showed a lack of consensus on the text and pointed to the need for revisions. And the public appeared to agree; a post-referendum survey conducted by Imasen showed that 78.9 percent of those polled agreed that the constitution should be modified prior to its enactment.[77]

The opposition's calls for a new dialogue and amendments to the constitution fell on deaf ears. Torres y Torres Lara spoke of possible amendments in the future, but only after the constitution was enacted. Congresswoman Martha Chávez scoffed at the opposition's calls for *concertación* in the aggressive manner that became the hallmark of her political career: "I do not call for *concertación* because I can't get together with those who espouse the interests of groups. I cannot get together with Sendero Luminoso, nor the extreme left, or with a leadership that is xenophobic and tries to restore its own privileges. I have no interest in talking with such leaders."[78]

Fujimori went ahead and signed the constitution on December 29, 1993. The signing ceremony, held in the presidential palace, lacked fanfare and pomp. No high-ranking foreign dignitaries were present. In a press conference called before the ceremony, CCD opposition leaders characterized the new constitution as "illegitimate" and presented an alternative text for a constitution.[79]

The formal recasting of political institutions was over, but it had not generated a new political consensus or jumpstarted democracy in Peru. Instead, the political processes of 1992–1993 repackaged the coup in the garb of new institutions. Even though the public at large still did not like to think of their country as being in the grip of an authoritarian regime, a significant part of the political class and the press did.

Culture of Cover-Up

Despite its flaws, the 1993 constitution was not a blueprint for authoritarianism per se. Like many other Latin American and previous Peruvian constitutions, the 1993 document provided the president with significant powers. But the 1993 constitution, in theory, also provided for countervailing powers to be exercised by autonomous institutions such as the congress, the supreme court, the Tribunal Constitucional, and the Defensoría del Pueblo. Torres y Torres Lara and his constitutional commission did, in the end, produce a document that mimicked most of the normal traits of a presidential system and met international standards of democratic design.

Authoritarianism in Fujimori's Peru was not a function of formal design. What made the political system authoritarian were the people who inhabited the institutions and the extremes to which they were willing to go in service to Fujimori. The countervailing powers among the three branches of government did not function because there was no one at the helm of institutions interested in or capable of making them work.[80] How low officials were willing to go in order to circumvent constitutional norms and undermine the principle of accountability in order to protect the regime's principals is made painfully clear in how they dealt with the government's first major human rights case—the case of La Cantuta.

The case began on July 18, 1992, when nine students and one university professor of the Universidad Enrique Guzmán y Valle (more popularly known as La Cantuta) "disappeared." The victims were kidnapped and killed in an operation undertaken by an elite military squad working under supervision of the army intelligence service. The individuals targeted, who allegedly were working with Sendero Luminoso, were summarily executed and their bodies were buried in unmarked graves outside of Lima.

Relatives of the disappeared looked to the legal system for answers, but found none. It was a matter of public record that military personnel were on the university campus on the night of abductions, but early on in the case there was no evidence definitely linking the military to the "disappearances." Three writs of habeas corpus were filed, but General Hermoza, head of the armed forces high command, fought off attempts to force officers to testify in the case by citing "security reasons." Because no bodies had yet been discovered, a judge ruled that the relatives had failed to produce evidence that the individuals in question had ever existed. The legal route concluded when the supreme court upheld a lower court ruling on March 29, 1993, which effectively closed down the case. The judicial halt to the investigation left the CCD as the only other institution that families could appeal to in their search.

Knowing that they faced an uphill fight, opposition legislators took up the cause. On April 1, 1993, Congressman Carlos Cuaresma of FIM prepared to introduce a motion calling on the ministry of defense to report to the CCD on the La Cantuta disappearances. During the debate, Congressman Henry Pease rose to announce that he had received a memorandum from a group of officers calling itself Comandantes, Mayores y Capitanes (COMACA). To the gasps of reporters and visitors in the gallery, Pease said that the memo confirmed that army intelligence operatives had executed the La Cantuta detainees and that Vladimiro Montesinos and General Hermoza authorized the operation.

Faced with the explosive charges that military officers were responsible for ten homicides, the CCD had to act. It created an investigative commission to look into the matter and, trying to project an image of impartiality, the C90-NM majority manned the commission with three opposition members and two *oficialistas*. Representing the opposition was the commission's president, Roger Cáceres, along with Gloria Helfer and Carlos Cuaresma. Gilberto Siura and Jaime Freundt represented C90-NM.

After some delay, General Hermoza showed up for tense testimony before the committee on April 20. He denied knowledge of any military involvement and speculated that military or paramilitary forces could have been involved, or that Sendero might have attacked the students, or that it could have been a stunt by the students, an *auto-secuestro* (self-kidnapping).

Obviously miffed at being called on the carpet by legislators, Hermoza faced reporters after his testimony and read a prepared statement. He blasted the COMACA document as false and accused congressmen of being involved in a campaign to discredit the army. On the following day, Hermoza ordered an unusual "tank parade" in downtown Lima. On the same day, the army issued an ominous statement lashing out at the congressional opposition and accusing them of abetting terrorists.[81]

Another strange parade of tanks and armored vehicles followed on April 22 around the Campo del Marte in downtown Lima. The event was not just for opposition consumption. It was a reminder to Fujimori and C90-NM that the armed forces would not tolerate any attempt to blame them for human rights abuses. Apparently getting the message from the tank parades, Fujimori denounced efforts at "tarnishing" the image of the military.[82]

This heavy-handedness in Lima backfired in Washington. Disturbed by the tank parades, the U.S. government did some signaling of its own. Bernard Aronson, secretary of state for inter-American affairs, called Fujimori with the message that the military's attempt to intimidate the legislature was unacceptable. In meetings with U.S. Treasury officials in Washington, Peruvian finance minister Jorge Camet heard the same warning.[83] The attaché in charge of the U.S. embassy in Lima, Charles Brayshaw, told the press that the situation could threaten the flow of international aid to Peru. Meanwhile, opposition party leaders and legislators met in a long session to discuss strategy, including the idea of quitting the CCD altogether in protest.

With events threatening to undo his efforts to reestablish Peru's good standing in international circles, Fujimori tried to defuse the conflict. In a nationally televised address bereft of his usual insults and threats, Fujimori called for civility and respect for institutions. General Víctor Malca, the minister of defense, suddenly showed up in the CCD and pledged the military's cooperation in the investigation.

But conciliatory gestures could not put an end to the growing controversy. In early May, General Rodolfo Robles went public with information confirming the existence of a death squad, called Grupo Colina. Robles said that the squad, composed of army intelligence operatives and led by

Major Santiago Martín Rivas, was responsible for the La Cantuta homicides. Robles charged that the group operated under direct orders from Vladimiro Montesinos and with the knowledge of General Hermoza. Fearing retribution, Robles and his family sought refuge at the U.S. embassy in Lima, and later moved to Buenos Aires.[84]

Army officials reacted ferociously. The military's high court, the Consejo Supremo de Justicia Militar (CSJM), laid a slew of charges against Robles that included insubordination, insulting the armed forces, and making false statements. On May 11, fifty-four army generals signed a statement calling Robles a coward and a felon, unworthy to wear the uniform of the armed forces. In a televised interview, CSJM judge General José Picón said that Robles was suffering from a "mental problem" and that his accusations were probably fueled by thwarted career ambitions. Picón concluded that if he were in Robles's shoes, he would be ashamed and would commit suicide.[85]

Apparently no one in the armed forces felt obliged to suspend judgment before the investigation concluded. Neither did CCD president Jaime Yoshiyama. On a trip to Washington, Yoshiyama tried to assure U.S. officials of the integrity of the investigation while confessing his disbelief in the charges against Montesinos and Hermoza.[86] Fujimori proclaimed that he had "absolute confidence" in Montesinos. Many Peruvians were less confident. An Apoyo poll taken in April reported that 38 percent of those polled believed that an army death squad was responsible for the deaths, while only 22 percent rejected the accusation.[87] A May poll by Imasen showed that, among people who said that they were familiar with Robles's accusations, 52 percent believed them to be true and 73 percent supported the congressional investigation.[88]

Efforts to derail the congressional commission intensified. The three opposition members of the commission—Cáceres, Helfer, and Cuaresma —received anonymous threats, delivered by phone and indirectly through social acquaintances. Meanwhile, congressional colleagues stonewalled their investigation. In an obvious move to limit the evidence available, Víctor Joy Way and Martha Chávez introduced a resolution that restricted the CCD to calling only high-ranking officers in human rights investigations. Their C90-NM colleagues dutifully passed the measure, ensuring that low-ranking officers could not offer testimony damaging to those higher up in the chain of command. Opposition members walked out of the debate in disgust, charging that the CCD majority was effectively abdicating its responsibility to investigate. Congressman Henry Pease said that the CCD was treating the military as a "separate state within the state."

In another move to restrict testimony, the CSJM issued an order forbidding Vladimiro Montesinos from appearing in front of the commission on the pretext that his testimony would interfere with ongoing judicial proceedings. In his second appearance before the commission, General Hermoza also cited ongoing CSJM proceedings as the ground for limiting his testimony.

Despite all the efforts to quash the investigation, the three opposition members filed a majority report that identified army intelligence operatives as the perpetrators of the La Cantuta disappearances. The report called for indictments of the operatives as well as felony charges for all officers involved in the planning of the operation and the cover-up of evidence. Filed by *oficialistas* Gilberto Siura and Jaime Freundt, the commission's minority report declared that the evidence was insufficient to come to a conclusion about the disappearances at La Cantuta. The minority report repeated some of the hypotheses offered up earlier by General Hermoza—that the students might have been the targets of a paramilitary or terrorist attack, or that they might have gone underground to become terrorists or to avoid terrorists. Years later, Freundt acknowledged that the minority report drew on information provided directly by Vladimiro Montesinos: "We asked him [Montesinos] for information [and] he gave us information, excellent information, unfortunately it was a lie, but at that time how were we supposed to know it was a lie, there was no way to know."[89]

Not surprisingly, the majority report was dead on arrival. The C90-NM majority voted to accept the minority report by a margin of thirty-nine to thirteen on June 26. Just when the case appeared to have hit a dead end, however, another leak of crucial information to the press brought it back to life.

One major obstacle in the course of the investigation was the lack of physical evidence to prove the homicides—most importantly, the victims' bodies. Acting on information and a map provided by an anonymous source, the director of *Sí*, Ricardo Uceda, and his team of journalists made a grim discovery in the case. Using the map, the journalists uncovered human remains in unmarked graves on a hillside in the outskirts of Lima. Years later, the anonymous creators of the map were revealed. Justo Arizapana, a local garbage recycler, saw the bodies being dumped in the dead of night. He alerted a friend, Guillermo Catorca. The men decided to draw a map and get it into the hands of investigators. The map was routed to the congressional office of Roger Cáceres and passed on to *Sí*.[90]

The discovery forced Attorney General Blanca Nélida Colán to reopen the investigation. From the start, however, reporters from *Sí*, *Caretas*, and *La República* questioned the handling of the crime scene investigation and wondered about the forensic evidence. Colán turned down offers of expert assistance from Amnesty International, the U.S. embassy, and the highly respected Argentine forensic anthropology team. As the investigation dragged on, evidence found in the graves led to the certain conclusion that the remains were those of the ten "disappeared" from La Cantuta. Relatives identified their clothing, and keys found at the site fit the residence of one of the victims. Several skulls found at the scene showed that the victims had been shot in the head at close range.

What happened to the bodies had to be explained, and the idea of laying the blame on Sendero resurfaced. The counterinsurgency division of the national police contended that the information regarding the location of the graves provided to Ricardo Uceda had to have come from Sendero, and thus the evidence could have been planted.[91] Fujimori seemingly endorsed the view in his annual speech to the congress on July 28 when he referred to Cieneguilla (the area where the graves were located) as one of the sites of Sendero massacres.[92]

Like the congressional investigators, the leading journalists following the case (Ricardo Uceda and his team at *Sí*, Cecilia Valenzuela of *Caretas*, and Mónica Vecco of *La República*) became targets of anonymous acts of harassment and death threats. Congresswoman Martha Chávez suggested that a criminal case could be filed against Ricardo Uceda because, by uncovering the graves, he disturbed the crime scene.[93]

As evidence in the case mounted, Attorney General Colán made an obvious move to contain the investigation. On August 24, Colán informed the congress that the civilian investigation of La Cantuta would be shut down so as not to duplicate the work of the CSJM, which had opened its own proceedings in the case.[94] Despite the shutdown of the case, the special prosecutor in charge of the gravesite investigation, Víctor Cubas Villanueva, continued compiling materials for his final report. The stage was set for a legal battle over whether the civilian or military judiciary would have jurisdiction in the case.

That the La Cantuta case intersected with the constitutional referendum of 1993 complicated matters considerably for the administration. Just as Fujimori was preparing to normalize the regime with the new constitution and proclaim to the world that Peru had returned to democracy, the La Cantuta case telegraphed a very different story and renewed international criticism. After the discovery of the bodies in July, a *New York Times* editorial lambasted Fujimori for leading a regime with the worst human rights record on the continent and called on the Clinton administration to keep up the pressure on Peru to make good on its promise of democratization. The editorial coincided with similar calls in the U.S. Congress from Senator Patrick Leahy and Representative David Obey.[95]

As the international scrutiny mounted, the cover-up needed to be rejigged. In late October, Fujimori broke the news through the *New York Times* that four military officers, including Major Santiago Martín Rivas, were under arrest in conjunction with charges in the La Cantuta case. His announcement turned out to be false, and arrests in the case only came later. But Fujimori's changed story showed that the administration was preparing to offer up some limited prosecutions in order to lay the case to rest.

Fujimori made it clear how limited the concessions in the La Cantuta case would be in December 1993 when he reconfirmed, rather than replaced, General Hermoza as head of the armed forces high command. In the traditional ceremony held on Army Day, Fujimori elegized the general's accomplishments in Peru's war against terrorism. He also laid out the new line on La Cantuta, one that depicted the crimes as the aberrant acts of individuals: "The discovery of the cadavers in Cieneguilla and Huachipa are part of an investigative process that must follow its legal course. None of these condemnable individual and isolated acts will diminish the pacification work of the Bolognesi army."[96]

The official attempt to portray the crimes as the work of individuals was a sham. As the exhaustive investigation by Peru's Comisión de la Verdad y Reconciliación (CVR) later showed, Grupo Colina was formally constituted as a special unit and administratively recognized as such.[97] Any genuine investigation would have rapidly turned up its existence, and also would have shown the long list of officials in the Dirección de Inteligencia de Ejército (DINTE) that Colina operatives took orders from and reported to. At the top of the chain of command were General Hermoza and Vladimiro Montesinos, two men that reported directly to the president.

Víctor Cubas Villanueva, the civilian prosecutor in the case, filed his final report on December 11, 1993. In the report, Cubas brought kidnapping and murder charges against eleven individuals involved in the execution of the operation at La Cantuta. Cubas also argued that civilian courts should retain jurisdiction over the case. The original indictment did not include charges against higher-ranking commanding officers. Attorneys for the families of the victims filed a request that additional charges be laid against another twenty-five individuals in the intelligence and army intelligence services, including General Hermoza, General Julio Salazar Monroe, and General Luis Pérez Documet. Cubas annexed the request to his original indictments and forwarded them to the judge assigned to review the case, Carlo Magno Chacón. Twenty-four hours later, Judge Chacón issued indictments for ten of the eleven people listed by Cubas. Chacón's decision was unusually speedy, considering that the documentation provided by Cubas included two thousand files.

Given the competing jurisdictional claims between military and civilian courts, the final decision on where the case would be heard rested with the penal division of the supreme court. But how the supreme court might rule on the case was anyone's guess, especially if the case were postponed until January 1994 when two new, perhaps independent-minded members were slated to take up their scheduled rotations onto the court.

Chacón's lightning-speed ruling in the case appeared to be a move aimed at getting the supreme court to rule before the personnel rotations took place. Reporting by José Jara and Angel Páez in *La República* had already cast doubt on Chacón's impartiality. Chacón, who was abruptly assigned to the case in early December, had political ties to the Fujimori administration that included leading a march, organized with the help of the SIN, supporting the 1992 coup.[98]

Heriberto Benítez, the attorney for the victims' families, filed a motion to have Chacón removed from the case. Chacón, in turn, accused prosecutor Víctor Cubas of incompetence and delaying the investigation. Some analysts wondered if the Chacón-Villanueva feud was being staged to discredit the civilian investigation and assure that the case would be assigned to a military court. Chacón was eventually removed from the case in January 1993, but by that time the legal imbroglio meant that the supreme court would rule on jurisdiction with its two new members in place.

On February 3, 1994, the penal division of the supreme court rendered a split decision of three to two in favor of military jurisdiction. The vote did not settle the matter, however, since supreme court rules stipulated that four votes were necessary to make a determination on jurisdiction. In such situations, other senior judges—in this case, Carlos Giusti and Manuel Sánchez Palacios—were assigned the responsibility for casting the final vote. Giusti was slated to make the first ruling, but if he sided with the minority, Sánchez would make the final determination. Neither Giusti nor Sánchez seemed disposed to grant military jurisdiction and the military prosecutor sought to have Giusti removed from the case.

Giusti scheduled oral arguments for February 10. On February 7, a briefcase full of dynamite exploded in the garden of Giusti's home. The attack on Giusti served as the pretext for the CCD to upset the judicial process. At 10:30 p.m., Congressman Julio Chú Mériz proposed a bill to alter the voting procedures of the supreme court.

It was a legislative ambush. Opposition members had not been told about the bill or that it would come to a vote in the evening session. The bill modified the supreme court's rules to allow jurisdictional votes to be decided by a simple majority, rather than the four-vote rule. Chú Mériz, a congressman who had been kicked out of FIM and who was part of a caucus of independents called Somos Independientes, later confirmed that SIN officials had handed him the bill to present that night.

Opposition members of congress walked out in protest, and the bill passed with forty-five votes in favor and six against. Among those casting negative votes was Congressman Carlos Ferrero, one of a few dissenters in the C90-NM caucus.[99] Congressional vice president Víctor Joy Way justified the measure on the grounds that it would be impossible for any judge to act objectively in casting the tiebreaking vote in light of the attack on Giusti's home.[100]

Legal experts and civic groups were flabbergasted by the CCD's blatant intrusion in the case. Lima's bar association, Colegio de Abogados de Lima (CAL), deplored it as "a virtual coup d'etat by the legislature against the independence and autonomy of the judicial branch." Similarly, the jurist group Comisión Andina de Juristas denounced the measure as unconstitutional on the grounds that the law allowed for its retroactive application in order to disrupt ongoing legal proceedings. Opponents in congress argued that the way in which the bill was passed violated the legislative rules of procedure.

On the same night that congress passed the bill, President Fujimori signed it as Law 26291. Alfonso Bustamante, the president of the cabinet of ministers, declined to sign the law and resigned his post, but he was the only dissenter. On February 11, the supreme court met again and, applying the new voting rules prescribed in Law 26291, voted to send the La Cantuta case to military court.

The U.S. Department of State called on the Peruvian government to "show complete respect for the principles of the separation of powers and judicial autonomy contained in the 1993 constitution," but to no avail.[101] The immediate criticisms by state department officials or American congressmen were of little consequence; the Fujimori administration officials knew by 1994 that it was unlikely that Peru would suffer any real retribution for the egregious actions in the La Cantuta case. The CCD election had been effective in providing the Fujimori administration with a cover of political normalcy, and Peru's relationship with the Clinton administration had improved considerably. By 1994, Peru had become the largest recipient of foreign aid in Latin America, and American officials were impressed by Fujimori's successes in counterinsurgency and neoliberal economic reform.[102]

Grupo Colina defendants got a speedy military trial. Just ten days after the supreme court resolution on jurisdiction, the CSJM found nine of the ten individuals charged in the case guilty on various counts. The officers directly in command of the operation, Major Santiago Martín Rivas and Major Carlos Eliseo Pichilingue, received sentences of twenty years imprisonment and fines. The rest received sentences that ranged from one to fifteen years. Voicing the government's view, Congressman Carlos Torres y Torres Lara lauded the verdicts as a groundbreaking moment in the history of military jurisprudence in Peru because no court had ever handed out tougher sentences. But Archbishop Augusto Vargas Alzamora of the Roman Catholic Church called the sentences "benign" in light of the grievous crimes involved. Human rights advocates speculated that the sentences would be commuted once the publicity surrounding the case died down, and that prediction came true when Fujimori signed a 1995 amnesty law that freed the perpetrators.

In a final act of disrespect, the remains of those killed from La Cantuta were returned to their families in cardboard cartons. But the callous and half-baked cover-up did not put the controversy to rest. The military trial ended the legal process, but the larger questions looming in the case remained unanswered. What was going on inside Peru's intelligence agency? Were Hermoza, Montesinos, and perhaps even President Fujimori responsible for authorizing the crimes or the cover-up?

Immediately after the sentencing, opposition political leaders and human rights advocates began strategizing about how the case could be reopened or appealed abroad in the Inter-American Court of Human Rights. They had been stymied in the CCD, but they were not about to give up on the effort to uncover and publicize the abuses of the regime. Neither would the small band of investigative reporters at *Sí, Caretas, La República,* and *Oiga,* who believed that La Cantuta was just the tip of the iceberg—one of many crimes begging to be unearthed.

5

PERU CAN'T STOP

ALBERTO Fujimori had good reason to love public-opinion polls. He basked in his high job-approval ratings after the 1992 coup, and he used them effectively against his critics. From 1993 through 1994, his polling numbers were steady, showing that between 60 to 70 percent of Peruvians approved of his job performance. His approval slipped only once, dipping to 58 percent in February 1994 as the La Cantuta controversy raged.

The president of the CCD, Jaime Yoshiyama, shared the president's fascination with polls and focus groups. He made extensive use of both to gauge probable reactions to the congress's controversial measures. What he discovered was that human rights problems, and the La Cantuta case in particular, were issues that the government could afford to ignore. Even though polls showed the public's disapproval of the handling of the case, focus-group research revealed a public that was resigned and unprepared to mobilize against such measures. Opposition legislators and the independent media could go ahead and howl about La Cantuta, but Yoshiyama and his advisors concluded that it was an issue destined to fade out in the course of the 1995 presidential campaign.[1]

Poll after poll showed that the most salient issues in the minds of voters were economic ones, with unemployment at the top of the list of concerns. The primacy of the economy as an issue bode well for Fujimori's reelection campaign. While Fujimori's poll figures on managing the economy were never as high as his personal job approval ratings, they stood above 40 percent in the first half of 1994, and broke through to over 50 percent in the second half of 1994.

Despite the polls, Fujimori and his advisors understood that the 1995 reelection could not be taken for granted. The narrow margin of the 1993 vote on the referendum, and especially the losses in the provinces, served as a reminder of the volatility of Peru's electorate. Moreover, winning the presidential race was not enough in itself. To consolidate the new political model, Fujimori needed to keep a solid, loyal congressional majority—one that could be counted on to lend an air of legitimacy while rubber-stamping the measures necessary to reproduce the regime. International public opinion clearly was not inclined to allow Fujimori yet another closure of congress should he lose control of it. President Jorge Serrano's 1993 attempt to pull off an auto-coup in Guatemala had met sharp reactions from the United States and the OAS. Fujimori wanted a big, decisive win in 1995—one sufficient to silence his critics and secure his control over the incoming congress.

All the President's Powers

Until just before the October 1994 deadline to register as a presidential candidate, Fujimori was coy when questioned about whether he would run again. He laughed at reporters' questions and simply refused to answer. But he also liked to remind them that reelection was constitutional and that "the people" were encouraging him to run.[2]

But the reelection bid was not the cakewalk that *oficialistas* had originally hoped it would be. By early 1994, polls were showing a gap between Fujimori's job-approval performance and support for his reelection bid. While the president's job-approval rating remained in the 60 percent range, less than 50 percent of Peruvians supported his reelection. In early 1994, Javier Pérez de Cuéllar, Peru's premier diplomat and secretary-general of the United Nations, emerged as the leading challenger in the presidential race. In polls taken in the first quarter of 1994, Fujimori trailed slightly behind Pérez de Cuéllar, who, like Fujimori, had not yet announced his decision to run.

Congressional president Jaime Yoshiyama acknowledged that the 1993 referendum was a "warning bell" triggering a new, concerted effort to rebuild provincial support in advance of the 1995 elections.[3] The political strategy would be a model of simplicity: President Fujimori had to become unequivocally identified as the candidate who "delivered the goods." To that end, public spending was directed to shore up support for Fujimori, especially in the regions where the government had fared poorly in the referendum.

The president already had all the resources in hand for a spending spree. The Ministerio de la Presidencia, the superministry created after the coup, was a deep well. Accounting for 9 percent of the national budget in 1992 and 1993, this ministry's budget was equal to the combined total slated to the ministries of health, education, labor, and agriculture.[4] The Ministerio de la Presidencia administered Peru's programs aimed at poverty alleviation and welfare, all of which involved discretionary spending that could be used to channel money to communities for food aid, public works, temporary employment programs, and subsidized housing construction. School construction was one of Fujimori's favorite projects.

The reelection strategy and the real needs of some of Peru's poorest communities conveniently converged in 1994–1995. The spending targeted the needy, the voters that Fujimori needed to win over. Scholars Carol Graham and Cheikh Kane found that discretionary expenditures were redirected after the 1993 referendum to areas where Fujimori lost the 1993 referendum and entailed a "substantial redistribution of public resources from the capital city of Lima to remote regions of the country previously neglected by various Peruvian governments."[5] In another study that focused on antipoverty funding, Norbert Schady concluded that expenditures ebbed and flowed along with elections during Fujimori's first term in office, with one of the largest spikes in spending occurring in the period prior to the April 1995 elections.[6]

To reduce the resources in the hands of potential rivals, Fujimori tightened the central government's grip over discretionary public spending. In December 1994, congress passed Legislative Decree 766, the Municipal Tax Law, which completely restructured municipal finances. The law reduced local taxes on property and sales, and made municipal governments more dependent on the central government via the Municipal Compensation Fund. The rationale behind the reform was to redirect resources to the country's poorest areas, but in doing so the government was targeting those areas where it had fared poorly in the 1993 referendum. With the fate of their public works projects now hanging in the balance, municipal officials needed to be careful about their relations with the central government. The new law dealt a punishing blow to Lima mayor Ricardo Belmont, who had emerged as a potentially troublesome challenger to Fujimori. Under the new system, Lima's share of transfers from the central government dive-bombed; municipal income decreased by 40 percent in 1994.[7]

Fujimori's spending for the 1995 campaign had to be conducted in a way to make sure that voters associated the president, and by extension C90-NM, with their good fortune. To fix that association in the minds of voters, Fujimori and his ministers had to be free to act in ways that made the point—by inaugurating new schools, cutting ribbons on new roads, and handing out clothes and food.

Long before the kickoff of the official campaign season, the C90-NM majority in the CCD made sure that the justice system would not stymie the president's electioneering. Keeping Attorney General Blanca Nélida Colán in her post was deemed vital. Colán was one of many officials who owed her rapid ascent to the 1992 coup. Before the coup, she was serving as a provincial judge in Callao; in her new job as attorney general, Colán quickly gained a reputation as someone who toed the government's line. Impressed by Colán's loyalty under fire, Montesinos said that she was someone "who would give her life, would die with us."[8]

But arranging another term for Colán required some creative legal maneuvering. The new constitution mandated that the position be filled by a vote of the Junta de Fiscales Supremos (Prosecutors' Board). In a January 1994 vote, Colán tied with rival Miguel Aljovín. C90-NM congresswoman Martha Chávez came to Colán's rescue with a made-to-order piece of legislation mandating that, in the case of a tie vote, the winner would be designated on the basis of seniority.[9] That provision gave the victory to Colán. The opposition dubbed the new bill *"Ley Colán."*

The president and his partisans now were free to proceed as they wished; there were no authorities, institutions, or rules that could hold them back. Despite the enactment of the 1993 constitution, there was no system of checks and balances. Inaction on the part of congress kept three important entities mandated by the 1993 constitution inoperative throughout 1994: (1) the Tribunal Constitucional (TC); (2) the Defensoría del Pueblo (DP); and (3) the Consejo Nacional de la Magistratura (CNM). All three offices were charged with important oversight responsibilities. At least in theory, the institutions could have had an impact on the conduct of the 1995 election had they been in place.

Of the three, the most glaring absence was that of the TC, the highest judicial body charged with ruling on the constitutionality of laws. With no functioning TC, the congressional majority enjoyed a legal carte blanche. There was no legal authority with the power to declare laws unconstitutional. Meanwhile, the entire judicial system remained in a post-coup limbo. Prosecutors and judges functioned as "provisional" appointees. A temporary board, the Jurado de Honor de la Magistratura, had been created to work on the problem in 1993, but it had made little progress in tenuring new personnel. In 1994, more than half of all judges still remained in provisional appointments.[10] Given their job insecurity, officials were unlikely to use their powers to rein in fellow government officials during the campaign. Even more troubling was the fact that many provincial prosecutors, by virtue of their responsibility to head the provincial election boards, would be directly involved in the vote-counting process. *Caretas* reported that thirty-six of the forty-seven provincial election boards were under the direction of provisional appointees in October 1994.[11]

Absent the TC, the congress, controlled by C90-NM, was the final arbiter of rules governing the election. It could write and rewrite election laws at will. The entity charged with organizing the 1995 elections was the JNE. In theory, the JNE was supposed to function as an autonomous body and was the ultimate authority in all matters related to elections. But it was bound to uphold the electoral laws passed by congress, and the congress was poised to overrule the JNE if necessary.

Campaigning from Above

Fujimori went back on the hustings with a vengeance in early 1994. While Javier Pérez de Cuéllar remained in Paris, contemplating his presidential run from afar, Fujimori was in full campaign mode, traveling through the provinces and inaugurating public works at every stop.

On one of his campaign stops, Fujimori reflected on his own frenetic pace, noting that he had inaugurated ten new schools in four hours and that Peru just "could not stop." The phrase *"Perú no puede parar"* became his campaign slogan. And in case voters needed further evidence of the president's seemingly endless energy and largesse, there were frequent reminders. A government-sponsored advertising blitz in mid-1994 touted the country's improvements with the catchphrase, *"Perú tiene su oportunidad"* (Peru has its chance).[12] There were ubiquitous billboards of the Ministerio de la Presidencia (in the orange and white colors also used by C90) adorning each public work in progress.

Generous public spending and the mobilization of public employees were the keys to Fujimori's campaign. To have any hope of "leveling the playing field" in the 1995 race or discrediting the election, the opposition needed to make an issue of Fujimori's use of public servants and money and force the JNE and OAS election observers to pay attention. In mid-1994, the push began, with opposition calls for the president to *bajar al llano* (come down)—that is, take a leave of absence from the presidency in order to campaign like any other candidate.[13] No one seriously expected that Fujimori would heed the call to step down. Nonetheless, the idea circulated in the print media and served as a prelude to the opposition's attempt to put pressure on the JNE to regulate the president's conduct during the campaign.[14]

The publication of a photograph of General Howard Rodríguez added fuel to the debate about the violation of election laws. In September 1994, a photographer from the local newspaper *El Correo* caught the uniformed Rodríguez, the commander of the First Military Region, in an apparent violation of the prohibition on political activity by the military. He was handing out calendars featuring Fujimori's picture during a presidential tour in Piura. Congressional opponents decried the general's actions as part of a bigger plan to use state resources and personnel to assure the reelection. Congressman Henry Pease observed, "What's so serious is that this is not an isolated act but one among many oriented to favor the candidacy of Fujimori, his reelection, and in the last instance, the fraud."[15] Earlier in the year, Pease had denounced Army General Raúl Diez, commander of the first infantry division of Sullana, for actively campaigning for the president. According to Pease, Diez and a contingent of soldiers appeared at a community meeting where Diez delivered a speech enumerating the government's public works in the area and urging support for the president's reelection.[16]

Underscoring the need for clear rules to regulate the conduct of the president and other public officials during the campaign, Javier Pérez de Cuéllar met with JNE members and called for other international observation teams to join in election monitoring along with the OAS. Pérez de Cuéllar also asked the JNE to remedy another troubling problem: thousands of voter cards issued to military personnel, ostensibly for security reasons, could be illegally used to vote in the elections.[17]

Meanwhile, Fujimori brushed off all suggestions to "come down" from the presidential heights or restrict his activities. He insisted that his appearances at events in his role as president could be clearly differentiated from campaign appearances. As the official start of the campaign season approached, Fujimori became more agitated on the subject. In late November, he denounced the suggestion that he stop inaugurating public works: "I prefer to open schools rather than political headquarters and I will continue, without stopping, because this is what differentiates this government from all the useless talk."[18]

Given Fujimori's intransigence and the mutual distrust between government and opposition groups, it was hardly surprising when the campaign to get all political organizations to sign onto a voluntary code of ethics fizzled. Transparencia, a new citizens' group founded to monitor the election process, had proposed the idea of an "honor pact" among parties. Representatives from seven political organizations signed the pact, most notably Javier Pérez de Cuéllar of Unión del Perú.[19] But AP and APRA refused to sign up, criticizing the pact as vague and useless. Raúl Diez Canseco, the presidential candidate of AP, characterized the pact as meaningless since it did not stipulate rules regulating the president's use of state resources. APRA officials balked at a provision in the pact professing "confidence in the integrity of the JNE." As expected, C90-NM was a no-show for the pact signing, and Congresswoman Martha Chávez, now the official representative of C90-NM and the number-one candidate on its congressional list, blasted Transparencia as a front for government opponents.[20]

Reacting to the growing controversy about the president's conduct in the campaign, the JNE sent a draft of its recommendations on electoral law to the congress in early December. The JNE proposal contained a provision expressly prohibiting the president from inaugurating public works in the ninety days prior to the April election. The recommendations included giving the JNE the power to fine and remove presidential or congressional candidates from the ballot if they were found guilty of three violations of the election law.

Fujimori fired back immediately, saying that the proposed restriction would be "negative because it would paralyze the rhythm of work for three months." But he added that he would, in the last instance, obey whatever law the congress passed.[21] Congressional president Jaime Yoshiyama quickly indicated that the C90-NM members drafting the final law should not stick with the JNE version: "As prestigious and autonomous the JNE is, I think that it should not paralyze a president who must make good on his mandate until the 28th of July 1995."[22]

Whether or not the JNE board members believed that their recommendations would be taken seriously was unclear. An editorial in *Oiga* magazine suggested that the draft of the law was an elaborate "pantomime," a ruse by the JNE to create the appearance of being tough while knowing all along that the congress would strip the bill of its most prohibitive prescriptions. JNE president Ricardo Nugent did not seem especially fired up about policing the election. He was disinterested in the idea of seeking additional international election observers apart from the OAS, saying that they were unnecessary because their presence would imply that some type of irregularities were going on.[23] After Nugent handed over the JNE's proposed election law, he sounded more resigned than combative, conceding that congress would make the final decision and that the JNE would "follow the law."[24]

Fujimori cast the proposed law as a nefarious plot to keep the president from "his people." He criticized the JNE in his campaign speeches. In a stop in Ayacucho, he told voters: "There's a proposed law sent to congress by the JNE that would stop me from visiting Paucara, and that's inconceivable after 500 years when no public official showed up here . . . today the president goes to the people to help them. They can't stop me because from the first day of my government, I have been with the people." In a campaign visit in Cañete, Fujimori emoted: "They can attack me but let me work for people. Don't bother me. But, damn it, how can I not be able to see things if this allows me to see what is needed and later bring development to the people?" He concluded with a question to whip up the crowd: "Who is in favor of continuing the inauguration of public works?" Predictably, the villagers raised their hands.[25]

Like the villagers, the C90-NM congressional caucus understood what the president wanted. The legislators passed the final version of the election law with forty-nine votes after opponents walked out of the vote in protest. The law stripped away the JNE's provision prohibiting the president from public works inaugurations and replaced it with a rule barring the president from making explicit references to opponents when acting in his official capacity as president. The congressional version also removed the provision allowing the JNE to remove candidates from the ballot for violating election laws. In addition to stripping away restrictions, the new law added a provision considered to be extremely favorable to the president: it stipulated that photographs of the presidential candidates be included on the ballot.

Fujimori's photograph had been plastered on calendars and school notebooks and distributed throughout Peru. Distributing the items was standard practice whenever Fujimori made public appearances. Fujimori's opponents understood the enormous electoral advantage that accrued to the president by having his photo appear on the ballot. The photo alone could garner Fujimori an extra 2 or 3 percent of the vote, a gain that might be sufficient to boost his votes over 50 percent so he could win on the first round of the election.[26]

Commenting on the new law, the JNE observed that it made it impossible for the JNE to "regulate and sanction" violations of the law. After duly noting its own powerlessness, the JNE fell silent, offering no opinion on the inclusion of candidate photographs on the ballot.

Santiago Murray, the head of the OAS election observation mission, showed no interest in weighing in on questions of election law, no matter how much the opposition cried foul. Murray affirmed the "normalcy of all the juridical-legal framework" governing the upcoming elections.[27] But Susana Higuchi de Fujimori found her encounter with election law anything but normal.

Shutting Down Susana

Among the president's opponents, none was more volatile and potentially threatening than his own wife, Susana Higuchi de Fujimori. The diminutive Higuchi had long been a loyal helpmate, managing the family's finances and standing by her husband in his long-shot bid for public office in 1990.

She was startled when he actually won, and grew more perturbed as she observed what was going on inside the presidential palace.

Higuchi's trajectory as a whistle-blower began in March 1992, when she charged the president's relatives with mismanaging and trafficking in the charitable donations of clothing from Japan. Private donations in cash and kind from Japan were channeled through two nongovernmental organizations founded by Fujimori in 1990–1991, Apenkai and Aken.[28] Making the accusations during a live press conference, Higuchi fingered the president's sister Rosa Fujimori for diverting funds from the charitable activities she headed. The opposition in congress promised an investigation, and a special prosecutor was named to look into the allegations. But the April coup scotched any inquiry, and Higuchi disappeared from public view for months. Years later, she revealed that she had been kidnapped and held at the SIN.[29]

The marriage that had already crumbled privately was dissolving publicly by early 1994. Higuchi returned to public view, giving interviews criticizing the administration's authoritarianism and failure to help the poor. With Higuchi sounding more like a political candidate than a disgruntled wife, the CCD legislated a hasty addition to electoral law in mid-July 1994. It enacted a provision prohibiting close relatives of the president from being a candidate for president, vice president, or congress. The law was quickly dubbed *"Ley Susana."*

Higuchi denounced the law as unconstitutional. The 1993 constitution made no such proscriptions on the family members of a president. She petitioned Attorney General Colán to take legal action on her case. Colán said that the matter was outside of her jurisdiction, and most likely was something to be resolved by the still nonexistent Tribunal Constitucional.

Higuchi added fuel to the fire with new allegations of corruption and abuse. She characterized Vladimiro Montesinos as being "bad for Peru" and said that the nation's intelligence service had been turned into a "political police." She claimed that her telephone was tapped and that members of her staff were under surveillance and being harassed.[30] But perhaps the most damaging accusations had to do with corruption and her claims that cabinet ministers were taking bribes and involved in other money-making scams.[31] The charges flew in the face of Fujimori's insistence that he and his officials were squeaky-clean technocrats. During a neighborhood tour, Fujimori poured out his anger at Higuchi. He defended the honesty of his ministers and lashed out at "people who don't work and criticize."

He warned: "Don't anybody tell me that there's been bad management because anyone who accuses along these lines will go to hell."[32]

Fujimori tried to end what had become both a national soap opera and a growing political scandal in a nationally televised address, during which he officially deposed Higuchi as first lady. He said that his wife was unstable and that she was under the influence of unscrupulous (but unnamed) persons who were using her for political purposes.[33] Several days after the speech, Higuchi was barred from entering her office in the presidential palace.

Despite Fujimori's effort to portray his wife as misguided, flaky, and disloyal, Peruvians did not dismiss Higuchi altogether. In an August poll taken by Apoyo, 67 percent of respondents said that they believed Higuchi's allegations about ministerial corruption while just 22 percent of the respondents said they were false. In regard to the claim of telephone tapping, 41 percent of respondents said they believed her to be a victim while 34 percent rejected her claim. Higuchi also garnered a clear majority in support of her legal position: 52 percent of those interviewed expressed support for the elimination of the law barring her candidacy, while 39 percent opposed.[34]

Even though Peruvians found many of her claims credible, the public was split over what spouse to blame in the marital breakup, and support for Higuchi as a presidential candidate was modest. At the height of the scandal in August, Apoyo's presidential poll showed Higuchi at 6 percent support, Fujimori at 48 percent, and Pérez de Cuéllar at 25 percent. Higuchi was no real threat to her husband as a candidate, but her stories about the Fujimori family and Montesinos continued to garner embarrassing press coverage.

By enacting *Ley Susana,* the C90-NM majority gave the JNE the necessary legal cover to deny Higuchi a place on the ballot. But Higuchi vowed to challenge the law. She formed her own political movement, felicitously named Harmony 21st Century, and proceeded to gather the signatures required to obtain legal status. With the support of the Asociación Pro Derechos Humanos (APRODEH), a noted human rights organization, she filed a petition with the OAS Inter-American Commission of Human Rights in Washington DC, asking that it issue *medidas cautelares* (preventative measures) to ensure her right to participate in the elections.[35]

On October 6, the OAS commission recommended that the Peruvian government give Higuchi a "rapid judicial or administrative review" should the JNE fail to register her candidacy after the deadline date of October 11. Meanwhile, judicial officials were making sure that Higuchi's allegations about ministerial corruption were discredited. Prosecutor Julia Eguía terminated the investigations of former minister of the presidency Raúl Vittor and Vice Minister of Justice Miriam Schenone after a reported meeting with Attorney General Colán.[36]

Instead of invoking the controversial *Ley Susana,* the JNE issued a ruling on October 18 that rejected the presidential candidacy of Susana Higuchi on technical grounds. The JNE claimed that Highuchi's Harmony 21st Century movement had failed to collect the 100,000 valid voters' signatures necessary to be placed on the ballot. The movement submitted a total of 147,840 signatures, but the JNE ruled that only 11,851 were valid.

Higuchi charged that the SIN was behind her problem with the JNE and that SIN agents had infiltrated her movement. She impugned the JNE in an interview with *Oiga,* saying that it was "under control." She identified JNE board member Romulo Muñoz Arce as the "intermediary" between the JNE and the government because of his friendship with the president's brother and advisor, Santiago Fujimori. Muñoz angrily denied the charges, saying it was "false, absolutely false that I have connections with the executive branch."[37] After the fall of the Fujimori regime in 2000, videos showed that Muñoz did develop a clandestine relationship with Vladimiro Montesinos and consulted with him about matters pending at the JNE. Documents also surfaced that confirmed Higuchi's suspicions about the SIN. She had been the target of "Operation Campaign," a plan that planted clandestine SIN agents in her entourage and subjected her to twenty-four-hour electronic surveillance. Montesinos confided that Fujimori was obsessed with his ex-wife, and asked for daily reports on her telephone taps again when she ran for congress in 2000.[38]

But in 1994 Higuchi had no concrete proof to back up her suspicions about SIN involvement. Moreover, fourteen other movements were denied registration on the same grounds, making it harder to argue that Harmony 21st Century had been singled out. Since the JNE was the only body with jurisdiction over electoral matters, Higuchi could not appeal her case. She announced that her movement would seek legal status once again, in order to register a list of congressional candidates by the January 9, 1995, deadline. But once again, the JNE ruled against Higuchi, arguing that her list of congressional candidates was full of typographical errors that rendered it invalid.

Higuchi said she was dumbfounded by the errors. Her attorney Heriberto Benítez suggested that the mistakes had been arranged by the government to keep Higuchi off the ballot. The JNE refused to consider a correction of the list, a decision contested by legal experts who argued that the JNE did indeed have the discretion to allow for a resubmission of the list in the case of a "material" error.[39]

In a desperate move, Higuchi started a hunger strike on January 17 after the JNE literally closed the doors on her and refused her appeals. The hunger strike took its toll on the frail Higuchi. After a public fainting spell, she was hospitalized. Her hospitalization attracted intense media attention and expressions of sympathy by opposition leaders, including Javier Pérez de Cuéllar, who called on the JNE to provide further explanation of their decision. OAS election mission chief Santiago Murray visited Higuchi in the hospital and promised to consult with the JNE on her case.

Santiago Murray met with JNE members on January 24, and the Higuchi case was one of many items on the agenda. At least publicly, Murray did not take Higuchi's side. JNE officials made it clear that they were not prepared to reopen the case, but they told Murray that they would provide the OAS mission with a more extensive legal reasoning on the ruling.[40]

By barring her from the election and terminating legal inquiries into the corruption allegations, the government effectively silenced Higuchi. She was no longer a news story. With no campaign to follow and with no fresh evidence in hand, Higuchi lost the media spotlight in January 1995, as reporters turned their attention to the other presidential candidates and another dramatic story—the outbreak of a border war between Ecuador and Peru. Still, other presidential hopefuls sensed that Higuchi was right, that Fujimori was using the intelligence service to undermine them and put a lock on the 1995 election.

The "F" Word—Fraud

Unlike the CCD election of 1992, there was no heated debate among opposition leaders on the question of whether or not to participate in the 1995 elections. The results of the 1993 referendum evoked new optimism about the prospects for defeating the regime at the ballot box. Even the "maximalist" opposition parties that had abstained from the 1992 CCD election (APRA, AP, PUM) were ready to participate.

How all the groups seeking to unseat Fujimori would approach the election was an open question.[41] Some analysts were convinced that Fujimori could not win on the first round, and that offered the tantalizing possibility of an upset in the second round. There was considerable talk among opposition groups about unifying around a single presidential candidacy in the first round. The political buzz focused on Javier Pérez de Cuéllar, who had actually pulled slightly ahead of Fujimori in the polls of early 1994.

Opposition leaders were never sanguine about the conditions they would face in the elections. When they spoke of the 1992 CCD election or the 1993 referendum, the government's congressional opponents freely used the word "fraud." Fraud, in its dictionary definition, means "deliberate deception for unfair or unlawful gain." And in their view, "fraud" was the appropriate word to describe the manifold ways in which the resources of the state had been used unlawfully to produce the government's electoral victories. Still, the opposition could not arrive at a strategic or tactical consensus regarding how best to contest the 1995 election and challenge the conditions under which it was being conducted. Despite the initial enthusiasm for fielding a single presidential candidate to challenge the regime, the proposal was dead in the water by December 1994. Pérez de Cuéllar aspired to be the unity candidate, but he balked at explicit alliances with the "traditional parties" so demonized by Fujimori—namely, APRA, AP, and the PPC. Pérez de Cuéllar and his advisors feared that any formal alliance, like the one struck by Mario Vargas Llosa in his failed 1990 presidential bid, would tarnish his image as an "independent" candidate.

Under the circumstances, the leaders of other political organizations could see no advantage to staying on the sidelines in the presidential race. On the contrary, conventional wisdom held that running a presidential candidate on the ticket helped to garner votes for parties' congressional candidates. In line with previous practice, the congressional election was scheduled concurrently with the first round of the presidential election in April. When the October 19 deadline for registering presidential candidates came, twenty-seven organizations lined up to register their nominees. Along with Pérez de Cuéllar of Unión por el Perú (UPP), the leading presidential candidates included: Raúl Diez Canseco (AP), Lourdes Flores (PPC), Mercedes Cabanillas (APRA), Ricardo Belmont (Movimiento Obras), and Alejandro Toledo, who merged his own País Posible party with José Barba Caballero's CODE in order to get on the ballot. When the JNE finished sifting through the registration petitions, fourteen candidates were ruled eligible.

Trying to carve out a space in the crowded field, the candidates pursued their own campaigns. There were no coordinated efforts among opposition groups to take on the JNE or engage the OAS observation mission on issues related to the conduct of the campaign or the organization of the election. Instead, each of the candidates made periodic *denuncias* (allegations) about violations of election law, and the independent print media (primarily the newspaper *La República* and the magazines *Caretas, Oiga,* and *Sí*) reported the allegations and dug up their own stories on election abuses.

Oficialistas roundly dismissed any use of the word "fraud." Javier Pérez de Cuéllar's references to fraud were especially alarming, not just because he was the leading candidate of the opposition, but because his distinguished diplomatic career gave him international credibility sufficient to call the legitimacy of the elections into question, if he chose to do so. From the start of the campaign, Pérez de Cuéllar voiced his suspicions about the election conditions. He denounced the use of government resources and personnel to promote Fujimori's reelection, and let it be known that he believed that the government "would not hesitate to use underhanded means" to secure that end.[42]

In November 1994, Pérez de Cuéllar took his case to the JNE. He vigorously backed the proposals to radically restrict the president's conduct during the campaign and underscored that the president's uncontrolled use of state resources constituted a "deception" of the electorate and, thus, "fraud."[43] In a blitz of new appearances during a trip to Madrid, he repeated the idea that "fraud" could be constituted by the totality of the conditions in the campaign: "Fraud is not something that happens only when the votes are being counted. The campaign, in itself, can constitute a fraud."[44]

Not surprisingly, Pérez de Cuéllar's comments evoked a backlash by *oficialistas* back home. *Expreso* columnist Manuel D'Ornellas said that the ex-diplomat sounded like a loser who was using the fraud charge to divert attention from his dive in the polls. In an editorial, *Expreso* characterized his use of the word "fraud" as inaccurate and said that "inequities" more properly described the problem in the campaign.[45] As usual, Fujimori scoffed at the suggestion of fraud. He liked to point to the participation of the opposition as the ultimate proof of the democratic nature of the regime and the legitimacy of the election, as did other *oficialistas* who had welcomed the Pérez de Cuéllar candidacy as a kind of imprimatur.[46]

Pérez de Cuéllar was not the only person complaining. As the campaign began in September, leftist leader Javier Diez Canseco charged that SIN was actively targeting opposition candidates for "dirty tricks" and keeping them under surveillance.[47] In December, both Pérez de Cuéllar and Alejandro Toledo charged that they were being subjected to a "dirty war" directed by the SIN. Pérez de Cuéllar said that he was under constant surveillance and that hired troublemakers were following him on the campaign trail and disrupting events.[48] He reported that he and other UPP leaders had received telephoned death threats. Likewise, Toledo claimed that he and his family were targets of an SIN smear campaign and that the intelligence service was fabricating false documentation to implicate him in wrongdoing. But because there was no way to force an investigation of the SIN, there was little in the way of concrete proof that the candidates could offer to back their *denuncias*.

When disturbing evidence that the government was illegally orchestrating the reelection finally did come to light in January, opposition leaders quickly pounced on it. Starting on January 2, *La República* began reporting that regional officials appointed by the central government were, under orders, using their offices illegally to promote the president's reelection campaign. Responding quickly, the JNE asked Attorney General Colán to investigate the charge. Meanwhile, the government depicted the report as an "isolated incident" and fired one of the alleged wrongdoers.

But *La República* reporters kept digging, and its editors kept using the word "fraud." On the morning of January 6, 1995, the newspaper ran the banner headline, *"Fraude en marcha"* (Fraud Underway). One of that day's stories came from presidential candidate Raúl Diez Canseco, who called on the JNE to investigate the government's plan to distribute six million *"Fuji-cuadernos"* (school notebooks) featuring a color photo of the president. The stories kept coming. *La República*'s lead story on January 8 was about a videotape showing another government appointee, Tomás Gonzáles Reátegui, rallying local coordinators of the president's reelection campaign. Reátegui had also been implicated in a scheme to distribute *Fuji-cuadernos*.

However newsworthy, the *denuncias* were doomed to an institutional dead end. JNE president Ricardo Nugent disposed of the *denuncias* by turning them over the attorney general's office, arguing that criminal wrongdoing was not in his jurisdiction. Attorney General Colán, an ally and friend of Montesinos, could be counted on to bury the cases in her office.

Warning again of the "threat of an enormous deception, an enormous fraud," Pérez de Cuéllar took his complaints straight to OAS mission chief Santiago Murray. In a meeting on January 23, he turned over new documents that appeared to confirm the charges that local government appointees were being turned into coordinators and organizers of the president's reelection. The new documents included a letter from the mayor of Chachapoyas to a regional prefect that outlined upcoming campaign activities. UPP campaign chief and vice presidential candidate Guido Pennano said that the Chachapoyas case was one of many, and that the UPP had similar complaints from Ilo, Chaví, Loreto, and Huánuco.[49]

Oficialistas fumed. C90 congresswoman Martha Chávez characterized the talk of fraud as a last-ditch effort by losing candidates: "We see various candidates crying about a supposed fraud because they lack proposals. They have a poor image of the Peruvian people, whose votes for a candidate can't be bought with calendars or notebooks." Manuel D'Ornellas, writing for *Expreso,* called on Pérez de Cuéllar to withdraw the UPP ticket from the election if he honestly believed that the election would be a sham.[50]

OAS mission chief Santiago Murray weighed in on the debate over how to define "fraud," and in doing so he challenged Pérez de Cuéllar's framing of the issue. In remarks after a meeting with Pérez de Cuéllar, Murray took an important rhetorical turn while underscoring the mission's deference to local authorities: "Fraud is a very serious word and one has to be a little more measured [in its use]. . . . In my view, to speak of fraud does not seem correct to me because basically we are talking about irregularities. If there is an irregularity, the correct procedure is to seek to identify the proof, submit it to the authorities or the observer mission so that we turn it over to the same authorities."[51]

Murray viewed the role of the OAS mission as limited, and maintained that it did not include emitting opinions about the electoral process prior to the election.[52] He never openly questioned the conduct of the JNE or the attorney general's office in their handling of the *denuncias.* In fact, he always insisted that the JNE, not the OAS mission, had the primary responsibility to investigate specific allegations and pronounce on them.[53]

The 1995 border war between Peru and Ecuador, begun in late January, brought the discussion about fraud to a halt, and paralyzed the campaign altogether. Fujimori turned all of his attention to the war. The event offered him a greater opportunity to dominate the news and he took advantage of it. The president headed to the war zone, tramping through the jungle with journalists in tow. The public rallied around the troops, and opposition candidates fell silent as the military conflict unfolded.

The war effectively overshadowed all other political issues throughout February. By the time a ceasefire was secured, there was a little more than a month to resume campaigning before the April 9 elections.[54] Accusations about the illegal involvement of local officials in Fujimori's reelection campaign continued.[55] A provocative series of articles in the magazine *Sí* highlighted corrupt practices in the JNE's acquisition of election materials, suggesting that a "mafia" was operating inside the institution.[56] Still, neither Pérez de Cuéllar nor the other candidates threatened to pull out of the election in protest. Pérez de Cuéllar still clung to the hope that he might garner enough votes to force Fujimori into a second-round runoff. Moreover, none of the political organizations had any interest in pulling their congressional lists out of contention. There was no real threat of an opposition boycott of the election. The dream of a second round and the drive for congressional seats trumped all other considerations among Fujimori's competitors, even their own somber argument that they had already been set up to lose.[57]

Containing the Huánuco Scandal

By January 1995, the combination of government spending and Fujimori's incessant campaigning was paying off. Surveys showed Fujimori with about a twenty-five-point lead over his closest rival, Pérez de Cuéllar, and the other contenders languishing in the single digits. Pérez de Cuéllar and Toledo roundly criticized Fujimori's handling of the border war with Ecuador, but to no effect. Voters rallied around the president, and by mid-March, Fujimori enjoyed 46 to 50 percent support in the polls as Pérez de Cuéllar trailed behind in the 17 to 20 percent range.

Fujimori's campaign was masterful while Pérez de Cuéllar's floundered. Pérez de Cuéllar had a late start, undertaking what his political advisor and son-in-law Alfredo Barnechea imagined as a Gandhi-like tour of the provinces beginning in Cusco. As everyone acknowledged, Pérez de Cuéllar was not a natural-born campaigner. Voters respected the former diplomat, but his refined manners made him seem remote. Fujimori harped on the many years that Pérez de Cuéllar spent abroad as a way of underscoring his disconnection from Peru, calling him an "illustrious spectator."

Style was not the only source of difficulties in the Pérez de Cuéllar campaign. The biggest problem was that Pérez de Cuéllar failed to make a compelling case that he could do a better job than Fujimori in delivering the concrete economic benefits and neighborhood improvements that voters wanted. Pérez de Cuéllar was no foe of neoliberal economic reform, and he acknowledged that he had urged president-elect Fujimori to accept International Monetary Fund (IMF) dictates and implement neoliberal reforms in 1990. That made Pérez de Cuéllar vulnerable to critics who argued that his candidacy was simply a form of *Fujimorismo sin Fujimori* (Fujimorism without Fujimori) or *Fujimorismo Lite*.

Those characterizations were surely unfair; Pérez de Cuéllar differed with Fujimori on other key issues. He spoke frequently of the need to restore *institucionalidad democrática* (democratic institutions) and to advance political decentralization; the problem was that those issues were less salient to voters than the bread-and-butter issues that worked in favor of Fujimori. Pérez de Cuéllar promised to create two million jobs if elected, but the promise of jobs in the future could not compete with Fujimori's breakneck inauguration of public works in real time.

Internal conflicts inside the UPP further muddied the public's view of the Pérez de Cuéllar candidacy. In an attempt to make the UPP a "big tent" of opposition, the UPP congressional list was a hodgepodge of candidates from left to right. The inclusion of well-known leftists like newspaper publisher Gustavo Mohme and Cusco mayor Daniel Estrada gave C90-NM leaders the ammunition to blast the UPP ticket as extremist.

The other major candidates in the presidential race—Ricardo Belmont and Alejandro Toledo—also failed to make inroads with Peru's voters. Neither had been especially outspoken voices of the opposition prior to the election. Lima mayor Ricardo Belmont, who had begun his career as a popular radio and television host, fumbled badly in managing the city after the central government restructured municipal finances. His job approval rating plummeted to less than 30 percent in the months prior to the April election.

Like Belmont, Alejandro Toledo was an independent candidate who launched his own political vehicle, País Posible, to run in the 1995 election.

Referring to himself as *"el cholo de oro"* (the golden *cholo*), Toledo tried to mix race, culture, and economics in his appeal to voters.[58] As a dark-skinned Peruvian who rose from humble origins to earn a Ph.D. from Stanford, Toledo embodied the upward mobility to which so many Peruvians aspired. Like Fujimori, Toledo liked to portray himself as a technocrat with the skills to get things done. At the start of his campaign, he balked at openly identifying himself with the opposition, trying to stake out a middle position between the opposition and Fujimori. But Toledo's campaign stalled, and polls showed him stuck with support from 5 percent of the voters.

Whatever the mistakes of the opposing candidates, not all of their problems were of their own making. The SIN was, in fact, spying on them and harassing their campaigns. In 1997, Frecuencia Latina television broke the story of an elaborate telephone-tapping scheme operating in 1995 that targeted at least 197 individuals.[59] The list included Pérez de Cuéllar and UPP congressional candidates as well as many members of the media. Yet the lack of concrete proof made it difficult for either candidates or political analysts to assess the extent of the SIN's illegal operations and the damage it was doing to opposition efforts.[60]

Would the government's underhanded acts include a manipulation of the vote count on election day? Fujimori's commanding lead in the polls militated against the possibility of vote tampering in the presidential race simply because there appeared to be no need for it. But days before the April 10 balloting, a vote-tampering scandal threatened to upset the election. On Thursday, April 7, news broke that seventeen individuals, including local notables and JNE workers, had conspired to alter the voting results in the provincial town of Huánuco. The scheme involved the theft from the JNE of 3,024 *actas* (the official tally sheets used on election day to report the aggregate vote count from each polling station).

Of those stolen, 360 *actas* had been fully or partially filled in with numbers and another 56 had erasures; the remaining 2,608 forms were blank. Hypothetically, if all of the *actas* had been filled out, they could have been used to submit 604,800 fraudulent votes—approximately 4.79 percent of the total national vote. In the presidential race, the pilfered *actas* assigned 3,225 votes to Fujimori and fewer votes to the remaining presidential candidates. On the congressional side, the candidates who benefited from the creative accounting were Horacio Cánepa of the PPC and C90-NM congressional heavyweight Víctor Joy Way. C90-NM congressman Pablo Tello Tello was identified as one of the masterminds behind the scheme.[61] Cánepa, Joy Way, and Tello Tello were native sons of Huánuco.

News of the scandal could not have come at a worse time. The OAS's secretary-general, César Gavíria, was scheduled to arrive on the following day to lead his organization's observation mission on election day. Government spokesmen immediately swung into action. Cabinet president Efraín Goldenberg announced that both Attorney General Colán and JNE board member Manuel Catorca were en route to Huánuco to lead an investigation. Meanwhile, the police arrested twelve of the seventeen suspects in the case but the remaining five vanished, including Cánepa.

Even before the investigation began, Goldenberg hinted at what the investigators would conclude. He said that the government viewed Huánuco as an "isolated incident" authored by a "band of thugs," but that the incident did not compromise the integrity of the elections. The interior minister, General Juan Briones Dávila, concurred, saying that the incident involved "just a group of swindlers." C90-NM congressman Víctor Joy Way denounced those involved as "delinquents" and scoffed at the notion that he needed any illicit help in garnering votes in his own hometown.[62]

Once on the ground in Lima, César Gavíria indicated that he was taking the scandal seriously. He told reporters: "This goes beyond an act of political proselytism and could constitute fraud, something that could endanger the legitimacy of the election." Gavíria also noted that the OAS had received reports that similar vote-tampering operations had been uncovered in Huancavelica and Cerro de Pasco.[63] In emergency meetings with Gavíria, Pérez de Cuéllar and fellow presidential contenders pressured for a postponement of the election until the situation could be clarified.

By Saturday morning, the government investigation was completed. Following the line already suggested by Goldenberg, Catorca and Attorney General Colán concluded that what had happened was an "isolated act of common criminals." Their public pronouncements failed to note, however, that the criminals involved were a band that had operated since 1990 and were believed to have been active in the 1992 CCD election and the 1993 referendum. That inconvenient fact, left out of the JNE report, clearly should have raised questions about who might have had prior knowledge about the gang and why neither law enforcement nor the JNE had taken action to prevent a repeat of the crimes.[64]

In making the results of the investigation public, JNE president Ricardo Nugent insisted that, notwithstanding the opposition's calls for a postponement, the election would take place on Sunday. Anticipating a possible boycott by opposition candidates, Nugent said that the election would be held even if "there were only one candidate."[65]

Emergency meetings between Gavíria and the presidential contenders continued late into the evening of Saturday night at the Sheraton Hotel in downtown Lima. As the day wore on, it became clear that OAS officials were not prepared to challenge the government's version of Huánuco as an aberrant, local crime. Other than moral persuasion, the presidential contenders had little leverage in the meetings since there was no real prospect of organizing a meaningful or effective boycott of the election. The logistics of a boycott were impossible; the ballots were printed and distributed and each political organization was concerned about how it would fare in the congressional race. Neither Pérez de Cuéllar nor Toledo expressed serious interest in boycotting the race the day before the election.

After a frustrating day of talks with Gavíria, the seven presidential contenders left the Sheraton. As a small group of protestors gathered in front of the hotel, chanting *"El fraude ya se dió"* (The fraud is already done), the presidential candidates voiced their frustration with the OAS team. They said that the government was using Gavíria and the OAS to endorse an "ongoing electoral fraud."[66]

The protest was too little, too late. On the following morning, television cameras showed a dutiful Pérez de Cuéllar casting his ballot and a relaxed Fujimori breakfasting with his children. Election day television coverage was almost completely devoid of references to what had happened on the previous day. The inability and unwillingness of the protesting presidential candidates to withdraw from the race undercut their characterizations of the process as a "fraud." Only Ricardo Belmont, owner of television station Channel 11 (RBC Televisión), seemed interested in trying to whip up a fraud frenzy. His news director Guillermo Thorndike, accompanied by television hostess Laura Bozzo, turned the station's election coverage into a nonstop, hysterical harangue, in stark contrast to the mellow coverage by every other station.

Just minutes after the polls closed at three o'clock, exit polls confirmed what everyone had expected: a solid victory for the incumbent president.

When the counting was done, Fujimori had his first-round victory, winning 64 percent of the valid vote.

Preelection polls taken several days before had already prepared contenders for the loss. But what no one was prepared for were the results in the congressional race. Contrary to the predictions of almost every pollster, the C90-NM congressional list won a majority of seats in the legislature. It was an astounding development. As the surprising results were scrutinized, more questions about what had gone on in the JNE emerged.[67] But by the time all the messy details came to light, the international press corps was long gone, and OAS officials readied to wrap up their mission.

The Other Results

Before heading back to Washington, Gavíria held a news conference confirming that the 110 observers fielded by the OAS had encountered few problems during Sunday's balloting. OAS mission chief Santiago Murray happily pronounced that the elections "had reinforced democratic institutionality" and that Peru had moved beyond its previous status as an "emerging democracy."[68]

Gavíria's assessment was the same as that rendered by the newly created national election observation organization Transparencia. Transparencia fielded more than nine thousand volunteer poll watchers in the election. In its own report, Transparencia confirmed that the irregularities at polling places were minimal. Transparencia's own "quick count" of the presidential returns coincided with pollsters and those of the JNE, showing Fujimori with 64 percent of the valid vote.[69]

Transparencia's quick count also confirmed the surprising results in the congressional race—a whopping 52 percent of the valid vote in favor of Fujimori's C90-NM. That number translated into an absolute majority of 67 seats for C90-NM in the 120-member unicameral congress. UPP trailed significantly behind, winning just 14 percent of the valid vote and 17 seats. Every other party polled in the single digits. None of the preelection polls predicted such a staggering victory for C90-NM; most pollsters projected that *oficialistas* would win only about one-third of the seats.

In the Fujimori camp, the prospect of losing control over congress in the

1995 election was worrisome. The 1992 coup was staged to rid Fujimori of an obstreperous legislature. So considerable time and effort went into the task of making sure that congress would not become a problem once again. Fujimori turned to congressional president Jaime Yoshiyama to do the job, and Yoshiyama turned to consultants to find the perfect candidates to run on the C90-NM list. Yoshiyama and his team sifted through the résumés of around one thousand "applicants" for the C90-NM congressional slots. With the aid of a psychologist, the list of possible candidates was narrowed. One of the criteria used for the selection was that the person be deemed "apolitical," and thus more likely to accept Yoshiyama's directions. The team then conducted polls and focus groups to determine the candidates most likely to be viewed negatively by the public. The process winnowed out seventeen of the forty-four incumbent legislators of the C90-NM caucus in the CCD and replaced them with new faces.[70]

In addition to its own C90-NM seats, the government also anticipated bringing allies on board from smaller political organizations who might win some seats. One was the center-right Renovación, led by Rafael Rey, which had frequently voted with C90-NM in the CCD. Other marginal organizations also appeared to be likely recruiting grounds for allies, including the one that placed dance-hall star Susy Díaz at the top of its ticket. Even groups that ran against Fujimori, including the UPP, included individuals who seemed ripe to become "defectors" in the future congress.[71]

The JNE count of the congressional results was slow, complicated by the system of preferential balloting. In addition to casting their vote for a chosen party, voters could also indicate preferences for two individual candidates of their chosen slate. As the official count proceeded, the peculiar characteristics of the congressional election emerged. The staggering victory of C90-NM was based, in part, on an unprecedented number of invalidated votes. Nearly 41 percent of all the votes cast for congress were declared invalid.

JNE officials explained the high number of invalid ballots as a function of confusion among local officials about how to count and record the preferential votes on the official form used to tally results, the *acta*. In many instances, the two candidate preferences chosen by voters were counted erroneously as two separate votes—thus, hundreds of *actas* were submitted to the local elections boards that showed the number of congressional votes exceeding the number of voters assigned to polling stations. When such a discrepancy occurred, the JNE's computer program automatically rejected the results and invalidated the votes. Because all individual voting ballots were destroyed after each *acta* was completed at every polling station, no recount of the actual ballots was possible.

Another indication of the enormous confusion in counting and recording results came when the final results of the presidential and congressional elections were compared after they were officially announced by the JNE on April 18. Since both the presidential and congressional choices were contained on a single ballot, the number of voters in both contests should have been the same. But there were 835,964 more votes cast in the presidential race than in the congressional race. In theory, any discrepancy between the two sections in the ballot should have been reflected in the null/blank votes of the congressional race, but this was not the case. Once again, JNE officials blamed the problem on local poll workers. According to the JNE, many local election officials had computed only the preferential votes in the results for congress. However, many voters did not make use of their preferential votes and simply cast a single vote for a slate. Mistakenly, according to the JNE, those votes were not added into the overall congressional totals.[72]

The JNE's postelection problems were not confined to the errors in counting and documenting the votes. With questions mounting over the integrity of the count, another major scandal surfaced on April 21. A technician working for the firm Otepsa, a company hired by the JNE to handle computer operations, charged that 206 fraudulent *actas* from the province of Juliaca had been used to alter the preferential vote in favor of a local C90-NM congressional candidate. He implicated two C90-NM officials in the vote tampering.[73] Four employees of the provincial election board (Jurado Provincial Electoral Integrado de San Román), including its computer manager, were later indicted.[74]

The Juliaca incident was followed by an even more explosive story. On April 26, the newspaper *El Comercio* reported on a JNE inventory taken just two days prior to the election. The inventory showed that 37,000 *actas* for the general election and 40,557 *actas* used to report the preferential vote for congress were missing from JNE storage facilities and could not be accounted for. Along with the *actas,* other missing materials included thousands of bottles of indelible ink (used to mark voters' fingers), hundreds of official seals, and thousands of official envelopes. JNE officials had not reported their findings to the police or the attorney general's office.[75]

Only after *El Comercio*'s story did JNE board members come forward with their version. They claimed that lower-level JNE personnel had covered up the missing materials. The JNE admitted that its supply director, Hilda Otoya, had vanished just days after the election. The attorney general's office named a special prosecutor to investigate the case. By mid-May, a total of twelve JNE officials were indicted on charges related to the missing *actas* and wrongdoing in the purchasing of election materials.

In light of the Huánuco and Juliaca incidents, the disappearance of massive quantities of election materials was suspect. News of the missing *actas* broke just as the OAS and Transparencia readied to issue their final reports on the elections. Both groups suspended the submission of their final reports pending further clarifications by the JNE. On behalf of the UPP, Javier Pérez de Cuéllar called on the JNE to recount the congressional vote.[76]

A few opposition leaders went even further. PUM leader Javier Diez Canseco suggested that the irregularities in the conduct of the congressional election were so profound that a nullification of the results was warranted. Diez Canseco argued that, in addition to the 37,000 missing *actas,* thousands of other *actas* remained unaccounted for because the JNE had ordered an excess of election materials. He also pointed to inexplicable anomalies in the incidence of invalidated ballots across electoral districts, suggesting that provincial voting boards diverged significantly in how they applied criteria in determining whether or not an *acta* was valid.[77]

As the evidence of incompetence, negligence, and malfeasance mounted, the JNE finally agreed to recount all *actas* to ensure that no fraudulent ones had been slipped into the system. The recount involved a comparison of an original copy of each *acta* with the "scanned" version in the JNE computer files. No more fraudulent *actas* were uncovered in the JNE's recount. The finding gave little comfort to congressional hopefuls, including those from C90-NM, who complained that JNE personnel and the parties' legal representatives had colluded in altering the preferential votes assigned to individual candidates.[78]

The controversy over what had happened in the elections dissipated when the OAS mission and Transparencia issued their final reports. Both entities concluded that there was no evidence of systematic vote tampering. The OAS mission report adhered to the government's finding that the incident at Huánuco was a low-level criminal conspiracy. Transparencia's own "quick count" results collected by their volunteers at individual polling stations almost perfectly matched the official results reported by the JNE. The matching results undermined the hypotheses that fraudulent *actas* had been submitted or that some kind of computer fraud had taken place, since such *actas* would have produced huge discrepancies in the final results reported by both entities.

The findings of the OAS and Transparencia effectively closed off any further challenges to the election results. Without any institutional support, critics such as Javier Diez Canseco had nowhere to go for answers to the questions that still lingered. Had the government prepared a secret contingency plan that could have been put into motion to alter the results if deemed necessary, and did the missing and floating *actas* figure into the plan? Had the government anticipated the confusion in the reporting of results, figuring that disorder would work in its favor? How had the provincial election boards, in many instances overseen by appointees beholden to Attorney General Colán, behaved during the confused counting? Had the preferential vote been manipulated in a way that ensured a pliant C90-NM majority and a pool of potential defectors from other parties?

It was abundantly clear that there would be no congressional hearings or blue-ribbon presidential panel to study what had gone wrong in the 1995 election. On the contrary, Fujimori and *oficialistas* were intoxicated by the victory. If there were election problems, a bunch of grifters from Huánuco were to blame—*unos malos* (bad boys), as Attorney General Colán liked to say.

Lost in the victors' self-congratulations was any concern about how many Peruvians had been disenfranchised or altogether forgotten in the 1995 elections. The CCD had enacted an important change in the voting rules used to calculate vote percentages. The calculation was based on the valid vote (which involved subtracting null and blank votes) rather than the total number of votes cast. When viewed through a different mathematical lens, Fujimori's touted *victoria abrumadora* (overwhelming victory) took on more modest dimensions. Fujimori's 64 percent of the valid vote meant that only 39 percent of the electorate had cast a ballot for him if abstention, null, and blank votes were taken into account. Similarly, the 52 percent allotted to C90-NM turned into a mere 18.5 percent of support from the total electorate—hardly a mandate for the controversial legislating to come.

Consolidating Power

Reveling in the victory, Fujimori could look forward to another five years in power. He had won congratulations from the OAS and the American government on the elections.[79] Now it was time to consolidate power, reward his military allies, and put all the naysayers in their place.

Sending a message to dissenters inside the armed forces, the CSJM indicted three high-ranking officers, General Walter Ledesma, General Carlos Mauricio, and General Luis Mellet Castillo. They were charged with insulting the armed forces because they criticized the conduct of the war with Ecuador. Both Ledesma and Mauricio were active supporters of Pérez de Cuéllar's presidential bid; Mauricio had been a congressional candidate on the UPP list. The indictments were widely viewed as political payback and as a sign that dissent in the armed forces, even if voiced by retirees, would not be tolerated. Ledesma served forty days in prison. Mauricio fared worse, receiving a one-year prison sentence and a hefty fine.

The drive to put a damper on dissent continued. In the early morning hours on May 25, C90-NM legislators unexpectedly unveiled and passed Law 26457, which mandated a government-directed reorganization of public universities, beginning with the Universidad Nacional Mayor de San Marcos (the national university) and Universidad Enrique Guzmán y Valle (La Cantuta). *Oficialistas* justified the move as a way to clamp down on any remaining guerrilla groups. To the opposition, the law looked like another attempt to extend surveillance and ensure political control. The president signed the law on the same day, and it went into effect immediately; *El Peruano* published it in that morning's edition.[80]

In another move anticipating the unconventional legislating ahead, the constitutional commission headed by Carlos Torres y Torres Lara introduced a package of new rules governing legislative debate. The new rules included a provision that allowed new items to be placed on the agenda by a majority vote of representatives present on the floor. The measure reversed an earlier rule that disallowed the introduction of previously unapproved items onto the schedule. UPP congressman Henry Pease predicted that the new rules would be used to unveil even more surprise "midnight laws."[81]

Pease was right—another controversial human rights case loomed. In an unusual show of judicial independence, a prosecutor and judge reopened the investigation into the Barrios Altos case. In November 1991, Grupo Colina—the same military intelligence squad involved in the La Cantuta killings—massacred fifteen civilians, including children, at a neighborhood chicken dinner in Lima. These killings supposedly targeted members of Sendero Luminoso. As in the La Cantuta case, the government initially denied any involvement.[82]

In response to legal motions filed by the victims' families, prosecutor Ana Cecilia Magallanes and Judge Antonia Saquicuray reopened the case in April 1995. But once again, military officials refused to testify. General Julio Salazar Monroe refused Saquicuray's order to appear on the grounds that, as director of the SIN, he enjoyed ministerial status and that his testimony could not be compelled. The joint chiefs commander, General Hermoza, used a court order issued by the military's CSJM that barred him from testifying on grounds that the civilian court did not have jurisdiction.[83] Both Magallanes and Saquicuray responded with rulings that reasserted the court's right to order the testimony of the two generals.[84]

The government majority used a sweeping measure to bring the judicial inquiry into Barrios Altos, and all human rights cases, to a halt. In the early morning hours of June 14, C90-NM congressman Gilberto Siura introduced a bill granting blanket amnesty to all military and police personnel implicated in human rights abuses during the course of Peru's war against counterinsurgency since 1980. Only Jaime Yoshiyama and few other *oficialistas* had even seen the text of the law prior to Siura's presentation. Siura and other *oficialistas* portrayed the bill as an exercise in forgiving and "national reconciliation."[85]

Also included in the amnesty were the military "dissenters," meaning the officers imprisoned for the failed coup attempt of November 1992 and the generals indicted for insulting the armed forces. Thus, the officers who had been outspoken in the criticisms of the government, the armed forces, and Montesinos—General Jaime Salinas, General Rodolfo Robles, and General Carlos Mauricio—would be "forgiven" in the same piece of legislation that absolved the convicted assassins in the La Cantuta case.

A furious floor debate ensued. PPC congresswoman Lourdes Flores voiced the opposition's rage at the content of the law and the ambush-style tactics used by the government. She concluded: "What's happening is that this law is nothing but one more example of the political model that we are living in Peru: the project of a democracy under military control and a parliament that is its instrument."[86]

At three o'clock in the morning, the vote on the floor began. The amnesty passed with forty-seven votes, as many opposition deputies walked out in protest. In one of the rare moments of dissent, five C90-NM deputies voted against the measure. Fujimori quickly signed the bill, making it Law 26479.[87]

Public reaction to the amnesty was uniformly negative. Human rights groups and Foro Democrático joined with church leaders and the Colegio de Abogados in denouncing the measure. Every major newspaper, including *Expreso,* deplored the amnesty in their editorials. Polls showed near-complete public disapproval. An Apoyo poll showed that 87 percent of respondents disagreed with an amnesty benefiting those convicted in the La Cantuta case; 69 percent said that the government should consider reversing the measure. International human rights groups Human Rights Watch and Amnesty International protested the measure, as did the U.S. State Department.[88]

Despite the negative reaction from all quarters, the administration showed no sign of relenting. Fujimori said that he was "bored" by his critics who had done nothing to defeat terrorism in Peru and that he failed to understand how the U.S. government could criticize Peru as it contemplated its own antiterrorist measures in the wake of the Oklahoma City bombing of April 1995. The amnesty, according to Fujimori, was part of Peru's broader counterterrorism strategy.[89]

American officials were annoyed with the amnesty, but unwilling to turn it into a major issue. They doubted that Fujimori would back down and worried that a confrontation would undermine cooperation in other areas, especially counternarcotics. A cable from the American embassy in Lima to the State Department described the tradeoff:

Our reaction needs to be conscious of the diversity of our interests here including Fujimori's important commitment to deal conclusively with counternarcotics in the next five years. No one—least of all this mission—underestimates the difficulty of dealing with Fujimori, and his penchant for sudden moves based on a cold-eyed calculation of what he sees as overriding state interests. However as much as we are troubled by this "in your face" attitude toward our views on human rights and the legislative role, the fact remains that he retains overwhelming support from a public which cares little about these matters. It is also a reality—albeit uncomfortable—that we have a massive national security problem—drugs—which at this point requires his cooperation to ease, if not resolve.[90]

Not everyone, however, was resigned to accepting the amnesty. Judge Saquicuray tried again. On June 19, Saquicuray ruled that the amnesty law was inapplicable to the Barrios Altos case, arguing that it was unconstitutional. The army's armored division responded with a brief "tank parade" on June 20.

Jurists and prosecutors went on record in support of Saquicuray's ruling. Prosecutor Carlos Augusto Mansilla of the Eleventh Circuit of the Superior Court of Lima upheld Saquicuray's finding on appeal. Attorney General Colán did not share the view; she suggested that Saquicuray might find herself indicted on corruption or obstruction of justice charges because of her ruling.[91]

Reminiscent of its conduct in the La Cantuta case, the C90-NM congressional majority swung into action again. On the evening of June 28, C90-NM congressman Víctor Joy Way introduced another surprise piece of legislation. It was an "interpretive" law, asserting that the amnesty law was not subject to judicial review and that it must be applied. The bill passed with just thirty-five votes.[92]

The new law effectively shut down any further judicial action on the Barrios Altos case. On July 14, two judges of the Eleventh Circuit upheld the amnesty law and dismissed any further action against General Julio Salazar Monroe and the officers associated with the clandestine Grupo Colina. Still, the attempt to shut down the debate on amnesty was not completely successful. Coordinadora Nacional de Derechos Humanos, the umbrella organization of Peru's human rights groups, announced that it would lead an effort to collect the one million signatures necessary to call for a national referendum on the law.[93]

Attorney General Colán was rewarded again for her loyal service. In yet another "interpretive" law, the C90-NM majority extended her term as attorney general. The extension was a violation of article 158 of the constitution that stipulated the term.[94] The measure was immediately dubbed *"Ley Colán II."*

The CCD officially concluded its session in late July, turning over its duties to the newly elected congress. In its cover story on the departing CCD, the magazine *Caretas* summed up its legislative record in a banner headline—"Submission Accomplished."[95]

Fujimori's right-hand man, Vladimiro Montesinos, in a rare television appearance. Courtesy *Diario Oficial El Peruano*

Fujimori on the campaign trail accompanied by dancing girls, April 2000. Courtesy *Diario Oficial El Peruano*

Presidential candidate Alberto Andrade promises "Work for all Peruvians" in a campaign flier, April 2000. Courtesy Thomas Crupi

In a show of solidarity, opposition presidential candidates appear with Alejandro Toledo on election night, April 9, 2000. From left to right: Víctor García Belaúnde, Alberto Andrade, Alejandro Toledo, Luis Castañeda, Máximo San Román, Abel Salinas. Courtesy *Diario Oficial El Peruano*

Eduardo Stein, head of the OAS election observation mission, in a press conference with leaders of Transparencia on April 10, 2000. Courtesy *Diario Oficial El Peruano*

Resistencia created this traveling mural of government officials as a "Wall of Shame" and invited the public to add their own messages and grafitti.
Courtesy Thomas Crupi

The deadly fire set at the Banco de la Nación in downtown Lima on inauguration day, July 28, 2000. Courtesy Thomas Crupi

Police teargas demonstrators during La Marcha de los Cuatro Suyos in Lima on July 28, 2000. Courtesy Thomas Crupi

President Alberto Fujimori (center) with cabinet president Federico Salas (left) and defense minister General Carlos Bergamino (right), 2000.
Courtesy *Diario Oficial El Peruano*

Demonstrators from Sociedad Civil washing the Peruvian flag in protest of the administration's "dirty tricks." The flag washing, staged in front of the presidential palace, began in May 2000 during the controversy over the second round of the election. Courtesy Thomas Crupi

Opposition leader Alejandro Toledo joins in the flag-washing protest, September 2000.
Courtesy Thomas Crupi

Fujimori loyalists rally as the government deals with the video scandal, September 2000. Courtesy Thomas Crupi

Protestors march with posters that denounce the 2000 election as a fraud and portray Fujimori and Montesinos as the leaders of a corrupt dictatorship. Courtesy Thomas Crupi

After Fujimori's departure in November 2000, protestors show the deposed president as a wanted criminal. Courtesy Thomas Crupi

6

THE REELECTION PROJECT

HEADY as it was, the 1995 reelection was not enough. In early 1996, the buzz began that something else was being planned. Suddenly, political insiders were talking about what at first seemed liked a far-fetched idea: Fujimori would seek yet another reelection in 2000 and govern until 2005.

Publicly, Fujimori denied any desire to stay in power and routinely cut off reporters' queries on the subject.[1] But the mood behind the scenes was entirely different. After his arrest in 2001, Vladimiro Montesinos testified to congressional investigators that, on direct orders from the president, reelection became the "primary political objective."[2] Montesinos said that, as a "solider," he acted on those orders and devoted his energies to pursuing the objective.

To pursue another reelection, Fujimori needed many more soldiers like Montesinos—people willing to do whatever was necessary to win. As an attorney, Montesinos was acutely aware of the substantial legal obstacles that lay in the path of the reelection project. Fujimori always liked to depict his government as one of technocrats, but he depended heavily on the legal profession. He needed lawyers willing to craft questionable rules and judicial officials ready to rule in his favor. Everyone in the political game was aware that actors in the international community still had their eyes on Peru. For the government, maintaining a veneer of legality, as thin as it became over time, was critical to the viability of the reelection project. For the opposition, the law offered at least some openings, albeit limited, to challenge this project.

As opposition challenges mounted, the government radicalized the reelection project. More extreme measures had to be taken, more officials had to be lured into the conspiracy, and more lies had to be told. Each excess made it more difficult to maintain the illusion of normal politics. As the trickery and abuses accumulated, those involved understood that there was no turning back, that they had reached, as Montesinos noted, a "point of no return."[3]

The relentless pursuit of the 2000 reelection was the defining feature of Fujimori's second term in office. No issue or policy came close in importance. The 1992 coup set Peru on the path to authoritarianism, and the decision to force continued control sealed it. But while most Peruvians had gone along with the coup, the reelection project came up against resistance.

Why Reelection?

Fujimori never fully explained why he ultimately made the controversial decision to seek a third term as president. Hubris, an occupational hazard of politicians everywhere, certainly played a part in the decision. By 1996, the war against Sendero Luminoso was essentially over. The government's neoliberal economic policies had reestablished price stability, and economic growth had resumed.[4] If saving Peru from economic collapse and terrorism were the president's central objectives, then his goals had been accomplished and there was no need for him to remain in power.

Oficialistas argued that continuity—the need to sustain the policies— was the reason behind reelection. But the argument that only Fujimori could guarantee continued policy successes underscored a fatal flaw in the president's "antipolitics" model. Because Fujimori had no real political organization other than the ersatz vehicles he used for elections, there was no political party capable of carrying on his policies and generating future leaders. Fujimori's carefully selected political lieutenants took care never to overshadow the president. CCD president Jaime Yoshiyama was viewed as a potential successor; but after he lost the Lima mayoral race to Alberto Andrade in 1995, his political fortunes faded and he quit the government altogether in September 1996. Around the same time, Santiago Fujimori, the president's brother, who labored behind the scenes as an advisor, also stepped aside. Montesinos never expressed a personal interest in diving into electoral politics. Presumably, his shady past ruled him out as a viable successor to Fujimori. Other *oficialistas*—Víctor Joy Way or Martha Chávez—may have dreamed of being anointed as Fujimori's successor, but none seemed close to having the great electoral appeal of their boss.

Continuing Fujimori's policies became the official mantra of the reelection, but other concerns were certainly on the minds of those at the top of the regime; one concern was facing retribution for their conduct. As the 1995 amnesty law demonstrated, the military's top officials were adamant that there should be no public accounting or punishment for their conduct during the counterinsurgency war. As commander in chief of the armed forces, Fujimori would be a likely target in any future human rights investigations related to the war, as would Montesinos. It was important to keep the amnesty in place.

Losing the presidency meant running the risk of being held accountable. And by 1996, there were simply too many crimes too hide. There were also too many opportunities for profiteering to call it quits. With the judiciary and police firmly under control, officials used their positions to cash in.

As Peruvian investigators have documented, Peru was, by 1996, well on the way to becoming a kleptocracy, or a "Mafia state," with at least three compartmentalized spheres of corruption.[5] In one sphere, Montesinos shared the spoils with top-ranking military officers, including General Hermoza. Among their operations were multimillion-dollar kickback schemes from arms purchases and other procurements. Military officers plundered millions of dollars from their own pension fund, the Caja Militar.

The ministry of the economy and related agencies became another site of corruption in the system. Jorge Camet, the minister of the economy from 1993 to 1998, presided over the convoluted deals that profited government officials and their associates in the private sector. Almost every government transaction—from procurement to privatization to the repurchase of Peru's debt papers—became a realm for illicit gain by officials who enjoyed insider information and privileged access to business deals.

In another realm, the Fujimori family and their close associates enjoyed the opportunities opened up by political power. Fujimori's sister Rosa and her husband Víctor Aritomi (appointed as Peru's ambassador to Japan) became directly involved in managing the multimillion-dollar accounts of Apenkai and Aken, two nonprofit, charitable foundations created by Fujimori. The foundations' bookkeeping was haphazard at best, and included transactions that routed financial donations in and out of the personal bank accounts of family members. Financial practices inside the presidential palace were equally opaque. Susana Higuchi reported that she found $110,000 in cash tucked in a safe inside the family quarters of the presidential palace in 1993.[6] Montesinos later alleged that he routinely sent briefcases of cash to the palace at Fujimori's request. Montesinos's secretary Matilde Pinchi Pinchi confirmed the practice. The monthly deliveries, in amounts of $500,000 or more, came from SIN slush funds. To date, none of the monies have been accounted for.[7]

Reelection would keep the cash flowing and the deals going. It was also the way to ensure that no one would have to explain the peculiar bookkeeping or lack thereof.

The "Authentic Interpretation" of the Constitution

Back in 1993, Congressman Manuel Moreyra warned that reelection provision in the constitution allowing for two consecutive presidential terms contained potential for subterfuge. Moreyra cautioned that *oficialistas* could open the door for Fujimori by arguing that the 1993 constitution should not be applied "retroactively" to his first election in 1990.

By early 1996, it was clear that Moreyra had been prescient, not paranoid. The first intimations of the reelection project came from high-profile C90-NM legislators. In a speech on his home turf in Huánuco, congressional president Víctor Joy Way took the first step. He asserted: "The government plan of President Fujimori is for twenty or thirty years." Then he added: "All of us should entertain the hope that President Fujimori will go beyond ten years."[8]

The press latched onto Joy Way's comments. Fujimori loyalists such as Congressman Luis Delgado Aparicio and Congressman Gilberto Siura endorsed Joy Way's views. Other *oficialistas*, however, acknowledged the legal barrier posed by the two-term limit in the constitution. Both Congresswoman Martha Chávez and Congressman Carlos Ferrero stated publicly that the constitution would have to be amended to allow for a 2000 bid by Fujimori.[9]

Amending the constitution to allow for another reelection was a tall order, even with the C90-NM's absolute majority in congress. The 1993 constitution provided only two routes to amendment. One way was by winning a two-thirds majority vote in congress in two successive legislative sessions. The other route was by winning approval of an amendment in a national referendum, followed by a subsequent ratification of the amendment in congress by a simple majority.

The first option—getting a two-thirds majority vote in congress—would not be easy. C90-NM enjoyed a sixty-seven-seat majority in congress, but that still fell considerably short of the eighty votes necessary. The second option—a national referendum—was risky and the chances of victory were slim. After nearly losing the 1993 referendum on the constitution, *oficialistas* did not want another embarrassing experience that might backfire and defeat reelection. Public-opinion polls did not bode well for a reelection referendum. A CPI poll taken in January 1996 showed that 58 percent of the public opposed the reelection proposal. Compounding the difficulties was the slide in Fujimori's job approval rating. It dropped more than ten points between January and February as the controversy about the proposed privatization of the state-owned oil company PETROPERU heated up.[10]

During the first six months of 1996, desertions from the ranks of the opposition and "independents" increased the number of votes that C90-NM could potentially count on for an amendment vote in congress. In fact, Congressman Henry Pease, a noted UPP leader, sounded the warning that the government was trying to induce congressional deputies to flip to the government side in order to patch together the eighty votes it needed.[11] Still, the government was at least five votes short of the two-thirds majority in August 1996.

With a straightforward constitutional amendment seemingly out of reach, C90-NM legislators reverted to the more controversial route, floated publicly by Congressman Luis Delgado Aparicio months earlier: perhaps all that was needed was a law to "interpret" the constitution to allow for reelection. The new law would establish that President Fujimori's election in 1995 was his "first" election within the terms of the 1993 constitution, thus allowing for a consecutive term beginning in 2000.

The first foray into the murky constitutional waters was barely comprehensible. Congressman Oscar Medelius, chair of the judiciary commission, became Montesinos's point man.[12] Medelius shepherded through the obscure Law of General Norms of Administrative Procedures (Law 26654) on August 15, 1996. The law stipulated: "when a public law norm makes the exercise of a right conditional upon previous acts that the only previous acts subject to the application of the norm are those posterior to the enactment of the norm." According to Medelius, Law 26654 established the principle of non-retroactivity, which effectively permitted President Fujimori to stand for reelection in 2000 since the 1993 constitution did not apply to his first election in 1990.

Still, the reelection project was too important to be left hanging on the obtuse language of Law 26654 and the assertions of Congressman Medelius alone. After a meeting of the C90-NM caucus on the evening of August 19, leaders emerged with the Law of the Authentic Interpretation of Article 112 of the Constitution, which came to be known as *Ley de interpretación auténtica.*" Among the sponsors of the law were the leaders of C90-NM: Víctor Joy Way (president of the congress), Carlos Torres y Torres Lara, Martha Hidelbrandt, Oswaldo Sandoval, Oscar Medelius, Luz Salgado, Luis Delgado Aparicio, and Gilberto Siura.[13]

Law 26657 came to a vote on the floor of the congress in the early morning hours of August 23, 1996. It stipulated that Article 112 of the constitution, the provision that limited a president to two consecutive terms in office, could not be applied retroactively to the 1993 constitution. Thus, Fujimori's 1990–1995 term would not be counted as his first term, rendering him eligible to stand for reelection in 2000. Opposition legislators walked out of the vote in protest. The law passed with seventy votes; the only dissenting vote in the C90-NM caucus came from Congressman Carlos Ferrero, who insisted that reelection could only be sanctioned through a constitutional amendment.

Ferrero's colleagues did not share his commitment to consistency, and they lined up to defend the measure regardless of their previous positions on the matter. During the 1993 debate in the CCD, Congressman Carlos Torres y Torres Lara, the law professor who chaired the constitution commission, unequivocally stated that Fujimori's first term in office "counted" and that another Fujimori reelection in 2000 would be off-limits. When queried about his turnaround on the issue and his support for Law 26657, Torres y Torres Lara complained that his previous remarks were misunderstood. He also suggested that if Law 26657 was unconstitutional, then it could be easily overturned by the high court with jurisdiction over such matters, the Tribunal Constitucional.[14] Meanwhile, Congresswoman Martha Chávez, who had previously argued on many occasions that a constitutional amendment was required for reelection, dismissed reporters' queries. She reiterated her belief in unlimited reelection—an idea that she, along with Víctor Joy Way, tried to promote unsuccessfully during the CCD debate in 1993.[15]

Torres y Torres Lara was right on at least one point; he knew that numerous legal challenges lay ahead. Though pro-Fujimori forces inside the government were dominant, the 1993 constitution provided legal channels that the opposition could try to use to battle the reelection.

Resistance through Referendum

Reelection was not the first issue to inspire a push for a citizens' referendum. Human rights organizations coordinated a nationwide petition drive calling for a referendum to overturn the 1995 amnesty law. But the effort fizzled. Over one hundred thousand signatures were collected, but the figure fell fall short of the necessary mark of over one million.

From the government's viewpoint, the more bothersome grassroots campaign was the one mounted in early 1996 to oppose the privatization of the state-owned oil company PETROPERU. Polls showed over 70 percent of the public opposed to privatization. A diverse collection of high-profile leaders from the APRA party and the left began rallying around the referendum proposal. The oil workers' union Federación Nacional de Trabajadores Petroleros y Afines del Perú (FENPETROL) and the national trade union confederation Confederación General de Trabajadores del Perú (CGTP) joined them. Even the prelate of the Roman Catholic Church, Cardinal Augusto Vargas Alzamora, weighed in and declared his support for the referendum, as did Lima mayor Alberto Andrade.

As the antiprivatization campaign gained ground, the C90-NM caucus took preventive legal action. It came in the form of Law 26592, sponsored by Congressman Gilberto Siura (and subsequently dubbed *"Ley Siura"*), passed in April 1996. The law added a new caveat to the constitutional provision for a citizen-sponsored referendum: it required forty-eight or more congressional votes in order for any referendum to be approved. Setting the bar at forty-eight votes effectively ensured that no referendum could pass without the support of the government.

Despite the failure of previous referendum initiatives, Congressman Javier Diez Canseco proposed a referendum on reelection on the floor of the congress. Attorney Alberto Borea of the nongovernmental organization Foro Democrático quickly picked up on the idea and organized a cadre of leaders to pursue it. Congressman Diez Canseco, Congresswoman Lourdes Flores, APRA leader Mauricio Mulder, and Alberto Borea made their way to headquarters of the national electoral office Oficina Nacional de Procesos Electorales (ONPE) on September 2, 1996. They requested the official forms required for collecting voter signatures. On the following day, Borea announced that Foro Democrático would spearhead the campaign for a referendum to overturn the reelection law.

Now that the petitions were in the hands of the opposition, the legal battle was underway. Montesinos managed the government's legal strategy, which meant making sure that every judicial and electoral institution was unquestionably under his control.

From the start, ONPE was anti-referendum. José Portillo López, the portly, Bible-quoting computer professor who headed the agency, refused the opposition's request for the petitions. He pointed to *Ley Siura,* which stipulated that a referendum required congressional approval with at least forty-eight votes. But the JNE, the entity charged with overseeing election law, ordered Portillo to make the petitions available on the grounds that the language of *Ley Siura* was imprecise. Upset by the JNE's interpretation, the C90-NM caucus fired back and accused the JNE of acting illegally and siding with the opposition. Congressman Carlos Torres y Torres Lara promised that new legal maneuvers were on the way: "There are ten solutions and we are going to apply one."[16] He underscored the legal lengths the caucus was willing to employ: "There will be other laws and as many laws as necessary until [the JNE] understands."[17]

The solution was Law 26670, a reworked and more carefully worded version of *Ley Siura.* The new law (now sponsored by Congressman Ricardo

Marcenaro and referred to as *"Ley Marcenaro"*) reasserted the requirement mandating congressional approval of referendum initiatives by a minimum of forty-eight votes. ONPE chief Portillo invoked *Ley Marcenaro* to cancel the reelection referendum, but found himself overturned again by a unanimous JNE ruling. Led by JNE president Alvaro Chocano, JNE officials reasoned that *Ley Marcenaro* could not be applied retroactively and that the petitions, already in the hands of Foro Democrático, could not be recalled.

Unexpectedly, all saber rattling by the C90-NM caucus stopped. The JNE's status as the arbiter of electoral law was clearly prescribed in the 1993 constitution; and the prospect of further wrangling between congress and the JNE had the potential of turning into a full-blown constitutional crisis. Under better circumstances, the C90-NM congressional leaders might have pressed on, but the political atmosphere was turning more troublesome by the last quarter of 1996. Allegations that the military was involved in drug trafficking dominated the news, especially after drug kingpin Demeterio Chávez ("El Vaticano") implicated Vladimiro Montesinos in taking kickbacks. Some opposition leaders even wondered if the hoopla over reelection was a smokescreen—a way to draw attention away from the narco-trafficking scandals.[18] Fujimori's popularity continued the downward plunge commenced in January 1996. By November, his approval fell below 50 percent for the first time since the 1992 coup. According to polls, 60 to 70 percent of the public favored the idea of a referendum.[19]

Fujimori scotched the potential constitutional crisis by saying that he would accept a referendum, but also suggesting that *Ley de interpretación auténtica* might simply be rescinded by congress in order the save the country the cost of holding a referendum. By the end of 1996, the reelection issue appeared to be on hold. *Oficialistas* fell silent on the matter, and Foro Democrático took up the daunting task of collecting more than a million signatures in support of the referendum.

Events focused the public's and the government's attention elsewhere. On December 17, 1996, a handful of guerrillas from the near-defunct Movimiento Revolucionario Tupac Amaru (MRTA) staged a spectacular attack on a cocktail party at the home of the Japanese ambassador in Lima. In the days immediately afterward, the guerrillas released hundreds of the terrified guests, but kept seventy-two high-profile hostages, including Foreign Minister Francisco Tudela, the Bolivian and Japanese ambassadors, six congressmen, and six members of the supreme court. Fujimori took a hard line, refusing to accede to the guerrillas' demands. The four-month-long hostage crisis that followed became a media event of international proportions. Journalists and photographers camped out in the streets around the residence. Lounging in lawn chairs day after day in Lima's summer heat, they waited to see how the drama would conclude. In the background, the legal struggle over reelection continued.

Taking Down the Tribunal

Holding a referendum was one legal recourse, but not the only one available to the opposition to stop reelection. After the enactment of *Ley de interepetación auténtica,* Lima's bar association, CAL, announced its plan to challenge the constitutionality of the law in the Tribunal Constitucional (TC).

The TC was a newly reinstated entity, still working through a backlog of more than one thousand cases left unresolved since the closure of the TC in the 1992 coup. The 1993 constitution mandated the creation of the tribunal. Putting together the requisite eighty votes in congress to select the seven members had been problematic, especially when C90-NM leaders tried to push the candidacy of Augusto Antonioli, a former SIN director. That effort failed, and the C90-NM legislators had little alternative but to get the TC in place by bargaining with the opposition. The selection of court members was one of the few instances in which *oficialistas* and opposition legislators reached a consensus on anything—thus, the nominations produced a mix of jurists who were neither entirely predictable in terms of how they might vote on issues nor exclusively beholden to the *oficialista* elite.

The TC was, effectively, a wild card in the reelection game. By the end of 1996, press reports said that the TC was preparing to rule in favor of CAL's legal challenge. As the uncertainty mounted, bizarre incidents involving TC members suggested that the SIN was up to "dirty tricks." In November 1996, tribunal president Ricardo Nugent, formerly the head of the JNE, was the target of a suspicious attack by unidentified assailants near his home; he survived unharmed, but two bodyguards died in the shootout.[20] As the tribunal prepared to rule in mid-January 1997, TC magistrate Delia Revoredo charged that documents relevant to the deliberations on Law 26657 had been stolen from her office and that she had reason to believe that her home was under surveillance. Revoredo implicated fellow TC magistrate José García in the theft. The twisted congressional investigation that ensued over the following months turned into a snare to sack Revoredo and fellow magistrates. Just days before the ruling, forty C90-NM legislators signed a letter urging the TC not to overturn the reelection provision. Opposition legislators complained that the letter invoked the TC to violate its own organic law that expressly forbade the TC to act on instructions from other governmental branches.

In the already-tense atmosphere, the TC magistrates split on the reelection ruling, making the status of the decision open to interpretation. On January 16, three of the seven TC magistrates issued a ruling that Law 26657 was "inapplicable" to reelection. The magistrates making the ruling were Manuel Aguirre Roca, Delia Revoredo, and Guillermo Rey Terry. President Ricardo Nugent did not sign the ruling, nor did magistrates Luis Díaz Valverde, Francisco Acosta, and José García. The three magistrates issued their ruling as "unanimous," that is, having a majority of the emitted votes cast. The number of votes mattered. In designing the TC, the congress laid down rules making it extremely difficult for the TC to overturn legislation by requiring a vote of six of its seven members on matters involving the constitutionality of laws.

On the same day, José García and Francisco Acosta filed a separate decision that ruled against the CAL challenge. To add to the confusion, the government's official newspaper of record, *El Peruano,* published both findings, effectively giving legal status to both decisions. But the anti-reelection finding was published with typographical errors that muddled the meaning altogether. Although he had abstained from signing either decision, TC president Nugent denounced *El Peruano* for what he believed to be deliberate typesetting errors designed to obfuscate the ruling against reelection.

Total confusion regarding the status and the meaning of the two contending TC rulings made for a legal quagmire on the reelection issue, one that *oficialistas* were quick to exploit. That the three-person ruling declared Law 26657 "inapplicable" instead of "unconstitutional" was interpreted as victory. President of the congress Víctor Joy Way said that he was happy because there was no finding of unconstitutionality by six members of the TC. In his view, the law was still standing.

But behind the scenes, the confused outcome was suboptimal. Montesinos and his advisors always prepared multiple "scenarios" when strategizing on reelection. As a counterweight to the adverse ruling, Montesinos wanted a reverse finding from another legal authority that *oficialistas* could brandish if necessary. He turned to Congresswoman Martha Chávez, an attorney. She filed an appeal of the TC's "inapplicability" ruling in the public law circuit court. It was a dubious legal move since the TC was the highest legal authority on constitutional matters. Chávez insisted that her legal battle was her own initiative. Montesinos later divulged that all the case materials were prepared by the SIN and passed on to Chávez.[21]

Chávez's case was rejected, but her appeal eventually moved on to the supreme court, an institution squarely under the control of Montesinos. In December 1997, the supreme court issued a ruling in favor of Chávez's challenge of the TC ruling, an opinion that shocked every constitutional expert because of the obvious jurisdictional error.

Meanwhile, no matter what its legal status, the adverse TC ruling was an unwelcome complication, so Montesinos looked for another solution. The goal was simple: ensure that the TC would not be an obstacle to reelection or block key government policies in other areas. But eviscerating the country's primary judicial body was not easily accomplished. Certainly, just shutting down the TC was not an option, since that would predictably provoke the ire of the international community and accusations of another auto-coup. So once again, Montesinos turned to the C90-NM congressional caucus to concoct a legal way around the 1993 constitution.

Magistrate Revoredo's charge that her office had been robbed during deliberations on the reelection matter served as the pretext for opening a congressional investigation into the matter. Congresswoman Martha Hidelbrandt was chosen to chair the commission. Hidelbrandt, a noted linguist and the only bona fide intellectual in the C90-NM caucus, would add gravitas to the proceedings. She expanded the scope of the investigation to include other "irregularities" in the TC. The commission hit on a seemingly obscure issue: the legal propriety of the publication of a text by Aguirre Roca, Revoredo, and Rey Terry. The document was a response to a request by the CAL to explain the reasoning underlying their finding on reelection. TC president Nugent authorized the publication of the opinion.

The opportunity to take down the TC came in May, while Fujimori's popularity ratings soared. On April 25, Fujimori brought the four-month hostage crisis to an end by giving military commandos the green light to attack the ambassador's residence. The operation was, in the eyes of most people, a spectacular success. Security forces had spent months constructing an elaborate underground tunnel and rehearsing the raid. Using explosives, the commandos blew their way through the residence, gunned down all the guerrillas, and whisked the hostages to safety. Only one of the seventy-two hostages died in the rescue.[22]

It was a public relations bonanza for Fujimori. Peruvians huddled around televisions and radios, riveted by the live coverage of the attack. As soon as the rescue concluded, the president was on the scene, riding on the bus taking the hostages to safety. Fujimori later toured the grisly scene of the operation, with television cameras filming the cadavers of the guerrillas lying at his feet. In a rare public appearance, Montesinos made his own pilgrimage to the residence. The successful operation had come at a perfect time. Fujimori, Montesinos, and General Hermoza were once again audacious leaders in the fight against terrorism. Fujimori reveled in describing his role in personally planning the details of the attack.

Exploiting the president's bounce in the polls, *oficialistas* proceeded with the controversial move against the TC. Congresswoman Hidelbrandt joined with three other legislators to present a motion to charge four of the seven TC members (Aguirre Roca, Revoredo, Rey Terry, and Nugent) with breaching the constitution. The accusation was based on their alleged improper conduct in the publication of the reply to CAL. Outside *oficialista* circles, the motive underlying the accusation was obvious. Tribunal president Ricardo Nugent characterized the accusation as a coup d'état aimed at eliminating the tribunal, the equivalent of another *auto-golpe*.[23] Nugent laid out the logic: "We [the tribunal] represent an obstacle to *oficialismo*. But to elect our replacements, two thirds of the votes in congress is necessary. And if it took two years to elect this Tribunal, to elect another four members will take three years. That means that there will be no Tribunal until 2000."[24]

In a style that had become all too familiar, C90-NM legislators raced ahead with the plan to take action against the offending TC members, regardless of public opinion opposing the action. C90-NM legislator Luz Salgado and Congressman Dennis Vargas, the former radio host who had recently defected from CODE-País Posible to join the government ranks, led some hasty hearings on the matter, then passed the "constitutional denunciations" to the floor for a vote.

The debate on the floor of the congress was a strange spectacle. As if to add to the humiliation of the proceeding, the accused magistrates were consigned to seats behind a table at the back of the chamber, where they listened to a barrage of insults. Leading off the harangues was Congressman Enrique Chirinos Soto of Renovación, an ostensibly "independent" political group that frequently voted with C90-NM. Chirinos Soto, often lampooned in the press for his weight and his drinking problems, was a longtime friend of Manuel Aguirre Roca, a fact that made his role in the proceedings look cruel and pathetic.

In the early hours of May 29, 1997, the proceedings ground toward their predictable end. By a vote of a simple majority—fifty-two votes in favor, thirty-three votes opposed, and one abstention—the congress voted to remove Aguirre Roca, Revoredo, and Rey Terry from the TC. Congressional president Víctor Joy Way ignored the procedural objections of opposition legislators, who argued that the removal of the magistrates should require the same number of votes it took to elect them—namely, a two-thirds majority (eighty votes). Joy Way concluded the tense session with a vote to censure opposition Congressman Fernando Olivera for deriding Joy Way as *un miserable* (a scoundrel) for his heavy-handed management of floor debate.

Tribunal president Ricardo Nugent was spared the impeachment since he had neither voted on the reelection matter nor coauthored the opinion on the ruling. Keeping Nugent in place was a crafty stroke. By doing so, the TC retained four members and thus could continue to rule on matters such as habeas corpus motions. At the same time, however, the TC was rendered unable to pronounce on questions regarding the constitutionality of laws because a minimum of six votes was required for such rulings.

The outcome ostensibly gave *oficialistas* some room to argue that they had not breached the constitution. They had left the TC intact, at least technically speaking. But the argument fell flat. All of the principal newspapers, including the usually progovernment *Expreso,* condemned the impeachment. So did the government's human rights ombudsman, Jorge Santistevan, and Roman Catholic Cardinal Augusto Vargas Alzamora. A wide range of organizations joined the chorus of opposition to the impeachment, including Foro Democrático, CAL, and the trade union federation CGTP.

Polls showed strong opposition to the impeachment. Imasen polls taken immediately after the impeachment in the Lima metropolitan area showed

74 percent of the public opposed to the impeachment. When asked why the impeachment took place, 80 percent of the respondents agreed that it was because the magistrates had ruled against the reelection. Of those polled, 76 percent agreed with the statement that the action was "part of a strategy of the government to weaken institutions" rather than just an "isolated case." In the same poll, 77 percent of respondents agreed with the statement that the impeachment was a "signal to intimidate all those who oppose the government." When asked if the government was democratic, 62 percent of the public said no.[25]

Fujimori was conspicuously silent during the public debate on the TC. Peruvians didn't like the impeachment, but Fujimori had little reason to be concerned about international reaction to the events. Dennis Jett, the American ambassador who, during his tenure from 1996 to 1999, came to be regarded as a critic of Fujimori, characterized the impeachment as a "step backward" for Peruvian democracy. But Jett conceded that he was voicing his own personal opinion and that it was unlikely that U.S. aid would be endangered by the move.[26] When the OAS general assembly met in Lima in June 1997, the ongoing events in Peru were a non-issue.

As he almost always did, Fujimori happily distanced himself from the controversy, leaving C90-NM legislators to deal with the political fallout. "I am part of the executive," he explained, "I don't want to interfere in what the members of the legislature do and their responsibility to the whole country, which they must assume."[27] As the impeachment proceedings got underway, Fujimori was on a trip to Bangladesh and India and unavailable to reporters. One political cartoon showed a content Fujimori, with suitcases in hand. In the cartoon, the president mused: "Ah, there's nothing like coming home after a pleasure trip and finding all the dirty work done."[28]

But there was more dirty work to come. And the public and the media were making it harder to do it. Since the coup, the government had counted on dealing with a passive, demobilized citizenry—people tired of politics, fearful of the violence once associated with it, and preoccupied with eking out a living under trying economic circumstances. Even when public opinion had opposed government conduct (as in the case of La Cantuta or the military amnesty of 1995), no significant mass protests took place. But by 1997 the atmosphere was changing. The TC impeachment provoked demonstrations in Lima and the provinces. University students, thought to be apolitical and alienated, marched through the streets of Lima. They asserted their new and rightful presence in politics with the chant, *"Somos estudiantes, no somos terroristas"* (We're students, not terrorists).[29] People were starting to believe that the reelection project had gone too far, and some of them were willing to stand up and say so.

Recasting the JNE

With the TC out of the picture, the only institution that could still complicate Fujimori's 2000 reelection bid was the national election board, the JNE. As mandated in the 1993 constitution, the five-member executive board of the JNE was the final arbiter of all electoral processes.

Each of the JNE board members was a representative of one of five "corporate" entities: (1) the law faculties of public universities; (2) the law faculties of private universities; (3) the bar association; (4) the supreme court; and (5) the board of national prosecutors. Members of each entity elected their representative. In the case of the law school representatives, current and retired law school deans were entitled to vote. On the supreme court and prosecutors' board, voting members included current and retired members. The JNE term was four years, but members were eligible for reelection for one additional term. Members were obliged to resign at the age of seventy, even if time remained on their term.

Given the diverse constituencies electing the members, the JNE board did not automatically fall under the direct control of the executive branch. Indeed, the JNE's 1996 ruling that disregarded *Ley Siura* and *Ley Marcenaro* demonstrated the willingness of some JNE members to overrule the C90-NM congressional majority. Montesinos knew that the JNE had to be fixed for the reelection and he proceeded to do so. According to Montesinos, the process involved both corrupting individuals (*trabjando la persona*— "working the person") and manipulating the institutional rules governing the JNE elections.

"Working the person" meant co-opting individual members. Montesinos struck up a clandestine working relationship with JNE board member Romulo Muñoz Arce. Muñoz, the JNE representative of the CAL, was scheduled to remain on the board until June 2000. As the CAL representative, Muñoz was a high-profile member of the JNE and liked to profess his "independence" to the press. But behind closed doors, Muñoz was anything but independent. Videotapes of his 1998 meetings at SIN headquarters show Muñoz strategizing with Montesinos on how to circumvent the reelection referendum. In exchange for the favor, Muñoz received money to finance his daughter's studies abroad and jobs for his son and wife.[30] Montesinos also struck up what he termed a "friendship" with Walter Hernández, the JNE representative of the law faculties of public universities.[31]

It was fortuitous that three of the JNE members, including the president, were scheduled to conclude their terms in 1998–1999. The vacancies offered an opening for Montesinos to make sure that JNE members were individuals who could be counted on in the reelection. To do this, Montesinos sought a foolproof way to influence the internal elections in the two government entities, the supreme court and the prosecutors' board. According to Montesinos, Congressman Oscar Medelius devised the legal strategy to make sure that progovernment candidates won. On December 10, 1997, legislation was introduced to alter the rules governing the election of JNE members. Law 26898 gave voting rights to prosecutors and judges holding provisional appointments.

The objective of the legislation was apparent. Provisional appointees interested in preserving their jobs could be easily pressured to cast their votes for Montesinos's handpicked candidates. Congressional opponents immediately dubbed Law 26898 as *"Ley de fraude"* (Fraud Law). To protest the measure and the irregularities in the floor debate, opponents scrawled handmade placards that read *"No al fraude"* (No to fraud) and posted them on their seats. Carlos Torres y Torres Lara, serving as congressional president, suspended the legislative session. The suspension continued on the following day when the defiant legislators refused to remove the signs.

The slogan *"No al fraude"* became the mantra of the opposition. The chant was heard again on May 21, 1998, when C90-NM took another turn to rein in the JNE. Legislation was introduced to change the voting rules inside the JNE. The new measure required that legal challenges to candidacies could only be approved by a vote of four of the five members, rather than a simple majority of three out of five votes. In essence, this meant that almost any legal challenge to Fujimori's presidential candidacy would be doomed, since at least two of the JNE members—those of the supreme court and the prosecutors' board—were sure to be aligned with the government. Once again, opposition legislators disrupted the session by yelling and waving signs that read *"No al fraude, Sí a la democracia"* (No to fraud, yes to democracy).

By mid-1998, Montesinos had put almost all of the legal pieces in place to allow for reelection. JNE president Alvaro Chocano, who led the board in its unanimous 1996 decision to authorize the referendum, reached the obligatory retirement age of seventy. Luis Serpa Segura, a longtime administration loyalist and associate of Montesinos, replaced Chocano. Representing the prosecutors, José Carlos Bringas was elected in mid-June 1998. Ramiro de Valdivia Cano, the JNE member representing the law faculties of private universities and thought to be the most independent member of the board, was elected to a second term in 1998. But with the remainder of the JNE firmly on the side of Montesinos, Valdivia was of little concern. Moreover, as Montesinos and Valdivia later confirmed, Valdivia participated in meetings that Montesinos held with JNE members, giving Montesinos a heads-up on how he would rule.

By "working" individual members and changing the rules, Montesinos rendered the JNE a reliable partner in the reelection project. Now Montesinos and *oficialistas* could turn their full attention to a last task before the 2000 campaign: shutting down the grassroots referendum project.

Burying the Referendum

Collecting the 1,200,000 valid voter signatures necessary for a referendum on the reelection issue was a monumental task. Given the failure of the previous two attempts at referendum campaigns on amnesty and privatization, there was good reason to believe that the effort might simply lose momentum over time and fall short of the necessary signatures.

The still-uncoordinated state of the opposition added to the difficulties in organizing the campaign to collect signatures. The opposition was diverse and dispersed. The most prominent leaders were those of the congressional opposition. They came from across the political spectrum, from longtime leftist Javier Diez Canseco to Christian Democrat Lourdes Flores. But the key problem of congressional opponents was the debilitated state of their own political organizations. As verbally combative and personally committed as they were in their fight against *Fujimorismo*, congressional opponents did not have strong party organizations capable of activating supporters to back them up.

Foro Democrático took on the responsibility for the campaign. But it did not have a broad-based organization, as it had previously focused its efforts largely on academic events and contacts with university students. For the petition drive, Foro Democrático would have to rely on the help of politicians, trade unions, and other grassroots organizations. While opposition politicians from across the spectrum had joined in the initial flurry of public events that launched the campaign in September 1996, the painstaking process of collecting the signatures was an entirely different matter. Suspicion that Alberto Borea, the leader of Foro Democrático, might use the success of the group as a launching pad for his own presidential candidacy left some politicians less than enthusiastic about the idea of helping Borea become the de facto leader of the opposition. But for others, the importance of the cause outweighed other considerations; Congressman Javier Diez Canseco and Congresswoman Lourdes Flores threw themselves fully into the campaign, as did Congressman Alejandro Santa María of APRA and General Rodolfo Robles.

The campaign languished in the first half of 1997, due in part to the tactical difficulties of launching the drive while the hostage crisis dragged on. But with the end of the hostage crisis and the growing public disaffection with the regime after the TC impeachment, the campaign to collect signatures came back to life in the last months of 1997. Inserting the petition form as a supplement in the Sunday editions of newspapers revived the effort.[32] To counter the identification of the referendum with Borea's political aspirations, Mario Roggiero, a businessman and former congressman, spearheaded a renewed signature drive across the country called Pro-Democracia. Raúl Diez Canseco, leader of AP, and leaders of UPP joined Roggiero. In early December 1997, Foro Democrático confirmed the collection of nine hundred thousand signatures for the referendum.[33] Roggieros's fundraising and other contributions bankrolled the new phase of the campaign, making it possible for Foro to add to its volunteer force by hiring people to work in signature-collecting "brigades."

On July 16, 1998, leaders of Foro Democrático arrived at ONPE headquarters to present petitions for the referendum. ONPE was the first stop because it was the entity charged with confirming the validity of the signatures on the petitions. The petitions contained 1,441,535 signatures; at least 1,200,000 signatures, amounting to 10 percent of the electorate, had to be judged as valid in order for the referendum to go forward.

The verification of the signatures alone offered endless possibilities for ONPE to stymie the referendum, had Montesinos opted for that route. Instead, he took a different tack. On July 30, a former C90 congressman, Manuel La Torre Bardales, filed a complaint with ONPE. He argued that *Ley Marcenaro* should be applied to the referendum process, despite the previous JNE ruling that the law could not be retroactively applied. As he had in 1996, ONPE chief Portillo seemed eager to apply *Ley Marcenaro* and prepared to send the referendum documents to congress for a vote. Foro Democrático leaders had little doubt that Portillo was acting on orders from above. Spokesman Mauricio Mulder denounced Portillo's decision as "one more set-up from the [presidential] palace."[34] Foro filed its appeal of the ONPE decision with the JNE, the entity with the power to overrule ONPE.

Although it was not public knowledge at the time, the planning to stop the referendum was very finely calibrated. Montesinos had the JNE ruling on the case prepared at SIN headquarters even before the JNE board met to hear the arguments. He met with JNE president Luis Serpa Segura and board member José Carlos Bringas on August 14 and instructed them on how to dispose of the appeal in summary fashion. Describing the upcoming hearing, he advised them: "Now, don't forget that there's no rebuttal or re-statements. They [the lawyers] just talk, goddamn it, the time that you give them, their thirty minutes or hour, and the stupid thing is over, brother. Ring the bell, vote, and you already have the decision. Throw them out of the room, goddamn it, and pull out this crap. The resolution is already made up, brother."[35]

The JNE dutifully followed the Montesinos script. On August 20, the JNE heard oral arguments from lawyers on the Bardales challenge. Most of the government's arguments simply rehearsed the previous arguments laid out back in 1996.[36] One novel twist was the argument that the referendum initiative did not officially begin when Foro leaders picked up the petitions in 1996, but when they submitted the petitions in July 1998—thus rendering *Ley Marcenaro* applicable. Just as Montesinos had instructed, the JNE members did their work swiftly, delivering a reversal of their 1996 decision just three hours after final arguments in the case. By a vote of four to one, the

JNE upheld that *Ley Marcenaro* required a congressional vote in order for a referendum to go forward. Ramiro Valdivia cast the lone dissenting vote.

The congress was the last stop for the referendum. At least in theory, there were forty-eight legislators who might line up in favor of the referendum. The pro-referendum position could reliably count on votes from what remained of UPP, AP, APRA, the PPC, and the left. The conduct of the self-declared "independents" was a question mark. There was no question, however, about the state of public opinion on the referendum. Polls showed that 75 percent of the public favored a referendum on the reelection issue.[37]

Montesinos left nothing to chance. He coordinated with congress president Víctor Joy Way to guarantee that there would not be forty-eight legislators in favor of the referendum on the floor of congress. To do so, they struck clandestine agreements with three legislators to be absent on the day of the vote. Montesinos later confessed to making at least one payoff and influencing trafficking. Congressman Luis Chu received payment on an apartment of approximately $130,000 from an SIN slush fund, according to Montesinos. In the same testimony, Montesinos said that he helped pending legal cases involving the business owned by Congressman Miguel Ciccia in return for his absence. Susy Díaz, the flamboyant showgirl-turned-legislator, simply agreed to be absent on "personal matters."[38]

University students staged a vigil outside of congress, trying to keep the pressure on any wavering legislators. Press reports had already identified Ciccia and Chu as possible deserters.[39] As the time of the vote approached on the evening of August 27, hundreds of demonstrators joined the students in chants of *"¡Sí al referéndum, no al fraude!"* (Yes to referendum, no to fraud!)

Inside the building, Joy Way presided over yet another acrimonious debate. In the most emotional moment of the evening, Carlos Ferrero, the long-standing dissident of the C90-NM caucus, broke ranks again and cast his vote in favor of the referendum with a shout: *"¡Que el pueblo decida! Sí al referéndum."* (Let the people decide! Yes to referendum.)[40] The referendum went down to defeat in a vote of sixty-seven opposed and forty-four in favor, leaving the opposition just four votes shy of the required forty-eight votes.

Meanwhile, Fujimori was off on vacation, visiting his children, who lived in Boston. When the referendum was torpedoed, there was no official reaction from the U.S. State Department.[41] At that point, the Clinton administration was far more concerned with Peru's international relations than its domestic affairs. Along with other Latin American countries, the United States had been active in trying to facilitate a peace accord between Peru and Ecuador to settle the longstanding border conflict that had plunged the countries into a brief war in 1995.[42] After a long process of negotiation, an agreement finally fell into place. President Fujimori joined President Jamil Mahuad of Ecuador in a celebratory signing of the historic peace treaty in Brasilia on October 26, 1998.

Toasted by his fellow Latin American presidents and lauded by President Bill Clinton and UN secretary-general Kofi Annan for his contribution to continental peace, Fujimori had managed to distance himself from the unpleasant politics back home.[43]

Fujimori headed to Ottawa, where he was the honored guest at a glittering state dinner hosted by Prime Minister Jean Chrétien in the National Gallery of Canada. But on the following day, Fujimori got a reminder that not all international observers were caught up in the peace treaty euphoria. Pressed into attending a meeting with Canadian human rights activists and academics, Fujimori grew annoyed with their questions on government abuses and the military amnesty.[44] When asked to comment on the blocked referendum, Fujimori was curt. Peru's congressional representatives were free to legislate as they pleased, he said.

Governing as Mockery

No one apart from those directly involved knew the details of Montesinos's conspiracy to block the referendum. For the opposition, though, the outcome of the legal struggle against reelection left no doubt that the 1993 constitution was a fiction, a nicety to be dispensed with or warped when it got in the way of reelection.

Another conclusion emerged from the legal struggle over reelection: the government was willing to openly defy public opinion, no matter how substantial, if it ran contrary to reelection. *Oficialista* willingness to manipulate rules and legislate against mainstream public opinion was not new; the handling of the La Cantuta case and the military amnesty were prime examples. In the case of reelection, however, the duplicity of the *oficialista* political elite and their readiness to thumb their noses at the public reached a new level. Legislators who had unequivocally argued that another reelection would be impossible without amending the constitution reversed themselves entirely, with virtually no explanation of their sudden change of heart. Fujimori, who had extolled the virtues of the referendum back in 1992 when he saw it as a way to rubberstamp the coup, fell silent on the topic as his political lieutenants constructed a legal maze to block citizens from using the referendum. That more than one million Peruvians actively supported the referendum by signing petitions, and that polls corroborated overwhelming support, simply did not matter.

In a *La República* column anticipating the referendum's demise, Mirko Lauer pointed to the pervasive cynicism of *oficialistas* and their insulting style of governing: *"Burla, burlando van gobernando"* (Mock, mocking, they go on governing). He wrote that the reelection drive was effectively turning the state into a "kind of grand, permanent chicanery." In its coverage of the referendum vote, the news magazine *Caretas* underscored the feeling: "The sensation that public opinion was mocked, however, spread nationwide."[45]

Montesinos and his associates went to great lengths to shroud the process in legal formalities. The operations securing reelection were secret, but the legal contortions were visible to the public and plainly outrageous. Polls showed that Peruvians viewed the reelection measures as obvious manipulations to keep the regime in power. Peruvians acknowledged the growing authoritarianism, rescinding the view that their government was democratic. And just in case Peruvians needed additional confirmation of how weird their government had become, all they had to do was turn on the television.

7

KIDNAPPING THE MEDIA

FUJIMORI always insisted that freedom of the press was untrammeled in Peru. And he liked to point to the newsstands of Lima as proof positive. As international criticisms of his government's treatment of the press intensified in 1997, Fujimori defended his record at a meeting of the OAS general assembly in Lima: "Contrary to what our detractors assert, democracy can be seen on every street corner, on every street. Just go out and take a ride downtown in the capital or on the outskirts and you can find a surprising number of daily or weekly publications. Their headlines contradict, in the most eloquent way, any assertion about the lack of press freedom in this country."[1]

Any visitor perusing the newsstands might have been tempted to agree. Opposition newspapers—*La República, Referéndum,* and later, *Liberación*—relentlessly pummeled the president and his *oficialistas.* So did the newsmagazine *Caretas,* which routinely mocked Fujimori and Montesinos on its covers.[2]

The freedom on display at Lima's newsstands was undeniable. At the same time, it was deceptive. Among the lessons learned from the 1992 coup was that press freedom was a significant marker for how the regime was regarded abroad. For the Fujimori administration, freedom of the press was an annoying but unavoidable convention. But, like the constitution itself, it could be established, then undermined. As the march toward the reelection advanced, Vladimiro Montesinos masterminded a complicated and expensive strategy to do just that. He used the SIN to lash out at the independent press and created an elaborate system of payoffs and favors to create a network of loyal clients among Peru's media moguls. But what Montesinos failed to grasp fully was how his own strategy to "kidnap" the media (in the words of 2000 presidential candidate Alejandro Toledo) would be undermined by its obviousness. Crafty as Montesinos was, he could not achieve complete control over the "wild complex" of Peru's public sphere.

Under Pressure and Under Surveillance

If there was anything that journalists of all political stripes agreed on during the Fujimori era, it was that they were under surveillance. The belief was pervasive. Long before the first solid evidence of the government's electronic eavesdropping came to light in 1997, editors and reporters were convinced that their telephones were tapped. Everyone in the news business, even journalists sympathetic to the government, had stories about strange clicks on their telephone lines or vans with darkly tinted windows that appeared regularly in the streets around their offices.

The stories about government surveillance, frequently dismissed by *oficialistas* as paranoid tales, turned out to be true. The avalanche of information that came to light after the fall of the regime in 2000 confirmed that Montesinos used the resources of the SIN to spy on the independent press. Simple surveillance, however, was not all—intimidating journalists, media owners, and those who might provide information to the press was also part of the mission. Harassing the press was necessary because so many people in the government had so much to hide, especially those in the intelligence services and the armed forces. Montesinos regarded investigative journalism on television as a danger since the stories always seemed to swirl around him. In 1996, a series of embarrassing news reports linked high-ranking military officials and Montesinos to accusations of involvement in narco-trafficking. On August 16, one of Peru's notorious drug kingpins,

Demetrio Chávez made the charges during a court appearance.[3] Chávez said that he made payments of fifty thousand dollars per month to Montesinos in exchange for the protection of his drug operations. In the courtroom, reporters from every media outlet were on hand, including television stations. No news organization, including the progovernment ones, could ignore the explosive story. The Chávez revelations immediately revived media interest in the long-standing questions about exactly what Montesinos did and what his formal job description was. Contradictory statements by administration officials, including Fujimori, contributed to the confusion regarding Montesinos's exact status.[4]

Not surprisingly, the news prompted a flurry of denials. High-ranking administration officials were trotted out to defend Montesinos, including Finance Minister Jorge Camet, General Hermoza, Minister of Justice Carlos Hermoza, Interior Minister General Juan Briones Dávila, and Attorney General Blanca Nélida Colán. But the public relations damage in Washington was evident as the human rights organizations Americas Watch and the Washington Office on Latin America called for inquiries into Montesinos's connections to the CIA and other American agencies.[5]

More revelations linking Montesinos and the military to narcotrafficking followed. In September, two of the highest-rated television stations aired audiotapes of alleged conversations between drug dealers and military officers. *La Revista Dominical*, the Sunday night newsmagazine on Channel 4 (América Televisión), hosted by the popular and usually progovernment journalist Nicolás Lúcar, aired the tape, as did the Sunday morning *Contrapunto* on Channel 2 (Frecuencia Latina).

The decision to air the tapes on *Contrapunto* was a watershed for the Frecuencia Latina network, which until then had been known for its obsequious coverage of the armed forces. The station's principal stockholder and executive was an Israeli-born naturalized citizen, Baruch Ivcher. Ivcher was known to be close to top administration officials—so close, in fact, that critics scorned Frecuencia Latina as the SIN network.

For reasons that still remain a subject of speculation in Peru, Ivcher ordered a shift in the station's editorial line in late 1995.[6] Staffing changes reflected the station's new turn. Julián Cortez, the longtime news director known to have strong ties to the armed forces, left the station. Joining the new staff was former newspaper editor Fernando Viaña and a team of journalists with extensive backgrounds in investigative reporting: Luis Ibérico,

José Arrieta, Roxana Cueva, and Iván García. Rounding out the *Contra-punto* team was its new host and fresh face, Gonzalo Quijandría.

General Tomás Castillo Meza, the minister of defense, denounced the drug tapes as fakes. The CSJM declined to investigate the charges. Castillo Meza recommended that any civilians associated with the alleged forgery be prosecuted. That was interpreted as a direct threat aimed at the news staffs of *Contrapunto* and *La Revista Dominical*. In another ominous signal from the armed forces, the military guards that had long been posted at the television stations as a precaution against terrorist attacks were removed, just hours after *Contrapunto* aired the recordings.

It became clear that the administration was gearing up to stop further public discussion of Montesinos and narco-trafficking when the president of the council of ministers, Adolfo Pandolfi, appeared before congress. He refused to answer any questions about Montesinos on the grounds that his duties at the SIN were a state secret.[7] Then Demeterio Chávez reappeared in court on August 23. In contrast to previous appearances, Chávez was disheveled and incoherent, unable to repeat his earlier accusations. Chávez's strange conduct provoked speculation that he had been tortured or sedated by prison officials.[8]

With Chávez gone silent and no legal inquiries launched, the story hit a journalistic dead end. Montesinos's high-profile appearance at an October 1996 meeting between Fujimori and General Barry McCaffrey, the U.S. drug czar, was a rejoinder to the onslaught of bad publicity and a reminder to the opposition that the United States had not openly repudiated Montesinos.[9] A *New York Times* editorial noted unhappily that the McCaffrey visit had been interpreted as support for Montesinos, and that it had helped stave off the opposition's calls for an investigation by congress.[10]

As the Chávez case showed, controlling the press was not always an easy task for the government. Unflattering revelations did occasionally make it to the airwaves. Even progovernment stations covered them when the allegations reached scandalous proportions and when a failure to cover the story risked placing an outlet at a competitive disadvantage. To effectively control the news and lay the groundwork for the reelection project (so likely to be fraught with potential scandals), Montesinos needed to tighten his grip. That meant using the intelligence service to put more pressure on the independent press and to make sure that people with damaging information would have reason to fear becoming whistle-blowers.

The first indication of how far Montesinos and the SIN were willing to go in the campaign of intimidation came in Puno on October 18, 1996. Three packs of dynamite exploded in sequence in front of a television station, the local affiliate of Global Televisión. No one was killed, but the blasts damaged the television transmitter and blew out the windows in nineteen nearby homes. No group claimed responsibility for the attack, but it had all the earmarks of an intelligence operation. Global Televisión had just launched a controversial news program, *La Clave,* hosted by César Hidelbrandt. Hidelbrandt, the maverick journalist and an ardent supporter of Mario Vargas Llosa in 1990, had left Peru after the 1992 coup. *La Clave* marked his return to the airwaves. From the government's viewpoint, his was an unwelcome return. Hidelbrandt attracted an audience, especially among middle-class *limeños,* and spoke nothing but invective when it came to the subject of Fujimori and Montesinos.

In what was certainly an unexpected turn of events for the culprits, local police officers made arrests in the Puno case. The arrests confirmed the suspicions of intelligence involvement. All three men detained were army intelligence operatives attached to the SIN. The scandal intensified when retired General Rodolfo Robles identified one of the men as a former member of the clandestine Grupo Colina. Robles, a whistle-blower in the La Cantuta case, was now a full-fledged opposition activist and crusader in the campaign for the reelection referendum.

The reprisal against Robles was swift. Five days after his declarations on the Puno incident, on November 26, Robles was arrested in broad daylight on his morning walk to a neighborhood newsstand. Agents gassed Robles, punched him, and forced him into a car. Robles yelled out to shocked bystanders, "They're from Intelligence! Tell journalist Hidelbrandt!" The arrest warrant for Robles had been issued by the CSJM. The retired general was charged with insulting the armed forces, disobedience, and giving false information. As Robles's son observed after the arrest, "Telling the truth in this country is a synonym for insult."[11]

The Robles arrest was meant to send the message that the SIN and the army would not tolerate whistle-blowers. But the arrest, and the manner in which it was carried out, became yet another public relations disaster. The Robles affair provoked widespread condemnation in Peru and from human rights organizations abroad. Opposition leaders in congress called for an immediate investigation, and editorials in every newspaper condemned the arrest. Even the progovernment *Expreso* called for a release of Robles. *Expreso* columnist Manuel D'Ornellas went even further, warning that Fujimori had gone too far in ceding to armed forces and that it was time for Montesinos and General Hermoza to go.[12]

In an unusual move, Fujimori temporarily broke ranks with the military, looking for a way out of the growing controversy. Opinion polls showed that nearly three-quarters of those surveyed believed that the arrest of Robles violated the right to freedom of expression. But far more troubling than the public support for Robles was the damage being done to the president's job-approval rating. Between November and December, Fujimori's approval rating dropped by six points, from 52 percent to 45 percent. According to pollster Alfredo Torres, Robles's jailing significantly eroded the president's poll numbers.[13]

Fujimori's solution was to send a new "amnesty" law to congress, specifically written to the particulars of the Robles case. The final version, prepared by the president of the justice commission, Congressman Oscar Medelius, extended amnesty to all retired military personnel accused of insulting the armed forces, disobedience, or providing false information. It also granted amnesty to any members of the judiciary (including the CSJM) for any legal actions having to do with their questionable conduct in the case. The amnesty was an ad hoc solution. It allowed Fujimori to quash the controversy depressing his poll numbers while avoiding a head-to-head confrontation with the military on the CJSM's jurisdiction and powers. To ease tensions with the military, Fujimori announced that the top commanders in the armed forces would retain their posts and not be subject to the customary December rotations.[14] After two weeks in jail, Robles was released.

As the Robles case drew to a close, *La República* published reports pointing to more sinister conduct by the SIN. Edmundo Cruz, a veteran investigative journalist who had worked on the *Sí* team that located the bodies in the La Cantuta case in 1993, filed the reports. Cruz reported that a confidential source, an agent from the army intelligence service, had divulged details of an intelligence operation aimed at threatening journalists.[15] The operation, launched in December 1996, was named Plan Bermuda, a play on the Spanish words *ver muda* (literally, to "see mute"). According to Cruz's source, César Hidelbrandt was among the principal targets. Others targeted in the plan included the director of *La República* and left-wing congressman Gustavo Mohme, and *La República*'s investigative reporters

Angel Páez and Miguel Gutiérrez. Both reporters had been actively investigating corruption in the military related to arms deals.

The plan purportedly did not include assassinations, but involved staging threatening incidents—such as muggings, car accidents, robberies, or damaging leaks of personal information—to instill fear in the targets and let them know that they were under surveillance. Cruz's source also confirmed that the attack on Global Televisión in Puno was part of yet another SIN operation named Plan Narval, designed to harass César Hidelbrandt.

Cruz's reportage provoked another round of what had now become the standard operating procedure for scandals. There were calls for investigation by the opposition and flat-out denials of any wrongdoing by the government. Henry Pease, opposition congressman, called for a commission to investigate the charge. Adolfo Pandolfi scoffed at the story, asserting that "nothing" like that was going on in the SIN, as did Víctor Joy Way.[16]

The long hostage crisis that began with the MRTA attack on the Japanese ambassador's residence in late 1996 monopolized the media's attention and put Cruz's story on the back burner. But in a follow-up, Cruz reported that intelligence agents were being detained for questioning by army intelligence to determine who was involved in leaking the Plan Bermuda story to the press. Among the agents rounded up was a female with the last name of La Rosa, who was being kept under wraps at a military hospital.[17]

Cruz's February report on the search for leaks inside the SIN went largely unnoticed as the MRTA hostage crisis continued. But when the handless and headless cadaver of an intelligence agent named Mariela Bareto was discovered, the rest of the media could no longer ignore the story. For the first time, television boldly followed the story and the government's campaign to squash the coverage assumed epic proportions. Viewers at home watched the battle for freedom of the press in prime time.

Taking Down Frecuencia Latina

The medium that mattered most to the Fujimori administration was television. Most Peruvians relied on television as their primary source for news, followed by radio, then the print media. Montesinos understood the central role of television. In his discussions of political strategy, he often noted how little people read.[18] As irritating as the Fujimori administration found the print media to be, it could ignore most negative stories as long as they were kept off television. If television were to get out of hand, there was no telling where it could lead or how damaging it could be to the reelection project.

When *Contrapunto* began covering the narco-trafficking allegations against Montesinos and the military in the latter half of 1996, the shifting editorial line of the highly rated Frecuencia Latina network was identified as a problem. According to Baruch Ivcher, the station's chief executive officer and majority stockholder, Montesinos sent an "emissary" to the station on August 16, 1996, to ask Ivcher not to cover the Chávez allegations in exchange for an exclusive SIN video on the hunt for Chávez and his capture in Colombia. Ivcher refused, and *Contrapunto* aired the Chávez story on August 18. That was followed on September 15 with the report featuring audiotapes of alleged conversations between military officers and drug traffickers.[19]

Behind the scenes, the pressure continued. On December 12 and December 17, Ivcher recorded videos in the presence of several Channel 2 reporters, explaining that he was being told by authorities to stop the station's critical coverage of the administration. Ivcher's tug of war with Montesinos halted, however, when Channel 2 turned its energies to reporting on the MRTA hostage crisis.

Contrapunto's investigative reporting on the SIN came back to life when the mutilated corpse of army intelligence agent Mariela Bareto was found dumped in the outskirts of Lima. Bareto was a member of the intelligence unit under suspicion of having leaked information earlier to *La República*. On April 6, 1997, *Contrapunto* aired an explosive report that included coverage of the Bareto murder and the revelation that she had been the longtime girlfriend of Major Santiago Martín Rivas, the leader of Grupo Colina, who had been freed in the 1995 amnesty. That report was followed by an exclusive interview with Leonor La Rosa. La Rosa, a colleague of Bareto, gave the interview from her bed at a military hospital. La Rosa claimed that she had been tortured during her interrogation by fellow army intelligence agents.[20]

The discovery of Bareto's body and La Rosa's allegations coincided with a string of strange events, all of which suggested that the SIN was acting along the lines reported months earlier by Edmundo Cruz in *La República*. The carjacking and burning of a vehicle owned by opposition congressman

Javier Diez Canseco was suspicious, as was unexplained gunfire aimed at former government minister Gustavo Saberbein. A bizarre four-hour kidnapping of the *La República* editor Blanca Rosales made little sense, especially since nothing was stolen from her during the ordeal. General Juan Briones Dávila, the minister of the interior, insisted that "common criminals" were responsible for the odd crimes.[21] Fujimori reiterated the view and denied the existence of any state-sponsored paramilitary units.[22]

Government reaction to the *Contrapunto* story was swift, by no means subtle, and included the bizarre explanations that had become typical of *oficialista* spin. A few days before the La Rosa story aired, police officials of the tax administration began soliciting accounting information from Channel 2. The station promptly reported on the incident, though president of the council of ministers Adolfo Pandolfi denied it had taken place. Pandolfi hastily retracted the denial when the station showed the agents' signatures on the entry and exit logs to the station. Proceeding as if the agents had acted without orders from above, Pandolfi announced that they had been removed from their jobs and were being investigated by a military court. He reiterated the government's commitment to freedom of the press.

The impromptu tax audit of Channel 2 was shelved, but what followed showed how unforgiving armed forces officials were. The day after the *Contrapunto* story aired, military helicopters began low-level flights over Productos Paraíso, a mattress factory owned by Baruch Ivcher. The official explanation was that the flights were routine maneuvers, but as Ivcher and local residents noted, no such flights had ever been staged before.

Meanwhile, with opposition legislators howling for an investigation of the Bareto-La Rosa case, efforts began to bury the case and smear the victims. A military court quickly found four lower-level officials guilty of torturing La Rosa, but simultaneously started proceedings against La Rosa for leaking intelligence information. Tomás Castillo Meza, the minister of defense, bristled at the idea of a congressional investigation of the case. He argued that it was the job of the military court system to handle such wrongdoing and told legislators to mind their own business.[23] He also called La Rosa's credibility into question, maintaining that La Rosa was suffering from psychiatric problems and that her ailments were psychosomatic. Congresswoman Martha Chávez followed Castillo's lead, speculating La Rosa's physical ailments were self-inflicted.[24]

But the strained efforts to bury the Bareto-La Rosa case did not resolve the larger problems posed by Ivcher and his renegade Channel 2. *Contrapunto* followed up with breaking news on another scandal involving Montesinos. In the show aired on April 13, Roxana Cueva reported that, based on insider information leaked from the national tax administration, Vladimiro Montesinos's income was far in excess of the salary scale for public-sector employees. Given the earlier allegations by Demeterio Chávez tying Montesinos to drug trafficking, the *Contrapunto* report begged for some official explanation of where Montesinos's money was coming from. An Imasen poll reported that 89 percent of the public favored an investigation of Montesinos's income.[25]

Adolfo Pandolfi was called to congress to provide the official explanation. One way to explain Montesinos's income was to claim that he was working as an attorney for private clients when he was off-duty (even though Montesinos would later maintain that he worked twenty-four hours a day at the SIN). But as in the previous volley with congress, Pandolfi refused to answer any specific queries at all about Montesinos's income. Pandolfi maintained that the principles of confidentiality precluded him from discussing Montesinos's tax returns or his exact duties at the SIN. Moreover, Pandolfi argued that he could not discuss any aspect of Montesinos's private legal practice since that would involve a breach of lawyer-client confidentiality if the clients' names were revealed.[26]

By exposing the illicit conduct of the intelligence service and Montesinos, Ivcher and Channel 2 threatened the entire power structure of the regime. Anticipating what was about to unfold, *Contrapunto* reported on May 11 that a so-called "Operation Bulldozer" was being prepared by the SIN to silence everyone thought to possess information embarrassing to the government. Surely, the idea that the government was prepared to do almost anything to stanch the embarrassing revelations and secure the reelection project seemed highly likely in view of the other events transpiring in May 1997. At the same time that the government was preparing to move on Ivcher and Channel 2, the C90-NM congressional caucus was busy sacking the magistrates in the TC who had opposed reelection.

Fearing imprisonment or worse, Baruch Ivcher left Peru on May 13, even though he had been summoned to testify in the military court case of the tax police officers accused of threatening to audit Channel 2. Concerned about how the military court might treat him or interpret his testimony, Ivcher disregarded the summons to appear, opening the door to legal action against him by the court.

Armed forces officials were not appeased by Ivcher's departure. The news team at Channel 2 continued its aggressive reporting in Ivcher's absence. In an extraordinary show of ire, the armed forces high command issued an official communiqué on May 23 denouncing "the naturalized Peruvian" Ivcher for defaming the armed forces.[27] The communiqué appeared in every major newspaper and was read on all television stations.

On the same day that the communiqué was issued, Supreme Decree 004-97-IN was published in *El Peruano*. The decree stipulated that a person's citizenship could be revoked for acts damaging "national security" or the "public interest" or for violating any of the procedures in the naturalization process. That the decree had been written with Ivcher in mind was apparent. According to Peruvian law, only citizens could own and operate media outlets. If Ivcher's citizenship could be revoked, he could not control Channel 2.

Samuel and Mendel Winter, brothers and businessmen, were the minority stockholders of Channel 2; together they owned 46 percent of the company's stock. Seeking to distance themselves from the troubles descending on Ivcher, the Winter brothers hand-delivered a letter to the Comando Conjunto headquarters expressing their disagreement with the views being aired on the station. General Hermoza, head of the Comando, met with the Winter brothers, along with air force commander General Elesban Bello Vásquez and navy commander Admiral Antonio Ibárcena.[28]

Meanwhile, progovernment media outlets were preparing the way for a legal assault on Ivcher. *Sí,* the once-independent news magazine that had been at the forefront of the La Cantuta investigation, had changed drastically under new management. News director Marcelo Gullo took the magazine in another direction—so much so that opponents now spoofed it as *SIN*. Following the military communiqué, *Sí* ran a cover story linking Baruch Ivcher to Ecuadorian general Francisco Moncayo and implicating Ivcher in arms trafficking to Ecuador during the Peru-Ecuador conflict.[29] At the same time, the celebrity magazine *Gente* prominently featured a story questioning the circumstances surrounding Ivcher's naturalization, entitled "Baruch Ivcher Is a Phony Peruvian."[30]

Contrapunto responded with a report from Ecuador that refuted the charges against Ivcher and included an interview with General Moncayo, who said that the documents published by *Sí* were forged. In response, C90-NM congressman Gilberto Siura introduced a surprise motion in congress, censuring Channel 2 for broadcasting the statement of "foreign military officers that is an affront to the national press well as Peruvian security institutions."[31] The motion passed, signaling that the *oficialista* congressional caucus was on board for the anti-Ivcher campaign.

Fujimori said nothing to distance himself from the attacks on Ivcher. On the contrary, he used his speech at the Lima meeting of the OAS in June to take on the press. Amid hoots and whistles from the assembled press corps, Fujimori accused journalists of misinforming the public, taking bribes, and serving as a "shield of corruption."[32]

General Fernando Dianderas, the national police director, opened up an investigation into the matter of Ivcher's citizenship. Not surprisingly, he concluded that Ivcher had failed to renounce his Israeli citizenship and that there were other "irregularities" in the documentation for Ivcher's naturalization.[33] The *prensa chicha* (tabloid press) jumped on the issue of Ivcher's nationality, making explicit the anti-Semitism that had simmered in the case all along. The newspaper *El Mañanero* maintained Ivcher was a "Jew down to his bones."[34] In another headline, *El Mañanero* proclaimed, "Jew Baruch Ivcher Never Was Peruvian."[35]

The final straw came on Sunday, July 13, when the still-defiant *Contrapunto* staff aired a program with evidence that a massive wiretapping operation targeting journalists and opposition politicians had been in place during the 1995 election campaign.[36] The evidence included recorded telephone conversations of Fujimori's challenger, Javier Pérez de Cuéllar. Although *Contrapunto* reporters could not confirm at the time that it was a SIN operation, the scope and the sophistication of the operation strongly suggested government involvement. Congresswoman Martha Chávez headed a congressional investigation into the matter that went on for close to a year. Chávez finally concluded that it was impossible to determine who was responsible for the wiretapping. Montesinos later said that he prepared Chávez's report on the case. "She knew that there had been wiretapping," Montesinos observed. "Her job was to cover it up."[37]

A few hours after the *Contrapunto* broadcast, an immigration official revoked Baruch Ivcher's citizenship, purportedly for the irregularities in documentation. The order revoking the citizenship was published in the Sunday edition of *El Peruano,* which did not appear on newsstands until after the *Contrapunto* broadcast aired. Stripping Ivcher's citizenship set the stage for a takeover of Channel 2 by the minority shareholders, Samuel and Mendel Winter. Attorneys for Ivcher and his wife fought the Winter brothers in court, losing appeal after appeal. On September 19, 1997, the Winter brothers led police and private security guards in taking over the buildings of Channel 2. In a final protest, the *Contrapunto* team and news staffers filed out of the station and greeted a crowd of supporters with their resignation letters in hand.[38]

But rather than ending the controversy, stripping Ivcher's citizenship and the takeover of the station was just the first installment in a conflict that dogged the Fujimori administration until its collapse. From exile in Miami, Ivcher mounted a sophisticated campaign to tell his story to an international audience, especially to officials in Washington. Not surprisingly, the international press corps and international press organizations were appalled by the events and covered the Ivcher case.[39] Editorials in the *New York Times, Los Angeles Times,* and *Washington Post* derided the Fujimori government. Joining in the condemnation was an array of international press organizations that included Freedom House, the Inter-American Press Association, the Committee to Protect Journalists (CPJ), Reporters sans Frontières, and others.

To help make his case in Washington, Ivcher hired Elliot Abrams, a former Reagan administration official, as his consultant. Even before Ivcher's citizenship was revoked, the Ivcher case was making waves in the U.S. Congress. Senator Jesse Helms and Representative Benjamin Gilman wrote a fiery letter to Fujimori. They condemned the anti-Semitic tone of the campaign against Ivcher and called on Fujimori to "restrain those who undercut freedom of the press with reprisals against Mr. Ivcher."[40] There was no response from the presidential palace. Similarly, there was no response to the special mission sent by the Inter-American Press Association to investigate the case.

The silence was not indicative of a change in tactics. Rather than backing off the Ivcher case in light of the bad publicity it generated, government reprisals intensified. As Ivcher prepared to take his case to the Inter-American Commission on Human Rights of the OAS in the fall of 1997, criminal accusations of tax fraud were filed against Ivcher in Peru. In a hasty trial, he was convicted in absentia. His wife and children also became the targets of criminal charges, as did former employees. After further investigation, the commission referred the Ivcher case to the Inter-American Court of Human Rights in 1998 for adjudication.

The Ivcher affair was just one of several high-profile cases pending against the government of Peru that included the dismissal of the TC magistrates, human rights violations, and the handling of terrorist trials. When the Inter-American Court ordered the Peruvian government to grant new trials to four Chileans who had been linked to the MRTA and convicted of treason under antiterrorism laws, the Fujimori administration took advantage of the controversial ruling to thumb its nose at the court, and by extension the OAS. Rather than accept the court's ruling, the Peruvian government announced that it was "withdrawing" from the court's jurisdiction in July 1999.

The convoluted campaign to silence Ivcher had backfired. It drew more international attention to the press situation in Peru and intensified the discussion about media manipulation in anticipation of the 2000 election. Because the scandal involved a highly rated television station, it was an event unlike previous controversies because it played out in front of a mass audience. Night after night in the months from April through July 1997, Frecuencia Latina blasted the government in its evening newscasts. Polls taken just after the seizure of Channel 2 showed overwhelming public disapproval of the government's actions. A University of Lima poll reported 80 percent of those surveyed opposed the station's takeover. In an Imasen poll, 81 percent of the public agreed that the press was being subjected to reprisals by the government.[41]

Peruvians were beginning to understand how integral the manipulation of the media was to the administration, and so were those looking at Peru from abroad. The Ivcher affair, converging with the dismissal of the TC magistrates, triggered new concerns about what was happening in Peru in advance of the 2000 election. In October 1998, Representative Gilman and Senator Helms introduced Joint Resolution 609 in the U.S. Congress, which cited Peru for the lack of independence in the judiciary and the problematic state of press freedom as evidenced in the Ivcher case. In 1999, the resolution was resubmitted and approved as Resolution 57 in October. Senators voiced the same concerns in Senate Resolution 209. Signaling some annoyance on the Ivcher case, Secretary of State Madeleine Albright alluded to the case as an example of how insecure governments repress the media to avoid accountability.

Back in Peru, Montesinos joked that he had "buried" Ivcher and that the congressional resolutions were meaningless.[42] In his myopia, he did not see how much the Ivcher case was undermining the regime's claims to democratic normalcy. It was as if Fujimori and Montesinos had sent up a flare alerting international observers to just how askew their government was.

The Hidden Hand

As Fujimori's primary political strategist, Montesinos dedicated great time and considerable financial resources of the SIN to ensure that the media, especially television, were on board for the 2000 reelection project. In testimony to congressional investigators, Admiral Humberto Rosas confirmed that Montesinos was "preoccupied" with the media, and that armed forces and intelligence officials were required to collect information on the media relevant to the reelection campaign starting in 1999.[43]

Long before the kickoff of the campaign, Montesinos was meeting with the principal stockholders and executives of television stations in his offices at the SIN. The transactions, captured by the cameras mounted in Montesinos's office, were friendly and straightforward. Television executives from every major station commiserated with Montesinos, and agreed to provide the kind of television coverage he sought in exchange for bribes or other favors, usually consisting of help in pending legal cases. On numerous occasions, Montesinos personally counted out the cash to his grateful guests, stashing the U.S. dollars or Peruvian *soles* in envelopes or duffel bags.

Montesinos enjoyed an especially close relationship with the father-son team, José Enrique and José Francisco Crousillat, who controlled Channel 4, which was rated in the top three networks. In October 1998, Montesinos handed over a little more than $600,000 in cash to José Francisco Crousillat, promising that he could expect installments on a monthly basis. In November 1999, the relationship was formalized when Crousillat signed a contract that gave Montesinos complete control over all news programming on Channel 4. In the contract, Montesinos reserved the right to bar journalists and commentators and determine who could appear on the station's political programs. In return, Crousillat collected a hefty $1.5 million per month during the campaign season from November 1999 to April 2000. Crousillat later confessed that the sum total of money his family received from Montesinos during the course of their relationship was approximately $12 million.[44] In addition to direct payments, Montesinos agreed to weigh in on behalf of the station in its effort to restructure loans of several million dollars with the Banco Wiese.[45]

In similar fashion, other executives lined up to do business with Montesinos. In October 1998, the principal stockholder of Channel 9 (Andina Televisión) received $50,000 in cash from Montesinos. In the meeting, Julio Vera eagerly described his plans to lay off investigative reporters Cecilia Valenzuela and Luis Ibérico and to sue his former employee César Hidelbrandt in a contractual dispute. Valenzuela, originally known for her work at *Caretas,* doggedly investigated the mysteries surrounding Fujimori's place of birth. Ibérico had come to Channel 9 fresh from his work on *Contrapunto.* Montesinos heartily endorsed Vera's move. "Sure, you've got to throw out those assholes," Montesinos opined.[46]

Getting journalist César Hidelbrandt permanently off the air was a topic of great interest, as evidenced in the interchanges between Montesinos and Genaro Delgado Parker in 1999. Delgado Parker, an owner of Channel 13 (Red Global), offered to fire Hidelbrandt from his nightly show in exchange for Montesinos's help with an ongoing business dispute he had with his brother, Manuel.[47] Manuel Delgado Parker had been a shareholder in Channel 5 (Panamericana Televisión) and Radio Programas, Peru's most popular radio station. Like his brother, he came calling on Montesinos to discuss business disputes and pending lawsuits. Joining him in the meeting was Ernesto Schutz, the principal stockholder of Channel 5. Schutz later negotiated payment with Montesinos for $1.5 million per month, for a total of $9 million during the 1999–2000 presidential campaign.[48]

In return for the pay and the favors, Montesinos micromanaged daily television news coverage. He was in constant contact with executives and provided explicit directions on what issues should be covered and how news that was negative for the government should be minimized. Montesinos scrutinized the media closely and received daily logs summarizing the coverage. The logs included data on how much broadcast time was allotted to government and opposition personalities.[49]

In the case of América Televisión, Montesinos's interest extended beyond the normal newscasts to its midday talk show, *Laura en América*. Hosted by the histrionic blond star Laura Bozzo, the show won some of the highest ratings in Peru's television industry and appealed to low-income women, a key constituency in the electorate.[50] Montesinos worked with Crousillat to use the Bozzo show as a platform to praise Fujimori, even in the most absurd ways. In one strategy session, Montesinos proposed the following scenario. Bozzo's studio audience should include a girl without a leg. Bozzo would pity the girl and promise to bring her plight to the attention of President Fujimori. In the next show, the girl was to appear with a new prosthesis, courtesy of the president.[51] Bozzo was also called on to remind viewers of the government's accomplishments by hosting "specials" on successes in the war against terrorism. Montesinos sent expensive jewelry to Bozzo in appreciation of her service.

Television executives were acutely aware that what they were doing was illegal. Montesinos often spoke about the need for secrecy and the importance of "deniability" if accusations ever surfaced. When it came to the payoffs, Montesinos dealt one-on-one with the executives. The meetings were top secret, thanks in part to a hidden garage in the SIN headquarters where the executives could come and go undetected.

Keeping the relationships clandestine allowed media executives and government officials to staunchly assert one of the great fictions of the 2000 election—that media coverage was a product of autonomous editorial judgments, not government interference.

By the fall of 1999, Montesinos had completely assembled what he referred to as a "team" of television station owners to work on behalf of the reelection. In a conversation with General Bello Vásquez in late November of 1999, Montesinos described how his control extended over television station owners:

> Sure, they're all lined up now. Everyone signed up on paper, the whole deal. We made them sign papers and everything. This is a serious game here.
>
> All of them, all lined up. Every day, I have a meeting a 12:30. I have a meeting with them here [at the SIN] at 12:30 and we plan the evening news. I already have the schedule until the 15th of December.[52]

The "team" also included a new entrant into the cable news industry in Peru, Cable Canal de Notícias (CCN). In November 1999, Montesinos put together a clandestine deal to channel two million dollars out of the budget of the ministry of defense to buy up CCN's stock from its major stockholder, Manuel Ulloa of the newspaper *Expreso*.[53] Montesinos would use his newly acquired cable station to act as a counterweight to Canal N. Owned by the newspaper *El Comercio*, Canal N had been launched in July 1999 as an "independent" news and talk cable station. Now with CCN and all the major broadcast stations under control, every segment of the television audience—highbrow, middlebrow, and lowbrow—was within the reach of Montesinos and the campaign to reelect the president.

Montesinos's Media

Television was the primary pillar in the reelection strategy, but the drive to control the media was not confined to broadcast news. Even if many people in Peru were not part of the "reading public," Montesinos recognized the value of an attention-grabbing headline. Many Peruvians did not buy newspapers, but gathering around newsstands to eyeball the headlines was a morning ritual for thousands of Lima's commuters. Montesinos knew that the print press could be used to smear his opponents and send a not-so-subtle warning that they were in the crosshairs of the SIN.

Using the same approach applied to the television stations, Montesinos paid off the executives of print outlets to plant stories favorable to the government and to attack opponents. In the mainstream press, the newspaper *Expreso* played a critical role in Montesinos's communications apparatus. Although *Expreso*'s circulation lagged significantly behind *La República*'s by the end of the 1990s, the newspaper was de rigueur reading for Lima's political class and was found at kiosks around the city. *Expreso* was progovernment after the 1992 coup, but struck a more critical posture after the 1995 election. Two of its most noted columnists, Jaime Althaus and Manuel D'Ornellas, soured on the reelection project. Althaus and D'Ornellas left *Expreso*, signaling the swing back to an unadulterated progovernment position.

Montesinos secured his hold over *Expreso* through his close relationship with its director, Eduardo Calmell del Solar. Calmell accepted at least one hundred thousand dollars in cash from Montesinos in 1999, money that was supposed to be used by Calmell to become the majority stockholder in the newspaper.[54] Calmell and Montesinos talked frequently about how to attack Fujimori's rivals in the presidential race, beginning with the early front-runners, Lima mayor Alberto Andrade and former Social Security chief Luis Castañeda. Calmell proved useful to Montesinos in another way; he dutifully rose to the defense of the government when it was attacked on freedom of the press issues. In international forums, Calmell adamantly denied any problems, enduring the ridicule of colleagues.

Expreso delivered Montesinos's messages to a middle-class readership in Lima, but Montesinos looked to other newspapers to reach the broad low-income electorate. He turned to the sensationalist tabloid press, the *prensa chicha*. Generally speaking, the tabloids catered to a readership interested in show business, crime, and sex, not politics. So when the tabloids turned to political stories, most observers immediately suspected that the stories came courtesy of the SIN. The politicization of the tabloids took off in 1997 during the conflict with Baruch Ivcher, when the papers launched anti-Semitic attacks against Ivcher.

The tabloids' attack journalism intensified with an unusual series of special supplements published in the biggest-selling tabloid, *El Chino,* under the editorship of the veteran tabloid journalist José Olaya. Entitled "Serie Coleccionable" (Collectable Series), the supplements featured insulting stories about some of Peru's most prominent commentators and journalists who were critics of Fujimori and opposed to reelection. Manuel D'Ornellas, the columnist who had defected from the ranks of *Fujimorismo,* was derided as an alcoholic. César Hidelbrandt, one of the journalists most despised by Montesinos, was described as a *chato mental* (a "mental shorty" —an insult that obviously referred to Hidelbrandt's short stature). Cecilia Valenzuela, the investigative journalist who dug into questions about Fujimori's citizenship, was a "devil."[55]

Attacks by the *prensa chicha* continued in the first half of 1998, responding in part to more embarrassing revelations about the SIN. Reacting to the anonymous death threats he had received, José Arrieta, formerly a journalist at Frecuencia Latina under Ivcher, fled to Miami. In Miami, Arrieta found a new source willing to talk about wrongdoing in the SIN, former intelligence agent Luisa Zanatta. In conversations with Arrieta and Edmundo Cruz of *La República* in March 1998, Zanatta confirmed the existence of a massive wiretapping operation inside the SIN and provided a photograph of herself in the room where it took place.[56] Even before the photograph appeared in *La República,* the tabloids set out to discredit Zanatta, the reporters, and the photograph. To make the point that photographs can be doctored, three different tabloids (*El Tío, El Mañanero,* and *La Chuchi*) published a picture of the same room in the SIN showing international supermodel Claudia Schiffer, not Luisa Zanatta.[57] The use of the same doctored photograph by three competing papers and the fact that the tabloids had gotten wind of *La República*'s scoop ahead of time smacked of a SIN operation.

The incident sparked a new wave of tabloid attacks on reporters Arrieta and Cruz, along with *La República* contributors, including its publisher Gustavo Mohme. The reporters were accused of being anti-patriotic and *tontos útiles* (useful idiots—an expression that had been used frequently in Peru to describe guerrilla sympathizers or collaborators) and were said to be plotting with Baruch Ivcher to destabilize the country. Fernando Rospigliosi, an academic and columnist specializing in the military and intelligence, stood accused of being a terrorist and coup plotter.

The tabloid hysteria directed at *La República* continued with attacks on its military affairs reporter Angel Páez, who was constantly digging up stories on corruption in the armed forces. On an almost daily basis from mid-April until the end of June 1998, *El Tío* made Páez its whipping boy. Managed by José Olaya (the former director of *El Chino* who had produced the notorious "Serie Colecionable"), *El Tío*'s insults ran the gamut, but the most unsettling one was the persistent charge that Páez was guilty of treason—a serious criminal offense.

The ferocious, nonstop attacks on mainstream journalists mobilized press organizations in Peru and abroad. Representatives from the CPJ, the Freedom Forum, and other Latin America media came to Lima in June 1998 to express their solidarity with Peruvian journalists and to call on the government to protect freedom of the press.[58] In a private meeting, Fujimori assured the international press representatives that journalists would be fully protected. After the meeting, the tabloid attacks came to a dead halt.

At the time, it seemed probable that Montesinos paid off the tabloids to attack, but proving it was another matter. One worker from *El Tío* leaked a fax to *La República* that contained the text of an article subsequently published verbatim by *El Tío*. The fax had come from the office of Augusto Bresani, a publicist rumored to be an associate of Montesinos. Bresani hid from the press and there was no investigation of the matter. After his arrest in 2001, Montesinos confirmed his elaborate use of the tabloid press to congressional investigators. Montesinos fingered Bresani as one of his operatives.[59] Former tabloid editors came forward with details on how payoffs were structured. Montesinos agreed to pay $3,000 for every concocted headline. A headline with a caricature went for $4,000 and a complete interior page of text cost $5,000. On the basis of these figures, one tabloid alone— *El Tío*—was estimated to have raked in at least $1.5 million in payoffs from March 1998 through February 2000.[60]

The tabloid attacks of 1997–1998 previewed what was in store for political challengers to Fujimori in the 2000 election. Nothing was off-limits. Lima mayor Alberto Andrade suffered a constant string of epithets in the tabloid headlines, among them *chancho* (pig). Luis Castañeda was slammed as effeminate, crazy, and obsessed with his pet canines—a detail that Montesinos found especially hilarious and one that he loved to use in the smear campaign against Castañeda.

Beyond Belief

Wheeling and dealing behind the closed doors of the SIN, Montesinos assembled an integrated political communications system for the 2000 reelection, most of it located in the private sector.[61] State-run television and radio, as well as the government newspaper *El Peruano,* were part of the system, but the audience reached by those outlets could not rival that of commercial television and the tabloids. To dominate the media during the election cycle, Montesinos needed media owners willing to sell out. Apart from some very notable exceptions (*La República, El Comercio, Caretas, Gestión,* CPN Radio, and Canal N Televisión), Montesinos found executives ready to oblige.

Because the locus of the communications system was in the private sector, the "dirty war" (as it came to be called by the opposition) could be represented as something else—as the product of editorial decisions made autonomously by owners for either business or journalistic reasons. At least that is what government officials and the offending executives repeated over and over.

As Machiavellian as Montesinos believed himself to be, he failed to appreciate the problems inherent in the system that he worked so diligently to create. First, it was a system without subtlety. The manipulation was so blatant that no one contemplating it could fail to see the underpinnings. Neither the Peruvian public nor international onlookers believed it to be a coincidence that the sudden "discovery" of irregularities in Baruch Ivcher's citizenship documents came as Frecuencia Latina took a critical turn in its coverage of the administration. Nor did it seem plausible that tabloid newspapers would spontaneously decide to attack exactly the same people at the same time with exactly the same headlines and photographs. Like most *oficialista* explanations of what was going on in Peru, the lies told about the media fell flat.

Second, as much as Montesinos boasted about his control over the media, it was never complete. Montesinos never effectively shut down the public debate about the nature of the regime. Independent outlets were allowed to operate because their existence helped muddy the waters about what was going on in Peru and gave Fujimori and *oficialistas* a way to refute critics when challenged on the state of press freedom in Peru. Montesinos might have like to shut down the independents altogether but he didn't dare, so he was forced to deal with their stories.

The campaign of intimidation did have some effects. Off the record, reporters admitted to some self-censorship and confessed to thinking twice about pursuing sensitive stories, particularly those involving Montesinos and the SIN. They acknowledged that editors and owners toned down coverage at times. The detention of General Rodolfo Robles and the Bareto-La Rosa case made it harder for reporters to find sources willing to cooperate.

Nonetheless, despite the anxiety that Montesinos created, the independent press never stopped its critical reporting on him, the SIN, or the Fujimori administration at large. On the contrary, the attempts to repress the press only produced more scandals, more scrutiny by the international press, and more concern in politically attentive quarters in the United States. Still, Montesinos was prepared to shrug off all the bad reviews, just as long as there was no "smoking gun" to tie him and his collaborators to the crimes they were committing. He sometimes joked with his associates that they would be hung if their nefarious deeds were discovered.

Absent a smoking gun, the international criticisms on the matters of press freedom or the state of democracy in Peru were of no great importance to him. Montesinos maintained that, in the final analysis, counternarcotics and counterinsurgency were the prime concerns of the United

States. He was acutely aware of how important it was to U.S. policymakers that Peru continue its cooperation in the American-led aerial interdiction program, the operations used to disrupt drug transport by air.[62] Montesinos reasoned that the United States could not afford to lose a good ally like President Fujimori, or a seasoned intelligence expert like himself. In the great scheme of things, Montesinos reasoned, Peru did not exist—that is, Peru was a country so irrelevant to the United States outside of the realm of counternarcotics that Fujimori's reelection would end up as a non-issue.[63]

Like Fujimori, Montesinos dismissed the importance of "talk," believing that action mattered more than words. Montesinos wagered that Peru's cooperation on counternarcotics would be enough to make the United States look the other way on the matter of the reelection. In the short run, Montesinos was right. Neither the United States nor the OAS was about to take a principled stand against the *re-re-elección*.

In the long run, however, Montesinos was wrong to dismiss the power of talk. What people knew and what people said about what was happening in Peru did figure in the final demise of the regime, albeit in circuitous ways. Inside Peru, adversarial talk, earlier confined to a small group of elite opponents, spread to a broader audience as abuses and affronts to common sense accumulated. And, while it was true that Peru rarely appeared on the radar screen of American policymakers, the controversies that raged on civil liberties and the reelection did not go unnoticed, thanks in great part to outraged journalists and activists. The radical disconnection between words and deeds—the untruth in what Fujimori and his officials told people at home and abroad—progressively came to light. With each revelation, the government's credibility suffered yet another blow. By the time the 2000 reelection arrived, the problem was acute. While the credibility crisis did not make a political transition inevitable, it did make it possible. It made it more difficult to keep up the lies.

From the comfort of his state-of-the-art war room at the SIN, Montesinos prepared methodically for the 2000 reelection. What his arrogance could not let him see was that he was acting out an old cliché, the one about winning the battle but losing the war.

8

PERU 2000

AFTER nearly four years of nonstop controversy, no one was surprised when Fujimori finally announced that he would seek a third term. On December 27, 1999, television stations aired the president's videotaped statement. Dressed in a blue suit and red tie, Fujimori tilted uncomfortably toward the camera, punctuating his sentences with a tight smile. He said that his decision to run was motivated by a desire to build on his administration's achievements and that the opposition offered nothing but "improvisation" and "neopopulism." At the conclusion, Fujimori pulled out a white placard with red letters that bore the name of his new electoral front for the election, Perú 2000.

Fujimori had teased the public for years about whether he would run, acting as if he had not decided. Rumors about the President's health came and went, making even hard-core *oficialistas* wonder if the reelection ruckus was much ado about nothing because he would not run in the end.[1] As much as Fujimori enjoyed fueling the uncertainty, he could not conceal his ambition altogether. In mid-July of 1999, a Colombian reporter asked Fujimori what his life would be like as a former president. Fujimori said that he could not even imagine being an ex-president.[2]

In retrospect, it is easy to understand why Fujimori failed to imagine another life. Unlike the Colombian reporter, he knew that all the resources of the state would be brought to bear to make the reelection happen. By mid-1999, the vast conspiracy designed to assure the reelection was in place, under the expert direction of Vladimiro Montesinos.

The Reelection Machine

Fujimori obligatorily waved the placard of Perú 2000, but the political organization was just one of the many fictions of the 2000 election. There was no grassroots movement, nor was there a multiparty coalition backing the president. The organizational center of the campaign was the SIN, and among the many hats worn by Montesinos was that of campaign manager.

By 1999, Montesinos had transformed the SIN headquarters and installed his equivalent of a "war room" for the reelection campaign. The venue, complete with state-of-the art technology, including satellite communications links across the country, cost one hundred thousand dollars to equip. Every day Montesinos tracked the activities of opposition candidates. Cabinet ministers, the top commanders of the armed forces and police, intelligence officials, pollsters, and media executives joined Montesinos daily to plot out the campaign. According to Montesinos, Fujimori checked in at night to review and modify the plans.[3] All this activity went on while Fujimori and his officials repeatedly denied any use of public resources in the reelection campaign.

As in any political campaign, money was the lifeblood of the reelection project. Lots of it was needed to fund wide-ranging operations. Millions of dollars were spent on polling and focus groups, as well as enormous bribes paid to media executives. To feed the reelection machine, money was rerouted clandestinely from ministries to the slush funds operated by Montesinos in the SIN. A study by the Superintendencia de Bancos later estimated that close to $146 million in public monies flowed into the government's campaign coffers in the period from 1992 through 2000.[4] The principal entities tapped for the illicit transfers were the ministry of defense, the ministry of the interior, and the high command of the armed forces.

Montesinos used state resources to compensate for the absence of a real political party and built an organizational grid across the country well in advance of the election. The reelection required an infrastructure to ensure that every aspect of the electoral environment was under control. At the behest of Montesinos, Peru's entire security apparatus—the armed forces, police, and intelligence agency—was mobilized for the reelection. In the years following the coup, Montesinos worked diligently to establish his de facto control over the Peruvian armed forces by manipulating promotions and retirements. Montesinos's power grab was completed in August 1998. After several highly publicized disagreements between Fujimori and General Hermoza over the terms of the 1998 agreement that ended the Peru-Ecuador border dispute, the general was abruptly forced into retirement. That ended his unprecedented tenure of nearly seven years as the head of the armed forces high command.[5] Hermoza's exit cleared the path for Montesinos's former military academy classmates to assume control of every top-ranking post in the army. By 2000, nine of the twelve top commanders in the army were classmates of Montesinos. The group included Montesinos's brother-in-law, General Luis Cubas Portal, who took over as commander general of the second military region headquartered in Lima in December 1999.[6]

Montesinos met regularly with high-ranking officers to confer on the reelection campaign. He made no bones about using the military and police for all kinds of jobs. He ordered military and police officers in the provinces to submit regular reports about political coverage in the local media; the police also provided intelligence about local conditions and the activities of opposition candidates. Government slogans were painted on the properties of military installations. The army's engineering division was ordered to build neighborhood sports facilities to boost the government's popularity. The police organized community events in poor neighborhoods, where attendees received free food along with a visit from political organizers. Montesinos even used the military to recruit and pay civilians to pose as Perú 2000 partisans and act as the organization's poll watchers on election day.[7]

In the same bald-faced way, other agencies were put at the service of the reelection campaign to deliver goods and progovernment propaganda. In 1999, government agencies sponsored what was ostensibly an advertising blitz to make citizens aware of programs and services available to them. The slogan of the campaign was *Perú país con futuro* (Peru, country with a future). The slogan found its way onto billboards, public buildings, and even military installations. The slogan-painting spree was a bone of contention. Opposition candidates identified the painting as thinly disguised campaign propaganda, while Fujimori publicly defended the effort as a spontaneous show of civic-minded optimism by concerned citizens.

Because so much of Peru's population depended on food aid to survive, the assistance programs and their connection to community organizations, especially the *comedores populares* (soup kitchens), were key to the government's strategy to secure votes. According to the government's own 1998 statistics, 46 percent of all households in Peru received aid from at least one food program. In 1999, more than ten million people nationwide received some aid from food programs.[8] Targeting these poor voters, Montesinos channeled money to the national food program run to distribute cooking pots to housewives and community soup kitchens. The government's largest ministry, the Ministerio de la Presidencia, coordinated with Montesinos on how to direct its social assistance expenditures during the campaign period. Cabinet ministers were routinely dispatched to the provinces, often on the heels of a local appearance by an opposition candidate, to make speeches and hand out food, tools, cooking utensils, or clothes.[9]

Local politics and power structures were by no means neglected in the grand schemes hatched at SIN campaign headquarters. The administration already had a loyal cadre of local power brokers in place, the nonelected prefects and governors appointed directly by the president. At the municipal level, however, the situation was complex. The 1998 municipal elections produced a mixed bag of results, with about a third of municipalities under the control of the government's vehicle, Vamos Vecino, and the remaining two-thirds divided between Alberto Andrade's organization, Somos Perú, and other "independent movements."

To get more mayors onto the reelection bandwagon, pro-Fujimori mayors of Vamos Vecino organized a takeover of the national mayors' organization, Asociación de Municipalidades del Perú (AMPE) in January 1999. Luis Guerrero, the Cajamarca mayor critical of the administration, was deposed and replaced by Chimbote mayor Guzmán Aguirre. Fujimori signaled his approval of the bureaucratic coup in AMPE by subsequently holding a meeting with its new officials.

Subterranean efforts to lure or coerce mayors into supporting Fujimori followed the AMPE takeover. Mayors supporting the presidential candidacy of Alberto Andrade began deserting his cause. At least thirty-two mayors affiliated with Somos Perú officially dropped out of the organization from August through October 1999.[10] Some mayors explained their move as a simple change of heart, but reports of harassment and threats against un-cooperative mayors were widespread.[11] In an understated explanation, one deserter noted that his town would be deprived of funding if he did not support Fujimori: "It's a bit difficult, if not impossible, to obtain support from the government being a mayor of Somos Perú. That's why I have decided to resign to obtain support from the central government, and thus work in favor of my people."[12] Minister of the Presidency Edgardo Mosqueira denied any government pressure on the mayors. But given the dirty tricks being visited on Somos Perú personnel around the country, the mayors' desertions looked like yet another carefully crafted operation to undercut Andrade.

Because the reelection machine revolved around the constant commission of crimes (misuse of public funds, illegal deployment of government employees, violations of election law, etc.) and cover-ups, Montesinos's control over the judiciary was vital to the campaign. After Santiago Fujimori and Jaime Yoshiyama left the government in 1996, Montesinos assumed a greater role in overseeing the judicial system. By 1999, judicial corruption was staggering. Prosecutors, superior court judges, and supreme court justices were on Montesinos's private payroll, receiving regular monthly payments in the thousands of dollars. Montesinos's staff members delivered the payments in cash to the homes of participating officials.[13]

Whenever opposition leaders turned to courts to complain about suspected abuses, the cases either disappeared in the judicial bureaucracy or were thrown out altogether. And often, the people who complained found themselves subject to legal harassment in return. In October 1999, Alberto Andrade petitioned for a judicial inquiry into the tabloids' defamatory attacks on him. He and his attorney were named subsequently as parties in a legal action brought by tabloid owners who accused them of obstructing freedom of the press. Journalists heading the watchdog group Asociación de Prensa Libre turned over evidence to the JNE documenting the harassment of presidential candidate Luis Castañeda on the campaign trail, then found themselves the targets of a prosecutor's investigation after the military tribunal charged that they had fabricated the evidence.[14]

As the principal regulator of the electoral process, the JNE was the centerpiece in Montesinos's plans. In November 1999, Alipio Montes de

Oca replaced Luis Serpa Segura as president of the JNE board. Eighteen months earlier, Montesinos had met with Montes de Oca to offer him the post, along with payments of ten thousand per month while he served. In exchange, Montesinos expected his full support in facilitating the reelection.[15] Montesinos had already established working relationships with the other JNE board members, Walter Hernández, Romulo Muñoz Arce, and José Carlos Bringas. Together, they had coordinated the maneuvers to stop the 1998 referendum.

By the end of 1999, one last legal hurdle remained in the way of Fujimori's candidacy. Peruvian election law established a short period between the time that a candidate filed to appear on the ballot and the time that the JNE accepted the filing. During the interim, *tachas* (formal challenges to the candidate) could be filed if there were grounds that the candidate had failed to meet the legal requirements set out in the election law. No one in the opposition honestly believed that the legal challenges would be successful, but the *tachas* were duly filed with the JNE after Fujimori announced his candidacy. The JNE quickly rejected the eighteen separate *tachas* filed to contest the Fujimori candidacy, refusing to deal with the question of the constitutionality of a third presidential term. According to Montesinos, all five JNE members—including the occasional dissenter Ramiro de Valdivia Cano—met with him secretly at SIN headquarters to prepare the official findings rejecting the *tachas*.[16]

As the formal campaign season kicked off in January 2000, the results of all the years of careful plotting came together. The entire apparatus of the state was geared up and ready to execute the plans. In the private sector, *la prensa secuestrada*—the "kidnapped" press so carefully managed by Montesinos in his daily meetings with the media executives—was already active. More than a year before the election, the tabloids' dirty war against opposition candidates and independent media outlets had begun. In 1999, in a renewed effort to discredit its aggressive investigative reporting, tabloids revived their attacks on *La República* and its director, Gustavo Mohme. José Olaya's *El Tío* published a series of reports entitled "The Liars of Politics," which accused Mohme and his staff of fabricating false stories about the government and defaming the armed forces.[17] The stories about Mohme included allegations of homosexuality and insulting caricatures of him. Anonymous publications (*La Repúdica* and *El Repudio*) that parodied *La República* and attacked Mohme were distributed gratis in neighborhoods in downtown Lima.[18]

Even before any opposition candidate officially announced his intention to run against Fujimori, the tabloids set their sights on the two front-runners in the race, Alberto Andrade and Luis Castañeda. Both men were widely respected as serious politicians and effective administrators. Andrade, an affable businessman who headed a family-owned leather goods factory, was the popular mayor of Lima who won the post in 1995 by defeating the government's handpicked candidate, Jaime Yoshiyama. Castañeda was a business executive and former head of Peru's social security agency.

The tabloids took aim at Andrade with headlines that slammed him as *pituco* (a slang expression for an upper-class snob), *gordo* (fatty), and *turista* (tourist—implying that he neglected his duties as mayor of Lima). The same tabloids depicted Castañeda as mentally unstable. Suggestions of homosexuality lurked in the constant references to an alleged relationship between Castañeda and show-business personality Jimmy Santi. Both candidates were accused of being corrupt, although no criminal charges were ever filed against either of them. *Expreso* joined in on the tabloid attacks blasting the two for corruption.

Starting in April 1999, the tabloid attacks were reproduced verbatim on a Miami-based Web site ostensibly run by the Asociación Pro Defensa de la Verdad (APRODEV), or the Pro-Defense of Truth Association. The director of the project was an Argentine national said to be an "astrologer" with a shady past, Héctor Faisal. Investigative reports by *La República* and cable news station Canal N found evidence linking Faisal to the SIN. Gustavo Mohme joined with other plaintiffs in filing a defamation suit against Faisal, who adamantly denied any links to the SIN.[19] Not surprisingly, the suit was dismissed when a judge ruled that Faisal was not responsible for the content of the material because he was just reproducing the text of previously published tabloid texts. At Faisal's criminal trial in 2002, various witnesses confirmed that Faisal enjoyed a close relationship with Montesinos, that he was on the SIN payroll from 1998 through 2000, and that he even enjoyed the use of an office at the SIN.[20]

In mid-1999, Peruvians got their first glimpse of how the reelection machine would work, and how public resources and the media would be wielded during the reelection campaign. The occasion was an official celebration of President Fujimori's birthday held on July 27, 1999. A crowd of twelve thousand people packed into a park in Lima's San Juan de Miraflores district for a concert in honor of the president. Among the performers was Rossy War, Peru's great star of *tecnocumbia* music. Dressed in her signature white cowboy hat and boots, War introduced a new song whose refrain, *Perú país con futuro,* was identical to the government's own advertising slogan. Television stations Channel 2 and Channel 4 covered the event live in its entirety, giving viewers a chance to see the president take an awkward turn at dancing—something that became standard fare in his campaign appearances.

The birthday event prefigured many of the abuses to come in the 2000 election campaign. *La República* reported that thousands of revelers were bused to the event on orders from government officials in the social assistance agencies. Attendees were rewarded with soft drinks, cookies, and fruit. Some participants reported that local soup kitchens were threatened that they would lose their government food supplies if they failed to send volunteers to the event. Estimates put the total cost of the event at around five hundred thousand dollars, but no official explanations were forthcoming about where the money for the event originated.[21] Television station managers also chose not to explain their decision to broadcast an event that had no news content but that was so obviously favorable to the president.

On the following day, July 28, President Fujimori made his annual Independence Day speech to the congress. But what Peruvians saw and heard that day was a far cry from the carefully controlled scene of the night before. Regardless of how well-laid the reelection plans were, some elements still remained beyond the control of Fujimori and Montesinos. Raising his voice, Fujimori was forced to repeat parts of his speech over the jeers of the opposition legislators. Their desks were posted with placards that read: "No to fraud, no to the re-reelection."[22] Despite years of frustration and setbacks, opposition leaders were still standing, ready to confront the reelection machine.

Government, Opposition, and Observers

To the dismay of many observers watching developments in Peru from abroad, opposition leaders never achieved the organizational unity equivalent to that of the Chilean opposition under Pinochet. In Chile, leaders struck the multiparty alliance, Concertación. The coalition successfully challenged Pinochet in a 1988 referendum that ended the dictatorship and then united around presidential candidate Patricio Alywin. In Peru, the elite-based opposition that emerged after the coup was disparate and disorganized, and it remained so.

Opposition politicians ruminated frequently on the need for unity and a *candidato único* (single candidate) to take on Fujimori in 2000, but the likelihood of such an agreement was always remote. Alberto Andrade, the early front-runner, believed that a single candidacy might actually help Fujimori's campaign by focusing all of the government attacks on a single target. And if the election did proceed to a second round, the opposition would rally around the challenger, effectively turning him into the *candidato único* anyway.

Political rivalries inside the opposition were deep, but equally strong was the conviction that Fujimori had to be stopped. While the opposition lacked a formal, permanent organization, the struggle against the regime did bring political leaders together episodically around important issues. In the halls of congress, the minority members worked together and protested together—contesting every legislative pillar of the regime, from the 1993 constitution to the Amnesty Law to *Ley de interepetación auténtica*. Solidarity across partisan lines was also evident in the campaign for the referendum; and fourteen political organizations signed onto the Governability Pact in December 1999, pledging to work together on future democratic and economic reforms.[23]

Organizations in civil society challenged the regime in different ways and venues. Foro Democrático and the Colegio de Abogados played a major role in the legal challenges to reelection. Human rights organizations (working together under the umbrella of the Coordinadora Nacional de Derechos Humanos) and press watchdog organizations produced documentary records chronicling the abuses committed during the reelection drive.[24] One such project was spearheaded by Carlos Basombrío at the Instituto de Defensa Legal (IDL). It involved a running compilation of election abuses that was distributed through a listserv to hundreds of individuals, media outlets, and institutions.[25] Student organizations played a major role in the street protests following the TC dismissals, the takeover of Channel 2, and the 1998 referendum.

So while there was neither a unified opposition nor a single unity candidate, an underlying consensus on certain fundamentals emerged among anti-Fujimori forces during the rough-and-tumble circumstances of the presidential race. Opposition leaders agreed that they had to make use of the "space" opened by the 2000 reelection to confront the regime and to keep up pressures from the international community. The hope was to create conditions (with a forceful presence of international observers) that would either allow for an outright defeat of the regime in the election, like that of Pinochet in 1988, or provoke international repudiation of the elections sufficient to spur some kind of political transition. Contesting the election conditions and questioning the legitimacy of the process were essential components of the opposition strategy from the start.

There was, of course, no lack of things to complain about, thanks to the dirty tricks served up daily by SIN operatives. As the early front-runner in the polls, Lima mayor Alberto Andrade was the prime target for what he and his aides referred to as a "demolition" operation. Demolition was an apt description because it involved every conceivable form of harassment. From the unofficial start of his campaign in mid-1999, Andrade complained of constant police surveillance. Rock-throwing mobs suspiciously appeared at his campaign events. To add to his troubles, Andrade's family-owned leather goods factory came under investigation for tax charges. There was no doubt in Andrade's mind that all his troubles, from taxes to tabloids, originated at the SIN, and he was vociferous in his denunciations.[26]

As he climbed in the polls, Luis Castañeda suffered the same treatment meted out to Andrade—smears in the tabloids, threats of litigation on corruption charges, vandalism of campaign headquarters, and harassment on the campaign trail. In September 1999, Castañeda released a videotape documenting harassment during several campaign appearances. The incidents included the police blocking his entry to towns and an inexplicable power failure during one campaign appearance. Castañeda turned over the video to the national election observation organization, Transparencia, for verification.[27] In one of the most bizarre incidents in the campaign, Castañeda chased and caught someone he claimed had been stalking him and his family. The individual turned out to be a plainclothes policeman. The culprit denied following Castañeda and claimed that Castañeda assaulted him. Everyone from President Fujimori to the national police chief, General Fernando Dianderas, lined up to dismiss Castañeda's version of the events. The incident provided more grist for tabloid accusations that Castañeda was "nervous."

Other candidates joined Andrade and Castañeda in making the same kind of charges. Alejandro Toledo, the presidential candidate of Perú

Posible, also reported police surveillance and disruptions at public appearances. Federico Salas, the mayor of Huancavelica and presidential candidate of Perú Ahora, a newly created party, charged that the government had mounted a "Gestapo" of prefects, governors, police, and military in the provinces to undermine the opposition and pressure local officials to work on behalf of the president's reelection.[28]

In short, no one in the opposition was prepared to concede that the electoral environment was fair or that the candidates were competing on anything approximating a level playing field. All the candidates agreed on the need for expanded election monitoring by the international community. Andrade, Castañeda, and Toledo called incessantly for an early arrival of international missions to offset what they feared would be yet another short-lived, rubber-stamp mission from the OAS in the style of its previous efforts.

On the government side, no one was willing to admit that anything was wrong, and nobody was in a hurry to see international observers in place. Instead, President Fujimori led *oficialistas* in a concerted effort to discredit opponents by depicting them as liars and whiners. Fujimori admonished his opponents: "Stop claiming to be victims."[29] Coming to the defense of the SIN, he suggested that the criticism was part of a systematic effort to undermine the intelligence agency.[30] Whenever he was queried about the opposition criticisms, Fujimori dismissed them as politically motivated lies and exaggerations—a "string of complaints."[31] If anything bad did occur in the course of the campaign, the president conceded that wildly enthusiastic and uncontrollable *ayayeros* (sycophants) were surely to blame.

The official dismissals and denials did not stop the complaints that were starting to attract attention abroad. Issues related to freedom of the press in Peru were highlighted in the 1999 reports issued by international watchdog organizations. In its annual international report, CPJ listed President Fujimori in the eighth position on its top-ten list of the world's "Enemies of the Press." That assessment came along with the news that Freedom House, the international organization that monitors civil liberties, demoted Peru in its standings from having a "partially free" press to having an "unfree" press—placing Peru in the same category as Cuba. Santiago Cantón, the Rapporteur on Freedom of the Press of the OAS, concurred with the bleak assessment.[32]

The bad press on Peru continued to accumulate through 1999, and more voices weighed in on the matter. During an August visit to Lima, U.S. drug czar Barry McCaffrey refused to the discuss the SIN, but did express concerns about human rights in Peru and met with rights activists. Elliot Abrams, the former Reagan administration official working with Baruch Ivcher, blasted the Fujimori government as undemocratic on a Spanish-language CNN network broadcast, then repeated his charges for the Peruvian media.[33] Luigi Einaudi, the former special envoy of the United States in the peace negotiations between Peru and Ecuador, acknowledged the Fujimori government's authoritarian tendencies in testimony before the U.S. Senate. He noted that, seven years after the auto-coup, questions about freedom of the press, the separation of powers, and the autonomy of the judiciary still dogged the Fujimori government.[34]

Senator Jesse Helms again weighed in on Peru and reintroduced Resolution 209 in October 1999. The text slammed Fujimori as "having manipulated" institutions for the purpose of seeking a "third term in office." It enumerated the controversies related to press freedom, including the attacks of the tabloid press and the actions taken against Baruch Ivcher. The resolution recommended a reevaluation of bilateral and multilateral relations with Peru if the upcoming elections were deemed to be "inconsistent with the standard of representative democracy" in the hemisphere. The Senate unanimously approved the resolution on November 8.

Back in Lima, *oficialistas* snapped. Congresswoman Martha Chávez called on the U.S. Senate to "stop sticking its nose into the internal affairs of countries."[35] In the same vein, Fujimori dismissed the Senate's admonitions as hypocritical: "When democracy was in danger in Peru, from the 1980s to 1993, there were no declarations from the Senate or from international organizations. Sendero and the MRTA were everywhere. Nobody said anything. Now that we are in a process of consolidating democracy, because it still is not perfect, they emit resolutions."[36] Fujimori later directed his ire toward the opposition for looking to the United States for help: "Members of the opposition think that the United States is the Pope when we have been a sovereign nation since 1821."[37]

Fujimori's resentment of foreign interference surfaced throughout the campaign. But as noxious as the international criticisms were to *oficialistas,* they could not be ignored altogether without putting the reelection project at risk. The lesson learned in the 1992 coup could not be ignored: the government would have to affect the appearance of goodwill and compliance with international norms. At the same time, the government would have to deflect the demands for fairness and transparency and muddy the waters sufficiently to make it difficult for observers to disqualify the election as a fraud.

Recognizing the need for some fresh gamesmanship on the international front, Fujimori named a new cabinet head in October 1999. José Alberto Bustamante, a gravelly-voiced attorney with experience representing Peru before the Inter-American Human Rights Commission, was tapped for the job as president of the council of ministers along with a portfolio as justice minister. At his swearing-in ceremony, Bustamante acknowledged the government's need to project a positive image in anticipation of the 2000 election: ". . . like Caesar's wife, we must not only be virtuous in the electoral process, but moreover we must appear to be so."[38]

Rehabilitating Peru's image was no small task, and Bustamante sought professional guidance. After the U.S. Senate passed Resolution 209, the Peruvian government signed contracts with two American firms to lobby on its behalf in the United States. One contract was with a Washington-based law firm, Patton Boggs. The other was with a New York firm, Shepardson Stern Kaminsky. Patton Boggs collected thirty thousand dollars per month in fees from October through December 1999, then fifty thousand dollars monthly starting in February 2000. Shepardson signed on for an initial payment of one hundred thousand dollars from October through December 1999, and collected thirty-five thousand dollars per month from January through April 2000.[39] As the denunciations about the election conditions piled up back in Lima, selling the idea that the Fujimori government was a picture of democratic normalcy was a stretch even for the savviest Washington lobbyists. In its annual report, the Inter-American Dialogue, a prestigious Washington think tank, labeled Fujimori as an "autocratic president" and underscored the debilitated state of political institutions in Peru.[40] A more extensive and blistering analysis of the collapse of democracy under Fujimori came from the Washington Office on Latin America, authored by Coletta Youngers.[41]

Oficialista attempts to represent the electoral process as normal were being complicated considerably by the national election observation organization, Transparencia. With funding from international organizations and governments including the United States, Transparencia was able to assume a more ambitious agenda of monitoring the preelection environment than it had done in 1995, and thus was in a position to confirm the veracity of many of the opposition's complaints. For example, Transparencia sent investigators to the countryside to corroborate Castañeda's charges of campaign harassment.

Even more startling was Transparencia's documentation of unfair media practices, especially the highly unbalanced coverage in favor of the president. Starting in November 1999, Transparencia published quantitative data proving that the major stations were wildly disproportionate in the time they allotted to coverage of the president versus the time allotted to opposition candidates. The November report showed that presidential coverage accounted for 78 percent of all the time devoted to candidates in nightly news coverage on Lima's six principal television stations.[42]

Transparencia's sober quantitative reports on many key election issues (e.g., government expenditures on advertising, government slogan painting, etc.) corroborated the claims of opposition candidates that the electoral process was unfair. Transparencia's director Rafael Roncagliolo was blunt in his early assessment that the electoral process was the most "unbalanced" in Peru's history. "Peruvian elections have never been a ballroom dance," he observed, "but there has never been such generalized harassment, so systematic and practically every place in the country where any opposition candidate goes."[43]

Transparencia's damning findings undercut the government's position that everything was on track for a normal election in 2000. So the government turned its energies to undercutting Transparencia. Fujimori led the charge. He questioned the "democratic credentials" of Transparencia leaders, pointing to the fact that some had worked in positions in the government-controlled media during the military dictatorship in the 1970s.[44] (That some of the president's own collaborators worked in the military government was, of course, never mentioned.) Unwilling to cede any ground to the organization, Fujimori said Transparencia needed to be monitored. "You have to observe the observers," he noted.[45] Taking the president's cue, the chief of ONPE, José Portillo López, followed up with a notarized letter, cautioning Transparencia to act appropriately during the election.[46]

Before any official international observer set foot in Peru, opposition candidates, Transparencia, and the independent press had already gone a long way in establishing the unfairness of the electoral environment. And that negative assessment had, to a great extent, become part of international public opinion. With so many of the key problems in the electoral environment already in plain view of Peruvians and the international community, the international election observation began in December 1999. The Carter Center joined with the National Democratic Institute (NDI) in a joint mission led by the former president of Uruguay, Luis Alberto Lacalle. The mission met with Fujimori, who already seemed to anticipate the confrontations ahead. Fujimori concluded that the mission would have "few observations" because the government was committed to a free and fair electoral process. He also repeated his position that observers did not have the right to "interfere in internal matters."[47]

In its first report, the Carter Center–NDI mission had more than the few observations that Fujimori predicted. The mission concluded that the preelection environment had "serious flaws" that would require "concerted and sustained efforts" to correct if the government sought to meet international standards. The report echoed the opposition's "string of complaints" almost in its entirety. The problems listed included: "(1) lack of media access for opposition candidates; (2) biased news coverage; (3) lack of coverage in the press of issues that could affect voters' choices; (4) violation of press freedoms; (5) problems with the legal framework and judicial remedies; (6) lack of confidence in electoral institutions; and (7) use of state resources to gain electoral advantage."[48]

Returning to Washington for an appearance at the Inter-American Dialogue, Bustamante tried to fend off journalists peppering him with questions about freedom of the press. Bustamante conceded that his government was in "damage control mode," admitting to "serious errors" in the past.[49] But Bustamante insisted that remedies to the real or perceived election problems were on the way.

Selling the idea that the Fujimori government would deliver acceptable elections was essential. After Fujimori announced his intention to run, the U.S. State Department issued a statement indicating that it was "neutral on whatever government is elected in Peru, but not neutral about the process."[50] It was clear that the Clinton administration was not going to plunge into debates about the constitutionality of Fujimori's reelection bid, but the actual election had to meet minimal standards.

Behind the scenes, Montesinos had already gotten reassurances about American neutrality and was writing off the importance of the Senate resolution on Peru. In November, Montesinos told military officials that he had spoken with the newly appointed American ambassador John Hamilton, who indicated that the United States had no plans to react adversely to Fujimori's bid. Montesinos rendered his version of the exchange with Hamilton:

> He [Hamilton] said: Look, [regarding] the position and discussions in dispute, I'm neutral. This is my profile now and it will continue to be so on this topic. In the end, it's the people of Peru who will decide. If the Peruvian people want it to go ahead, well, I have no reason for us to get involved in these things.
> That's the position that I have, the instructions that I have.[51]

Whatever the two men actually said in the meeting, Montesinos had reason to feel that the reelection was on track. All he had to do was simulate an electoral process that was somewhat convincing or, if not convincing, so confusing that that American and OAS officials would shrug it off and let it slide. Fujimori's reelection per se was not the problem. The problem was staging the process.

Campaign 2000

For Peru's opposition, any hope for a political transition depended on either rendering Montesinos's reelection machine inoperable (through intense international scrutiny) or exposing its crimes and making the elections illegitimate in the eyes of the world. The battle lines were clearly drawn. On one side, there was an opposition desperate to expose the election abuses. On the other side stood a government obsessed with covering them up. The key issue of the 2000 campaign was the conduct of the election itself.

That the campaign, now a struggle over regime transition, would be the most contentious in Peru's history was a given. It would be furious and fast. The JNE finalized the legal registration of presidential candidates in early January 2000; the general elections for president and congress were scheduled for April 9. In the tradition of previous presidential elections, a second-round runoff would take place in the presidential race if no candidate received the required "50 percent plus 1" majority in the balloting. Along with Fujimori, nine other candidates won a place on the presidential ballot. Alberto Andrade, Luis Castañeda, and Alejandro Toledo were considered to be Fujimori's principal challengers from the start of the race, even though Andrade and Castañeda were already suffering the effects of the smear campaigns against them.

As the official race got underway, the stakes in the public discussions about electoral conditions grew exponentially. Every new scandal added to the accumulating evidence that could be marshaled to show that Peru was failing to meet international standards for a free and fair election. Already troubled by Transparencia's studious documentation of abuses, Montesinos turned to the Mendel brothers, the owners of Channel 2, to mount an attack on the top leaders of Transparencia. In mid-January, the television station ran reports during their regular newscasts depicting Transparencia leaders as part of a *telaraña roja* (red spiderweb), former communists dedicated to undoing the government by fabricating false information about the election. And just in case viewers were not getting the point, a cartoon spiderweb was superimposed on the photographs of the Transparencia leaders used in the reports.

Human rights ombudsman Jorge Santistevan was also included in the *telaraña roja* reports. Elected by congress in 1996 to be the head of the Defensoría del Pueblo, Santistevan had maneuvered skillfully to keep his agency independent by focusing selectively on certain issues and developing strong links to international donors.[52] The agency stayed out of the legal battles on reelection. But as 2000 approached, Santistevan positioned his office to take a more active role in election-related activities, arguing that the agency did have an obligation to protect rights related to the electoral process. Responding to the chronic complaints by candidates that they were being harassed, Santistevan created a registry in the Defensoría to keep track of complaints and investigate them. Annoyed with Santistevan's initiative, Bustamante argued that the agency had no jurisdiction in the area. Nonetheless, Santistevan stood his ground, and tapped international donors for funding. Like Transparencia, the Defensoría office began producing empirical reports and bulletins corroborating the government abuses.[53]

Like the Transparencia leaders, Santistevan enjoyed credibility in international circles for his professionalism. He could not be dismissed simply another "crybaby" of the political opposition. If the objective was to discredit or intimidate Transparencia and the Defensoría, the obviously staged baiting backfired. The loony television news coverage only confirmed the media's collusion with the government. Rather than undermine Transparencia, the media attack prompted American ambassador John Hamilton to come to the defense of the organization, characterizing its work as "impartial."[54]

The chronicling of abuses by Transparencia and the Defensoría did not stop the clandestine reelection operations. But intense scrutiny made it more difficult to hide those operations from the public. Reporters dug in. The intrepid Edmundo Cruz at *La República* uncovered how deeply the SIN was involved in the day-to-day operations of the campaign. Cruz and his colleagues located a factory in downtown Lima producing Perú 2000 T-shirts and other campaign paraphernalia. They followed the factory's delivery trucks as they made their way to SIN headquarters. Cruz dubbed the T-shirts "Vladi-polos" in an obvious reference to Vladimiro Montesinos.[55]

Bustamante dutifully denounced *La República*'s story as "false, unfounded, a fabricated accusation," arguing that there was no incontrovertible evidence that trucks had indeed delivered campaign materials because Cruz had not actually been inside the SIN to witness the delivery.[56] But Cruz's story was right on the mark. Montesinos later confirmed that Perú 2000 promotional items, everything from shirts to calendars, were purchased with SIN slush funds.[57] The items were passed on to Perú 2000 congressional candidates. According to Montesinos, several candidates also received twenty thousand dollars in cash to fund their individual campaigns while visiting the SIN.

In the meantime, the official line was that no public funds were being used in the Perú 2000 campaign. When asked how he was financing his campaign, President Fujimori said that businessmen had sponsored the painting of the slogan *"Perú, país con futuro"* as a civic-minded gesture. Montesinos later revealed that the campaign contributions from businessmen were phony, fabricated to create a paper trail of receipts to make it look like the money had come from donors instead of the SIN.

On the heels on the Vladi-polos story, another sensational revelation rocked the campaign. This one involved the discovery of a *fábrica de firmas* (signature factory), an illicit operation mounted to forge signatures on petitions to register one of the Perú 2000 coalition partners, the Frente Independiente Nacional Perú 2000. The newspaper *El Comercio* broke the story after a young man employed in the scam contacted the Carter Center–

NDI office in Lima and the Defensoría. Daniel Rodríguez, the whistle-blower, provided details of the elaborate operations that employed scores of people to forge signatures. Their employer was a Lima city councilman from the Vamos Vecino political organization, another organizational partner of the Perú 2000 front.[58] Rodríguez described how the signatures were copied from the official ONPE voter-registration lists, documents that should have been inaccessible to the general public. His sister and mother corroborated his testimony, as did another witness, Erika Martínez, who identified other officials involved in the operation, including an employee of ONPE.[59]

The signature factory scandal had an element that the Vladi-polos incident lacked—participants who were willing to confess to wrongdoing and who could identify the bosses behind the scheme. At a minimum, the use of the ONPE voter-registration list to forge signatures and ONPE's acceptance of thousands of forged signatures on the petitions suggested incompetence and disarray inside ONPE. At a maximum, it implicated ONPE personnel in the commission of a crime. In addition, the organizers of the signature forgeries were associated with high-ranking political insiders, including Fujimori's top political operative, Absalón Vásquez, and Congressman Oscar Medelius—facts that suggested that the conspiracy was more than the work of *ayayeros*.

Under the circumstances, the government's standard routine of simple denials and dismissals would not suffice. There was at least some room for the government to argue with observers when it came to issues related to the preelection environment, but there was far less room to maneuver when it came to the mechanics of the election and the vote count. If international observers concluded that there was something wrong with ONPE, the entity responsible for counting the votes on election night, Fujimori's reelection would be in jeopardy. Somos Perú and Transparencia had already raised serious questions about inaccuracies in the voter-registration list and how the errors could tempt election-day fraud. Now ONPE and its blustering chief José Portillo were under a cloud too.

Fujimori and high-ranking C90-NM leaders scrambled to distance themselves from the scandal while asserting that the incident did not compromise the overall integrity of the electoral process. Fujimori conceded that a forgery might have taken place, called for an investigation, but claimed that the Frente's problems did not affect the legal status of the Perú 2000 alliance. And before any investigation got underway, JNE president Alipio Montes de Oca weighed in to say that the matter would not affect the election.[60]

The investigation quickly became as controversial as the crime itself. Mirtha Trabucco, a prosecutor with a provisional appointment in the public ministry, was assigned to the case. Dubbed *La Doctora Archivo* (Doctor Archive) by *La República,* Trabucco's work previously included disposing of cases against government officials, including Montesinos.[61] Living up to the nickname, Trabucco led an investigation that went nowhere, managing to extend the deadlines on the case to make sure that nothing substantial surfaced before the April election.

Meanwhile, the Montesinos-controlled media and *oficialistas* lashed out at those involved in revealing the scandal. The newspaper *Expreso* hounded Daniel Rodríguez, running front-page headlines depicting him as a homosexual felon who suffered from psychiatric disorders.[62] C90-NM legislators attacked Jorge Santistevan for alleged improprieties in his handling of the videotaped testimony in the case. Tabloids accused Santistevan of conspiring against the electoral process.[63]

The newspaper that broke the story, *El Comercio,* came under fire from Channel 2, now firmly under the control of the Mendel brothers. The program *Contrapunto* ran a story dealing with an ongoing legal dispute among *El Comercio* shareholders that implied criminal wrongdoing on the part of the management. *El Comercio*'s director Alejandro Miró Quesada went on the offensive, charging that the reports might be a prelude to a legal assault on the paper like the one mounted against Baruch Ivcher and Channel 2. U.S. ambassador John Hamilton hurried to declare support for *El Comercio.*[64] By the next day, Fujimori was backing off from the matter; he dismissed the *Contrapunto* report as the work of "false friends" and *ayayeros.*[65]

From the government's perspective, the timing of the signature factory scandal could not have been worse. It coincided with the official start of Misión de Observación Electoral (MOE), the electoral observation mission of the OAS. Strategically speaking, MOE was the most important player among the observers. Since the 1992 coup, the OAS had sent observation missions to every election, but the mission heads had kept a low profile and had been so guarded in their findings that most of Peru's opposition wrote off the OAS election observations as useless. Hoping for a repeat of those lackluster performances, Fujimori welcomed Eduardo Stein, the former foreign minister of Guatemala tapped by OAS president César Gavíria to head MOE.

In his first public statement in Peru, Stein acknowledged the "international tension" surrounding Peru's electoral process.[66] A second Carter Center–NDI mission, led by former president of Costa Rica Rodrigo Carazo, delivered another critical report in February. It concluded that the political conditions necessary for a free and fair election had not yet been established. At the top of the list of the Carter Center–NDI complaints was the opposition candidates' continuing lack of access to the media. But the mission's major recommendation, that public funding be provided to allow all candidates to purchase television time, was immediately rejected by Fujimori and Bustamante on the grounds that there was no provision for such a measure in Peruvian electoral law.[67] The Carter Center–NDI report was followed by an even tougher assessment by a mission of the International Federation for Human Rights (IFHR), which included the celebrity and political activist Bianca Jagger. The IFHR report condemned the SIN for its interference in the political process.[68]

During a trip to Washington DC in early March, Bustamante got a sense of how much clout the critics were acquiring. After meeting with Bustamante, the U.S. State Department issued back-to-back statements supporting Transparencia and the Defensoría. One high-ranking U.S. official reportedly told Bustamante that if, in the course of the election the U.S. government had to choose between believing the Peruvian government or Transparencia, it would opt for Transparencia.[69] The U.S. statements also expressed support for the findings of the Carter Center–NDI mission and urged the Fujimori government to take action on its recommendations.

The government's occasional feints at complying with the recommendations coming from election observers did nothing to change the perception that the electoral conditions were unfair. Responding to criticism that he was illegally campaigning when he inaugurated public works projects, Fujimori said that he would stop the inaugurations but reserved the right to "inspect" public works. After the deluge of criticism about television blackouts of opposition candidates, the JNE brokered a deal with the privately owned television stations. The stations agreed to provide some free airtime to all competing political organizations. Still, as Transparencia concluded, the "fifteen minute" solution did little to remedy the inequities, since the stations aired the free time close to 11:00 p.m., a move that ensured only a small viewing audience for the spots.[70]

To the government's dismay, MOE joined in the battle to keep up pressure for reform through its own *boletín* (bulletin). In its first mid-March bulletin, MOE concurred with other observers that the electoral conditions remained far from satisfactory, pointing to the growing lack of confidence in the JNE, ONPE, and the voter-registration bureau, Registro Nacional de Identificación y Estado Civil (RENEIC). The bulletin underscored the need for timeliness in the investigation of the signature factory scandal. Two subsequent MOE bulletins reiterated the same points and lamented the government's inaction. MOE noted that the election could lack "credibility" if the problems were not rectified.[71] Annoyed with the mission's preelection bulletins, ONPE chief José Portillo said that observers should be barred from making declarations before the election. In a curt rebuff, Eduardo Stein said that it was not his job to act as a "mute witness" to the process.[72]

Frustrated by their inability to quell the criticisms, *oficialistas* began blasting the observers, taking special aim at the Carter Center–NDI mission. The president of Peru's congress, Martha Hidelbrandt, accused observers of becoming spokesmen for the opposition. Francisco Tudela, the former foreign minister who had become Fujimori's vice-presidential running mate, joined in the attack: "I think that the Carter Center follows a political agenda. I'm not saying that all NGOs are totally irresponsible. What I'm saying is that the Carter Center is a private institution that does not represent the government of the United States, nor its citizens, or the OAS, or the United Nations. . . . Then, tell me, what in the devil do they represent?"[73] Congresswoman Martha Chávez and Archbishop Juan Luis Cipriani chided the Carter Center–NDI mission for arrogantly trying to impose foreign values on Peru.

Oficialista anger exploded again when Carter Center–NDI issued its third mission report on March 24. Characterizing the electoral environment as one of "polarization, anxiety and uncertainties," the report concluded that conditions for a fair election had not been established and that "irreparable damage" to the election process had already been done.[74] Congressman Carlos Torres y Torres Lara denounced the findings: "They come here with their minds made up and with prejudices. They arrive. They're here two days. They do a report and believe that they know all the problems of Peru and they do not have the faintest idea about politics or the reality of our country."[75] Seeking to dismiss the Carter Center–NDI altogether, Francisco Tudela concluded that the organization had "nothing to do" in Peru and said that the only legitimate electoral observation mission was that of the OAS.[76]

By the end of March, the Fujimori administration was losing its public relations battle to project the 2000 election as a free, fair, normal election. On March 28, the White House released a statement voicing its agreement with the "meticulous" evaluations of the Carter Center–NDI and OAS missions and declaring "profound concern" about the state of the electoral process in Peru.[77] On the following day, Republican senator Paul Coverdell of Georgia introduced a joint resolution in the U.S. Senate expressing Congress's "grave doubts about the transparency of the electoral process in Peru." The resolution proposed that the United States withdraw aid from Peru and reevaluate Peru's standing with international financial institutions should the April 9 election be deemed unfair by the international community.[78]

Furious, Fujimori played the nationalist card, telling crowds at his campaign stops that Peru did not need tutors or big brothers and could take care of itself. He fumed: "We are not going back, we are not going to depend on any power, no other country, no matter how much power it has in the world, that wants to tell us how we should develop Peru. The development of this country will be in our hands, in our heads and in the framework of an authentic democracy."[79] In the same angry vein, Bustamante told reporters that the Peruvian government was "losing its patience" and accused the American congress of fomenting instability.[80]

Patience and time were running out all around. MOE chief Eduardo Stein declared that there was little time left to fix the election problems and change the perceptions of Peruvians who were expecting a fraud. Trying to keep the pressure on the government, Stein reserved the option to declare that the electoral process had failed to meet international standards unless conditions improved appreciably in the final week leading to April 9.

Countdown to April 9

As the campaign drew to a close, Fujimori worked frenetically, crisscrossing the country in public appearances. The events were part show business, part populist politicking. At every stop, dancing girls entertained the crowds, shimmying to the strains of the hugely popular *tecnocumbia* anthem named after the president, *"El ritmo del Chino"* (Rhythm of El Chino). Dressed in a polo shirt and jeans, Fujimori whipped up the audience with promises of land titles and free health insurance, and railed against the "international conspiracy" against him. Handouts of food, clothing, and cooking utensils were de rigueur at every rally. Fujimori's renewed populism was not confined to rallies. The government had already announced a massive new program to give land titles to urban squatters; the program, launched in February, assured beneficiaries that their land claims would be finalized after the April 9 election.

A deluge of television advertising served up images of joyful crowds, delirious at the sight of Fujimori, along with the president's theme song and its incessant refrain, *"Y te gusta a ti, y me gusta mí, el ritmo del Chino es el de Perú 2000 . . . Chino, Chino, Chino, Chino, Chino"* (You like it, I like it, the rhythm of El Chino is Perú 2000). Fujimori claimed to have authored the catchy tune. No other candidate could match the media blitz.

The excess and overkill in the last days betrayed the nervousness in the Fujimori camp. Despite all the negative campaigning and the political mobilization of the entire state apparatus on Fujimori's behalf, a first-round victory for the president was by no means ensured (except by way of an outright election-day fraud). The scurrilous media attacks on Andrade and Castañeda accomplished their mission of sinking the two top front-runners of the opposition, but their decline did not significantly change Fujimori's own polling numbers. After a surge in support in November and December, Fujimori's polling numbers flattened out, leaving him with a solid but stagnant base of support of about 40 percent of the electorate. Fujimori polled best among low-income voters, people most directly dependent upon government assistance programs like food aid.

But not all of the electorate was caught up in the web of state-sponsored clientelism and coercion. Unemployment was the primary issue in the minds of most voters, and even low-income voters found Fujimori's record disappointing. Discontent with political aspects of *Fujimorismo* intersected with growing concern about Peru's poor economic performance. As the Andrade and Castañeda candidacies collapsed, Alejandro Toledo was able to capitalize on the political and economic frustrations of a public grown weary of a ten-year presidency. Toledo, a veteran of the 1995 presidential election, was appealing to voters for many reasons. He was an economist and told voters that he would devote his government to creating jobs, hence his slogan, *"Toledo-Trabajo"* (Toledo-Work). He loved talking about his humble origins, his struggle for an education that eventually led to Stanford and Harvard, and his pride in his indigenous identity and the Quechua language. Toledo campaigned alongside his attractive wife, Eliane Karp, a foreign-born anthropologist and fluent Quechua speaker.

Toledo began his upward swing in the polls in February, finally moving out of the single digits after languishing in the fourth-place spot for months. Toledo had enjoyed an important advantage by remaining marginal for so long; until he started climbing in the polls, the tabloids had ignored him, targeting Andrade and Castañeda instead.

That changed in March, when Toledo broke through in the polls, becoming the leading challenger to Fujimori. But the onset of tabloid attacks so late in the campaign did not affect Toledo's momentum. By the end of March, Toledo pulled within five percentage points of Fujimori. Given the margin of errors in polls, the race was, effectively, a dead heat.[81]

As the race tightened, concerns about the conditions at the polls and about a possible manipulation of the vote on election day grew exponentially among opposition leaders and observers. Toledo pointed to prospects of fraud in polling places in the countryside, where he estimated that at least 30 percent of all *mesas* (the individual tables at polling stations where voting takes place) would function without organized observers or poll watchers. Meanwhile, news stories surfaced about a possible "electronic fraud," detailing how computer hackers could manipulate ONPE software. Adding to the suspicions about ONPE was the news of the resignation of a regional director of the electoral agency who said that she had witnessed "irregularities" in her office.[82]

Meanwhile, as the worries about what was going on behind the scenes deepened, the visible abuses continued. There were nonstop reports of food handouts and government employees campaigning to ensure votes for the president. And despite Bustamante's much-ballyhooed commitment to ensuring more equitable media access, television viewers saw more than two hours of coverage of the president's final campaign rally in Lima. Private commercial channels (Channels 2, 4, 9, and 11) participated in the broadcast along with the state-owned network, Channel 7. None of the stations extended the same coverage to the other candidates.[83]

In the final days before April 9, MOE chief Eduardo Stein stopped short of his earlier threat to discredit the election ahead of time. Pointing to the public's desire to go to the polls and the fact that opposition candidates had not withdrawn from the race, Stein decided that there was no alternative but to go ahead with his mission to observe the elections. But MOE's last pronouncement before the election, issued on the evening of April 7, was far from the rubber stamp that the government had once hoped for from the OAS. Meeting with reporters gathered in the international press headquarters at the downtown Sheraton Hotel, MOE observers delivered a final, glum bulletin, blasting the government for its constant abuses, refusal to respond adequately to MOE recommendations, and consequent failure to imbue the electoral process with a "minimum of credibility." There was, in MOE's view, a serious "confidence deficit" with respect to the election.[84]

Two days later, the credibility crisis was more than just a conclusion in a report. It was plain for the world to see, and it was going on right in front of the Sheraton.

9

REELECTION AND RESISTANCE

Vladimiro Montesinos liked to think of his job in military terms. The reelection was a mission to be accomplished. Months before the first round, Montesinos told associates that the reelection was "substantively over." "The president is going to win," he flatly assured them.[1]

From the government's perspective, the ideal scenario would have been to recreate 1995: conclude with a first-round victory sufficiently sweeping to send international observers packing and leave opponents licking their wounds. By early April, however, that possibility had all but evaporated. Toledo and Fujimori were running neck and neck in the polls. Trouncing Toledo would be possible only through the grossest manipulation of the balloting and vote count, an event that international observers were poised to denounce.

Two days before the election, Augusto Vargas Alzamora, the now-retired archbishop of the Roman Catholic Church, voiced the widely shared skepticism about a possible first-round victory for Fujimori: "That's absurd and if it occurs, suspicion will be right. If that happens, the people have a right to say that the election was not legal. It appears that we are seeing a process in which people are looking to different candidates and as such, no single one could have a majority. It would be so scandalous that it would not be acceptable."[2]

Vargas Alzamora, a longtime foe of Fujimori, astutely summarized the problem of April 9. Any result short of going to a second-round runoff was likely to be seen as bogus by a majority of Peruvians and observers. But if going to the second round was the only legitimate outcome on April 9, it was repellent and risky for the government. A second round would mean more international observation, and more denunciations from the opposition. And in all likelihood it would require more government dissembling and cover-ups.

As the polls closed in the late afternoon of Sunday, April 9, the reelection project entered its final phase. The only question for the government was how to get it over with, how to confound the observers and enervate the opposition. In the tense days after the first-round balloting, Alejandro Toledo charged that Fujimori was trying to *ganar por cansancio*—win by default, by tiring everyone else out. Everybody did get tired as the battle over reelection dragged on, but losses in the war of attrition were not confined to the opposition.

The Politics and International Relations of Counting

The exit polls came first. Minutes after the polls closed at 4:00 p.m. on April 9, television stations rushed to broadcast projections by Peru's top polling firms. Their projections were based on surveys taken after voters had cast their ballots. All of the exit polls concluded that the vote for Alejandro Toledo exceeded that for Fujimori.[3] If the exit polls were correct, a second-round runoff was unavoidable. Meanwhile, pollsters readied a second wave of projections based on a "quick count"—samples of the actual vote count from selected polling places.

As the news of Toledo's victory sunk in, thousands of supporters began gathering in the streets around the Sheraton Hotel in downtown Lima. The hotel was the official headquarters for foreign correspondents and it had become the informal gathering place for opposition leaders. In the euphoria of the moment, Toledo donned a red headband, conjuring up the image of an Inca warrior. From the Sheraton's balcony, he spoke to the crowd below. Speculating that a first-round victory might be within reach, Toledo urged supporters to wait for the quick-count projection promised by the national election observation organization, Transparencia.

The jubilation was short-lived. The festive atmosphere gave way to shock and disbelief when the second wave of quick-count results rolled in. The same pollsters that had put Toledo in the lead were now reversing their projections, putting Fujimori in the lead with between 47 to 48 percent of the vote. Pollsters hastened to explain that the exit polls were within the standard margin of error. To Toledo's dismay, the Transparencia quick count confirmed the pollsters' readjusted numbers. Transparencia put Fujimori ahead with 48.73 percent of the vote to Toledo's 41.04 percent. The evening's reversal of fortune was stunning; Fujimori's lead placed him on the cusp of the 50 percent he needed to avoid the second-round runoff.

The evening wore on with no official word from ONPE about the results. For the opposition, it was no great leap to think that the official numbers were on their way to being cooked into a first-round victory for Fujimori. On the weekend of the election, Transparencia and MOE duly noted the failure of two successive computer simulations of ONPE's vote-tabulation software. On the day before the election, Transparencia reported that it had received information about the existence of a Web site that could be used to hack into the ONPE computer system. Eduardo Stein also confirmed that ONPE had not made provision for OAS technicians to monitor the operation of the vote-count software in real time.

The other presidential candidates in the race who fared poorly that day—Alberto Andrade, Abel Salinas, Víctor García Belaúnde, Máximo San Román, and Luis Castañeda—also showed up at the Sheraton to support Toledo. They joined Toledo in a press conference where he charged that ONPE was preparing an "electronic fraud." Outside, an estimated fifty thousand demonstrators gathered, and made their feelings known in thunderous chants of *"¡Fraude!"* Toledo vowed to lead protests demanding a second round. After midnight, Toledo led what was left of the rambunctious crowd to the presidential palace where police met the protestors with tear gas.

Broadcast television showed none of the drama that night. Montesinos's media executives were on the job. After announcing the first results right after the close of the polls, all of the principal non-cable television channels reverted to regular programming. A movie featuring the Mexican comic

Cantinflas and the film *Pulp Fiction* were among the fare that night. Only Peruvians with access to the independent local cable station Canal N or international media such as Spanish-language CNN got a view of what was happening on the streets that night.

Transparencia officials assembled, insisting that the quick count mandated a second round. At their press conference, they maintained that the margin of error in a quick count could be no greater than 1 percent, and that left the president short of a win. MOE chief Eduardo Stein agreed, and he underscored that the OAS mission could not verify the integrity of the ONPE vote count.

Reneging on his promise to hold the "best elections in the history of the republic" and deliver the official results quickly on election night, ONPE chief José Portillo emerged belatedly at a midnight press conference. From a special warehouse headquarters set up at the Feria del Pacífico in San Miguel, far from the reach of downtown protestors, he reported the results from less than 1 percent of Peru's polling stations. Portillo blamed the partial results on delays in the reporting of the vote count to regional computing centers. It was a dismal display by Portillo, and the torturous count had only just begun.

Despite the absence of any definitive official results, the morning headline in the government-run newspaper, *El Peruano*, declared that a second round would take place. But hope for a quick resolution in favor of a second round dissipated by early Monday afternoon, when Portillo reemerged to announce partial tallies from 39 percent of the polling stations. According to Portillo, Fujimori had polled 49.88 percent of the vote and Toledo had 39.88 percent. Later in the day, Portillo adjusted Fujimori's total downward slightly to 49.63 percent of the vote based on the count from 55.94 percent of polling stations. Nonetheless, the ONPE figures meant that Fujimori stood less than one-half of a percentage point away from being declared winner on the first round.

The struggle to stop Portillo from delivering a first-round victory to Fujimori began. On Monday afternoon, Eduardo Stein joined Transparencia officials in a joint news conference to repeat his conclusion that a second round was "inevitable." He blasted ONPE again for delays and unprofessional conduct and said that ONPE had given Peruvians reason to believe that "something sinister" was happening in the vote-counting process. Among the irregularities cited by Stein was ONPE's decision to suspend computing operations for a period on Monday morning, ostensibly to allow its workers some rest.[4]

With the integrity of the electoral process itself now in question, U.S. government officials in Washington endorsed the calls for a second round. U.S. State Department spokesman James Rubin deemed Transparencia's quick count reliable and said that the figures mandated a second round. The same message came from White House press secretary Joe Lockhart. In Lima, U.S. ambassador John Hamilton voiced faith in the quick-count numbers and Transparencia.[5]

Fujimori made no public appearance on election night. He reemerged on Monday night in a news conference to face tough questioning from the foreign press corps. Flanked by his two vice-presidential running mates Francisco Tudela and Ricardo Márquez, Fujimori refused to stipulate to the accuracy of the quick-count figure by Transparencia. He insisted that the final decision regarding a second round rested with ONPE and the JNE.[6]

With Fujimori refusing to back off from a first-round victory, American foreign policymakers issued more warnings. On Tuesday, Secretary of State Madeleine Albright expressed concerns regarding the "inconsistencies" between ONPE figures and the quick count, suggesting that differences between the numbers threatened to undermine the legitimacy of the election. On the same day, the U.S. House of Representatives passed Resolution 43, a measure previously passed by the Senate, which recommended a review of U.S.-Peru relations if international observers judged the election as unfair. General Barry McCaffrey, the U.S. drug czar, reiterated that aid could be withdrawn from Peru if the election failed to be judged as "clean and beyond reproach." Another White House press statement underscored the point that the absence of a second round would make the entire electoral process questionable.[7]

Europeans joined in pressuring for a second round. Both the European Union and the British Foreign Office issued communiqués voicing concerns about the electoral process.[8] French ambassador Antoine Blanc and Portuguese ambassador and EU representative Alexander de Almeida paid a high-profile visit to Toledo at his home, followed by an impromptu press conference to defend the role of the international community in monitoring the process.

Portillo delivered updates of the official results on Tuesday, but he could not allay concerns about what was transpiring behind the closed doors of

ONPE's warehouse. To date, it remains unclear exactly what did happen there. No official inquiry was ever conducted to determine whether or not the computer software was tampered with during the vote count. Eduardo Stein later said that, unbeknownst to him at the time, Montesinos had a team of experts working at the Feria del Pacífico site.[9] Recent research by political scientist Gregory Schmidt suggests that machinations in the vote count might have been engineered elsewhere; his statistical analysis indicates the possibility that election officials may have colluded with poll watchers from Perú 2000 to alter the votes recorded on the *actas*.[10] Votes cast by Peruvians abroad also could have been a tempting target for alterations.

With 90 percent of the polling stations accounted for by Tuesday afternoon, Fujimori remained within less than one-half of a percentage point of winning. The foreign press corps, still camped out at the Sheraton, awaited more returns. Toledo knew that he needed to keep the pressure on. He called on opposition leaders and supporters to continue their mass protests. On the evening of Tuesday, April 11, thousands of mostly young demonstrators jammed the streets in front of the Sheraton. They unfurled a gigantic red-and-white Peruvian flag that blanketed much of the crowd. In doing so, they created a perfect photograph—an icon of resistance—for the photographers and cameramen gathered above on the rooftop. Congressional deputies, Lima mayor Alberto Andrade, and even Susana Higuchi, the president's ex-wife turned congressional candidate, joined Toledo and the demonstrators holding vigil at the Sheraton. Toledo staked out his position on the ONPE results: nothing but results leading to a second round was acceptable.

By Wednesday, the waiting was both tense and tedious. Portillo scheduled, then postponed his second news conference of the day. In the press center at the Sheraton, one high-ranking source at the JNE confided that Fujimori's victory was "done," ready to be announced. Toledo called on supporters to gather in the downtown Plaza San Martín to await the results. Thousands of protestors returned.

At eight o'clock on Wednesday night, a frazzled Portillo faced the press to announce the official results from 97 percent of Peru's polling stations. According to ONPE, Fujimori polled 49.84 percent of the vote, with Toledo lagging behind at 40.39 percent. Portillo assured skeptical reporters that the second round was guaranteed, and that even the uncounted absentee ballots would not be sufficient to push Fujimori over the 50 percent mark.

The crowd gathered at Plaza Martín exploded in celebration. After years in the making, the reelection project had suffered its first real setback.

Strategizing the Second Round

The failure to secure the reelection in April had a profound impact. Not only had Montesinos's vast reelection machine been unable to deliver a convincing win in the first round, but the fractiousness of round one also ensured that securing reelection in the second round would be even more problematic. ONPE's strange conduct during the count guaranteed intense scrutiny from all observers, especially from Stein's OAS mission. And to make matters worse, the opposition now had a celebrity to rally around—Alejandro Toledo.

The Fujimori camp regrouped immediately, using its familiar dual-track strategy. On one hand, government spokespersons were conciliatory and tried to appear responsive to domestic and international critics. On the other hand, they reverted to all the well-worn tactics of "agenda denial" that the government had used so often and successfully in the past—stonewalling, foot dragging, and flat-out refusals to recognize problems.[11] And, as usual, they attacked critics using the tactic of nationalist appeal, impugning the patriotism of the opposition and denouncing foreign intrusion.

The public relations offensive began with rehabilitating the president's electoral vehicle, Perú 2000. An organizational shuffle ostensibly signaled a newfound commitment to reform and civility. Francisco Tudela, Fujimori's aristocratic and urbane vice-presidential running mate, was named to head the second-round campaign. In an effort to court foreign correspondents, Tudela inaugurated a new, press-friendly Perú 2000 headquarters in the upscale neighborhood of San Isidro. Tudela kicked off his duties with a flourish, announcing that the government was ready to act positively on recommendations from the OAS mission. He called on the media to provide equitable coverage for each candidate and confirmed that his organization was prepared to work out an arrangement for a presidential debate between Fujimori and Toledo.[12]

Tudela did not, however, disguise his irritation with what he viewed as collusion between Transparencia and U.S. officials to pressure for a second round, a move that smacked of turning Peru into a "banana republic."[13] Bustamante joined in denouncing European and American "interference" in the electoral process. Foreign Minister Fernando de Trazegnies called resident ambassadors on the carpet, lecturing them on what he said was the breach of international norms and customs during the elections— specifically, the highly publicized meeting of Alejandro Toledo with French and Portuguese ambassadors during the vote count.[14] De Trazegnies also began lining up Latin American counterparts to defend against foreign interference. Foreign ministers from Bolivia, Venezuela, Ecuador, and Colombia assembled at an Andean community conference to endorse the principle of nonintervention in domestic matters.[15]

For Toledo and the opposition forces allied with him, the second round was a risky, high-stakes game. If the government could manage to package the second round as "new and improved," then the abuses of the first round would be forgotten and Fujimori's victory was likely to be welcomed by the OAS and the United States. So if Toledo participated in the second round and lost, he risked legitimizing the reelection. On the other hand, if Toledo withdrew immediately from the second round, the JNE was legally entitled to declare Fujimori as the winner.

Toledo kept everyone guessing. He never conceded to losing the first round. *"Fraude"* was the word that Toledo used over and over again to describe the events. He said that he had been robbed in the first round and that his participation in the second round would depend on improvements in the electoral conditions. Trying to use his participation as a bargaining chip, Toledo frequently threatened to withdraw from the race. *"No me voy al matadero"* (I'm not taking myself to the slaughterhouse), he often told reporters and supporters.

Toledo's demands for improvements in electoral conditions might have been easier to ignore were it not for the chorus of similar demands coming from international observers. MOE chief Eduardo Stein repeatedly warned that any recurrence of the problems identified in the first round would not be acceptable to the OAS.[16] The Carter Center–NDI mission agreed and maintained that the runoff would fail to meet the minimum international standards for democratic elections unless "immediate and comprehensive improvements" were applied to the political environment as well as to ONPE's administration of the election.[17] Human Rights Ombudsman Jorge Santistevan joined in the calls for improved conditions. He sent a proposal to the JNE identifying five key areas for improvement, which included assuring media access and banning the use of public resources in the campaign. Santistevan urged the adoption of a code of ethics by the two candidates.[18]

From the government's perspective, striking a conciliatory tone was a necessary public relations move, but comprehensive reform was off the table virtually from the start. At most, Fujimori was prepared to admit to certain "imperfections" in the electoral process, but nothing more. The *oficialista* position was simple: there had been no fraud in the first round. To admit to wrongdoing and accede to the demands for reforms in the electoral conditions would put the reelection project in real danger. By early May, most polls showed Fujimori and Toledo in a statistical dead heat in the presidential race. Improving the electoral conditions to create the "level playing field" demanded by Toledo and observers risked tipping the balance to Toledo.

So, on the government's side, few risks could be taken. There was some improvement in media access. After Fujimori and Bustamante signaled that the media should provide fair access to candidates in the second round, television stations expanded their coverage of Toledo. But a lot of the news coverage was negative. The news magazine shows *Contrapunto* (Channel 2) and *Hora 20* (Channel 4) routinely ran negative stories on Toledo, his advisors, and even other media outlets that were identified as part of the *prensa toledista* (the pro-Toledo press). The tabloids continued to hammer Toledo as a liar, violent agitator, and terrorist sympathizer.

In other areas, the recommendations for reform went nowhere. Fujimori and Tudela quickly torpedoed the idea of a code of conduct and an ethics tribunal. They argued that no candidate could be responsible for the behavior of private actors during the campaign, particularly the media; in retrospect, it was a thoroughly disingenuous argument considering Montesinos's micromanagement of the media. Tudela and other representatives of Perú 2000 met with Perú Posible leaders, supposedly to arrange a presidential debate. But the talks broke down after just three days, with both sides charging that the other was acting in bad faith to sabotage the talks. There would be no presidential debate.

But all the controversies about the second round paled in comparison to the ones involving ONPE and the JNE. If the electoral machinery could be proven to be either unreliable or rigged, then neither Peruvians nor the rest of the world would accept the second-round win for Fujimori.

The Date, the Computers, Another Cover-Up

In contrast to ONPE's sluggish vote counting, JNE officials wasted no time in setting the date for the second-round runoff election. As soon as ONPE delivered the official consolidated election results on April 28, the JNE board called a hasty meeting. Later that evening, the JNE announced its decision to schedule the second-round runoff between Toledo and Fujimori for May 28, 2002, a little less than a month away. The rapid scheduling of the runoff favored Fujimori since it left little time to rectify all of the problems surrounding the electoral conditions and machinery that had marred the first round. Toledo called for a postponement of the date to sometime in June.

From the viewpoint of election observers, the rapid scheduling of the second round considerably complicated the problem of policing ONPE to ensure a clean count. Not only had ONPE failed to stage a timely and transparent count in the presidential race but its apparent mishandling of the congressional results also added to the suspicions about ONPE personnel and the vulnerability of ONPE software to manipulation. In its analysis of the congressional vote, Transparencia found instances in which parties ended up with fewer votes than those that had been tallied early in the vote counting. Reports published in *El Comercio* demonstrated discrepancies in different copies of ONPE's own reports of the vote counts.[19]

Under pressure to explain the strange vote count, ONPE director José Portillo admitted that at least twenty of his data entry operators were guilty of tampering with the preferential votes in the congressional races. The tampering favored twenty-four different candidates, half of which were on the Perú 2000 slate.[20] Nonetheless, Portillo insisted that the presidential count was unaffected by the shenanigans in the congressional count. But with all the messiness in the first round, Portillo's assurances would not suffice; it was evident that ONPE had to do something to reestablish its credibility in the second round, especially with Eduardo Stein and MOE. Portillo announced that ONPE would create three "working groups" that would include external observers to monitor ONPE's work on the second round. Representatives from Defensoría del Pueblo and a technical consultant from Perú Posible agreed to participate in the new working group charged with overseeing the computing system.

Scheduling the election on May 28 meant that it would be difficult, if not impossible, to undertake a thoroughgoing review of the computer system. On May 11, MOE chief Eduardo Stein said that the May 28 date did not allow for sufficient time to check ONPE's computer software. U.S. State Department spokesman Richard Boucher echoed Stein's concerns about the time frame for the election. Toledo reiterated his call for a postponement of the second round, repeating his threat to withdraw from the race so as not to legitimate a "fraud." Meanwhile, Fujimori insisted that the JNE was an autonomous entity, legally empowered to schedule the date, and that its decision was binding no matter what.

By mid-May, the timing of the election and questions about ONPE's computer software overshadowed all other concerns. On May 17, Stein made a bombshell announcement: MOE had concluded that there was insufficient time to run the necessary technical checks on ONPE's new computer program for the second round. Stein's vote of no confidence in the computer system gave Toledo the opening to declare the election unsound. In a dramatic midafternoon press conference on May 18, Toledo announced that he was withdrawing from the May 28 runoff, but with the proviso that he would continue to campaign and participate if a new date were set. On the same day, the JNE ruled against Toledo's official petition for a postponement.

Official reaction to Toledo's withdrawal was furious. In a joint campaign appearance in Chimbote on the day of Toledo's announcement, President Fujimori and vice-presidential candidate Francisco Tudela ridiculed Toledo as a "loser" and "crybaby," who was withdrawing to avoid a loss. Tudela told campaign supporters that postponement was out of the question because it would violate electoral law and require a change of the constitution.

In the following days, government officials kept repeating that there was no legal way to change the date. At the same time, ONPE officials tried to make the case that Stein's fears about the computer system were unfounded by staging two highly publicized simulations to test the system's software. The first simulation on May 20 failed to win the approval of either MOE or Defensoría del Pueblo, even though ONPE declared it to be a success. Another simulation was scheduled for May 25 at ONPE's warehouse headquarters. JNE and ONPE officials joined election observers and journalists for the tea and cookies served up by young, smiling hostesses at the event, then hovered over the assembled computer terminals to watch the second simulation. While the second simulation was judged to be technically sound by MOE technicians, Eduardo Stein concluded that MOE still needed at least ten days to complete its own independent review of the computer software program.

Stein's insistence on the need for more time to check the computer system heightened the already considerable pressures on the government to postpone the election. On the domestic side, thirteen political parties signed onto Toledo's call for a postponement, as did Transparencia. On the international side, the EU election observation mission and Human Rights Watch endorsed the call for a postponement.

In contrast, Clinton administration officials were less adamant on the question of postponement. As problematic as Fujimori's reelection drive had become, Toledo had failed to inspire confidence among American policymakers. Instead of lining up with the groups pushing for postponement, the U.S. State Department said that it "regretted" both Toledo's withdrawal and the JNE's "hasty ruling" on the election date.[21] Secretary of State Madeleine Albright avoided the question when reporters asked if the United States was pressing for postponement, saying only that she was "depressed about the way that [the Peruvian election] had been going on" and promised that the United States would be monitoring the situation.[22] It looked as if the United States was still clinging to hope that the "process" could be concluded in a way that would leave Peru-U.S. relations relatively unruffled, especially bilateral cooperation on counternarcotics.[23]

Meanwhile, Stein lobbied hard for a settlement, hoping to get Toledo and Fujimori to agree to at least a ten-day delay in the election date. As the final days to the election counted down, speculation that the government would cede to OAS pressures intensified. The JNE was scheduled to rule on more legal challenges to the election date, so there was one last opening for a change of heart. But the election date controversy was not the only problem threatening to unravel the reelection project. On May 24, journalist Fabian Salazar charged that he had been knifed by SIN agents and robbed of secret videotapes in his possession. He said that the tapes showed Montesinos in clandestine meetings with members of the JNE, media executives, and other high-ranking officials. Salazar claimed that a source inside the SIN leaked the videos to him.

As Peruvians eventually found out, Salazar was telling the truth. There were many videotapes documenting illicit meetings between Montesinos and scores of public officials, including members of the JNE. Equally true was Salazar's account of the SIN operation to recover those tapes from his residence. Montesinos orchestrated the operation, along with the subsequent cover-up. He concocted a media campaign using *Hora 20* to smear Salazar and depict his story as a fabrication. It was a close call. But Montesinos knew that Salazar's accusations could be buried as long as he had no videos to back them up.[24] With no "smoking gun," Salazar's story faded into the background as the showdown over the election date dominated the news. Montesinos's success in recovering the videos and discrediting Salazar kept the reelection project from being completely derailed in its final, tense days.

On the afternoon of May 25, the JNE put an end to the rumors that the government would back down. In a ruling approved by three of the five board members, the JNE declared that the election could not be postponed, nor would it permit Toledo to withdraw his name from the ballot. As news of the decision spread, street riots broke out in downtown Lima. Angry demonstrators attacked the JNE headquarters.

Not surprisingly, the decision to proceed with the election was the last straw for international observers. Eduardo Stein announced that he was recalling MOE team members from the field and suspending its activities on the grounds that the conditions necessary for a free and fair election on May 28 were not in place. Stein packed his bags and headed back to Washington. Officials of the Carter Center–NDI mission concurred and also suspended its observation, as did the EU mission. The Defensoría del Pueblo, while keeping offices open to register election-day complaints, called off its on-site polling observation activities. Human Rights Ombudsman Jorge Santistevan declared the election did not meet the criteria of a free and fair election.

After all the years of preparation, the reelection project was ending in a garbled mess. But the Fujimori administration was schooled in scandal. As troublesome as it appeared in the short run, the imbroglio still seemed manageable. As he had done so often in the past, it was time for Fujimori to dig in. The president would insist that everything was perfectly normal. And he would defy anyone who said it was not.

Victory Foretold

The May 28 balloting was a dreary affair. For the foreign correspondents who reassembled to cover the second round, most of the drama had already taken place during the preceding days, in the clashes over postponement and the final obstinate decision to go ahead. On Sunday, there were no international observers to follow around, no young Transparencia volunteers to photograph at the polls, and no uncertainties about the final results that José Portillo would deliver. Still smarting from the accusations that they were somehow involved in manipulating the projections in the first round, almost all polling firms sat out the second round.[25]

Nor could protestors repeat their performance for correspondents in front of the Sheraton. This time, the international press center was firmly under the control of the office of the president of the council of ministers, housed in its walled compound in a residential section of Miraflores. The facilities were comfortable, but access was tightly controlled. Waiters offered sandwiches and coffee to the reporters working at the computers and watching the big-screen television usually set on Canal N, the only local station offering continuous election coverage. Unlike the Sheraton, this closed government venue could not become an opposition headquarters or a place for protestors to unfurl the Peruvian flag to cameras from around the world.

Across Peru, Sunday's voting took place with no scrutiny other than that provided by ONPE and military guards. Trying to counter Toledo's initial call for a mass boycott of the election, ONPE waged a weeklong media campaign, reminding voters of the hefty fine (equivalent to US$33) levied on absentees. Realizing that the fine would be too much of a burden for most Peruvians, Toledo backed off the boycott, asking voters to spoil their ballots by writing in the slogan of the opposition, *"No al fraude."*

ONPE did not keep tabs on how many ballots were spoiled with that particular phrase. But when the first results rolled in, it was clear that Toledo's message had gotten through. Spoiled ballots accounted for at least 29 percent of the vote. The figure constituted the highest percentage ever in a presidential election. As stipulated by election law, the null and blank votes were tossed out of the final calculation, leaving Fujimori with 74 percent of the valid vote. Though Toledo maintained that he was not in the race, the JNE's refusal to authorize Toledo's withdrawal left his name on the ballot and his legal standing in the race intact. The official results showed Toledo with close to 26 percent of the valid vote.

Once the polls closed in late afternoon, the real story of the day was the riots, not the results. Police teargassed protestors gathered in Plaza San Martín in Lima's downtown. In the provinces, clashes between police and protestors mirrored the Lima disturbances. CPN Radio reported violent confrontations in the cities of Cajamarca, Trujillo, Chimbote, and Cusco. As in the first round, broadcast television stations did not cover the disturbances, nor did they show the late-evening gathering in Plaza San Martín, where the still-defiant Toledo addressed an estimated sixty thousand supporters. Toledo announced that it was the beginning of the "third round" —a campaign of civic resistance to overturn the election results and put an end to the illegitimate regime.[26]

Shuttered inside the presidential palace, Fujimori had nothing to say. He was a no-show at the arranged victory celebration set in the neighborhood of San Martín de Porres. The *tecnocumbia* dancers warmed up the crowd with *"El ritmo del Chino,"* but the event fizzled when Fujimori failed to appear.[27]

Even before Sunday's exercise, Fujimori had rehearsed the principal arguments to be used in the defense of the second round. In preelection interviews, he lashed out at Toledo for withdrawing and accused him of trying to sabotage the election and provoke a coup. Referring to the JNE ruling against Toledo's withdrawal, Fujimori maintained that he had not won the race as a *"candidato único"* (single candidate). He insisted that the OAS mission had not unearthed any systematic evidence of fraud either in the first round or in the days leading up to the second round.[28] In his first postelection interview on Monday night with Spanish-language CNN, Fujimori reiterated his position and unequivocally asserted that his reelection was "legal and legitimate."

Confronting the Critics

Just before the election, Francisco Tudela derided the growing international outcry over the second round as politicized and "hysterical."[29] The election did not end the controversy. On the contrary, Eduardo Stein's hasty departure back to Washington DC before the election virtually ensured a contentious debate back at the OAS. Backing off his attack rhetoric, Tudela reverted to a line that the administration had used before—the Peruvian government was woefully misunderstood. Tudela confessed to the press that he had failed to communicate effectively with the international community during the campaign. That's why, he explained, foreign observers succumbed to the misinformation being spread by Toledo and left-wing NGOs.[30]

In a nationwide broadcast on May 29, Fujimori similarly stated that a "campaign of demonization and disinformation" had been waged to discredit the election. But his adamant refusal to concede that anything improper had taken place in the course of the election was now accompanied by new promises. He pledged to "correct mistakes, for the purpose of strengthening democratic institutions." His third term would mark the beginning of "the most authentic democratization of the country."[31] Fujimori's promises to democratize were like those he had made in 1992, when it became obvious that concessions were required to placate the international community.

Fujimori had reason to be concerned about international reaction in the days immediately following May 28. An ominous, but anonymous, declaration by a U.S. State Department official on Monday, May 29 had gone so far as to characterize the election as "invalid." American officials toned down the rhetoric the next day, characterizing the elections as "flawed" instead of "invalid."[32] But even if the United States and OAS stopped short of demanding a new election per se, the prospect of continued international meddling and monitoring of Peru's internal affairs certainly was not attractive to anyone inside the Fujimori government. As in 1992, Fujimori and his cabinet ministers realized that they would have to act to contain and manage the demands that were likely to emerge from the OAS deliberations, scheduled to begin with the first MOE report to be delivered by Eduardo Stein on May 31. Fujimori's announcement of the "authentic democratization" was the first volley in the effort to preempt, mollify, and limit any future OAS project that might lord over Peru's political institutions.

Stein delivered his report to the Permanent Council of the OAS in Washington DC on May 31. He recited the litany of problems featured in MOE's periodic *boletines* that had so irritated Peruvian officials. Overshadowing everything was the government's decision not to postpone the second round to allow MOE's review of the computer software. Stein reiterated MOE's conclusion: that the election was "far from being considered as free and fair" by prevailing international standards. As unflattering as the report was, Stein did not have a "smoking gun"; he had no incontrovertible evidence that an election-day fraud had taken place. Stein later revealed that he had plenty of personal reasons to suspect wrongdoing in the election. He knew that his operation was under SIN surveillance.[33] But Stein had no concrete proof that vote tampering had taken place in the first-round election. The most damning evidence—the videotapes leaked to Fabian Salazar that showed the meetings of Montesinos with election officials—disappeared in the robbery and attack on Salazar.

Stein referred to "deficiencies, irregularities, inconsistencies, and inequities" in the election, but his reticence to apply the word "fraud" gave Peruvian government officials the opening they needed to mount their defense.[34] Peru's ambassador to the OAS, Beatriz Ramacciotti, vigorously defended the legality of the election. Then she sought to discredit MOE with attacks on Stein. She accused Stein of overstepping his jurisdiction as an observer and "intervening" into the electoral process by issuing his bulletins and appearing with Transparencia officials in their news conference after the first round.

Neither Ramacciotti's aggressive defense nor her attempt to discredit Stein shut down the OAS debate. Looking for some leverage to force concessions, U.S. ambassador Luis Laredo proposed that the Peruvian election be discussed within the framework of OAS Resolution 1080. This was the 1991 resolution authorizing the OAS to adopt "any decisions deemed appropriate" when a member country is deemed to have undergone "any occurrences giving rise to the sudden or irregular interruption of the democratic political institutional process."[35] But few Latin American countries were prepared to punish Peru, especially with controversial presidential elections in the offing in Venezuela and Mexico. The Brazilian ambassador joined with his Mexican and Venezuelan counterparts to fend off Laredo's proposal, and a compromise followed. The council voted to continue deliberations on the Peruvian situation in the June meeting of the OAS general assembly, slated to meet in Windsor, Ontario.

Facing yet another unpleasant round of scrutiny in Windsor, Fujimori and his cabinet members spoke effusively of their plans for democratic reform. In anticipation of the Windsor meeting, they announced the creation of a commission to strengthen democracy, manned by several cabinet ministers and Vice President–elect Francisco Tudela.[36] Fujimori outlined the reforms purported to be under consideration and, astonishingly, almost all of the government's controversial measures now appeared to be on the table for reconsideration. Fujimori claimed that the Tribunal Constitucional would be reconstituted, that the legal case against Baruch Ivcher would be shelved and ownership of his television station would be restored, and that the SIN would be downsized. Even more surprisingly, Fujimori suggested that Montesinos should come forward and publicly respond to questions about his role and activities in the government.[37]

Foreign Minister Fernando de Trazegnies took the lead in trying to derail the OAS debate on Peru in the general assembly meeting in Windsor. De Trazegnies reminded the delegates that Stein had not produced concrete evidence of fraud. He urged OAS delegates to shelve the "sterile discussion of a non-existent fraud" and reiterated the government's commitment to a broad plan of democratic reforms.[38]

But de Trazegnies's lobbying to shut down the discussion of Peru altogether fell short. The OAS's own Inter-American Commission on Human Rights weighed in with a report that concluded the electoral process in Peru did, in fact, "constitute a clear irregular interruption of the democratic process" and called for new elections.[39] Former U.S. president Jimmy Carter concurred with the call for new elections and sent a letter to the OAS meeting.[40] Joining in the intense jockeying at Windsor was Toledo's designated "truth squad," composed of Peruvian legislators Lourdes Flores, Diego García Sayán, and Anel Townsend. Sofía Macher and Ernesto de la Jara of Peru's respected Coordinadora Nacional de Derechos Humanos and Transparencia's Rafael Roncagliolo were also on hand in the effort to counter de Trazegnies.

The United States had floated the idea of invoking Resolution 1080 as a way of increasing the pressure on Peru, but the U.S. State Department officials assembled at Windsor were not pushing for a new election. Instead, they pieced together support for a proposal that would subject the Fujimori government to continued OAS scrutiny on issues related to democratic reforms. De Trazegnies had little choice but to accept. The OAS meeting concluded with a vote to send a new OAS mission to Peru to aid in "strengthening democratic institutions." The designations of OAS secretary-general César Gaviría and Canadian foreign minister Lloyd Axworthy were thought to lend weight to the project, making it more difficult for the government to brush it off.

That the OAS had not specifically invoked Resolution 1080 or called for a new election was cause for relief inside the Fujimori administration. On the other hand, there was no telling exactly where the OAS mission was headed or what kinds of demands it might make. Axworthy ruffled feathers in Lima when he declared that Peru's political future was "up to Peruvians" and would depend on Peru's congress to decide. That the OAS mission might somehow kick open the door to a process eventually leading to a new election, or replacing the president, could not be ruled out. Almost before the ink dried on the Windsor resolution, the official campaign to downplay the new OAS mission and offer a minimalist interpretation of its mandate began. Fujimori underscored that the mission had no mandate to review the recent election and that its job was to "look to the future" and help explore the prospects for institutional reform.[41] In a similar vein, de Trazegnies concluded that there was "nothing left to say" about the elections and that the OAS mission was simply one of "cooperation."[42]

All the government's glowing talk about Peru's democratic future was delivered in tandem with an unequivocal message: the regime was intact and Fujimori had no intention of relinquishing the presidency anytime soon, no matter what the OAS mission said or what the local opposition did. Fujimori, Montesinos, and the armed forces made the point loud and clear on June 8, right after the Windsor meeting. General José Villanueva Ruesta, chief of the armed forces high command, led troops in a ceremony swearing the allegiance of the armed forces to President Fujimori as commander-in-chief for the period 2000–2005. Montesinos looked on from the reviewing stand as Fujimori declared that Peru's political stability depended on "respect for the will of the people who cast their ballot for the government, with a majority in the first and second round." The timing of the ceremony was unprecedented since usually the event was scheduled only after a president was sworn in by congress on July 28. The opposition newspaper *Liberación* rendered its reading of the event in a stinging front-page headline: "Tanks 1, OAS 0."[43]

César Gavíria and Lloyd Axworthy arrived in Lima in late June to inaugurate the latest OAS mission to Peru. Rounds of meetings with government and opposition representatives produced a list of twenty-nine issues designated as priorities for democratic reform. If the reforms were indeed implemented, all the mechanisms that had kept the regime in place since 1992 (the control of the judiciary, the manipulation of the media, the SIN) would have to be dismantled.

Talking about reforms was one matter, but implementing them was another. Fujimori and Montesinos knew a great deal about the distance between talk and action. If the post-1992 interregnum were an example of OAS oversight, then they would have many opportunities for obfuscating and altering, or simply ignoring, the content of any proposed OAS reforms.

After a decade of watching Fujimori in power, opposition leaders were similarly versed in the disjunction between rhetoric and reality. Like Fujimori, they had reason to doubt that the OAS-sponsored talks would propel real change. Opposition leaders knew that high-minded discussions in a luxury hotel would not roust Fujimori from office. They knew that the talks had to be backed up with something more palpable, with actions to show the government and the OAS that lots of Peruvians rejected the reelection.

Not far from the luxurious Swiss Hotel where Gavíria and Axworthy set up shop, hundreds of women gathered in the streets. Symbolically mourning the death of democracy in Peru, they dressed in black. Police appeared and tear-gassed the crowd. Among the demonstrators choking in the gas that night was Eliane Karp, the wife of Alejandro Toledo.

The Third Round

Until April 2000, the opposition in Peru had no single star, no one leader who stood toe-to-toe with Fujimori. Fujimori's opponents came from across the spectrum of public life. At different junctures since 1992, congressional leaders, mayors, journalists, intellectuals, and professionals from a swathe of nongovernmental organizations all played important roles in the struggle against the regime.

By nearly beating Fujimori in the first round and by upsetting the second round with his withdrawal, Alejandro Toledo emerged as the de facto leader of the opposition. During the tense days after the first round, he had risen to the occasion. Tapping into the public's anger and frustration, Toledo called on Peruvians to join him in the streets. Many did.

The principal opposition leaders closed ranks with Toledo after the first and second rounds of the election, setting aside private doubts about Toledo's character at least momentarily. Inside Lima's political circles, Toledo was not well regarded or even liked. Prior to the 2000 election, he had not been a vocal critic of Fujimori nor had he worked on the opposition's major project, the referendum campaign to stop the reelection. As a professional economist, he was considered to be an intellectual lightweight, prone to gilding his résumé. His volatile personal life was rumored to include alcohol and drug abuse, along with sexual escapades. Indeed, immediately after the first round, Eliane Karp was assigned the unenviable task of preempting a scandal. She explained that television stations were poised to broadcast videotapes featuring her husband engaged in sex acts with prostitutes.[44] The tapes never aired. Still, questions about Toledo's character persisted. In the minds of some, Toledo seemed unstable, hotheaded, and too radical. The photographs of Toledo sporting his red bandana and leading protestors to the presidential palace on the night of April 9 made conservative middle-class *limeños* cringe, and left U.S. officials wondering about Toledo's temperament. Montesinos stoked the public's fears by directing the tabloids and television to hype negative stories on Toledo. The media responded with reports that Toledo was a violent left-winger and a deadbeat dad who refused to recognize his out-of-wedlock child.

Nevertheless, as the candidate famously wronged by Fujimori, Toledo was the center of attention. He was the obvious figure to spearhead the national and international campaign against the regime. Toledo wasted no time in assuming the mantle. On the evening of the second round, Toledo told the thousands of supporters in the Plaza de Armas that he would lead a campaign of nonviolent resistance to the reelection, in the style of Gandhi. He said it was time for *la tercera vuelta*—the third round.

On the following day, Toledo announced plans for an ambitious mass march to protest the inauguration of President Fujimori on July 28. The event was evocatively titled La Marcha de los Cuatro Suyos (March of the Four Corners), a reference to the four cardinal points of the Inca empire. To keep the march and himself in the spotlight, Toledo surrounded himself with a media "dream team" of advisors. Gustavo Gorriti, the prizewinning journalist who served as Toledo's press chief for the second round, stayed on as head of Toledo's "war room" headquartered in Hotel Cesár's in

Miraflores. Also part of the inner circle was Álvaro Vargas Llosa. Like his famous father, novelist Mario Vargas Llosa, Álvaro was an acerbic critic of the Fujimori administration.[45]

Everyone in the opposition agreed that, in order to keep the pressure on the government and on the OAS, mass mobilization had to continue. The public support for Toledo that was evidenced in the first and second rounds needed to be tapped by the opposition and integrated into a political strategy aimed at creating the conditions for unraveling the regime. On May 31, eleven political organizations joined with major trade union organizations in denouncing the second round as a fraud. They called for peaceful resistance to the regime and a new election.[46] Coordination among parties, social movements, trade unions, regional associations, and Toledo's organization to promote the *marcha* got underway. Former presidential candidate and Lima mayor Alberto Andrade endorsed the march. Carlos Bruce, a leader in Andrade's political organization Somos Perú, came onboard as national director of the *marcha*.

Calling for a new election was the obvious demand for the opposition to make. Deciding on exactly what political strategy was most likely to produce that result was the puzzle. Initially, Toledo was vague on the subject of how a political transition should be pursued. He called for a new election to be staged within two months, but said that he was open to discussion of routes to an eventual election. Speculation inside the opposition focused at first on the prospects for an OAS-brokered "Balaguer solution." That was the deal struck after a fraudulent presidential reelection in the Dominican Republic in 1994. The OAS and former U.S. president Jimmy Carter brokered an agreement with President Balaguer to cut short his term in office and hold new elections in 1996.

Hopes for a "Balaguer solution," at least in the immediate run, dimmed by the end of June. Despite Eduardo Stein's negative report on the election, the Fujimori administration had successfully warded off an OAS mission with an explicit mandate to seek a new election. Instead, what the opposition had in hand was the twenty-nine-item list of democratic reforms that the Gavíria-Axworthy mission designated as priorities for an OAS-led dialogue between the government and opposition. Toledo always maintained that he was ready to work with the OAS, but he did not hide his skepticism. He frequently alluded to the importance of "not putting all the eggs" in the basket of the OAS. After the second round, he traveled to Europe to cultivate contacts with EU leaders.

Without an OAS- or American-led push for a new election, the opposition looked for leverage elsewhere. La Marcha de los Cuatro Suyos was one way of showing the Fujimori administration and the world that Peruvians were fed up and ready to challenge the legitimacy of the regime. But overthrowing the regime would take more than a single march. As they had in the past, opponents considered legal strategies. Congressman Fernando Olivera pointed out two possibilities. One option was to launch a new referendum campaign to challenge the results of the election. The other option was to use a provision in the constitution that allowed congress to remove a president from office on the grounds of "moral incapacity."[47]

Once again, the congress was set to become a battleground. Montesinos went to work to make sure that congress was under control. Montesinos could not know that he was about to set a trap for himself and the regime that he had so diligently crafted.

Turncoats and Moles

Montesinos's grand plan had not gone well. He had accomplished his mission of reelecting the president, but there were still too many loose ends. Fujimori could look forward to months, if not years, of continued scrutiny by the OAS. Then there was the real prospect of ongoing confrontations with a more mobilized, combative opposition.

April 9 produced another important, immediate problem that required fixing. The congressional elections, run concurrently with the first round of the presidential election, produced 52 seats for the president's Perú 2000 organization. The number fell short of the absolute majority the government previously enjoyed.[48] Theoretically, if they worked together, the remaining political organizations elected to congress could constitute a majority. They held 68 out of the overall total of 120 seats in the unicameral congress.

The chances were not good that the opposition could secure a stable majority in the congress. Many of those elected were motivated primarily by their own ambitions, and they had no real commitments to the parties or movements with which they affiliated in order to get on the ballot. If previous experience was a guide, many legislators could be convinced to jump ship and either formally affiliate with the Perú 2000 caucus or vote with it, if the enticements were sufficient. Montesinos later maintained that Fujimori directly gave the order to begin "Operation Recruitment" in order to secure the votes needed to keep the congress under control. Montesinos said that he regularly briefed Fujimori on the details of Operation Recruitment.[49]

The operation was nothing new for Montesinos. He had been paying off judges, election officials, and other assorted politicians for years. With the help of his military cronies and other advisors, Montesinos identified the candidates who were most likely to be persuaded and invited each to a meeting in his office at the SIN. As the prospective client sunk into the beige leather sofa, Montesinos made his pitch, offering money and favors in return for the promise that the legislator would join the government caucus. Some legislators needed little coaxing to sign up as *tránsfugas* (turncoats, as the opposition labeled them). Others were more reticent to be so blatantly allied with the government right after the reelection, and opted instead to be among the *topos* (moles who passed on information about the congressional opposition and who could be counted on to be absent when the opposition needed votes). Montesinos found plenty of collaborators, though at least a few of the invitees had the fortitude to decline.

But, for most, the offers were hard to refuse. As if recruiting major-league sports figures, Montesinos offered "sign-up" bonuses to legislators ranging from reimbursements for campaign expenses to the cost of a new car or a Lima apartment and the furnishings to go with it. Those perks came in addition to the monthly bribes that ranged from ten to twenty thousand dollars, which Montesinos pledged would continue until the end of the president's term in 2005. Under those terms, an individual legislator could look forward to earnings of as much as one million dollars or more in addition to his/her regular salary and perks.

To ensure the required return on his investments, Montesinos made his newfound clients sign an "honor pledge" confirming their commitment, just as he had them sign receipts for the payments they received. To make sure that the legislators were not fudging the records, Montesinos had the legislators' signatures verified against other official documents.[50] And, as the legislators found out later, the meetings in Montesinos's office were videotaped. Montesinos carefully documented their corruption, and in the course of doing so, his own.

By the time that the new congress was set to begin its term, Montesinos had secured more than enough votes to control all the key positions and to protect Fujimori from any legislative effort to remove him. The smashing success of Operation Recruitment was evident in the vote for congressional offices held in late July. Leading the Perú 2000 slate, Congresswoman Martha Hidelbrandt was elected as the president of congress. The seventy votes cast for the Perú 2000 slate was proof positive that the corruption worked, and that Montesinos had fabricated an absolute majority for Perú 2000 when the election had not produced one.

Operation Recruitment was, of course, meant to be a secret. But the results were hard to hide. With legislators ditching their political organizations to switch to Perú 2000 or become "independents," it was no great leap to assume that something was amiss. Several members of Toledo's Perú Posible caucus who turned down the bribes confirmed that they had been approached. But the defecting legislators kept up the front, insisting that they were motivated by a suddenly discovered affinity with the government. Congressman Alberto Kouri, a dropout from Perú Posible, said his decision was motivated by a desire to promote "governability and stability," and with the hope that his cooperation with the government would allow him to continue his "efficient and effective social work" with the poor.[51] Kouri howled when Toledo publicly accused him of accepting a $160,000 bribe and filed a defamation suit against Toledo.

Operation Recruitment worked, but with trickery so evident that it generated a backlash. The independent media covered the story extensively, chronicling the growing roster of *tránsfugas* and *topos*. One measure of public awareness was how rapidly the topic became grist for satirists and comics. One popular joke told of a meeting of legislators in downtown Lima. Cries of "Traitor! Turncoat! Mole! Sellout!" ring out. One passerby asks another: "Are the legislators arguing?" "No," the other man replies, "that's the roll call."

Enraged at the deceit, opposition legislators vented their anger at the swearing-in ceremony for the new congress in late July. As Kouri and the other defectors filed to the front of the hall to take their oaths of office, opposition legislators hurled coins at them and chanted, "Traitor." Congresswoman Martha Chávez led *oficialistas* in equally insulting taunts of opposition leaders. But the word *tránsfuga* was now entrenched in Lima's political lexicon. In the eyes of many, the presidency and the congress were the products of fraud. The day after the fractious swearing-in, *La República*'s banner headline referred to the "illegitimate majority" in congress and declared: "The Fraud Is Sealed."

All the election and postelection gyrations took their toll on the public's views of Fujimori and the regime. More Peruvians registered disapproval of the president's job performance than approval. One Lima poll showed that 54 percent of interviewees believed that the presidential election results did not accurately reflect the will of the electorate. In the same survey, 53 percent of the public favored either a shortening of Fujimori's term in office or holding new elections immediately. When asked whether the government intended to make good on the promises of democratization, 51 percent said no.[52]

It was an inglorious start to the president's third term. Peruvians contemplated a government born of a scandalous election, run by unscrupulous people. They did not like it, and many were ready to make those feelings known through something other than a poll.

La Marcha de los Cuatro Suyos

Organizers conceptualized La Marcha de los Cuatro Suyos as a dramatic challenge to the government's claim of democratic legitimacy and its arrogant exercise of power. They hoped that the sight of thousands of defiant citizens on the streets would keep international attention focused on Peru, and ratchet up the pressure on the government to make real concessions in the OAS-directed talks on democratic reforms scheduled to start in August.

In the weeks after the second round, the streets of Lima showcased the changing public mood. Groups in civil society organized to protest the reelection. While most of the groups had small memberships, they were active, and their creativity in organizing striking symbolic protests was notable. The Frente Democrático Nacional de Mujeres brought together a number of women's groups that staged protests. Sociedad Civil, a group composed mostly of artists, staged a weekly flag-washing ritual in front of the presidential palace, welcoming passersby to join in. Resistencia, an umbrella organization for protestors, created the *Muro de Verguenza* (Wall of Shame). It was a mural of government officials on which the public was invited to add messages and graffiti. The same group also promoted the "Minute of Resistance," a Friday-night event staged in the center of Miraflores in which people honked their car horns and beat on pots and pans to protest the reelection.[53] Young people turned to the Internet to express their resistance to the reelection; more than 350 Web sites were linked in a clearinghouse site called "Opposition."[54]

As the opposition worked toward staging its greatest spectacle of resistance, La Marcha de los Cuatro Suyos, Montesinos countered with a strategy to thwart the protest and smear its leaders. To keep the number of protestors down, he directed police to impede traffic en route to Lima.[55] Montesinos directed a media campaign to generate distrust and fear. The *prensa chicha* launched more attacks on Toledo. The idea was to blame Toledo and the opposition for anything that might go wrong during the *marcha*. Banner headlines accused Toledo of being in cahoots with narco-traffickers. The newspapers claimed that Toledo was masterminding a plan to loot and burn the downtown and that he wanted people to die in the *marcha* in the hope of embarrassing the government. Toledo and his advisors, in turn, warned the press that the government was likely to plant troublemakers to disrupt the *marcha* and incite violence. But not even Toledo could have guessed how accurate the *prensa chicha* was in telegraphing Montesinos's plan. The dire predictions of looting, fire, and death came true.

The *marcha* was planned as three days of protest to coincide with Fujimori's inauguration on July 28. The events began on Wednesday, July 26. Labor unions rallied downtown, while a women's march brought thousands of female protestors to the Plaza Bolognesi. Amid the festive crowd were students on stilts, outfitted in white, carrying signs with the unofficial slogan of the *marcha*: "¡Democracia Ya!" (Democracy Now!) Clowns joined the stilt-walkers with banners reading *"Fujimori es un payaso"* (Fujimori is a clown).

By Thursday, protestors from across Peru were streaming into the four camps in central Lima that had been constructed to house them during the event. The attendees represented trade unions, peasant associations, youth groups, and political organizations. Many protestors told stories of the difficulties that they had encountered en route. Anticipating confrontations with the police, many came with homemade gas masks fashioned out of empty plastic soda bottles.

On Thursday night, the protestors paraded from the camps to the Paseo de la República, stopping in front of the Sheraton Hotel. There was a reviewing stand, flanked by huge television screens. Opposition leaders greeted and cheered the groups from the stand as they filed by in parade. An estimated 250,000 demonstrators were on hand for the evening's events of music and speeches. They listened as a twelve-year-old girl, dressed in a white gown, led an oath pledging allegiance to the struggle for democracy in Peru. Alejandro Toledo spoke last, closing the evening with a call for new elections, the restitution of the Tribunal Constitucional, and getting rid of Vladimiro Montesinos. He urged supporters to join in the "peaceful resistance" to Fujimori's inauguration on the following morning, including a march on congress and the presidential palace.

Meanwhile, the government was working on its own version of the week's news. Hoping to overshadow the start of the demonstrations and project the new image of reform, Fujimori announced the appointment of Federico Salas, mayor of Huancavelica, as his new head of the cabinet. Months earlier, Salas had been among the pack of presidential contenders challenging Fujimori in the first round and denouncing the SIN as the "Gestapo." On the streets, demonstrators were unimpressed and mocked Salas as yet another *tránsfuga*.

While Canal N provided live coverage of the *marcha* activities, broadcast television limited coverage to news snippets and critical commentaries. In the newspapers, *Expreso* countered celebratory accounts by *Liberación* and *La República* with gloomy coverage and photos that suggested a meager turnout for the *marcha*. An official ban on helicopter flights over Lima ensured that neither local nor international news organizations would have aerial shots showing thousands of protestors in attendance. On the morning of Fujimori's inaugural on July 28, all television cameras, except for those of Canal N, were trained on the official ceremonies, not on the altercations taking place in the streets nearby.

Despite the government's effort to put the best face on its ceremonies, it was a sour inauguration day. The poor celebrity turnout for the day's events reflected the international unease with the reelection. Apart from the regular diplomatic corps in residence in Peru, few high-ranking dignitaries showed up. Only President Gustavo Noboa of Ecuador and President Hugo Banzer of Bolivia made fleeting appearances.

By the time of the first official event—the traditional Te Deum Mass in Lima's downtown cathedral—police were battling scattered groups of demonstrators with tear gas and water cannons. The gas wafted through the cathedral. Archbishop Juan Luis Cipriani used his homily to make a not-so-veiled reference to Montesinos and the SIN: "There is an immense tutelary power over which the people have no control, and the absence of accountability generates a suffocating oppression that we are obliged to stand up to."[56]

The inaugural ceremony, set in the main hall of congress, was unruly. Opposition legislators greeted Fujimori with catcalls and homemade placards. Congressman Jorge del Castillo donned a gas mask in an obvious reference to the events transpiring outside. When Fujimori began his address, the opposition legislators walked out to join the embattled protestors.

What the legislators found outside was chaos. Toledo and other organizers, equipped with gas masks, were zigzagging through the streets in the company of protestors, but they had no apparent plan about how to deal with the aggressive police tactics or what to do in the confusion. In scattered locations downtown, vandals attacked buildings. The Palacio de Justicia, Banco de la Nación, and the Jurado Nacional de Elecciones were on fire. Terrified employees at the Jurado were able to escape. But the Banco collapsed, leaving six employees dead in the blaze. Later in the day, mobs attacked the offices of television stations Channel 4 and Channel 5.[57]

The violence was shocking. Equally disturbing was the slow response by police and firefighters. Viewers of Canal N watched for forty minutes while the Palacio de Justicia was torched, with no police in evidence. As the fire at the Banco de la Nación blazed out of control, Canal N and CPN Radio reporters pleaded on the air for firemen to rescue the people inside.

The official inaugural luncheon was canceled. Fujimori disappeared for the remainder of the day. On the day after, Fujimori came out swinging. Montesinos was on hand to watch. Addressing a luncheon of the top military brass, Fujimori blasted the *marcha*'s organizers as dangerous leftist terrorists and explicitly accused them of planning to burn down the congress during the inauguration.[58] Fujimori's comments signaled that criminal indictments of Toledo and his associates could be on the way. The minister of the interior, General Walter Chacón, showed up in congress with a videotape in hand. It was full of news clips and police footage. Chacón made a case that Alejandro Toledo, Eliane Karp, and other organizers were guilty of inciting violence in their speeches, not only on the day of the *marcha* but also well in advance of the event.[59] Congresswoman Martha Moyano of Perú 2000 filed charges against Toledo for instigating the homicides and the property damage in the *marcha*.

The attack was intended for international as well as local consumption. With the OAS-sponsored "dialogue" on democratic reforms scheduled to begin in August, administration officials believed that smearing Toledo might be a way of marginalizing or perhaps completely eliminating him and his Perú Posible organization from the proceedings. Cabinet president Federico Salas suggested that the OAS "evaluate" Toledo's behavior and prospective standing as a participant in the OAS talks. Minister of Justice José Alberto Bustamante was even more blunt about where he thought the opposition stood, observing that it would "be difficult to sit down with people who walk out of Congress and go to burn public buildings."[60]

Toledo countercharged that the SIN masterminded the sinister events of July 28 to discredit the opposition. According to the *marcha* organizers, SIN personnel worked with vandals while the police were ordered to stand back and let the violence get out of control. Toledo speculated that the collapse of the Banco de la Nación was caused by dynamite stored inside the building and called for an independent investigation of the fire.

The attempt to eliminate Toledo and Perú Posible from the OAS proceedings fell flat. In an August visit to Lima, OAS secretary-general César Gavíria dismissed the idea of criminal wrongdoing by Toledo, alluding to the tarnished record of the judiciary. He said that he presumed Toledo and other *marcha* organizers to be innocent of criminal accusations in the absence of any findings to the contrary from an "impartial and independent investigation."[61]

No one really expected to see an independent investigation of the events of July 28. It would have turned up exactly what Montesinos labored to hide. After the regime fell, the national chief of police, Fernando Dianderas, admitted that the opposition's suppositions about what had happened were correct, that SIN agents had infiltrated the *marcha* and recruited vandals for the violence.[62]

The reelection project was inelegant, but it worked. When the ruckus subsided, Alberto Fujimori was at his desk in the presidential palace. And just in case OAS officials or anyone else hoped otherwise, Fujimori reminded all that he planned to be there until his retirement in 2005.

Montesinos had no imminent plans to retire either; he was already thinking about the 2005 election. Fujimori was getting old and tired, and Montesinos looked forward to handpicking a successor.[63] Montesinos believed that he had hit on a winning formula that could be endlessly reproduced by virtue of his control over congress, the judiciary, the military, and the media. With or without Fujimori, the regime could on and so could he. At least that was the plan.

10

FUJIMORI FALLING

AFTER a decade in power, Alberto Fujimori was still standing. When he took the presidential oath for the first time in 1990, Fujimori was a political novice. No one knew for sure where the president and his government were headed. By the time Fujimori swore his third oath as president, Peru's political trajectory was painfully clear. Analysts from the CIA, Freedom House, and other organizations came to the same conclusion: Fujimori's presidency had circumvented democratic institutions and practices.[1] Eduardo Stein's OAS election report delivered a stinging confirmation of Peru's political degeneration. By failing to meet the minimal standards of a free and fair election, Peru flunked the basic litmus test of democracy.

Whenever foreign observers decried the demise of democracy in Peru, Fujimori dismissed them as wrong-headed or misinformed. According to the president, if abuses had occurred, then misguided supporters were to blame. Peruvian democracy was imperfect and unconsolidated, Fujimori conceded, but that would be remedied with his agenda of democratic reforms.

When Fujimori justified the 1992 coup as a way to renew Peruvian democracy, his promise was fresh. By 2000, the rhetoric was tired and, more importantly, implausible. As hard as Montesinos labored to control people and information, he could not manipulate everyone and everything all of the time. Though relentlessly distorted by SIN operations, Peru's public sphere was still a "wild complex." Occasionally the truth slipped out in unexpected ways and with undesirable consequences for the government. In an era of globalization, the uncomfortable truths traveled beyond Peru's borders. Baruch Ivcher took his complaints to the U.S. Congress, the impeached magistrates took their case to the Inter-American Court of Human Rights in Costa Rica, and repressed journalists found colleagues in New York and London who took up the cause of press freedom in Peru. At home, more Peruvians found alternative views on cable television, talk radio, the Internet, and in the defiant journalism of *Liberación, La República,* and *Caretas.*

The re-reelection mess had left, if not a catastrophic crisis of credibility and legitimacy, a lingering miasma hanging over the body politic. At least half of the country believed that the elections were tainted. When asked if the elections were "fair," 50 percent of respondents said they were not, and 62 percent maintained that Fujimori had not competed on a "level playing field" with other candidates. In a subsequent survey, 62 percent of respondents remained skeptical about Fujimori's promised reforms, concluding that the situation would stay the same or get worse; only 26 percent expressed confidence that a "democratic opening" was possible.[2] Noting the state of public opinion, the Carter Center–NDI mission issued a final report, arguing that the Peruvian government was "facing a crisis of legitimacy" as a result of the election process that "failed dramatically to meet the minimum international standards."[3]

Did the apparent erosion of the regime's credibility and legitimacy really matter? From the viewpoint of the Fujimori administration in August 2000, the answer was probably not, or at least not as much as opponents insisted it did. Fujimori and Montesinos had weathered every previous crisis. They had no reason to think that they could not keep on doing the same. The armed forces were still on board. And thanks to the *tránsfugas,* the congress was under control. The reelection had made the opposition more visible and mobilized, but domestic dissent still appeared manageable. The dreadful conclusion of La Marcha de los Cuatro Suyos and the absence of any clear evidence as to who was to blame gave Montesinos material with which to pummel the opposition in the tabloids and on television. Given the public's unhappiness with the outcome of the *marcha,* it was unlikely that opposition leaders would be able to muster widespread support for more demonstrations, at least in the short run.

On the international side, Fujimori and Montesinos had grown accustomed to the tongue-lashings from human rights organizations, journalists, and even the U.S. Congress. They had wagered correctly that neither the OAS nor the American government would be willing to take proactive measures to undo the reelection. Eduardo Stein had not produced the proverbial smoking gun.

When a smoking gun was discovered, however, it changed everything. In the face of incontrovertible evidence, the well-worn routines of denial no longer sufficed. Suddenly, the government's lack of credibility and legitimacy mattered a great deal.

The Montesinos Problem

Montesinos thought of himself as a workaholic living in the shadows; the archetypal intelligence specialist laboring behind the scenes for the good of his country. He told acquaintances that he lived ten years of his life sequestered in the SIN, that he had sacrificed his youth, his family, and his personal life for his job. "For those of us who work in intelligence," he mused, "our recognition is the recognition of silence. It's the satisfaction of silence. . . . We don't look for our names in the plazas. . . . You can't go out and say this or that is going on. You have to keep quiet."[4]

Montesinos loved the man-of-mystery image, but he never actually fit the profile. Although he rarely appeared in public, Montesinos was well known and widely feared. In 1992, Montesinos debuted in the twelfth slot of *Debate*'s annual ranking of the most powerful people in Peru. By 1993, he ranked as the second most important person in Peru, following Fujimori. He retained that rating through 2000.

Montesinos always attracted attention. His checkered background as a cashiered military officer and his reputed associations with drug dealers and the CIA made him an attractive target for Peru's investigative reporters. Once they started digging, they tied Montesinos to virtually every major scandal of the administration. *Caretas* dubbed him "Fujimori's Rasputin" in 1991, and later *La República* called him "Fujimori's Svengali." The critical coverage intensified after questions about Montesinos's income and his alleged links to drug trafficking resurfaced in 1996.[5]

Montesinos never responded publicly to all the questions about his conduct. He relied on his retinue of military and cabinet officials to defend him. Fujimori routinely sang his praises. When Montesinos showed up in public, it was to attend events that identified him with the armed forces and the administration's accomplishments in combating terrorism and narco-trafficking.

Montesinos had good reason to highlight those accomplishments. He understood the American foreign policy establishment and its ardent interest in combating armed insurgency and drug trafficking. Those objectives were embodied in the Clinton administration's Plan Colombia, the multimillion-dollar aid package aimed at quashing the guerrilla war and the drug trade in Colombia. As long as Peru was viewed as a staunch ally and supporter of the U.S. plan, Montesinos figured that Fujimori's presidency and his own career were safe.[6] Whining by the *New York Times* or bad reviews from Eduardo Stein would not be enough, Montesinos believed, to dislodge him or his president.

Montesinos was confident in his ability to handle U.S. officials; he had a long history of dealing with them. At the start of his military career, Montesinos cultivated contacts with the American embassy in Lima. He made his first trip to the United States thanks to an International Visitors' Leader Grant from the American embassy.[7] That visit ended his military career in 1976, when he was abruptly ordered back to Peru to face charges of disobedience, falsifying documents, and spying for the United States. After serving his sentence, Montesinos became an attorney known for defending drug traffickers. He rebuilt his network of contacts in the military and the intelligence service.

American officials were acutely aware of Montesinos's influence on President Fujimori. One early U.S. intelligence assessment cited high-ranking Peruvian army officers who characterized Fujimori as being in the "hip pocket of the SIN . . . and particularly influenced by Vladimiro Montesinos."[8] Montesinos and the constant controversy that swirled around him were recurrent subjects in the cable traffic from the U.S. embassy in Lima. It was duly noted that General Alberto Arciniega blasted Montesinos in

1993 and accused him of "destroying the country with the abuse of power."[9] Also noted was a report that Montesinos supervised the torture sessions of the military officers involved in the abortive coup plot of November 1992.[10] American diplomatic and intelligence reports consistently acknowledged the allegations about Montesinos, especially ties to drug trafficking, but concluded that there was no "incontrovertible evidence" that Montesinos was a criminal.[11]

Contrary to the advice of some officials inside the U.S. State Department and the Drug Enforcement Administration who remained suspicious of Montesinos, CIA officials struck a working relationship with him. In 1991, Montesinos was invited to CIA headquarters in Langley, Virginia, to discuss the new counternarcotics programs. The visit set the stage for ongoing collaboration, including a new program that joined the Peruvian military and CIA operatives in the aerial interdiction of drug-trafficking operations.[12] Over the decade, the CIA channeled ten million dollars directly to Montesinos's counternarcotics operations in the SIN.[13]

Montesinos had turned himself into a fact of life, someone that had to be dealt with because he was enormously powerful. In mid-July of 1999, a U.S. embassy cable from Lima described the dynamics: "Montesinos is part of the equation. . . . If Fujimori views Montesinos as a political liability one would not know it from his public statements about his national security advisor. In fact, Fujimori is depending on Montesinos to ensure his re-election . . . there is no one who stands toe-to-toe with Montesinos in the Peruvian government and nothing that the government does on intelligence, enforcement and security issues occurs without his blessing. Like it or not, *he is the go-to guy* short of the president himself on any key issue, particularly any major counter narcotics issue" [emphasis added].[14]

As the "go-to guy" of the administration, Montesinos was understood to be the master planner of the reelection. Everyone believed that he had been behind all the manipulation—from commissioning the tabloid attacks on candidates to directing elaborate campaign spending, to plotting the violent incidents of La Marcha de los Cuatro Suyos. Montesinos was not just a symbol of what was wrong with the government. In the eyes of many in Peru and abroad, he *was* what was wrong—the architect of abuse, corruption, and impunity.

As the OAS high-level mission readied to open the government-opposition discussions on democratic reform in August, the Montesinos issue loomed large. Anticipating the pressures, Fujimori talked about his commitment to reform the SIN. Cabinet president Federico Salas announced a reorganization of the SIN and even changed the organization's name to Central Nacional de Inteligencia (CNI).[15] But in all the official talk about restructuring the intelligence agency, Montesinos's name was conspicuously absent. When Montesinos surfaced, it was to remind everyone of his great achievements and that he was still the go-to guy.

Arms, the OAS, and the United States

Just hours before the scheduled start-up of the OAS talks on August 21, President Fujimori called a formal press conference. Flanked by Montesinos and other high-ranking military officials, Fujimori made a major announcement: the SIN single-handedly had dismantled a major arms-trafficking operation in the region. According to the president, Peruvian intelligence uncovered a smuggling ring selling weapons to the Fuerzas Armadas Revolucionarias de Colombia (FARC), the Marxist guerrillas in Colombia. The ring included low-level retired officers in the Peruvian army and foreigners. Fujimori detailed how the group purchased ten thousand Kalashnikov rifles in Jordan, shipped them to Peru, and later transferred the arms shipment by parachutes across the Colombian border.

The event provided an opening for Fujimori to show his unequivocal support of Montesinos. Fujimori praised Montesinos as the "architect" of the operation, promising that his advisor would continue his work on regional security.[16] When reporters attempted to ask Montesinos questions about the various accusations swirling around him, Fujimori dived in to defend him, insisting that he had not engaged in any wrongdoing. When asked if he would remove Montesinos from his post if requested to do so by the OAS and the opposition, Fujimori insisted that the greatest threats to democracy in Peru and the region were in the realm of security—a response tantamount to no.

The timing of the unusual news conference was no coincidence. Across town at the Hotel Country Club, Eduardo de la Torre was ready to begin the first meeting of the government-opposition "dialogue" on democratic reforms. De la Torre, the former foreign minister of the Dominican Republic, had arrived in Lima as head of the new OAS high-level mission charged with following up on the previous Gavíria-Axworthy mission. His job was to facilitate the talks between the government and opposition representatives and monitor the progress on promised democratic reforms. In the opposition's view, the presidential fanfare was designed to divert public attention from the OAS talks and send a message that there would be no negotiating about the future of Montesinos.

If the point of the presidential news conference was to refurbish the administration's image after the reelection and reestablish Fujimori and Montesinos as leaders in the hemispheric war on terrorism, it backfired terribly. Almost immediately, the official version of events delivered at the press conference came under fire.[17] Jordanian officials maintained that the arms sale was legal and that it was an official transaction with the government of Peru. From the United States, Assistant Secretary of State Thomas Pickering waded in, supporting Jordan's contention that the sale had been a government-to-government transaction.[18] If so, then the arms-smuggling operation had to involve not only retired military officers but also people higher up in the chain of command. The Fujimori administration's great intelligence coup started to look less like a triumph and more like a murky deal leading back to Montesinos. Two of the arms dealers involved in the ring later testified that Montesinos was involved. In retrospect, it appears that Montesinos may have led Fujimori to stage the press conference to try to preempt the discovery of his involvement.[19]

Instead of defusing the controversy about Montesinos, the dubiousness of Fujimori's grand announcement only added to it. In Washington, toleration for Montesinos was slipping away.[20] United States officials did believe, however, that Fujimori and his government could continue to function if Montesinos was removed.[21] National Security Advisor Sandy Berger and Secretary of State Madeleine Albright used the occasion of a United Nations conference in New York to make that case. In a private meeting with Fujimori, they pressed him to make good on his promise to "restructure" the SIN, which was one of the top priorities on the agenda of the OAS dialogue meetings.

Back at the Hotel Country Club, the OAS talks looked as if they were destined to drag on for some time. The government representatives made no dramatic gestures of goodwill or concessions, just vague assurances about being open to dialogue on the designated subjects, including the reform of the SIN. But the old politics-as-usual practiced by *oficialistas*—the foot-dragging, stonewalling, and denial—was about to come to an abrupt end.

The Video Scandal

With investigative reporters digging deeper into the arms trafficking story, Montesinos was vulnerable. For years, Fujimori administration officials had strived to maintain some "plausible deniability" when the government was accused of wrongdoing, even though their explanations became increasingly improbable as the scandals accumulated. Through it all, Montesinos had been successful in making sure that there was no direct documentary evidence to implicate himself, Fujimori, or other key players in criminal conduct. Cognizant of how devastating such evidence would be, Montesinos worked hard to make sure that none would be found. He joked with associates at the SIN about how they would be finished if the truth came out about what they had done.

Despite Montesinos's concern with secrecy and his own security, the SIN was not perfect. Like any bureaucracy, it fell victim to internal intrigues and even sloppiness in its handling of the great stores of information. The scandalous 1997 murder of the intelligence agent Mariela Bareto happened during the SIN's own internal investigation of leaks to *La República* reporters. Other disclosures were embarrassing, and in the case of the near-leak of incriminating videos just days before the May 28 balloting, it could well have proved disastrous were it not for the clandestine operation to recover the tapes.

The sheer scope of the SIN's surveillance operations produced a staggering amount of information. Scores of employees were involved in the surveillance and handling of the materials. As early as 1990, Fujimori authorized extensive wiretapping operations to eavesdrop on the conversations of opponents, media figures, and his own government officials. Montesinos chose Colonel Roberto Huamán to take charge of the operation. Every day, Montesinos received transcripts from the telephone intercepts done by army, navy, and air force intelligence.[22] With Huamán in charge of the SIN video-taping, Montesinos obsessively recorded his own meetings. At Fujimori's request, Huamán also installed videotaping equipment at the presidential palace, and untold numbers of videotapes piled up there. In short, there was no lack of incriminating evidence, and at least some employees at the SIN and the palace had knowledge of and access to the tapes. The problem for opponents had always been getting their hands on such evidence.[23]

The moment that opponents had long awaited came on September 14, 2000. A smoking gun was finally in hand, delivered to the public by legislators of the Frente Independiente Moralizador (FIM). Congressman Fernando Olivera, leader of FIM, called a late-afternoon press conference at the Hotel Bolívar, with two new colleagues at his side. Appropriately, both had a history of serving up bad news for Fujimori. One was Congressman Luis Ibérico, formerly an investigative journalist known for his work on Channel 2's *Contrapunto*. The other colleague was Congresswoman Susana Higuchi, the president's former wife turned political opponent.

As Canal N broadcast live coverage, Olivera played the videotape. The tape showed a windowless office. Seated on the brown leather furniture, two men conversed. One man was Vladimiro Montesinos. The other was Alberto Kouri, perhaps the most talked about *tránsfuga*. He was the congressman who had defected from Toledo's party to join the government caucus, purportedly to advance his social work with the poor.

Montesinos and Kouri were in the middle of making a deal. Montesinos mentioned the date; it was May 5, 2000, less than a month after the first round of the election. They were negotiating when Kouri would defect from the Perú Posible caucus and join the government majority. They settled on a price. Montesinos pulled wads of dollar bills out of an envelope and counted. The stack came to fifteen thousand dollars. Unashamed, Kouri haggled for more. He told Montesinos that he needed to recoup the costs of his congressional campaign, around sixty thousand dollars. "You spend a lot," Montesinos observed. "It's an investment," Kouri replied. Montesinos assured Kouri that he could expect the additional cash within days.[24]

Olivera and Ibérico would not say who had leaked the video to them. They later revealed that they paid their contact US$100,000 for the tape. Peru now had a functional equivalent of the Watergate scandal's "Deep Throat." Rumors were rampant about who was behind the leak. Among the initial suspects was Admiral Humberto Rosas. Rosas, the official head of the SIN, reportedly was tired of taking a backseat to Montesinos and infuriated over the arms-trafficking fiasco.[25] Some analysts believed that the CIA encouraged the leak as payback for Montesinos's entanglement in arms trafficking. It was later revealed that Montesinos's secretary, Matilde Pinchi Pinchi, had implicated herself in testimony to investigators.[26]

The mystery of who betrayed Montesinos paled beside the impact of the video itself. It was a bombshell. In congress, members of the government caucus were speechless, at a loss for how to react. Many of them, including Kouri, fled the building through side doors to avoid the swarm of reporters waiting at the entrance. At the presidential palace, Fujimori watched the video alone and then called a cabinet meeting. Watching from his office in the SIN, Montesinos was initially stunned, then infuriated. "We're fucked," he admitted to aides.[27]

The fifty-six minutes of videotape substantiated what the opposition had been saying for years about the nature of the regime and the extraordinary role that Montesinos played. Unlike previous scandals in which evidence and witnesses could be tampered with, the video was stark, incontrovertible evidence that directly implicated the president's advisor in the corruption of Peru's congress. There was nothing ambiguous in the video —no room for benign interpretation. "How much? How much? . . . You tell me," Montesinos said to Kouri as he counted out the cash.[28]

The televised scandal could not be ignored, especially with the OAS mission laboring over an agenda of democratic reforms. Congressman Olivera called on the opposition to boycott the OAS talks unless Montesinos was removed from his duties immediately. Other opposition members joined in the demand that Fujimori sack Montesinos. Business leaders, Roman Catholic Church officials, and U.S. ambassador John Hamilton called for an immediate, vigorous investigation. The OAS mission issued a statement warning that the viability of the OAS-sponsored dialogue would be in jeopardy if the Peruvian government failed to take effective action to deal with the scandal. The public's outrage poured out into the streets. Demonstrators gathered in front of the palace carrying posters showing Montesinos and Fujimori behind prison bars.

After so many years of relying on Montesinos as his chief political advisor, Fujimori was paralyzed, unsure as to how to react to the crisis unfolding around him. In the two days that followed the video broadcast, Fujimori sat huddled in the presidential palace with cabinet ministers, military officers, and his daughter, First Lady Keiko Sofia. She was tearful and adamant in her advice to her father: Montesinos must go.[29]

Sacking Montesinos—the obvious response to pressures pouring down on the administration—was easier said than done. As Fujimori and so many other *oficialistas* knew, Montesinos truly was the go-to guy; he was the person who managed the interlocking pieces of the regime (judiciary, military, congress, the media) and the day-to-day transactions that kept everything and everyone in place. For Fujimori and the government that remained, the risks involved in forcing Montesinos out were enormous. He seemed both irreplaceable and very scary. There was no one else who could easily replicate the relationships and reproduce the same level of control over the range of institutions and personnel that he had achieved. Moreover, as the leaked video inadvertently demonstrated, Montesinos had a cache of incriminating evidence at his disposal that could be wielded against colleagues and probably the president.

The slim hope that Montesinos might resign voluntarily evaporated quickly. Fujimori ordered cabinet chief Federico Salas to contact Montesinos and discuss his resignation. By the time Salas's call got through, Montesinos was already planning strategies to hunker down and use his power to defend himself. Salas later recalled Montesinos's fury and his chilling threats: "No president, much less a dinky president of a council of ministers has the power to fire me. . . . I have three thousand armed men and if I want to I can stage a coup." Implying that he had men at his command inside the presidential palace, Montesinos told Salas, "If you keep on insisting on this, you won't make it to the front gate of the palace."[30]

Fujimori probably did contemplate the risk of a coup; at least that is what he said later.[31] The two men had been political partners, but they were not friends. Each used the other, and the relationship had served them well. It had produced ten years of power and privilege, but both men kept parts of their lives secret from each other and carved out spheres where the other did not tread. Montesinos's labyrinth of corrupt business deals and kickbacks involved a network of military officers, family members, and other cronies. The president, in turn, kept Montesinos away from his family's activities in controlling charitable donations from Japan and from dealings with certain ministries like the ministry of the presidency. Secrets aside, each man had sufficient information to sink the other; the problem was that they had worked together on so many matters that it would be impossible for each to blame the other for wrongdoing without implicating himself.

Whether Montesinos genuinely believed he was in a position to stage a successful coup or whether the threat was a desperate bluff was never clear.

If it was a fiction, it was a useful one in the course of negotiating his exit. Well before the video scandal, Montesinos had worked with military officials on contingency plans for a coup that would maintain the regime even if Fujimori had to step down or somehow lost to Toledo. After the signature factory scandal in March, the SIN had laid plans for a military coup in the event that the reelection plan had to be ditched. The plan involved a military coup to be staged in the name of seeking "free and fair elections," followed by an interim government by former minister of the economy Carlos Boloña.[32] Later on, Montesinos contemplated a similar plan to prevent the inauguration of Toledo had he won the second round.[33]

Considering the 1992 coup and the recent aborted military coups in Ecuador and Paraguay, Montesinos had to know that the OAS and the United States would condemn a military takeover. Still, he played the part of coup-monger to the hilt. When cabinet chief Federico Salas showed up at SIN headquarters to make the pitch for resignation, Montesinos greeted him with top-ranking military officers standing at his side. The point was taken.

On Friday and Saturday, the president remained incommunicado in the palace, pondering the options with advisors and Keiko Sofia. Meanwhile, Montesinos was making headway on the cover-up. The staff of his favored television program, *Hora 20,* was instructed to put together a report suggesting that the Kouri tape had been altered to appear incriminating. Kouri faced the press, explaining that the money that he had accepted was not a bribe, but a loan. Montesinos even lodged an official request for an investigation of the incident with Attorney General Blanca Nélida Colán. As a longtime protégé of Montesinos, Colán could be counted on to make sure that all charges against Montesinos would be shelved; within days, the investigation was closed.[34] Meanwhile, the faithful government caucus rallied sufficient votes to quash six separate motions by the opposition to refer the Montesinos-Kouri video case to a congressional committee for investigation.

The crisis wound into its third day with no end in sight. Montesinos was still holding out, refusing to cede to Fujimori's ultimatums. While there were signs that some in the military were starting to distance themselves from Montesinos, Fujimori could not gauge whether the armed forces would side with him should he order Montesinos's arrest.[35]

Fujimori finally came to the conclusion that his long-standing relationship with Montesinos was no longer viable. But to fire Montesinos, he had to fire himself, or at least give the appearance that he was doing so. At 9:30 on Saturday evening, a little more than forty-eight hours after the Kouri video aired, Fujimori appeared on television. For the first time, he acknowledged that his ability to govern Peru had been affected by the discord over reelection and the opposition's unwillingness to accept it. Then he made the stunning announcement that he would "deactivate" the SIN, call for new general elections, and turn over power to a new government. "Even though I was elected by a majority of citizens, " Fujimori reflected, "I do not want to be disruptive factor, much less an obstacle to the strengthening of the democratic system."[36] Fujimori pledged that he would not be a candidate in the upcoming election.

Fujimori made no specific mention of Montesinos in his speech, but the message was clear. The president was plotting a prospective exit strategy for himself, and Montesinos would have to figure out his own next move. Fujimori's announcement may not have come as a complete surprise to Montesinos. In the days right after the messy first-round election in April, Montesinos said that Fujimori had floated the idea that he might resign, an option that Montesinos summarily dismissed. Montesinos likened the idea to a captain abandoning his crew on a sinking ship.[37]

A sinking ship was an apt metaphor for what was now taking place— and there was no telling exactly what the two cocaptains of Peru's ship of state were doing. Might Fujimori's offer be a smokescreen to resolve the crisis so that the regime could somehow be recomposed, either with Montesinos somewhere offstage or without him entirely? Fujimori fueled the confusion and speculation in a press conference on Monday, September 18. He told reporters that Montesinos was still in Lima and being afforded special security because, as a leader in the fight against terrorism, Montesinos was a target for assassination. At least officially, Montesinos was not under arrest, nor had he resigned or been fired. Armed forces officials remained conspicuously silent as the rumors of an impending coup multiplied.

With Montesinos's status and whereabouts unknown, there was ample reason for the opposition to doubt the authenticity of the transition offered by Fujimori. There was also reason to wonder if the coup threats were real or a fabricated scare tactic to make the opposition and international observers stop pressuring Fujimori and Montesinos any further. Adding to the uncertainty, Fujimori teased reporters with the suggestion that he might already be planning his presidential comeback for 2006. After the Monday press conference, Fujimori and Keiko Sofía awkwardly hoisted themselves atop the iron gate surrounding the presidential palace to greet supporters. The appearance looked as if Fujimori was ready to campaign again.

For any genuine transition to take place, opposition leaders knew that removing Montesinos was required. Otherwise the vast clientele network loyal to Montesinos could be mobilized to subvert the transition. Opposition legislators announced that they would boycott congress and the OAS dialogue meetings until Montesinos was removed officially from his post. In an emergency visit to Lima, OAS secretary-general Gavíria declared that, at a minimum, Montesinos had to be suspended. On September 20, the armed forces high command finally expressed support for Fujimori and the projected transition.

The tide was turning against Montesinos, but none of his colleagues, including Fujimori, could afford to abandon him altogether. Everyone who had dealt with Montesinos over the years had reason to fear him whether he was in power or not: surely he had more videotapes and embarrassing evidence to wield against those who crossed him. Opposition leaders called for the arrest of Montesinos, while Fujimori and his cabinet worked on arranging an attractive exile. Fujimori authorized a transfer of fifteen million dollars in government funds to Montesinos, ostensibly as a final bonus.[38]

On Saturday night, September 24, Montesinos boarded a private jet in Lima with an entourage of aides and his girlfriend, Jacqueline Beltrán. The plane headed to Panama, where Montesinos lodged a claim for political asylum. The Panamanian government reluctantly agreed to accept Montesinos temporarily after heavy lobbying by U.S. officials and OAS secretary-general Gavíria, who argued that Montesinos's continued presence in Peru would endanger the transition. United States ambassador John Hamilton maintained that the American role in helping to extricate Montesinos from Peru was motivated by fear of a coup.[39] Other reports suggested that American officials were trying to placate Montesinos, worried that he might go public with what he knew about them or U.S. intelligence operations in the region.

Montesinos's trip to Panama was no quick fix for Peru's political crisis. Simply extracting Montesinos from Lima did not guarantee a dismantling of the regime and a transition. Fujimori and the *oficialista* elite held on, looking for ways to reassert their control over the political process, salvage their careers, and protect themselves against future prosecutions. Montesinos wanted the same. With satellite phone in hand and a menu of threats, Montesinos remained a force to be reckoned with.

From the comfort of his luxurious residence in Panama, Montesinos agreed to sit for one, oddly staged photograph with a local newspaper.[40] Montesinos wore a black-and-white-striped sport shirt. He was reading a book, sitting next to a table with an exotic plant and a half-glass of water. Inside the open book in his hands, it looked like there might be a videotape cassette, but the outline was difficult to make out. Back in Lima, the photograph played as an ominous threat, a reminder that Montesinos still might have something in store for those who betrayed him.

Regime Unraveling

For everyone connected to the regime, the uncertainties unleashed by Fujimori's collapsing presidency were considerable. How would the transition play out? Might there be a way to reconfigure the regime, or at least impose safeguards against future retribution? Or was it time for everyone to abandon ship and reinvent themselves by using, rather than resisting, the transition? No one knew the answers. Without Montesinos, the government was rudderless.

Fujimori's bid to reinvent himself as the leader of the transition to democracy generated little enthusiasm inside Peru. After years of deception and double-talk, Peruvians found it impossible to believe that Fujimori was committed to democracy. Nor was it clear that Fujimori controlled the state apparatus even after Montesinos's departure. Alejandro Toledo, Alberto Andrade, and other opposition leaders argued that Fujimori was neither credible nor capable of leading the transition. They called for a transition government to oversee the new elections. The names of human rights ombudsman Jorge Santistevan and novelist Mario Vargas Llosa were floated as possible leaders of the interim government. From a legal viewpoint, however, the interim government proposal was problematic. Should Fujimori resign before the elections, the first vice president, Francisco Tudela, would be first in the line of succession, followed by the second vice president, Ricardo Márquez. Tudela was obviously complicit in the reelection, was not a neutral figure in the eyes of opponents, and was deemed unacceptable to head an interim government. To get rid of Fujimori and his two vice presidents quickly and legally, the congress would have to vote them out on the grounds of "moral incapacity." That option, previously impossible thanks to the *tránsfugas* and the unwavering discipline inside the government's caucus, began to look viable as legislators scrambled to distance themselves from the Kouri scandal by resigning from Perú 2000.

As his hold on power grew tenuous, Fujimori clung to his support from his most powerful external ally, the U.S. government. In the midst of Montesinos's coup-mongering, U.S. ambassador John Hamilton and Marine General Peter Pace, commander of the U.S. Southern Command, paid a visit to the beleaguered president to emphasize American willingness to stand by him.[41] In a surprise visit to Washington at the end of September, Fujimori met with Secretary of State Albright and National Security Advisor Berger. The tone of the meetings was cordial, and Fujimori reiterated his commitment to leading the political transition. Clinton administration officials were still backing the notion of a Fujimori-led transition.[42] Senator Jesse Helms, chair of the Senate Foreign Relations Committee, challenged the administration's support, but to no avail. In a letter to Albright, Helms endorsed the opposition's view that Fujimori could not guarantee the integrity of the transition and that a caretaker government should supervise the new elections.[43]

Fujimori returned from Washington, supposedly buoyed by the outcome. The official spin was that his trip, and the backing that he had received from the American brass and OAS secretary-general Gavíria, had "neutralized" the coup threat against his government.[44] It also undermined the opposition's demands that Fujimori step down immediately. Since there was little hope that Fujimori would resign absent a big push from the United States, opposition leaders agreed to accept the president's formal stewardship of the transition in an OAS dialogue meeting on October 3.

Ceding a nominal role to Fujimori was as far as the compromise between opposition and government went. Fujimori was still president of Peru, but his government was hardly in a position to dictate the terms of the transition. To keep American support in place, the government would have to accept the framework hammered out in the OAS-sponsored dialogue meetings and have congress legally enact the proposed reforms. Among the first measures was a provision to ensure Fujimori's promised "de-activation" of the SIN. It was followed by an agreement to change the dates for congressional sessions. The seemingly minor technicality was necessary so that the Peruvian congress could amend the constitution, thereby making it legal to schedule new elections.

When what was left of the government majority in congress failed to pass the bill to change the legislative dates, the omission renewed fears that a plan was being hatched to backtrack on the transition. One day earlier, the government had fought off the attempt to unseat Congresswoman Martha Hidelbrandt as president of congress in a narrow vote of sixty to fifty-six. Hidelbrandt's win was critical to keeping Fujimori in power. As long as the government majority held together in congress, Fujimori could not be voted out of office.

The events in congress raised suspicions that Montesinos was still calling the shots. *Caretas* reported that Montesinos was busy telephoning cabinet officials and legislators, concerned that his request for permanent political asylum in Panama might be turned down and that legal problems might befall him back in Peru.[45] Montesinos later confirmed that he had indeed called legislators to corral votes for Hidelbrandt, but at the request of Fujimori.

OAS mission chief Eduardo de la Torre lashed out at the legislative backpedaling. He announced that the OAS dialogue would be suspended until the congress enacted the necessary schedule change, a move that threatened the government with an all-out confrontation with the OAS. Opposition leaders, convinced that Montesinos was mobilizing his loyalists to try to derail the transition, wanted more pressure on the regime. Inspired by the popular uprising that had just brought down President Slobodan Milosevic in Yugoslavia, Alejandro Toledo called for a new round of mass mobilizations against Fujimori. Lima mayor Alberto Andrade wanted Gavíria and other high-ranking OAS officials back on the scene to ratchet up the pressure.

Congress was not the only institution endangering the transition. As of mid-October, Fujimori still had not removed any of Montesinos's handpicked appointees in the armed forces or the police. It seemed likely that they might maneuver to protect their patron or themselves in the transition. Now serving as justice minister, José Alberto Bustamante used the OAS dialogue meeting to set out the military's claim to immunity from prosecution. He proposed a special amnesty measure to cover the military and police for any crimes committed during counternarcotics operations. Bustamante's proposal included a provision to incorporate the amnesty law into the constitution in order to thwart any future attempt to rescind it. Moreover, Bustamante stipulated that the amnesty law was a condition for any further reforms. De la Torre immediately dismissed the amnesty proposal and the conditionality attached to it, as did the outraged opposition representatives.

Impunity was also on the mind of Vladimiro Montesinos. On the morning of October 23, Peruvians awoke to astounding news: Montesinos had left Panama, returned to Peru, and was in hiding. Peruvians wondered about how to interpret the latest outrage. Did Montesinos's return mean that Fujimori was collaborating once again with his old partner on some new scheme? Or was it proof positive that Montesinos still controlled the armed forces and would use his remaining power to protect himself and his allies?

In a telephone interview with *Radio Programas* on October 24, Montesinos offered his interpretation of events. He was perturbed that the Panamanian government had not acted quickly on his request for political asylum and that his visa was set to expire. He claimed that he was returning to Peru because he feared for his life, that he was a target for left-wing terrorists and drug dealers. Montesinos confirmed that the Peruvian ambassador to Panama helped with the arrangements and that Fujimori cleared his return. He denied that he had any plan to interfere in the transition and said that he just wanted to return to private life.[46]

Peruvians regarded Montesinos's yearning for the private life as one more *burla*—another bad joke insulting their intelligence. Gavíria was not amused. Infuriated with Montesinos's cavalier decision to abandon his carefully arranged exile, Gavíria characterized the return as an "act of intimidation against the opposition and civil society."[47] Displeased with the turn of events, the U.S. Senate passed another declaration on the Peruvian situation, Resolution 155, which denounced "elements" seeking to subvert democracy and voiced support for a "credible transition . . . headed by leaders who are committed to democracy and who enjoy the trust of the Peruvian people."[48] Having Montesinos on the loose made Fujimori look incompetent and powerless—hardly an ideal figure to spearhead the transition.

What happened next was more farce than drama. On October 25, Fujimori donned a black leather jacket and announced he would personally lead the search for Montesinos. With daughter Keiko in tow, Fujimori roamed the outskirts of Lima in a Jeep, followed by police cars. At various stops, he jumped out of the vehicle to point and shout orders at the policemen. When the terrestrial search failed to turn up the advisor, he took to the air in a helicopter, circling around Lima. Peruvian television broadcast this search live. The wire service photos of Fujimori in black leather got worldwide play.

If the point was to reestablish Fujimori as a dashing, powerful man of action, the exercise disappointed. Montesinos was nowhere to be found, and the president's escapade only provided more material for Lima's prolific comics. Even at the time, many observers believed that the event was a concoction, a photo opportunity staged by Fujimori to strengthen Montesinos's case for political asylum abroad. *Caretas* reported that Fujimori was searching for videos and other incriminating evidence in Montesinos's stashes. That report was later confirmed by General José Villanueva Ruesta, Peru's chief military commander. He said that Fujimori's primary concern in the search was to find videotapes and locate Colonel Roberto Huamán, the officer who had supervised most of the taping and wiretap operations.[49]

The absurd stunt did make at least one thing clear: Montesinos still had some powerful allies left. Testimony later provided by military personnel confirmed that, as the presidential search was underway, Montesinos was being protected on orders from General Villanueva Ruesta. But Montesinos must have concluded that he was running out of time, options, and friends. No longer able to control events, Montesinos fled again. On October 29, Montesinos secretly boarded a private yacht at a club in Callao. The boat headed toward the Galapagos Islands off of Ecuador. From there, Montesinos made his way to an island off Costa Rica and then to Venezuela.[50]

The Montesinos episode highlighted what the opposition had been arguing all along—that in order to secure a real transition to democracy, the commanding heights of the state had to be purged of all the apparatchiks linked to Montesinos. If Fujimori wanted to stay in power and lay claim to leading the transition, he had to show that he was in charge. On the day that Montesinos left, President Fujimori relieved General Villanueva Ruesta of his duties as head of the high command of the armed forces. Also forced into retirement were the heads of the air force and navy. General Luis Cubas Portal, Montesinos's brother-in-law, was forced out as the commander of the second military region. The distress lower in the ranks was palpable. In Arequipa, Captain Ollanta Humala led one hundred troops in a short-lived rebellion to protest corruption in the armed forces.

Piece by piece, the regime was coming undone.

Final Days, Final Lies

In the midst of the Montesinos crisis, Gavíria flew to Lima. In a meeting with Fujimori, cabinet officials, and congressional leaders, Gavíria made it clear that there was no room for maneuvering. He told the group that there could be no more dealings with Montesinos, that there could be no foot-dragging on scheduling the elections, and that the agreements struck in the OAS dialogue meetings had to be implemented without conditions attached.[51] It was the endgame: Fujimori had to undertake the reforms necessary for a real transition to take place or risk an all-out confrontation with the OAS and, by extension, the United States.

Fujimori folded. The OAS talks quickly produced several agreements that laid the groundwork for new elections. The date for presidential and congressional elections was set for April 8, 2001. The executive commissions that had been used to control the judiciary and the prosecutor's office were eliminated. A new attorney general replaced the resigned Blanca Nélida Colán. New directors were named to take over the electoral machinery at the JNE, ONPE, and RENIEC.

To demonstrate the government's break with Montesinos, Justice Minister Bustamante announced the appointment of a special prosecutor, José Ugaz. Ugaz was charged with investigating Montesinos on money laundering after the Swiss government revealed that it had uncovered accounts in Montesinos's name of US$48 million. It was just the tip of the iceberg; numerous other offshore accounts were discovered. Fujimori claimed to be completely dumbfounded by the discovery.[52] The news got worse. Roberto Escobar, the brother of the slain Colombian drug don Pablo Escobar, confessed to the magazine *Cambio 16* that he had given one million dollars to Montesinos, allegedly to finance Fujimori's first campaign. The story, although not confirmed, was nonetheless another black eye.[53]

The Montesinos investigation served as a pretext for another weird foray into videotapes. On November 7, officials raided the apartment of Montesinos's ex-wife. The officers involved included a military official posted at the presidential palace who posed as a civilian prosecutor investigating the case. They confiscated dozens of suitcases, many containing videotapes and documents. In violation of all normal police procedures, the items were whisked off to the presidential palace. After six days, the items were finally turned over to the police and inventoried.[54] No one knew what the president may have rifled through and whether or not he had removed any incriminating evidence from the illegal search and seizure.

Oblivious to the legal impropriety and unseemliness of it all, Fujimori called a news conference on November 9 to exhibit some of the booty from the raid. Fujimori showed reporters Montesinos's collection of jewel-encrusted watches and Christian Dior menswear. Sixty suits, over one thousand shirts, and hundreds of Italian ties were on display. Fujimori must have believed that this was an impressive show, a final repudiation of his relationship with Montesinos for the whole world to see. For reporters, the news conference raised more questions than it answered. What videos did Fujimori have in his possession? How could Fujimori claim not to have known about the egregious corruption in his own government?

The president who had so often touted his managerial prowess and audacious leadership now looked vacuous, inept, and even pathetic. By early November, Fujimori's hold over congress, the cornerstone of the regime since 1993, was slipping away. Without Montesinos to keep caucus members in line, the government's majority succumbed to defections and infighting. The Kouri video triggered a first wave of defections, led by Cecilia Martínez, who blanched at the instructions by Congresswoman Martha Chávez to close ranks around Kouri.[55] After Montesinos's surprise return, Vice President Francisco Tudela, who had faded into the background, resigned from Perú 2000. The original cadre of C90-NM legislators clashed with Absalón Vásquez and his Vamos Vecino faction, and the Perú 2000 alliance formally disbanded. As the government caucus self-destructed, the stage was set for the opposition to take over the leadership of the congress and remove Fujimori on the grounds of "moral incapacity."

If the congress was lost, so was Fujimori. Rumors were rife that the president was preparing to leave the country permanently. Sources told reporters that Fujimori was in a packing frenzy, even wrapping up belongings in bed sheets after all the suitcases were full. Journalists and photographers staked out the palace, waiting to cover Fujimori's flight. But Press Secretary Carlos Orellana made sure that there would be no photographs of Fujimori's final moments in Peru. On November 13, Orellana primed reporters for a presidential appearance at a separate location while Fujimori made his way to the airport. He boarded the presidential jet with what was later described as an unusual amount of luggage, some of which were identified as suitcases seized from the illegal raid on Montesinos's apartment.[56] For official purposes, Fujimori was said to be on his way to attend the Asia-Pacific Summit in Brunei. His appearance in Brunei was brief. Canceling a scheduled appearance in Panama, Fujimori proceeded to Tokyo, ostensibly to negotiate new loans for Peru.

By the time Fujimori arrived in Tokyo on November 17, he knew it was his final trip as president. On the day of Fujimori's departure from Peru, the last domino fell. With support from newly incarnated "independents" and former *tránsfugas*, the opposition won the vote to censure and remove Martha Hidelbrandt as president of congress. In a significant show of unity, opposition leaders rallied around a consensus candidate, knowing that the new president of congress was in all likelihood on his way to becoming the next president of Peru. On November 16, Valentín Paniagua, the respected veteran politician from the Acción Popular party, was sworn in as the new president of congress.

Fujimori was said to be suffering from a head cold. His return trip home would be delayed. It sounded like a lie. The explanation evoked memories of the story told during the 1990 campaign—that Fujimori could not make an appearance to discuss his platform because he had eaten some bad codfish.[57] Federico Salas, president of the cabinet, and Carlos Boloña, minister of finance, signaled that a resignation could be imminent. When Salas emerged on the morning of Sunday, November 19, to confirm that Fujimori was resigning and remaining in Tokyo, it was no particular surprise.

Continuismo, keeping a link between the old and new regimes, was not an option. The new congressional leadership made it clear that a succession by either the first vice president, Francisco Tudela, or the second vice president, Ricardo Márquez, was unacceptable. Both men submitted their resignations to congress for ratification. The next person in the line of succession was Valentín Paniagua, the new president of congress.

One more matter was left to resolve. By resigning in advance, Fujimori sought to escape the final ignominy—being removed through a formal act of congress declaring him unfit for office. His ignominy was, to a degree, already assured by virtue of having become the first president to flee while still in office and resign from abroad.[58] No niceties would be extended to a president on the run. On November 21, congress rejected Fujimori's resignation and debated a motion to remove the president by reason of "moral incapacity." Martha Chávez and other diehard *oficialistas* took their last opportunity to laud Fujimori and sling some parting insults at the opposition. Defiant to the end, Chávez and others walked out as the voting began. At 10:43 p.m., it all came to an end. By a vote of sixty-two in favor, nine against, and nine abstentions, Fujimori was removed as president of Peru.

On November 22, 2000, Valentín Paniagua was sworn in as the new interim president of Peru. It was like the end of Watergate. The prevailing mood was that Peru's "long national nightmare" was over. Outside the presidential palace, Paniagua greeted jubilant demonstrators who had come one last time to wash their country's red-and-white flag in the ritual that had become one of the most recognized symbols of resistance.

In a brief and modest inaugural address, President Paniagua said that it was time to begin a new era in Peru, to start "reconstruction and democratic re-insitutionalization."[59] But to make a clean break with the past, Peruvians would have to start by taking a long, hard look at it.

11

EVERYBODY KNEW

> Nobody's a saint, no one can say that they were surprised, they
> took the money . . . everybody knew.
>
> *Vladimiro Montesinos, 2001*

THE Kouri video was just the beginning. In the months after the fall of
Fujimori, there were more videos. Night after night, Peruvians watched what
became a familiar show. They saw Montesinos, shoving cash into duffel bags
and envelopes, then passing them to his buddies while making it clear what
he expected in return. Everyone from business executives to middling bureaucrats scooped up the money and asked for more. Never in the history
of Latin America had the hypocrisy and venality of a ruling elite been so
thoroughly documented, and completely exposed on prime-time television.

With the videos came investigations, prosecutions, and the spectacle of
those who had wielded so much power being led off to jail. After months on
the lam, Montesinos was arrested in Venezuela in June 2001 and sent back
to Peru to face scores of criminal charges. Montesinos remained steadfastly
silent about crimes that carried long prison sentences: narco-trafficking,

arms trafficking, and homicides committed by Grupo Colina. But he confessed to investigators regarding the offenses caught on videotape. He described the SIN's political operations and provided detailed testimony on the payoffs he made to judges, election officials, legislators, and media executives.

Montesinos was not the only one talking. As myriad investigations unfolded, the confessions of wrongdoing, small and large, multiplied. So did the number of former luminaries incarcerated: attorney general Blanca Nélida Colán, armed forces commanders General Nicolás de Bari Hermoza Rios and General José Villanueva Ruesta, congressman and finance minister Víctor Joy Way, the Winter brothers of Channel 2, ONPE chief José Portillo, and JNE officials Alipio Montes de Oca and Romulo Muñoz Arce. Others, like Fujimori, fled prosecution.[1]

From the comfort of an apartment in Tokyo, Alberto Fujimori professed his astonishment over the crimes of his associates. Unlike his underlings caught on tape, Fujimori could claim ignorance and innocence. No videotapes of him had surfaced. He said that he knew nothing of all the machinations undertaken on behalf of his reelection. He bemoaned the corruption that he said had taken place behind his back. After ten years of working side by side with Montesinos, Fujimori now referred to his former advisor as the "cancer inside my government."[2]

From the vantage point of a jail cell, Montesinos saw things differently. He scoffed at the likes of Martha Chávez and Francisco Tudela for claiming to have known nothing of the machinations at the SIN when, he said, they had visited him there to plot political strategy. Montesinos hardly thought of himself as the "cancer" on the Fujimori presidency. In fact, he was just the opposite. He was, in his words, a "soldier" who had executed the president's orders and reported back to him regularly. And now, Montesinos was facing the music, acknowledging at least some of his misdeeds. He called on Fujimori to do the same:

> I followed orders and in every case there was a "co-authorship" because he [Fujimori] gave me orders and I carried them out. . . . So I say, come and let's both answer to the country. . . . I handed out money and handed out money . . . everything was so that *El Señor* was re-elected president, so that the presidency would not be declared "vacant," so that he would have a parliamentary majority, so that there was control

over the judiciary, the Public Ministry, the Constitutional Tribunal, the National Elections Board, to have a harmonious relationship with the armed forces, the police and the intelligence community. All those efforts weren't for my benefit, they were for the benefit of *El Señor*, and he was the president.[3]

Montesinos's version of events was, of course, as self-serving as that offered by Fujimori. Montesinos did not dwell on the millions of dollars that he made in illicit deals, the impunity he enjoyed, or the power that he wielded while he promoted Fujimori's political ambitions, and by extension, his own. But on one point, Montesinos was correct: Fujimori should not escape culpability. At the height of his career, Montesinos was an extraordinary fellow. He was crafty, creative, and tireless. But Montesinos did not single-handedly corrupt Peru or undo its democracy. He found willing partners everywhere, from the halls of congress to the halls of justice, from newsrooms to army barracks. His most important partner resided at the presidential palace. Fujimori was the president. As Montesinos rightly argued, Fujimori was responsible for letting his government run amuck.

If Fujimori did not know about the criminal underworld operating inside his government (an assertion that Montesinos hotly disputes), then that could only be true because he did not want to know about it. All the president had to do was pick up *Caretas* or *La República* over his morning coffee in order to figure out that something was awfully wrong.

A Regime Revealed

Fujimori and those who served him were obsessed with secrecy. But as the decade wore on, their government became weirdly transparent.[4] In the sorry attempts to cover up, the administration's transgressions came into focus. As the excesses and abuses mounted, so did the lies and the evidence.

In its cruelest manifestation, the evidence came as mutilated bodies—the disappeared of La Cantuta and army intelligence officer Mariela Bareto. Then there were the official explanations that defied common sense and made people feel that, in fact, the government was mocking them with its tall tales. It was a government that laid claim to extraordinary competence and efficiency, but one that could never get to the bottom of anything. After heading an official investigation for more than a year, Congresswoman Martha Chávez said that she just couldn't figure out who wiretapped scores of opposition figures in the 1995 election. Nor could Minister Adolfo Pandolfi say why irregularities were conveniently discovered in Baruch Ivcher's naturalization papers just at the time that his television station was taking on Montesinos and the SIN. And certainly no one, including the president, could provide a definitive answer about Montesinos's employment status —sometimes Montesinos was said to be working gratis, other times he was said to be a civil servant who was moonlighting as an attorney. But no matter what Montesinos's job title, his income was solemnly proclaimed to be a state secret.

Proof of the government's failed storytelling could be found in the polls, where the public's cynicism was on permanent display. Time after time, Peruvians said that they did not believe what their government was telling them. They thought Susana Higuchi was right when she claimed there was corruption. They thought Montesinos was creepy and that the stories about his links to narco-trafficking merited investigation. They believed that public monies were misappropriated to fund the reelection. They concluded that the government was manipulating the media. After the fact, even Fujimori mocked Montesinos's concoctions as unconvincing. From Tokyo, Fujimori complained that the media's "excessive and shameless sycophancy" had been so over the top that "even a child watching television could understand that 'support' from that toadyish media was useless."[5]

In retrospect, what was so remarkable about the Fujimori presidency was not how little everyone knew about what was going on, but how much everyone knew—so much that "even a child," as Fujimori put it, could figure out the scams. Was the weird transparency of the Fujimori government evidence of its own incompetence, intelligence failures, and glaring lack of talent in the modern art of spin control? Perhaps it was, at least in some cases. But there is another possibility—that the less-than-convincing lying was done on purpose. By committing crimes and sloppily lying about them, the Fujimori government was signaling that it could "do whatever" and get away with it. Demonstrating that it could act with impunity may have been the point at times. One of the leaders of Grupo Colina claims that at least one of their crimes, the 1991 Barrios Altos massacre, was aimed not just at Sendero, but also at sending a message that the government would not be cowed by human rights organizations.[6]

Whether Fujimori and Montesinos thought the lies were convincing or whether they understood them to be perverse but useful gamesmanship, the elaborate charades were an essential part of the process of reproducing the regime. It was part of what CIA analysts noted was "Fujimori's evident concern with maintaining a veneer of legitimacy."[7] Maintaining the veneer, no matter how thin, took great time and energy because hard-core opponents devoted equal time and energy to tearing away at it.

Many Peruvians labored long and hard to bring the regime to an end. Yet, professional observers of Peru's political scene often discounted the opposition in Peru as weak and incoherent. Even after the fall of the regime, analysts have underscored this point, particularly the evident weakness in the party system and the often self-serving calculations of Fujimori's political rivals.[8]

The opposition in Peru was, in fact, dispersed, numerically small (at least until the 2000 reelection), and without a unified strategy. There was no Solidarnosc, Concertación, or "People Power"—that is, there was no single heroic organization or movement that united leaders and the masses to bring down the regime. Neither trade unions nor political parties acted as the essential dramatis personae in Peru's peculiar political transition.

For most of its existence, the opposition was not one easily identifiable entity. It had no charismatic leaders or even a mass base to speak of. Fujimori's opponents did not jam the plazas, but they did move through public space. In the years leading up to the 2000 reelection, they circulated through the nebulous, "wild complex" of Peru's public sphere in the media, civil society, academia, NGOs, and remnants of political parties. They were reporters, editors, human rights activists, intellectuals, whistle-blowers, anonymous tipsters, and assorted public figures—all the individuals who refused to succumb to Fujimori's exhortations that they just shut up. They were annoying and contentious. They were not leading the masses to storm the presidential palace, but they were capable of making trouble. And they did, using every opening at their disposal to embarrass, expose, and mock the regime's claims to credibility and legitimacy.

Publishers and journalists were perhaps the biggest troublemakers of the lot. Early on, a handful of independent print outlets led the charge. Publisher Enrique Zileri let loose his *Caretas* reporters to cover Montesinos, the election shenanigans, and the legislative acrobatics of the C90-NM caucus. Over at *Oiga,* Francisco Iguartua published reports on the military's

Plan Verde. Led by Ricardo Uceda, the investigative team of *Sí* unearthed the remains of the missing of La Cantuta. Gustavo Mohme at *La República* published the groundbreaking stories filed by Edmundo Cruz and Angel Páez, who chronicled the SIN's crimes and military corruption. Under the leadership of Alejandro Miró Quesada, *El Comercio* tracked the election problems in 1995 and broke the most explosive story of the 2000 election—the signature factory scandal.

Joining the wave of investigative reporting was Baruch Ivcher's Frecuencia Latina. And, although confined to cable, Canal N established itself as the "television of record" in its exhaustive coverage of the 2000 election and La Marcha de los Cuatro Suyos. Listeners turned to CPN Radio for the independent reporting and critical commentary that so irked Montesinos.

Uncovering scandals was the work of journalists, but the reporters could not have done it without the help of individuals who dared to tell their stories. Susana Higuchi blew the whistle on the Fujimori family's mishandling of charitable donations. General Rodolfo Robles confirmed the existence of the Grupo Colina death squad. Leonor La Rosa rendered her terrifying story of a witch hunt inside the SIN. Luisa Zanatta described Montesinos's elaborate electronic eavesdropping system. Daniel Rodríguez stepped up to describe the operation of the signature factory. Journalist Fabian Salazar morphed from reporter to source after being beaten by intelligence agents in an operation to recover leaked videotapes on the eve of the 2000 reelection. Behind the scenes, anonymous sources leaked information on the covert intelligence operations aimed at the press and Montesinos's unusual income tax reports. Among the unsung heroes of the time were two average citizens, Justo Arizapana and Guillermo Catorca; after inadvertently discovering the bodies of the La Cantuta victims, they drew a map and sought a way to reveal the gruesome crime.

Legislators and lawyers were another link in the chain of people working to impede the consolidation of authoritarianism in Peru. By exploiting the formal aspects of the regime—its constitution and legal procedures—they forced the government's hand, obliging Montesinos to hatch a succession of plots to pursue reelection. Inside the CCD and the congress, opposition deputies labored tirelessly to confront the regime, speaking out and walking out. Inside the judiciary, a handful of magistrates made their mark. Judge Antonia Saquicuray's courageous rulings on the Barrios Altos case turned a spotlight on the government's crimes. The TC magistrates—

Manuel Aguirre Roca, Guillermo Rey Terry, Delia Revoredo—sacrificed their jobs to take a stand against reelection. Leading the legal offensive from civil society was the Colegio de Abogados and the Foro Democrático.

To stop his foes from uncovering the truth and thwarting the reelection, Montesinos had to buy off congressmen, bribe judges and election officials, and sack the Tribunal Constitucional. With every step, the recklessness of the reelection project became more obvious.

Fujimori spent a decade dismissing "talking heads," but he knew that his critics were shaping international perceptions of the regime. Fujimori berated nongovernmental organizations that chronicled the abuses of the regimes, saying they were havens for has-been leftists who were bent on "demonizing" his government; Transparencia bore the brunt of this criticism in the 2000 election cycle. As much as he tried to change the subject, Fujimori could not rid his government of the need to reply, at least in some form, to the homegrown critics and their listening audiences abroad.[9] The Defensoría del Pueblo, human rights organizations, press watchdog groups, and disgruntled academics kept alive the conversation about the nature of the regime both inside and outside of Peru.

Peru's opposition was disparate and fragmented. It did not topple Fujimori's regime in a straightforward way. But opponents did play a crucial role in wearing down the regime. They tarnished its image and contested its claims to "plausible deniability." The years of agitation, troublemaking, and truth telling took a toll. When the smoking gun finally appeared in the guise of the Kouri video, there was, to borrow a phrase that Christopher Hitchens has applied to another presidency, "no one left to lie to."[10] Even the practiced self-deception of *oficialistas* crumbled.

The opposition did not bring down Fujimori and Montesinos by itself. But it can take credit for its spadework in making a transition possible, for keeping the "wild complex" of the public sphere alive. The final crisis of the regime was a subjective one. It was a crisis because relevant elites, including Fujimori, judged it to be so.[11] The great fictions of the regime—that it was democratic, that it was not corrupt, that Montesinos was a benign public servant—were laid bare by the Kouri video. Things were just as the opposition had always described. There was no easy way to keep on dissembling. Unable to manage the crisis without Montesinos, Fujimori set in motion a transition that, in the end, he could not control.

Getting History Straight

The Fujimori era is over, but like previous experiences of authoritarianism in Latin America, it leaves behind a trail of nagging questions. If "everybody knew" about the rotten underpinnings of the regime, why did it last for so long? Why didn't more Peruvians recoil and resist early on? How do we explain society's toleration, support, and collusion in the reproduction of the regime?

Peruvians are leading the search for answers. Setting Peru's history straight was the principal mission of the Comisión de la Verdad y Reconciliación (CVR). Created during the interim government of President Valentín Paniagua in 2001, the CVR was charged with the enormous task of investigating the origins, conduct, and impact of Peru's counterinsurgency war of the 1980s and 1990s. The commission's nine-volume report, released in August 2003, is essential reading for anyone trying to understand contemporary Peru. In its exhaustive examination of every aspect of the war, the CVR painted the portrait of a country brutalized and desensitized by horrific violence, where human rights and the notions of democratic accountability were progressively eroded during the 1980s and where state security forces became accustomed to acting with impunity.

Desperate for a solution to the crisis enveloping Peru, voters elected Alberto Fujimori in 1990. It was a collective leap into the dark—a gamble by voters looking for a way out of the chaos that included hyperinflation along with political violence. Fujimori assumed office under circumstances that were ripe for the abuse of executive power. Peruvians wanted results—an end to the war and a stable economy—and they were willing to give Fujimori great leeway to secure those ends. In Fujimori's hands, that leeway morphed into an "end justifies the means" doctrine, the auto-coup, and the subsequent political model. According to the CVR: ". . . during the two administrations of Alberto Fujimori, and particularly after April 5, 1992, there was a functional relationship between political power and criminal conduct. Intentionally and progressively, the government organized a state structure to control all the branches, as well as all key bureaucracies, and utilized formal/legal procedures to insure impunity for violations of human rights first, and corruption thereafter."[12]

Did average Peruvians support Fujimori's political model? For the most part, they did not. Peruvians tempered their initial support for the coup with a belief in the need to restore the constitutional order and elections. In conjunction with external pressures from the OAS and the United States, Peruvian public opinion played a critical role in forcing Fujimori to backtrack from the institutional void of the coup. While Peruvians approved of aggressive counterinsurgency policies, they wanted the military to be accountable for their actions. At every juncture, Peruvians expressed their disapproval of the unconstitutional drive for reelection—the authentic interpretation of the constitution, the impeachment of the TC magistrates, and the suppression of the referendum.

That Fujimori scored high job-approval ratings, even when he defied public opinion on political matters, cannot be denied. Fujimori's popularity was buoyed by the public's approval of certain components of his economic program and the palpable progress made in combating the leftist insurgency. Moreover, the president adroitly managed to distance himself from controversial and unpopular political measures by having others take the blame—the congress, the courts, the JNE. Subjected to the cynical manipulation of social assistance programs, Peru's poor became a captive audience for Fujimori. Through broadcast television and the *prensa chicha*, low-income Peruvians were fed a steady stream of propaganda that highlighted the president's great successes and trashed opponents in every conceivable way.

The great popular support that Fujimori boasted about was of the most passive sort. Unlike populists of the past or his contemporary, President Hugo Chávez in Venezuela, Fujimori never attempted to lead a movement and empower his supporters by creating a lasting organization. Fujimori opted for media manipulation, especially control over television, in lieu of organization. As Steve Ellner has noted, Fujimori's political project was striking in its "institutional barrenness."[13] Militant *chavistas* mobilized to save their embattled president in Venezuela. In Peru, there was no grassroots groundswell of support for Fujimori as his presidency crumbled, no popular defense of the president who had prided himself on his popularity.

Average Peruvians were not cheerleaders for authoritarianism, nor were they naive enough to believe Fujimori's claim that his was a pristine model of good government. For most of the duration of the regime, Peruvians were apathetic and cynical and understandably so. After years of war and economic stress, Peruvians were weary of politics and their inept political class. At the beginning, they welcomed a respite from ills that Fujimori seemed to offer; then *Fujimorismo* swept through state and society, turning opposition into a remote and risky option for many.[14]

That average Peruvians acquiesced in the face of a political model they clearly did not endorse was a constant frustration to opposition leaders. But, as opposition leaders frequently liked to point out, Peruvians never swallowed *Fujimorismo* whole. Even with high personal-approval ratings and all the resources of the state at his disposal, Fujimori had difficulty rallying voters at the ballot box: consider the dubious (or more likely, nonexistent) margin of victory in the 1993 constitutional referendum, or the repeated failures of *oficialista* candidates in municipal elections.

To understand the sway of *Fujimorismo* and its staying power, we need to look for the answers higher up in Peruvian society—among the people who should have known better. In the study of Latin American politics, the "failure of elites" has been a long-standing topic, and the Fujimori era provides good reason to revisit this perennial problem.[15]

Latin America's troubled history of democratization is full of episodes in which elites have frequently said one thing and done another. An obvious point leaps to mind: elite hypocrisy is a common phenomenon, visible in all democratic politics, or any politics for that matter. Latin America's variant of the problem, however, has always been acute, and its roots can be traced to how democratic institutions emerged. As Leonardo Avritzer has argued, there is a long tradition of "instrumentality" in elite relations to democracy.[16] In the nineteenth century, Latin America underwent a process of "institutional emulation"—democracy was imported, and superimposed on a social and cultural reality that was hostile to it, one in which elites refused to make democracy meaningful by ceding power to their less privileged countrymen. No matter what the constitutional niceties, elites exercised the option to upset institutions when they felt threatened by them. Upsetting institutions via coups was not the only way elites blocked democratization. Even when democratic institutions stayed in place, elite practices undermined the integrity of democracy from within. The "other institutionalizations"—favoritism, clientelism, and racism—entrenched inequality and exclusion, and made the democracy dysfunctional.

Peru's history is one in which elites continually failed to construct a meaningful democracy, as Fujimori liked to point out. That elite failure was replayed again in *Fujimorismo*. The pillars of Peru's establishment, the so-called *poderes fácticos* (the military, business community, professionals, and technocrats) either openly or tacitly endorsed Fujimori's break with constitutionality. The coup, made in the name of the "national" interest, also served class- and corporate-based interests. Businesses, especially large conglomerates, were poised to benefit from Fujimori's privatization plans. The military and other security forces were content to be rid of the last vestiges of oversight. In short, Fujimori had little trouble convincing most of the Peruvian establishment to jettison democratic constitutionalism; the immediate advantages of doing so were evident and trumped any rhetorical attachments to the rule of law.

The collective failure to defend democratic principles—the acceptance of the coup—opened the door to authoritarianism. But consolidating the system depended heavily on another kind of elite failure: a surrender of judgment and morals. At every juncture in the making of this authoritarian regime, professionals were called on to do what many of them knew to be wrong. That so many of them complied was the secret of the regime's success. Some did it to keep their jobs or advance their careers. Others did it for the cash or favors bestowed by Montesinos. Still others were attracted by the glamour and power, the chance to be a political insider. And certainly, there were "true believers"; those who insisted that any means were justified if they served the ends of the president who had saved Peru.

Whatever the particular motives of individuals, the aggregate result was an astounding collapse in public ethics, morals, and common sense that enabled the regime. Legislators, with their beepers in hand, became the errand boys of Montesinos. Journalists concocted the news. Prosecutors and judges roamed the halls at SIN headquarters, working on their latest cover-up. Cabinet ministers dutifully trotted in front of the cameras so they could deny what they knew to be true. As Montesinos later observed, the administration's descent into illegality was an obvious, undeniable fact. Montesinos acknowledged that pursuing the reelection was to "leap across the porous border of legality, enter illegality and break the rules."[17] It's no wonder that Montesinos reserves a special disdain for his former colleagues who now claim that they didn't know that laws were being broken.

The CVR's final report concluded that Peru's armed conflict was a major contributor to the country's "moral decay" that culminated during the Fujimori administration. The conflict created a tolerance for authoritarian measures, a willingness to sacrifice legality, an indifference to the abuse of authority, and an overarching sense of impunity. Both elite and mass sensibilities were profoundly shaped by the war.

Yet, while the hangover from the war explains the disregard for democratic procedures and rights, the sheer venality of Peru's elite is a wonderment. Perhaps old-fashioned avarice was not the only impulse at work. If, as it is frequently argued, lower classes in Latin America became atomized and unhinged as a result of neoliberal economic reforms, then it stands to reason that the same syndrome descended on middle and upper classes coping with the economic uncertainties of the 1990s. Even among the relatively well off in Lima, job and financial insecurities were intense, and Montesinos's offers were hard to refuse. To cash-starved media executives trying to keep their heavily indebted companies afloat, Montesinos and his bags of money were a godsend. To bureaucrats and political appointees, just keeping one's post in the increasingly volatile job market was reason enough to play along.

Peru's elites, working together, could have stopped Fujimori and Montesinos. Instead, many opted to cash in or to accommodate and just keep quiet. Going along had its rewards; business insiders reaped the benefits of privatization and government contracts. Resisting certainly had its risks. Businessmen and professionals feared the tax audits or legal problems that could materialize out of the blue when one questioned the prevailing powers. As one astute observer of the political scene saw it, *"Oposición no es negocio"* (Being in the opposition is not [good] business).[18]

External actors—the United States government and the OAS—came to a somewhat similar conclusion. Going along with Fujimori had its benefits, and all-out confrontation was out of the question. Once the initial outrage over the coup dissipated, the United States and the OAS lost interest, giving Fujimori a free hand to "formalize" the coup in a rejigged institutional structure. Fujimori and Montesinos understood the game. As long as they kept the thinnest institutional façade in place, there was plenty of room to maneuver.

For the American government, the rewards of going along with Fujimori trumped the oft-expressed concerns about democracy in Peru. Judged in the light of the history of American foreign policy, it was not an unusual trade-off. American promotion of democracy in the region has always been tempered by economic and security interests.[19] In the minds of most American policymakers, Peru's participation in counternarcotics efforts, Fujimori's championing of neoliberal reform, and the 1998 peacemaking that ended the Peru-Ecuador border conflict overrode other considerations. The episodic "expressions of concern" about human rights and democracy delivered by American diplomats were just that: messages to deter Fujimori from even more egregious behavior, but nothing sufficient to make him change course. The Clinton administration never suspended foreign aid to Peru during the long destructive march to the 2000 election, or in the months thereafter as Fujimori settled in for another five-year term.[20]

Similarly, the OAS failed to back up its rhetoric on democratization with real action during most of the duration of the Fujimori regime. Sensitive to the geopolitics and their own concern with protecting sovereignty, member states hesitated to intervene. While the OAS can be credited for its role in forcing Fujimori to back away from his original project of one-man rule in 1992, its subsequent attempts at oversight were limited and sluggish. The objectives of the electoral observation missions in 1992, 1993, and 1995 were narrowly construed, and the complaints lodged by the opposition received scant attention. Indeed, the OAS's apparent unwillingness to take the opposition seriously stands as one of its most glaring mistakes.

In 2000, Eduardo Stein took a great step forward in forging a new kind of OAS electoral mission. Refusing to act as a "mute witness," Stein and his mission played a crucial role in documenting and publicizing abuses as they took place. For the first time in OAS history, a mission declared that a member country had failed to meet the international standards for a free and fair election.[21] Nonetheless, the politics inside the General Assembly did not produce a bold, unequivocal response—namely, a call for a new election. Instead, Fujimori was slapped with yet another OAS mission, one that he fully expected to dance around once more.

In hindsight, hemispheric leaders evidently failed to act decisively and effectively to stop the insidious type of authoritarianism that Fujimori crafted—a system disguised as civilian and wrapped in faux legality. After the fall of Fujimori, Peruvian diplomats spearheaded the effort to create a new framework in the OAS better suited to dealing with the problem of civilian-led authoritarianism.[22] The result was the Inter-American Democratic Charter, signed into effect in Lima on September 11, 2001.

The charter is a far-reaching accord that establishes democracy as a "right" of the people of the Americas. It prohibits member states from engaging in an "unconstitutional interruption of the democratic order or an unconstitutional alteration of the constitutional regime that seriously impairs the democratic order."[23] In effect, the language perfectly describes the evolution of the Fujimori regime, from the auto-coup to the steady evisceration of constitutional law. By recognizing that breakdown of democracy can take place through routes other than simple military takeover, the charter represents a major step forward in the collective defense of democracy in the hemisphere. Implementing the charter will be one of the OAS's greatest challenges in the twenty-first century. Whether the OAS will acquire the political will and the means to deal with the transgressions that governments will probably deny, just as Fujimori did, is an open question.

Alberto Fujimori remains in Tokyo. He has launched a Web site. He says that he is planning his political comeback and that he will be president of Peru again one day. The government of Peru is requesting Fujimori's extradition from Japan. If returned to Peru, Fujimori would face scores of criminal charges that include conspiracy, embezzlement, and twenty-five counts of homicide in the Barrios Altos and La Cantuta cases. Fujimori insists that all the charges are false and that he is the victim of political persecution.[24]

Whatever his future, Fujimori will not be forgotten, but not because he was a great president. Alberto Fujimori's greatest legacy is most likely to be the one that he will never acknowledge. Through the misdeeds and the moral failure of his presidency, Fujimori inspired a new collective consciousness about the threats to democracy in Latin America and a realization that what happened under his watch should not be allowed to happen again.

NOTES

Notes on Sources

Unless otherwise indicated, all translations from Spanish to English have been done by the author.

In citing works in the endnotes, short titles have generally been used after the first reference. Works frequently cited have been identified by the following abbreviations.

Vladimiro Montesinos's testimony to the congressional commissions was recorded in two documents, both of which were available on a section of the *El Comercio* Web site that has since been discontinued. Citations to the first document will be abbreviated as illustrated below:

> Congreso de la República, Primera Legislatura Ordinaria de 2001, Subcomisión investigadora de la Comisión Permanente del Congreso de la República, encargada de investigar la denuncia constitucional numero 6, presentada contra la Congresista Martha Chávez Cossío de Ocampo y otros por supuesto delito de receptación y otros en agravio del estado, December 20, 2001, *El Comercio,* http://www.elcomercioperu.com.pe/EcEspe/html/ montesinos (accessed February 15, 2002; site now discontinued).

will be abbreviated as

> Congreso de la República, Primera Legislatura Ordinaria de 2001, December 20, 2001.

Similarly, citations to the second document will be abbreviated as follows:

> Congreso de la República, Segunda Legislatura Ordinaria de 2001, Comisión investigadora de la influencia irregular ejercida durante el gobierno de Alberto Fujimori Fujimori (1990–2000) sobre el poder judicial, ministerio público y otros poderes e instituciones del estado vinculadas a la administración de justicia," April 25, 2002, *El Comercio,* http://www.elcomercio.com .pe/EcEspe/html/montesinos (accessed June 1, 2002; site now discontinued).

will be abbreviated as

> Congreso de la República, Segunda Legislatura Ordinaria de 2001, April 25, 2002.

Transcripts of videotapes and audiotapes clandestinely recorded by Montesinos were made available by the congress and posted on the *El Comercio* Web site, but that site has been discontinued. Readers should note that Peru's congress recently published a six-volume collection of the video and audio transcripts that includes portions that were cited as inaudible in the original congressional transcripts posted by *El Comercio*. For the new publication, see Congreso de la República del Perú, *En la sala de la corrupción: Videos y audios de Vladimiro Montesinos (1998-2000)* (Lima: Fondo Editorial del Congreso, 2004). Transcript citations will be abbreviated as illustrated below:

> Congreso de la República, Primera Legislatura Ordinaria de 2001, "Transcripción del audio B/1-A," n.d., *El Comercio*, http://www.elcomercio.com .pe/EcEspec/html/montesinos (accessed June 5, 2003; site now discontinued).

will be abbreviated as

> Congreso de la República, Primera Legislatura Ordinaria de 2001, "Transcripción del audio B/1-A," n.d.

News source *Foreign Broadcast Information Service-Latin America* will be abbreviated as *FBIS-LAT* followed by year and volume number (example: *FBIS-LAT-92-067*). *EFE World News Services* will be abbreviated as *EFE*.

Chapter 1: The Permanent Coup

1. *La República,* April 10, 1995.

2. Interview reprinted in *Expreso,* April 18, 1995.

3. Perot's antipolitical, technocratic discourse was strikingly similar to Fujimori's. On Perot, see Gwen Brown, "Deliberation and Its Discontents: H. Ross Perot's Antipolitical Populism," in *The End of Politics: Explorations into Modern Antipolitics,* ed. Andreas Schedler (London: Macmillan, 1997), 115–48. On Fujimori, see Carlos Iván Degregori, *La década de la antipolítica* (Lima: Instituto de Estudios Peruanos, 2000).

4. In a post-coup interview with the *Washington Post,* Fujimori confirmed that he would not seek a second term in 1995. Peru's 1979 constitution limited the president to serving a single term in office. The interview was reported in *Ojo,* April 13, 1992.

5. For an analysis of the regime as *democradura,* see Sinesio López, "A donde va la democradura," *Cuestión de Estado* 1, no. 3 (May–June 1993): 28–32; Sinesio López, "El regimen fujimorista y sus (monstruosas) criaturas," *Cuestión de Estado* 1, no. 2 (March–April 1993): 13–17. On presidential Caesarism, see Enrique Bernales, "Retorno al absolutismo," *Argumentos* 2, no. 9 (1993): 5–6. On the civil-military nature of the regime, see Henry Pease García, *Los años de la langosta: La escena política del fujimorismo* (Lima: Instituto para la Democracia Local, 1994), 244–47. On plebiscitary authoritarianism, see Julio Cotler, *Política y sociedad en el Perú: Cambios y continuidades* (Lima: Instituto de Estudios Peruanos, 1994), 165–235.

6. Jaime Yoshiyama, the president of the CCD from 1993 to 1995, happily identified himself as a member of the "management team of the firm called Peru." See his remarks, "La reingeniería del Perú," *Boletín Extraordinario CCD,* November 17, 1993.

7. For a complete analysis of the evolution of U.S.-Peru relations in this period, see Cynthia McClintock and Fabian Vallas, *The United States and Peru: Cooperation at a Cost* (New York: Routledge, 2003).

8. On Fujimori's popularity and neoliberal economic reform, see Kenneth M. Roberts, "Neoliberalism and the Transformation of Populism in Latin America: The Peruvian Case," *World Politics* 48 (October 1995): 82–116; Bruce H. Kay, "Fujipopulism and the Liberal State in Peru 1990–1995," *Journal of Interamerican Studies and World Affairs* 38, no. 4 (Winter 1996): 55–98; Kurt Weyland, "Neopopulism and Neoliberalism in Latin America: Unexpected Affinities," *Studies in Comparative International Development* 31, no. 3 (Fall 1996): 3–31; Kurt Weyland, "A Paradox of Success? Determinants of Political Support for President Fujimori," *International Studies Quarterly* 44 (2000): 481–502.

9. I am indebted to Harold Mah for his insight and elegant language. The quote is from Harold Mah, "Phantasies of the Public Sphere: Rethinking the Habermas of Historians," *Journal of Modern History* 72 (March 2000):153–82.

10. Many analysts used the term "permanent coup." It may have originated in a column by Mirko Lauer, "Campaña electoral permanente," *La República,* May 12, 1996. Javier Pérez de Cuéllar also used the term in the wake of the impeachment of the three magistrates of the Tribunal Constitucional in 1997. His remark appeared in *El Comercio,* November 17, 1997. For my own use of the term in reference to political developments in Peru, see "The Permanent Coup: Peru's Road to Presidential Reelection," *LASA Forum* 24, no. 1 (Spring 1998): 5–9.

11. For the noted discussion of how analysts have qualified the use of the word "democracy," see David Collier and Steve Levitsky, "Democracy with Adjectives: Conceptual Innovation in Comparative Research," *World Politics* 49 (April 1997): 430–51.

12. Fareed Zakaria, "The Rise of Illiberal Democracy," *Foreign Affairs* 76, no. 6 (November–December 1997): 22–43.

13. Guillermo O'Donnell, *Counterpoints: Selected Essays on Authoritarianism and Democracy* (Notre Dame, IN: University of Notre Dame Press, 1999), 164.

14. Romeo Grompone, "Al día siguiente: El Fujimorismo como proyecto inconcluso de transformación política y social," in *El Fujimorismo: Ascenso y caída de un regimen autoritario,* ed. Romeo Grompone and Julio Cotler (Lima: Instituto de Estudios Peruanos, 2000), 107–13. For the classic definition of authoritarianism, see Juan J. Linz, *Totalitarian and Authoritarian Regimes* (Boulder, CO: Lynne Rienner Publishers, 2000).

15. For the categorizations by Peruvian analysts, see the works cited in note 5 to this chapter, especially Julio Cotler's use of the term "plebiscitary authoritarianism." McClintock initially laid out this argument in "¿Es autoritario el gobierno del Fuji-

mori?" in *El juego político: Fujimori, la oposición y las reglas,* ed. Fernando Tuesta Soldevilla (Lima: Fundación Friedrich Ebert, 1999), 65–92. McClintock extends the argument in "Electoral Authoritarianism versus Partially Democratic Regimes: The Case of the Fujimori Government," in *The Fujimori Legacy,* ed. Julio Carrión (University Park, PA: Pennsylvania State University Press, forthcoming).

16. On the rise of technocratic ideas, see Michiel Baud, "The Quest for Modernity: Latin American Technocratic Ideas in Historical Perspective," in *The Politics of Expertise in Latin America,* ed. Miguel A. Centeno and Patricio Silva (London: Macmillan, 1998), 13–35.

17. Fernando Coronil, *The Magical State: Nature, Money, and Modernity in Venezuela* (Chicago: University of Chicago Press, 1997), 166–67.

18. Analysts have drawn comparisons between Peru under Fujimori and the Dominican Republic under President Joaquín Balaguer. In both cases, public monies were diverted to the presidents' campaigns; the money was also used to bribe officials and businessmen. For an in-depth analysis of the Balaguer regime, see Jonathan Hartlyn, *The Struggle for Democratic Politics in the Dominican Republic* (Chapel Hill: University of North Carolina Press, 1998).

19. Coronil, *The Magical State,* 154–58.

20. Deputy Assistant Secretary of Defense, Inter-American Affairs, "President Bush's Call to President Fujimori, 22 April, 1992" (declassified document, National Security Archive, George Washington University, Washington DC).

21. Steven Levitsky and Lucan A. Way, "The Rise of Competitive Authoritarianism," *Journal of Democracy* 13, no. 2 (2002): 51–65. The adjective "competitive" may be somewhat misleading to the reader, especially when applied to the Fujimori regime. While there was competition in elections, there is no evidence that regime incumbents were ever prepared to lose the elections at the national level. The regime compensated for losses in municipal and local elections through corruption (e.g., enticing local officials to ally with the government) and by measures that weakened local control over budgets. For a further discussion of regimes of this type, see Marina Ottaway, *Democracy Challenged: The Rise of Semi-Authoritarianism* (Washington DC: Carnegie Endowment for International Peace, 2003).

22. For discussions of the shifting patterns in U.S. foreign policy toward Latin America, see Peter H. Smith, *Talons of Eagles: Dynamics of U.S.-Latin American Relations,* 2d ed. (New York: Oxford University Press, 2000).

23. I formulated my initial ideas on the role of the public sphere in the Fujimori regime in two essays published midway during the Fujimori government. See, "Polls, Political Discourse and the Public Sphere: The Spin on Peru's Fuji-golpe," in *Latin America in Comparative Perspective: New Approaches to Methods and Analysis,* ed. Peter Smith (Boulder, CO: Westview Press, 1995), 227–55. Also see "Public Life in the Time of Alberto Fujimori," (Working Paper 219, Latin American Program, Woodrow Wilson International Center for Scholars, Washington DC, June 1996).

24. This definition restates the one offered by Daniel C. Hallin as a "particular

nexus of processes and institutions, the news media being the most important, which are involved in the construction of political meaning and the formation of opinion." See Daniel C. Hallin, *We Keep America on Top of the World: Television Journalism and the Public Sphere* (London: Routledge, 1994), 10.

25. Jürgen Habermas, *The Structural Transformation of the Public Sphere*, trans. Thomas Berger (Cambridge, MA: MIT Press, 1989).

26. See the essays in Craig Calhoun, ed., *Habermas and the Public Sphere* (Cambridge, MA: MIT Press, 1993). On the European critics of Habermas, see Peter Uwe Honhedahl, *The Institution of Criticism* (Ithaca, NY: Cornell University Press, 1982), 242–80. Also see Bruce Robbins, ed., *The Phantom Public Sphere* (Minneapolis: University of Minnesota Press, 1993). For historical studies of the public spheres see, for example, Mary P. Ryan, *Civic Wars: Democracy and Public Life in the American City during the Nineteenth Century* (Berkeley and Los Angeles: University of California Press, 1997); Michael Warner, *The Letters of the Republic: Publication and the Public Sphere in Early Eighteenth Century America* (Cambridge, MA: Harvard University Press, 1990). For an application of the notion of the public sphere in Latin American politics, see Philip Oxhorn, "When Democracy Isn't All That Democratic: Social Exclusion and the Limits of the Public Sphere in Latin America," (North-South Agenda Paper 44, North-South Center, University of Miami, April 2001).

27. On the concept of the counter-public, see Oskar Negt and Alexander Kluge, *Public Sphere and Experience: Toward an Analysis of the Bourgeois and Proletarian Sphere* (Minneapolis: University of Minnesota Press, 1993); Susan Herbst, *Politics at the Margin: Historical Studies of Public Expression Outside the Mainstream* (Cambridge, MA: Cambridge University Press, 1994); Black Public Sphere Collective, ed., *The Black Public Sphere* (Chicago: University of Chicago Press, 1995).

28. Jürgen Habermas, *Contributions to a Discourse Theory of Law and Democracy*, trans. William Rehg (London: Polity Press, 1996), 307.

29. Craig Calhoun, "Civil Society and the Public Sphere," *Public Culture* 5, no. 2 (Winter 1993): 267–80. Building on Habermas, Leonardo Avritzer examines the disconnection between the public sphere and state institutions in *Democracy and the Public Space in Latin America* (Princeton, NJ: Princeton University Press, 2003), 36–54.

30. The phrase is taken from Nancy Fraser, "Rethinking the Public Sphere: A Contribution to the Critique of Actually Existing Democracy," in *Habermas and the Public Sphere,* 134.

31. There are numerous works on this subject. For an excellent overview of how American politics has been shaped by the new political technology, see Steven Schier, *By Invitation Only: The Rise of Exclusive Politics in the United States* (Pittsburgh, PA: University of Pittsburgh Press, 2000).

32. Guillermo O'Donnell drew attention to the persistence of clientelism in his essay, "Another Institutionalization: Latin America and Elsewhere," (Kellogg Institute Working Paper 222, Helen Kellogg Institute for International Studies, University of Notre Dame, March 1996). The study of informal institutions in Latin America is at-

tracting renewed attention. See Gretchen Helmke and Steven Levitsky, "Informal Institutions and Comparative Politics: A Research Agenda" (paper presented at the conference, "Informal Institutions and Politics in Latin America," Helen Kellogg Institute for International Studies, University of Notre Dame, April 24–25, 2003).

Chapter 2: Fujimori Meets the Press

1. A home video made by Fujimori's son, Kenyi, showed his father in a white terrycloth bathrobe casually lounging on a bed with two television reporters during a trip to London in 1997. See "En un hotel en Londres," *Caretas,* March 11, 2004.

2. For a comparative view of the development of the press in Latin America, see Silvio Waisbord, *Watchdog Journalism in South America: News, Accountability and Democracy* (New York: Columbia University Press, 2000). For a discussion of accountability and the role that the media plays in contemporary Latin America, see Enrique Peruzotti and Catalina Smulovitz, eds., *Controlando la política: Ciudadanos y medios en las nuevas democracies* (Buenos Aires: Editora Temas, 2002).

3. For further background on Fujimori's career, see Luis Jochamowitz, *Ciudadano Fujimori: La construcción de un político* (Lima: PEISA, 1993); Sally Bowen, *The Fujimori File: Peru and Its President 1990–2000* (Lima: Peru Monitor, 2000); Raúl A. Wiener, *El reelectionista: Clima político y juego del poder en el Perú de los 90* (Lima: A-4 impresores S.R.L., 1998).

4. Pedro Planas emphasized Fujimori's relationship with García and APRA in his discussion of Fujimori's political ascent. See *La democracia volátil: Movimientos, partidos, líderes políticos y conductas electorales en el Perú contemporáneo* (Lima: Fundación Friedrich Ebert Stiftung, 2000), 295–301.

5. *El Comercio,* May 24, 1990.

6. The term *chino* is used frequently in Peru to denote a person of Asian descent. It can also be used broadly to denote a person of color.

7. Works that examine the dynamics of the 1990 presidential race include Jeffrey Daeschner, *The War at the End of Democracy: Mario Vargas Llosa versus Alberto Fujimori* (Lima: Peru Reporting, 1993); Carlos Iván Degregori and Romeo Grompone, *Demonios y redentores en el nuevo Perú: Una tragedia en dos vueltas* (Lima: Instituto de Estudios Peruanos, 1991); Maxwell A. Cameron, *Democracy and Authoritarianism in Peru: Political Coalitions and Social Change* (New York: St. Martin's Press, 1994); Gregory Schmidt, "Fujimori's 1990 Upset Victory in Peru," *Comparative Politics* 28, no. 3 (April 1996): 321–54; Mark Malloch Brown, "The Consultant," *Granta* 36 (Summer 1991): 88–95; Álvaro Vargas Llosa, *El Diablo en la campaña* (Mexico City: Ediciones El País, Aguilar Ediciones, 1993); Patricia Oliart, "Alberto Fujimori: The Man Peru Needed?" in *Shining and Other Paths: War and Society in Peru, 1980–1995,* ed. Steve J. Stern (Durham, NC: Duke University Press, 1998), 411–24; Martín Tanaka, *Los espejismos de la democracia: El colapso del sistema de partidos en el Perú* (Lima: Instituto de Estudios Peruanos, 1998), 167–200.

8. Malloch Brown, "The Consultant," 90–93; Mario Vargas Llosa, "A Fish Out of Water," *Granta* 36 (Summer 1991): 68–70.

9. John Sheahan, *Searching for a Better Society: The Peruvian Economy from 1950* (University Park, PA: Pennsylvania State University Press, 1999), 144, 161. For further discussion about the problems in the Peruvian economy in this period, see Carol Wise, *Reinventing the State: Economic Strategy and Institutional Change in Peru* (Ann Arbor, MI: University of Michigan Press, 2003); Eva Paus, "Adjustment and Development in Latin America: The Failure of Peruvian Heterodoxy, 1985–1990," *World Development* 15, no. 5 (1991): 411–34.

10. Peter Flindell Klarén, *Peru: Society and Nationhood in the Andes* (New York: Oxford University Press, 2000), 407. The number of fatalities was calculated from the statistics of the Comisión de la Verdad y Reconciliación.

11. On the left's problems, see Kenneth M. Roberts, "Economic Crisis and the Demise of the Legal Left in Peru," *Comparative Politics* 29, no. 1 (October 1996): 69–72.

12. Planas, *La democracia volátil*, 296–301.

13. Fujimori's place of birth was the subject of conjecture throughout his presidency, and spotty records on the subject only added to the intrigue. Fujimori insisted that he was a native-born Peruvian, but what he failed to reveal was that his parents had registered his birth with Japanese authorities, thus making him eligible to claim Japanese citizenship. When he fled to Japan in 2000, his dual citizenship status finally came to light.

14. The 1983 report was by Gustavo Gorriti, an investigative reporter, who was later arrested and detained at SIN headquarters during the 1992 coup. See Gustavo Gorriti, "Mouse Trap: Fujimori Goes for My Mac," *New Republic,* May 4, 1992, 14.

15. Mario Vargas Llosa, *A Fish in the Water,* trans. Helen Lane (New York: Farrar, Straus and Giroux, 1994), 504–5.

16. See the comments by Mariella Balbi and Luis Cisneros in the discussion reported in *Prensa y política: Crítica y autocrítica,* comp. Luis Jaime Cisneros and Oscar Malca (Lima: Fundación Friedrich Ebert, 1990), 37; Luis Jaime Cisneros, "El poder de la prensa," in *El poder en el Perú,* ed. Augusto Alvarez Rodrich (Lima: Editorial Apoyo, 1993), 130.

17. César Hidelbrandt, interview by author, August 15, 1996, Lima.

18. For a discussion of the shift to the paradigm of neutrality in American journalism, see Michael Schudson, *Discovering the News* (New York: Basic Books, 1978). For a history of the Peruvian press, see Juan Gargurevich, *Historia de la prensa peruana (1594–1990)* (Lima: La Voz Editores, 1991).

19. Roberto Miró Quesada, "Contradicciones al interior de la burgesía peruana a través del analisis de los diarios *El Comercio* y *La Prensa 1956–62* (Tesis de bachiller, Sociología, Universidad de San Marcos, 1974).

20. For further discussion of the Velasco period, see Dennis Gilbert, "Society, Politics, and the Press: An Interpretation of the Peruvian Press Reform of 1974," *Journal of Interamerican Studies and World Affairs* 21, no. 3 (August 1979): 369–93; Hélan Jaworski, "Democracia y socialización en los medios de comunicación," in *El Perú de*

Velasco, vol. 3, ed. Carlos Franco (Lima: Centro de Estudios para el Desarrollo y la Participación, 1983), 767–95; Luis Peirano et al., *Prensa: Apertura y límites* (Lima: DESCO, Centro de Estudios y Promoción del Desarrollo, 1978).

21. Deporting editors was a long-standing tradition in Peruvian politics. Doris Gibson, the founding editor of *Caretas* in the 1950s, was deported during the Odría presidency as was Francisco Igartua, founding editor of *Oiga*.

22. Ricardo Uceda, "Como se hizó el Diario de Marka," *Revista Chasqui*, April–June 1982; Ana María Diaz, "Informe sobre lectoría de diarios en Lima" (Facultad de Ciencias de la Comunicación, Universidad de Lima, 1984); Juan Gargurevich, "Cambios en el consumo de prensa diaria y sus efectos en la industria editorial" (Escuela de Graduados, Maestría en Comunicación, Pontifícia Universidad Católica del Perú, December 1996).

23. For an overview of media development in this period, see Cynthia McClintock, "The Media and Re-Democratization in Peru," *Studies in Latin American Popular Culture* 6 (1987): 115–33.

24. For a hilarious, thinly disguised fictional account of the newspaper's downfall, see Jaime Bayly, *Los últimos días de "La Prensa"* (Bogotá: Editorial Seix Barral, 1996).

25. The word *chicha* carries multiple connotations in Peru. It is used to denote something associated with popular culture and implies hybridity (a mix of elements). It is also used disparagingly to indicate something that is shoddy or low class.

26. Richard Webb and Graciela Fernández Baca, *Perú en números 1995* (Lima: Cuánto S.A., 1995), 780.

27. For the history of polling in Peru, see Fernando Tuesta Soldevilla, *No sabe, no opina: Encuestas políticas y medios* (Lima: Fundación Konrad Adenauer, Universidad de Lima, 1997).

28. José Perla Anaya, *Derecho y comunicaciones: La prensa, la gente y los gobiernos* (Lima: Universidad de Lima, 1987), 115.

29. For further discussion of the press in this period, see Carlos Oviedo, *Prensa y subversión: Una lectura de violencia en el Perú* (Lima: Mass Comunicación, 1989); Víctor Peralta, *Sendero Luminoso y la prensa* (Lima: CBC-SUR, 2000); Jorge Acevedo Rojas, *Prensa y violencia política (1980–1995)* (Lima: Asociación de Comunicadores Sociales Calandria, 2002).

30. *Index on Censorship* 20, nos. 4–5 (April–May 1991): 55.

31. *Expreso*, December 26, 1991.

32. *El Comercio*, July 6, 1991.

33. For more discussion of pre-1992 coup plans in the military, see Fernando Rospigliosi, *Montesinos y las fuerzas armadas: Cómo controló durante una década las instituciones militares* (Lima: Instituto de Estudios Peruanos, 2000).

34. The word *"doctor"* is often used in Peru as a sign of respect, to denote someone who is well educated even if the person does not have a Ph.D. or medical degree. In political circles and the press, Montesinos was often referred to as *"El doc."*

35. Fujimori also took an important preinaugural trip to New York and Wash-

ington, where he met with American and IMF officials who urged him to adopt neo-liberal policies.

Chapter 3: Dissolving Peru

1. Alan García later recounted his escape in a thinly disguised novel, *El mundo de Maquiavelo* (Lima: Mosca Azul Editores, 1994). The APRA leaders arrested in the coup included Abel Salinas, Jorge del Castillo, and Remigio Morales Bermúdez. Legislators arrested included Luis Negreiros, Aurelio Loret de Mola, and César Barrera. Ex-president Fernando Belaúnde was placed under house arrest. See *DPA*, April 6, 1992, in *FBIS-LAT-92-067*, April 7, 1992; and *Notimex*, April 7, 1992, in *FBIS-LAT-92-068*, April 8, 1992.

2. Gorriti discussed his arrest in an interview with Sarah Kerr, "Fujimori's Plot: An Interview with Gustavo Gorriti, *New York Review of Books*, June 25, 1992, 18–22.

3. For further analyses of the coup, see Philip Mauceri, "State Reform, Coalitions and the Neo-Liberal Auto-golpe in Peru," *Latin American Research Review* 30, no. 1 (1995): 7–37; Maxwell A. Cameron, "Self-Coups: Peru, Guatemala, and Russia," *Journal of Democracy* 9, no. 1 (January 1998): 9–139; Cynthia McClintock, "Peru's Fujimori: A Caudillo Derails Democracy," *Current History* (March 1993): 112–19.

4. "Manifiesto a la Nación del 5 de abril de 1992," in *Proceso de retorno a la institucionalidad democrática en el Perú*, ed. Eduardo Ferrero Costa (Lima: Centro de Estudios Internacionales, 1992), 129–35.

5. *Latin American Weekly Report*, November 22, 1990, 4.

6. "Clausura a cargo del Señor Presidente Constitucional de la *República*, Ingeniero Alberto Fujimori Fujimori" (Speech delivered to the Conferencia Anual de Ejecutivos, Lima, December 1990).

7. "Clausura a cargo del Señor Presidente Constitucional de la *República*, Ingeniero Alberto Fujimori Fujimori," (Speech delivered to the Conferencia Anual de Ejecutivos, Lima, December 1991).

8. *EFE*, April 16, 1992, in *FBIS-LAT-92-075*, April 17, 1992. For the "counter-coup" argument, see Carlos Torres y Torres Lara, *Los nudos del poder* (Lima: Desarollo y Paz, 1992), 73–100.

9. For a detailed analysis of the dynamics of executive-legislative relations during this period, see Charles D. Kenney, *Fujimori's Coup and the Breakdown of Democracy in Latin America* (Notre Dame, IN: University of Notre Dame Press, 2004).

10. For Montesinos's view on the coup, see Congreso de la República, Segunda Legislatura Ordinaria de 2001, April 25, 2002. For Hermoza's description of the coup planning, see Nicolás de Bari Hermoza Ríos, *Fuerzas Armadas del Perú: Lecciones del siglo* (Lima: Fimart S.A., 1996), 303. In an interview with Patricio Ricketts, Fujimori explained that his planning of the coup began with his jotting down of ideas at three or four in the morning and that it took a "relatively long time" to develop the idea. For the transcript of the interview, see *Panamericana Televisión*, May 25, 1992, in *FBIS-*

LAT-92-101, May 26, 1992. Some analysts have argued that the coup was modeled on a contingency plan authored by the military, the so-called Plan Verde. See Fernando Rospigliosi, *Montesinos y las fuerzas armadas: Cómo controló durante una década las instituciones militares* (Lima: Instituto de Estudios Peruanos, 2000).

11. Kenney, *Fujimori's Coup,* 197–98.

12. Alfredo Torres Guzmán, "The Coup in Peru and Its Popular Support" (Lima: Apoyo, 1992). The observation on Peruvians' passive reaction to coups is from Henry Pease García.

13. Ferrero Costa, *Proceso de retorno,* 140–44.

14. Lima Radio and Television Networks, April 9, 1992 in *FBIS-LAT-92-069,* April 9, 1992.

15. *Resumen Semanal,* April 10–14, 1992.

16. Alfonso de los Heros was the only member of Fujimori's cabinet to resign in protest of the coup.

17. *Radio Programas del Perú,* April 7, 1992, in *FBIS-LAT-92-069,* April 9, 1992; *EFE,* April 11, 1992, in *FBIS-LAT-92-071,* April 13, 1992.

18. See the interview with Oscar de la Puente, *Radio Programas del Perú,* April 18, 1992, in *FBIS-LAT-92-076,* April 20, 1992.

19. *Panamericana Televisión,* May 4, 1992 in *FBIS-LAT-92-086,* May 4, 1992. In an Apoyo poll taken a week after the coup, 54 percent of those polled characterized the government as "democratic"; only 30 percent opted for "dictatorial." See Apoyo, "The Fujicoup," (document, Lima, April 1992).

20. *La República,* April 8, 1992. This edition features photos of the military occupation of the newspaper with the caption, "The Black Night of Peruvian Journalism."

21. I have taken these observations on the character of the print press coverage of the coup from the excellent analysis by David Wood, "The Peruvian Press Under Recent Authoritarian Regimes, with special reference to the Autogolpe of President Fujimori," *Bulletin of Latin American Research* 19, no. 1 (January 2000): 17–32.

22. Fujimori urged journalists to go out and take their own readings of public opinion in his speech of April 9, 1992. For international press coverage of poll results, see, e.g., *New York Times,* April 9, 1992; *Washington Post,* April 17, 1992; *Washington Post,* May 2, 1992.

23. Lima Radio and Television Networks, April 22, 1992, in *FBIS-LAT-92-078,* April 22, 1992.

24. Mario Vargas Llosa, "The Road to Barbarism," *New York Times,* April 12, 1992.

25. *Radio Programas del Perú,* April 19, 1992, in *FBIS-LAT-92-076,* April 20, 1992.

26. See "Porcentajes en vez de democracia: El reino de las encuestas," *La República,* April 18, 1992; "Encuestas de jabón," *Caretas,* April 27, 1992. Also see Luís Alberto Sánchez, "Ahora hay que elegir por encuestas," *Caretas,* April 27, 1992.

27. *Panamericana Televisión,* April 13, 1992, in *FBIS-LAT-92-072,* April 14, 1992.

28. The parties that made explicit reference to the dictatorial nature of the

regime in their post-coup statements were Solidaridad y Democracia, Movimiento Libertad, Frente Nacional de Trabajadores y Campesinos, Izquierda Socialista, Izquierda Unida, Partido Popular Cristiano, Partido Unificado Mariateguista, APRA, and Acción Popular. The statements can be found in Ferrero Costa, *Proceso de retorno,* 146–60.

29. For U.S. reaction, see *New York Times,* April 7 and 11, 1992. The *New York Times* editorial appeared on April 7, 1992.

30. See Resolución del Consejo Permanente de la OEA, "Situación en el Perú," in Ferrero Costa, *Proceso de retorno,* 163–64.

31. For the text of the speech, see the memoir by Augusto Blacker Miller, *La propuesta inconclusa* (Lima: Consorcio La Moneda, 1993), 225–45.

32. *EFE,* April 12, 1992, in *FBIS-LAT-92-072,* April 14, 1992.

33. *EFE,* April 26, 1992, in *FBIS-LAT-92-082,* April 28, 1992.

34. *Panamericana Televisión,* May 4, 1992, in *FBIS-LAT-92-086,* May 4, 1992.

35. *Panamericana Televisión,* April 29, 1992, in *FBIS-LAT-92-083,* April 29, 1992.

36. Carlos Boloña Behr, *Cambio de rumbo* (Lima: Instituto de Economía de Libre Mercado-San Ignacio de Loyola, 1993), 138. Hernando de Soto was lionized in conservative circles as an advocate of Third World entrepreneurship. See his *The Other Path: The Invisible Revolution in the Third World,* trans. June Abbott (New York: Harper and Row, 1989).

37. "Informe de la Misión al Perú, del 17 de mayo de 1992," in Ferrero Costa, *Proceso de retorno,* 186–90.

38. As Charles Kenney discovered, large portions of Fujimori's speech denouncing the evils of *partidocracia* in Peru were plagiarized from the work of a political scientist, Michael Coppedge, who writes on Venezuelan politics. Presidential advisor Hernando de Soto was familiar with Coppedge's work. See Kenney, *Fujimori's Coup,* 220–23.

39. See the document, "Resolución MRE/RES. 2/92 de la Reunión Ad Hoc de Ministros de Relaciones Exteriores del 18 de mayo de 1992," in Ferrero Costa, *Proceso de retorno,* 203–4.

40. For further discussion of the evolution of government and policies, see Maxwell A. Cameron and Philip Mauceri, eds., *The Peruvian Labyrinth: Polity, Society, Economy* (University Park, PA: Pennsylvania State University Press, 1997); Henry Pease García, *Los años de la langosta: La escena política del fujimorismo* (Lima: La Voz Eddicones, 1994); Jo-Marie Burt, "Statemaking against Democracy: The Case of Fujimori's Peru," in *Politics in the Andes: Identity, Conflict and Reform,* ed. Jo-Marie Burt and Philip Mauceri (Pittsburgh, PA: University of Pittsburgh Press, 2004), 247–68.

41. *EFE,* October 24, 2003. Disaggregated figures on the transfers were included in Congreso de la República, Subcomisión investigadora de la denuncia constitucional numero 6, Comisión Permanente del Congreso de la República, *Informe Final,* January 14, 2002, Lima.

42. The congressional investigative commission headed by Fausto Alvarado noted this important but frequently forgotten aspect of the coup. See Comisión Inves-

tigadora de la influencia irregular ejercida durante el gobierno de Alberto Fujimori Fujimori (1990–2000) sobre el poder judicial, ministerio público y otros poderes e instituciones del estado vinculadas a la administración de justicia, *Informe Preliminar,* December 12, 2001, Lima, 4.

43. Americas Watch, *Human Rights in Peru: One Year After Fujimori's Coup* (New York: Americas Watch, Division of Human Rights Watch, April 1993).

44. See "La década de los noventa y los dos gobiernos de Alberto Fujimori," in Comisión de la Verdad y Reconciliación, *Informe Final* (2003), 85–87, http://www .cverdad.org.pe/ifinal (accessed September 20, 2003).

45. In keeping with his penchant for videotaping, Montesinos recorded the inaugural festivities. See *La República,* September 3, 2003.

46. Francisco Durand, *Riqueza económica y pobreza política: Reflexiones sobre las elites del poder en un país instable* (Lima: Pontifícia Universida Católica del Perú, Fondo Editorial, 2003), 458–63.

Chapter 4: Formalizing the Coup

1. Cynthia McClintock, "Presidents, Messiahs, and Constitutional Breakdowns in Peru," in *The Failure of Presidential Democracy,* ed. Juan J. Linz and Arturo Valenzuela (Baltimore: Johns Hopkins University Press, 1994), 382.

2. *El Mercurio,* August 16, 1992, in *FBIS-LAT-92-175,* September 9, 1992. For an overview of the early post-coup scholarly debates on developments in Peru, see Joseph S. Tulchin and Gary Bland, eds., *Peru in Crisis: Dictatorship or Democracy?* (Boulder, CO: Lynne Rienner Publishers, 1994).

3. *EFE,* April 24, 1992, in *FBIS-LAT-92-081,* April 27, 1992.

4. *El Peruano,* June 7, 1992, in *FBIS-LAT-92-119,* June 19, 1992. Also see César Arias Quincot, *La modernización autoritaria: La nueva institucionalidad surgida a partir de 1990* (Lima: Fundación Friedrich Ebert, 1994).

5. Lima Radio and Television Networks, *FBIS-LAT-92-106,* June 2, 1992.

6. *Global de Televisión,* June 13, 1992, in *FBIS-LAT-92-115,* June 15, 1992.

7. *Radio Programas del Perú,* June 16, 1992, in *FBIS-LAT-92-125,* June 29, 1992; *Global de Televisión,* June 24, 1992, in *FBIS-LAT-92-122,* June 24, 1992.

8. *Global de Televisión,* June 27, 1992, in *FBIS-LAT-92-125,* June 29, 1992; *Global de Televisión,* June 24, 1992, in *FBIS-LAT-92-122,* June 24, 1992.

9. *Panamericana Televisión,* July 1, 1992, in *FBIS-LAT-92-128,* July 2, 1992.

10. *Global de Televisión,* July 2, 1992, and July 4, 1992, in *FBIS-LAT-92-129,* July 6, 1992.

11. Mirko Lauer, *Días divididos: Columnas políticas de los años 90* (Lima: ADEC-ATC, 1994), 71–73.

12. *Televisión Nacional de Chile,* July 8, 1992, in *FBIS-LAT-92-131,* July 8, 1992.

13. Lima Radio and Television Networks, July 28, 1992, in *FBIS-LAT-92-147,* July 30, 1992.

14. *Radio Programas del Perú,* August 4, 1992, in *FBIS-LAT-92-151,* August 5, 1992.

15. *Global de Televisión,* August 5, 1992, in *FBIS-LAT-92-152,* August 6, 1992.

16. *Global de Televisión,* August 8, 1992, in *FBIS-LAT-92-154,* August 10, 1992.

17. *Global de Televisión,* August 9, 1992, in *FBIS-LAT-92-154,* August 10, 1992.

18. In the 1990 congressional election, FIM won a total of seven seats, SODE won three, and Convergencia Socialista won one. The Coordinadora Independiente was an improvised congressional group led by two dissidents elected on other party tickets. Thus, the accord was signed by political organizations that accounted for no more than 5 percent of the 240 elected legislators in the 1990 congress. Adding in the forty-six seats won by C90, the accord represented an agreement involving organizations that accounted for just a quarter of the 1990 legislature.

19. For the entire text, see "Ley de Elecciones para El Congreso Constituyente Democrático, del 21 de agosto de 1992," in Ferrero Costa, *Proceso de retorno,* 234–64.

20. *Global de Televisión,* August 26, 1992, in *FBIS LAT-92-167,* August 27, 1992.

21. *Global de Televisión,* August 29, 1992, in *FBIS-LAT-92,* August 31, 1992.

22. *Radio Programas del Perú,* August 29, 1992, in *FBIS-LAT-92-169,* August 31, 1992.

23. *Panamericana Televisión,* September 11, 1992, in *FBIS-LAT-92-817,* September 14, 1992.

24. Alberto Borea, interview, Lima, August 6, 1994.

25. *Panamericana Televisión,* September 7, 1992, in *FBIS-LAT-92-176,* September 10, 1992.

26. See the interview with Moreyra, "Se abre un panorama sombrío," *Quehacer* 84 (August 1993), 29–32.

27. *Global de Televisión,* September 10, 1992, in *FBIS-LAT-92-176,* September 10, 1992.

28. The official name of the new organization was Alianza Nueva Mayoría-Cambio 90. In the 1995, the organization reversed the name to Cambio 90-Nueva Mayoría. To avoid confusion, the organization is referred to as Cambio 90-Nueva Mayoría (C90-NM) throughout the book.

29. Víctor Joy Way, interview by author, Lima, December 12, 1994.

30. Carlos Torres y Torres Lara, interview by author, Lima, August 4, 1994.

31. *Radio Programas del Perú,* May 13, 1992, in *FBIS-LAT-92-094,* May 14, 1992.

32. Samuel Abad Yupanqui and Carolina Garcés Peralta, "El gobierno de Fujimori: Antes y después del golpe," in *Del golpe de estado a la nueva constitución,* ed. Comisión Andina de Juristas (Lima: Comisión Andina de Juristas, 1993), 176–77.

33. For an analysis of the images and text of the miniseries, see Imelda Vega-Centeno, *Simbólica y política: Peru 1978–1993* (Lima: Fundación Friedrich Ebert), 86–119.

34. Julio Carrión, "La campaña electoral y la opinión pública en El Perú actual" (paper delivered at the Twenty-second International Congress of the Latin American Studies Association, Miami, March 16–18, 2000).

35. Fujimori provided details of the plot in television interviews. See *Panamericana Televisión,* November 16, 1992, in *FBIS-LAT-92-224,* November 19, 1992.

36. Jaime Salinas Sedó, *Desde El Real Felipe: En defensa de la democracia* (Lima: Mosca Azul Editores, 1997), 17–20.

37. Abad Yupanqui and Garcés Peralta, "El gobierno de Fujimori," 180. Cynthia McClintock generously provided me with a copy of the 1992 CCD ballot from her files.

38. Organización de los Estados Americanos, Unidad para la Promoción de la Democracia, *Observaciones Electorales en el Perú 1992–1993* (Washington DC: Organization of American States, 1996).

39. Einaudi delivered his remarks to the OAS meeting on December 14, 1992. In hindsight, Einaudi conceded that the December decision to close the ad hoc foreign ministers' meeting on Peru might have been mistake. See Luigi Einaudi, "The Peruvian Transition and the Role of the International Community," in *The Crisis of Democratic Governance in the Andes,* ed. Cynthia Arnson (Washington DC: Latin American Program, Woodrow Wilson International Center for Scholars, 2002), 125.

40. *Frecuencia 2 Satelite Televisión,* November 23, 1992, in *FBIS-LAT-92-226,* November 23, 1992.

41. *El Comercio,* October 10, 1992, in *FBIS-LAT-92-204,* October 21, 1992.

42. Abad Yupanqui and Garcés Peralta, "El gobierno de Fujimori," 186–88.

43. *Global de Televisión,* November 24, 1992, in *FBIS-LAT-92-227,* November 24, 1992.

44. As a number of analysts have noted, a select group of female politicians became the most strident defenders of the president. Among the group were Congresswoman Luz Salgado, Congresswoman Carmen Lozada, Congresswoman Martha Hidelbrandt, and Minister of Women María Luisa Cuculiza. See Cecilia Blondet, *El encanto del dictador: Mujeres y política en la decáda de Fujimori* (Lima: Instituto de Estudios Peruanos, 2002). On Fujimori's connections to women's issues, also see Gregory Schmidt, "All the President's Women," in *The Fujimori Legacy,* ed. Julio Carrión (University Park, PA: Pennsylvania State University Press, forthcoming).

45. *EFE,* February 5, 1993, in *FBIS-LAT-93-024,* February 8, 1993.

46. The C90-NM commission members who voted to limit presidential reelection to one term were Carlos Ferrero, Samuel Matsuda, Pedro Vílchez, Ricardo Marcenaro, and Carlos Torres y Torres Lara. Lourdes Flores, Enrique Chirinos Soto, José Barba Caballero, and Roger Cáceres voted against the first motion to allow for presidential reelection. See *Resumen Semanal,* June 9–15, 1993.

47. *Sí,* April 5–11, 1993.

48. *El Comercio,* June 14, 1993.

49. The original interview in Spanish appeared in *Quehacer* 84 (July–August 1993): 29–32. An English translation of the interview was reprinted in *FBIS-LAT-93-197,* October 14, 1993.

50. The transcript of the debate can be found in Pedro Planas, *El Fujimorato: Estudio político-constitucional* (Lima: n.p., 1999), 393.

51. *Sí,* April 5–11, 1993, 20–23.

52. Comité por El No, "¿Por qué el No? ¡Porque queremos un Perú democrático!" (document, Lima, July 1993). The meeting held in Lima on July 12, 1993, was reported by *La República,* July 13, 1993, in *FBIS-LAT-93-142,* July 27, 1993.

53. *Caretas,* April 7, 1993, 9.

54. *Resumen Semanal,* July 14–20, 1993.

55. *Resumen Semanal,* July 21–August 3, 1993.

56. For a discussion of the 1993 race, see Henry A. Dietz, "Urban Elections in Peru, 1980–1995," in *Urban Elections in Democratic Latin America,* ed. Henry A. Dietz and Gil Shidlo (Wilmington, DE: Scholarly Resources, 1998), 213–16. For a laudatory appraisal of Belmont's political career, see Guillermo Thorndike, *El hermanón* (Lima: Editorial Libre, 1994).

57. *Agence France Presse,* September 1, 1993, in *FBIS-LAT-93-168,* September 1, 1993.

58. *El Comercio,* September 19, 1993, in *FBIS-LAT-93-192,* October 6, 1993.

59. Committee founders included former PPC congressional leader Roberto Ramírez del Villar, former IU senator and newspaper publisher Gustavo Mohme, economist Javier Tantaleán, and ML leader Javier Gonzales Olaechea. *Sí,* September 6, 1993, 13.

60. *La República,* September 12, 1993, in *FBIS-LAT-93-193,* October 7, 1993.

61. *EFE,* September 13, 1993, in *FBIS-LAT-93-176,* September 14, 1993.

62. *La República,* September 10, 1993, in *FBIS-LAT-93-192,* October 6, 1993.

63. *Radio Programas del Perú,* October 29, 1993, in *FBIS-LAT-93-209,* November 1, 1993.

64. *El Comercio,* September 18, 1993, in *FBIS-LAT-93,* October 6, 1993.

65. *La República,* September 19, 1993.

66. *Expreso,* September 15, 1993.

67. *Expreso,* October 2, 1993.

68. One cover story was entitled, "¿Puede rendirse Sendero Luminoso?" *Sí,* August 2–8, 1993.

69. Apoyo, "Informe de opinión" (document, Lima, November 1993), 25.

70. Imasen confidencial, "Flash de opinión pública del 23 al 25 de agosto de 1993"(document, Lima, August 1993).

71. Apoyo, "Referendum: Se acorta la distancia," (document, Lima, n.d.).

72. *Radio Programas del Perú,* November 1, 1993, in *FBIS-LAT-93-209,* November 1, 1993.

73. *Panamericana Televisión,* November 1, 1993, in *FBIS-LAT-93-209,* November 1, 1993; *Resumen Semanal,* November 3–9, 1993.

74. Ibid.

75. Organización de los Estados Americanos, *Observaciones Electorales,* 68.

76. *Resumen Semanal,* December 8–14, 1993.

77. *Caretas,* November 11, 1993, 15.

78. *Resumen Semanal,* November 3–9, 1993.

79. *Caretas,* December 30, 1993, 12–13.

80. For a discussion of how accountability evolves in democratic systems, see Andreas Schedler, "Restraining the State: Conflicts and Agents of Accountability" in *The Self Restraining State: Power and Accountability in New Democracies,* ed. Andreas Schedler, Larry Diamond, and Marc F. Plattner (Boulder, CO: Lynne Rienner, 1999), 333–50.

81. *Radio Programas del Perú,* April 21, 1993, in *FBIS-LAT-93-076,* April 22, 1993.

82. *Global de Televisión,* April 22, 1993, in *FBIS-LAT-93-076,* April 22, 1993.

83. For an analysis of the events of that week, see the report, "Aprendiz de brujo," *Oiga,* April 26, 1993.

84. For Robles's original statement, his commentaries, and other relevant documents, see Rodolfo Robles Espinoza, *Crimen e impunidad: El "Grupo Colina" y el poder* (Lima: Asociación Pro Derechos Humanos, 1996).

85. "General Picón dice que General Robles debería quitarse la vida," *La República,* May 16, 1993. The article is reproduced in Robles, *Crimen,* 172–74.

86. *Resumen Semanal,* May 12–18, 1993.

87. Of those surveyed, 40 percent refused to answer the question; this may have reflected widespread fearfulness of discussing of the topic. See Apoyo, "Informe de opinión," (document, Lima, April 1993).

88. *Resumen Semanal,* June 2–8, 1993.

89. The majority and minority reports are reproduced in their entirety in Robles, *Crimen,* 137–56. For Freundt's testimony to the Townsend Commission, see Congreso de la República, Comisión Investigadora sobre la actuación y el origen, movimiento y destino de los recursos financieros de Vladimiro Montesinos Torres y su evidente relación con el ex Presidente Alberto Fujimori Fujimori. The text is available on the Web site of the National Security Archive, http://www.gwu.edu/~nsarchiv/NSAEBB/NSAEBB72/final.doc (accessed August 1, 2004): 170.

90. César Romero and Ernesto Carrasco, "Reciclador de cartones y un artesano fueron los artífices del mapa de Cieneguilla," *La República,* December 5, 2004.

91. Americas Watch, *Peru,* 9.

92. *Sí,* August 2–8, 1993, 13.

93. *Resumen Semanal,* July 7–13, 1993.

94. *Resumen Semanal,* August 25–31, 1993.

95. *Resumen Semanal,* August 18–24, 1993.

96. *Resumen Semanal,* December 8–14, 1993.

97. The organization of the Grupo Colina is discussed at length in "Apéndice: El Destacamiento Colina," in Comisión de la Verdad y Reconciliación, *Informe Final* (2003), http://www.cverdad.org.pe/ifinal (accessed September 30, 2003).

98. Rúa, *El crimen,* 168–69.

99. C90-NM congressman Ricardo Marcenaro abstained from voting, while C90-NM congressman Reynaldo Roberts walked out with opposition members. The C90-NM congressman César Fernández Arce also opposed the measure, but he was not present during the vote on the bill. The five members of the Somos Independiente caucus—Julio Chu Mériz, César Larrabure, Mario Paredes, Eusebio Vicuña, and Pablo Cruz—voted with forty members of C90-NM in support of the bill.

100. *Resumen Semanal,* January 26–February 13, 1994.

101. Ibid.

102. Cynthia McClintock and Fabian Vallas, *The United States and Peru: Cooperation at a Cost* (New York: Routledge, 2002), 140–41; Kenneth Roberts and Mark Peceny, "Human Rights and United States Policy Toward Peru," in *The Peruvian Labyrinth: Polity, Society, Economy,* ed. Maxwell A. Cameron and Philip Mauceri (University Park, PA: Pennsylvania State University Press, 1997), 218–20.

Chapter 5: Peru Can't Stop

1. Interview with former consultant to Jaime Yoshiyama, December 4, 1997, Lima.

2. For Fujimori's remarks, see *EFE,* March 15, 1994, in *FBIS-LAT-050,* March 15 1994; *Estrategia,* March 14, 1994, reproduced in *FBIS-LAT-060,* March 29, 1994.

3. *Debate,* September–October 1994, 8–13 in, *FBIS-LAT-229,* November 29, 1994.

4. Bruce H. Kay, "Fujipopulism and the Liberal State in Peru, 1990–1995," *Journal of Interamerican Studies and World Affairs* 38, no. 4 (Winter 1996): 83.

5. Carol Graham and Cheikh Kane, "Opportunistic Government or Sustaining Reform? Electoral Trends and Public-Expenditure Patterns in Peru, 1990–1995," *Latin American Research Review* 33, no. 1 (1998): 99.

6. The study focused on expenditures by the Fondo de Compensación y Desarrollo Social. See Norbert R. Schady, "The Political Economy of Expenditures by the Peruvian Social Fund (FONCODES), 1991–95," *American Political Science Review* 94, no. 2 (June 2000): 289–304.

7. *EFE,* April 20, 1994, in *FBIS-LAT-087,* April 20, 1994.

8. Montesinos made the remark on an audiotape to an unidentified person. See Congreso de la República, Primera Legislatura Ordinaria de 2001, "Transcripción del audio B/1-A," n.d.

9. *Resumen Semanal,* January 12–18, 1994.

10. Marcial Rubio Correa, *Quítate la venda para mirarme mejor: La reforma judicial en el Perú* (Lima: DESCO, 1999), 174.

11. *Caretas,* October 20, 1994.

12. In the months of July and August 1994, the government spent a little over $220,000 to run these television spots, with more than half of the amount going to Channel 2 and Channel 9. See *Oiga,* September 19, 1994.

13. See the editorial of *La República,* July 10, 1994.

14. See, for example, the point and counterpoint essays on the topic by Luz Salgado and Raúl Ferrero, "¿El Presidente debe bajar al llano?" *Sí,* October 17, 1994, 20–21.

15. *La República,* September 8, 1994. When the photos came to light, Rodríguez explained that he was simply helping an old woman who was reaching for a calendar. When Rodríguez realized he had been photographed, he was irate and ordered that some of the film from the local photographers should be seized.

16. *Resumen Semanal,* May 4–10, 1994.

17. *La República*, November 4, 1994.

18. *Expreso*, November 29, 1994.

19. The signatories of the Pact of Honor were Javier Pérez de Cuéllar (Unión por el Perú), Lourdes Flores (Partido Popular Cristiano), Alejandro Toledo (CODE–País Posible), Carlos Cruz Garay (Frente Independiente de Reconciliación Nacional), Rolando Breña (Izquierda Unida), Máximo San Román (Obras), and Teresa Gonzales (Unión, Paz, y Desarrollo). See *La República*, November 30, 1994.

20. Ibid.

21. *La República*, December 7, 1994.

22. *Resumen Semanal*, November 30–December 6, 1994.

23. *Notícias Argentinas*, October 1, 1994, in *FBIS-LAT-193*, October 5, 1994.

24. *Resumen Semanal*, November 30–December 6, 1994.

25. Excerpts from the speeches were from *Resumen Semanal*, December 28, 1994–January 17, 1995.

26. *Gestión*, January 9, 1995.

27. *Expreso*, January 21, 1995.

28. *La República*, October 19, 2003.

29. The events are described in Sally Bowen, *The Fujimori File: Peru and Its President 1990–2000* (Lima: Peru Monitor), 102–4.

30. *Caretas*, August 11, 1994.

31. *Caretas*, August 25, 1994.

32. *Expreso*, August 18, 1994.

33. *Expreso*, August 24, 1994.

34. The results are from a monthly poll conducted by Apoyo in metropolitan Lima and reported in *La República*, August 18, 1994.

35. *Gestión*, September 29, 1994.

36. Reporters covering the story claimed that Eguía was preparing indictments on both Vittor and Schenone prior to the meeting with Colán. See *Caretas*, September 1, 1994.

37. The Higuchi interview with journalist César Hidelbrandt appeared in *Oiga*, October 24, 1994. Muñoz's denials were reported in *La República*, October 26, 1994.

38. Angel Páez, "Susana Higuchi fue espiada día y noche por el SIN," *La República*, September 25, 2002. For the transcript of Montesinos's testimony, see Congreso de la República, Primera Legislatura Ordinaria de 2001, December 20, 2001.

39. *Oiga*, January 23, 1994.

40. *Expreso*, January 25, 1994; *La República*, January 25, 1995.

41. See the transcript of the roundtable discussion with Enrique Bernales, Javier Diez Canseco, and Javier Valle Riestra, "¿Cómo ganarle a Fujimori en buena lid?" *Ideele* 66 (July 1994): 2–8.

42. "Javier encendió la esperanza," *Oiga*, September 26, 1994, 36.

43. *El Comercio*, November 4, 1994.

44. *Resumen Semanal*, November 9–15, 1994.

45. *Resumen Semanal*, November 16–22, 1994.

46. *Oiga,* September 26, 1994.

47. *La República,* September 16, 1994.

48. *La República,* December 12, 1994; December 13, 1994.

49. *La República,* January 23, 1994.

50. Manuel D'Ornellas, "El cuento del fraude," *Expreso,* January 25, 1994.

51. *Expreso,* January 25, 1994.

52. See the interview with Santiago Murray in *Caretas,* March 30, 1995, 27–28.

53. When queried about the handling of *denuncias,* Murray remarked: "The competent authorities have that responsibility [to judge] and it is not incumbent on us, that is not our mission." *La República,* January 25, 1995.

54. For an overview of developments in the complicated conflict, see Hal Klepak, *Confidence Building Sidestepped: The Peru-Ecuador Conflict of 1995* (Toronto: Centre for International and Security Studies, York University and The Canadian Foundation for the Americas, 1998).

55. *La República,* April 4, 1995; April 5, 1995.

56. For the reports on the irregularities in the acquisition of election materials in the JNE, see the following editions of *Sí:* February 20–26, 1995; February 25–March 5, 1995; March 6–12, 1995; March 13–19, 1995.

57. For a comprehensive report on election conditions compiled by the observer mission of the Latin American Studies Association headed by Cynthia McClintock and Steve Stein, see *The 1995 Electoral Process in Peru: A Delegation Report of The Latin American Studies Association* (Miami: North-South Center, University of Miami and The Latin American Studies Association, 1995).

58. In the Andean region, *cholo* is used to describe an indigenous person who moves to the city with aspirations for upward social mobility. Whites and *mestizos* often used the term in a pejorative way. By celebrating the term *cholo,* Toledo was attempting to reach out to rural migrants who compose a large part of the urban electorate.

59. For a partial list of those wiretapped, see *Caretas,* July 17, 1997, 26.

60. On February 25, 1995, *La República* reported that a special group, "Comando Charlie," had been created in the SIN to spy on candidates and fabricate false information to disseminate during the campaign. Targets included presidential candidates Pérez de Cuéllar, Toledo, and congressional candidates Gustavo Mohme and Javier Diez Canseco.

61. The figures were presented in a news conference by JNE officials and reported in *Gestión,* April 9, 1995.

62. *El Mundo,* April 8, 1995.

63. Ibid.

64. *La República* reported that JNE board member Manuel Catorca González had included this information in his original report, but that paragraph was stricken from the official statement released by the JNE concerning the Huánuco incident. The report was published in the newspaper's edition of April 14, 1995. A subsequent report by *El Comercio* revealed that three JNE employees implicated in the Huánuco scandal had been involved in the fraudulent use of election materials on previous oc-

casions. Officials of the JNE never clarified why the individuals were allowed to retain their jobs. See the report in *El Comercio,* June 3, 1995.

65. *Gestión,* April 10, 1995.

66. *Expreso,* April 9, 1995.

67. For an assessment of the election and its controversies, see the following collection of articles that appeared in *LASA Forum* 26, no. 2 (Summer 1995): Catherine M. Conaghan, "Troubled Accounting, Troubling Questions: Looking Back at Peru's Election," 9–12; Bruce H. Kay, "Observations on the 1995 Peruvian National Elections," 13–16; David Scott Palmer, "Peru's 1995 Elections: A Second Look," 17–20.

68. *Expreso,* April 10, 1995; *El Mundo,* April 11, 1995.

69. Transparencia, "Nota de Prensa No. 02: Informe de Resultados del Acto Electoral," April 9, 1995, Lima.

70. Interview with former consultants to Yoshiyama, Lima, April 27, 1995.

71. For a look at postelection speculation regarding possible defections, see Mónica Vecco, "¿Cambiarán de bancada?" *La Revista Domingo, La República,* July 23, 1995, 8–9.

72. *La República,* May 10, 1995.

73. *Gestión,* April 24, 1995; *Caretas,* May 11, 1995.

74. *El Comercio,* June 1, 1995.

75. *Resumen Semanal,* April 26–May 2, 1995.

76. *El Comercio,* May 2, 1995.

77. *La República,* May 8, 1995.

78. *La República,* May 11, 1995.

79. The U.S. State Department acknowledged the election results and underscored the contributions of the OAS and nongovernmental election observers on April 24. *Resumen Semanal,* April 19–25, 1995.

80. *Resumen Semanal,* May 24–30, 1995.

81. *Resumen Semanal,* June 7–13, 1995.

82. The massacre and its aftermath are described in Asociación Pro Derechos Humanos, *Y la verdad será nuestra defensa: El caso de Barrios Altos* (Lima: Asociación Pro Derechos Humanos, 1996).

83. *Resumen Semanal,* May 31–June 5, 1995.

84. *Gestión,* June 13, 1995.

85. "El Grupo Colina anda suelto," *Oiga,* June 19, 1995.

86. The remarks by Lourdes Flores were reproduced in "¡Qué tal congreso!" *Ideele* 77 (July 1995): 6.

87. The C90-NM dissenters were Carlos Ferrero, César Fernández Arce, Ricardo Marcenaro, Carlos Torres y Torres Lara, and Jorge Velásquez Ureta. *Resumen Semanal,* June 14–20, 1995.

88. For a review of the reactions and the Apoyo data, see "No, no, no, no, no, no, no . . . ," *Ideele* 77 (July 1995): 10–12.

89. *Resumen Semanal,* June 21–27, 1995.

90. U.S. Embassy (Lima), "Amnesty Law in Peru: Analysis and Recommenda-

tions," June 15, 1995, The National Security Archive, www.gwu.edu/~nsarchiv/
NSAEBB/NSAEBB72/montesinos2.pdf (accessed August 1, 2004).

91. Ibid.

92. *Resumen Semanal,* June 28–July 4, 1995.

93. *La República,* July 21, 1995; July 23, 1995.

94. *Resumen Semanal,* July 5–11, 1995.

95. See *Caretas,* July 20, 1995.

Chapter 6: The Reelection Project

1. In an interview for Brazilian television in February 1996, Fujimori denied that
he was thinking of another reelection and confirmed his departure from office in 2000.
He said that he would do antipoverty social work during his retirement; see *Gestión,*
February 20, 1996.

2. For Montesinos's testimony, see the transcript, Congreso de la República,
Segunda Legislatura Ordinaria de 2001, April 25, 2002.

3. See Montesinos's conversation with businessman Dioniso Romero: Congreso
de la República, Segunda Legislatura Ordinaria de 2000, "Transcripción de los videos
#1574 y 1575, Reunión del Señor Vladimiro Montesinos Torres con Dionisio Romero
Seminario, El General EO Saucedo Sánchez, General PNP Fernando Dianderas Ottone,
Almirante Ibárcena Amico, General EP Villanueva Ruesta y General EP Bello Vásquez,"
June 14, 1999.

4. On the evolution of economic policies in this period, see Efraín Gonzales de
Olarte, *El neoliberalismo a la peruana: Economía política del ajuste structural,
1990–1997* (Lima: Instituto de Estudios Peruanos, 1998).

5. For extensive discussion of the different spheres of corruption, see Francisco
Durand, *Riqueza económica y pobreza política: Reflexiones sobre las elites del poder
er un país instable* (Lima: Pontificia Universidad Católica del Perú, Fondo Editorial,
2003); Manuel Dammert Ego Aguirre, *Fujimori-Montesinos: El Estado Mafioso* (Lima:
El Virrey, 2001).

6. Higuchi claimed that the money could not have come from the family's own
finances. For Higuchi's revelation, see *La República,* September 11, 2003.

7. See Montesinos's testimony, Congreso de la República, Segunda Legislatura
Ordinaria de 2001, April 25, 2002.

8. *Resumen Semanal,* January 17–23, 1996.

9. Chávez repeated her views on the need for a constitutional reform for reelection on numerous occasions. Her remarks appeared in *La República,* April 23, 1995;
Gestión, February 25, 1996. In a press conference with foreign correspondents, she
stated: "I have a position in that I admit that legally the re-election of President Fujimori in 2000 is not possible . . . my technical position as an attorney is that a constitutional amendment is necessary in order to permit a re-election." See *El Comercio,*
March 1, 1996.

10. On the drop in Fujimori's approval, see *La República*, February 22, 1996; *Expreso*, February 22, 1996. The CPI poll on reelection is cited in *Resumen Semanal*, January 24–30, 1996.

11. *Resumen Semanal*, June 17–23, 1996.

12. Congreso de la República, Segunda Legislatura Ordinaria de 2001, April 25, 2002.

13. *La República*, August 20, 1996.

14. *Expreso*, August 22, 1996.

15. *La República*, September 1, 1996.

16. *La República*, October 5, 1996.

17. *La República*, October 13, 1996.

18. Mario Vargas Llosa noted the convergence between the reelection issue and the multiple scandals related to narco-trafficking; see "La reelección permanente," *Gestión*, September 19, 1996.

19. An Imasen poll taken in November reported that 65.7 percent of those surveyed favored a referendum on reelection. See *Resumen Semanal*, November 6–12, 1996. An Apoyo poll taken in September found support for a referendum among 72 percent of those surveyed. See *Resumen Semanal*, September 11–17, 1996. An Imasen poll taken after the enactment of the reelection law showed 54.5 percent of the public against reelection. See *Resumen Semanal*, September 18–24, 1996.

20. *Resumen Semanal*, November 13–19, 1996.

21. Congreso de la República, Segunda Legislatura Ordinaria de 2001, April 25, 2002.

22. Supreme Court Justice Carlos Giusti was the only civilian who died in the operation. Giusti was the judge whose home was attacked during the La Cantuta case. For coverage of the operation, see *Caretas*, April 25, 1997.

23. *La República*, May 7, 1997.

24. *El Sol*, May 9, 1997.

25. The Imasen polls were published in *Gestión*, May 31, 1997.

26. *Gestión*, May 30, 1997. Congressman Carlos Torres y Torres Lara, vice president of the congress, blasted Jett for his comments and for "interfering" in Peruvian affairs; see *Gestión*, June 4, 1997.

27. *Gestión*, May 25, 1997.

28. The cartoon by Heduardo appeared in *Gestión*, May 30, 1997.

29. The surprising mobilization of students prompted the news magazine cover story, "Rebelión estudiantil ¿Generación X dijeron?" *Caretas*, June 12, 1997.

30. See the following transcripts of Montesinos's meetings with Romulo Muñoz Arce, Congreso de la República, Segunda Legislatura Ordinaria de 2000, "Transcripción del video #916, Reunión Dr.—Oscar Medelius—Rómulo Muñoz Arce," July 21, 1988; "Transcripción del video #1318, Reunión Dr.—Oscar Medelius—Romulo Muñoz Arce," November 11, 1998; "Transcripción del video #1317, Reunión Dr.—Oscar Medelius—Romulo Muñoz Arce," November 11, 1998.

31. In an audiotaped meeting that included JNE board member José Carlos

Bringas, Montesinos spoke of how he had established friendships with JNE members Romulo Muñoz Arce and Walter Hernández, which effectively made them part of the "the team." Congreso de la República, Segunda Legislatura Ordinaria de 2000, "Transcripción de la cinta del audio #1196, Reunión Dr. Serpa—Dr. Bringas—Ing. Joy Way," August 14, 1998.

32. "Abriendo la cancha," *Caretas,* November 20, 1997.

33. *Gestión,* December 9, 1997.

34. *La República,* August 11, 1997.

35. Congreso de la República, Segunda Legislatura Ordinaria de 2000, "Transcripción de la cinta del audio 1196, Reunión Dr. Serpa—Dr. Bringas—Ing. Joy Way," August 14, 1998.

36. Silvia Rojas, "Papelón en el Jurado," *La Revista Domingo, La República,* August 23, 1998.

37. *El Comercio,* August 27, 1998.

38. Congreso de la República, Segunda Legislatura Ordinaria de 2001, April 25, 2002.

39. *El Comercio,* August 27, 1998.

40. In one of the meetings between Montesinos and Joy Way, Montesinos urged Joy Way to try to bribe Ferrero in return for a vote against the referendum. Congreso de la República, Segunda Legislatura Ordinaria de 2000, "Transcripción de la cinta del audio 1195, Reunión Dr.—Dr. Serpa—Dr. Bringas—Ing. Joy Way," August 14, 1998.

41. Cynthia McClintock and Fabian Vallas, *The United States and Peru: Cooperation at a Cost* (New York: Routledge, 2002), 145.

42. Luigi Einaudi was appointed to act as U.S. special envoy for the Ecuador-Peru peace process. Einaudi was recognized as playing a pivotal role in the negotiations along with Brazilian president Fernando Henrique Cardoso. For more on the process, see McClintock and Vallas, *The United States and Peru,* 78–84.

43. *Gestión,* October 27, 1998.

44. *Ottawa Citizen,* October 29, 1998. The author attended the Rideau Hall meeting, sponsored by the Canadian Foundation for the Americas, on October 28, 1998. Fujimori attacked Amnesty International for "defending terrorists" after Amnesty representatives questioned Fujimori about human rights abuses in Peru.

45. Mirko Lauer, "Burla, burlando van governando," *La República,* August 25, 1998; "La victoria de una derrota," *Caretas,* September 3, 1998.

Chapter 7: Kidnapping the Media

1. "Discurso del Presidente Alberto Fujimori en la inauguración del 27 Período Ordinario de Sesiones de la Asamblea General de la Organización de Estados Americanos," *El Peruano,* June 2, 1997.

2. Cover stories featuring Montesinos included the following: *Caretas,* April 11, 1996; August 22, 1996; September 5, 1996; September 26, 1996; December 12, 1996;

April 17, 1997. *Referéndum* was founded in 1998. Its title referred to the blocked referendum on reelection. Fernando Viana, Luis Ibérico, and José García, the journalists who gained notoriety as a result of their involvement with Channel 2 and Baruch Ivcher, created the newspaper. It ceased publication in October 1998 in the midst of disputes between the journalists and stockholders. Viana later joined with César Hidelbrandt to publish *Liberación*, a strident opposition newspaper that blasted Fujimori and Montesinos through the course of the 2000 election and after.

3. *La República*, August 17, 1996.

4. During the congressional investigation on La Cantuta in 1993, the director of the SIN, General Julio Salazar Monroe, stated that Montesinos worked "ad honorem" in the intelligence agency. Presumably, that status relieved Montesinos of any obligation to testify in the case. When queried about Montesinos in 1996, Fujimori said that he "supposed" Montesinos was a paid functionary of the SIN. Fujimori underscored that Montesinos was not his own personal advisor, but a legal attaché of the SIN. On the question of Montesinos's status, see "¿Yo señor? Historia de un asesor negado," *Caretas*, September 5, 1996.

5. *La República*, September 7, 1996. The charges against Montesinos came on the heels of several embarrassing incidents that suggested possible links between the military and drug traffickers. In May 1996, 174 kilos of cocaine were found on one of the planes used by the president and piloted by one of his military attaches. In June, 120 kilograms of cocaine were discovered on a Peruvian navy ship docked in Vancouver, British Columbia.

6. Rumors circulated that the falling out between Ivcher and Montesinos had to do with conflicts over business deals. Ivcher denied the stories. Journalists at Channel 2 maintained that Ivcher's decision was based on changes in his own political sensibilities and a desire to improve the image of his network.

7. *La República*, September 6, 1996.

8. One of the theories was that Chávez had been tortured with electric shock. See the cover story, "Tratamiento para que no hable," *Caretas*, August 29, 1996. Chávez was found guilty on October 11 of drug trafficking and forgery charges, receiving a sentence of twenty-five years in jail. He had been previously convicted on treason charges for collaborating with Sendero Luminoso and had received a thirty-year sentence. Chávez was not permitted to address the court after sentencing. Along with Chávez, retired general Jaime Ríos Araico was convicted on drug trafficking along with two other army commanders.

9. *Resumen Semanal*, October 23–29, 1996.

10. The *New York Times* editorial of November 25, 1996, was reprinted in the cover story on the detention of General Rodolfo Robles, *Caretas*, November 28, 1996.

11. *Resumen Semanal*, November 20–26, 1996.

12. *Expreso*, December 3, 1996.

13. *Resumen Semanal*, December 4–10, 1996.

14. Ibid.

15. Cruz's initial reports were published on December 9, 10, and 14, 1996, in *La República*.

16. *La República,* December 10, 1996.

17. *La República,* February 12, 1997.

18. In the video transcript of a meeting between Montesinos and television station owner Domingo Palermo, Montesinos reflected on how infrequently people read and how they depended on television for information. See Congreso de la República, Primera Legislatura Ordinaria de 2001, "Transcripción del video #1782, Reunión Dr.—Palermo," November 10, 1999.

19. A complete chronology of events was published on Ivcher's web site, *Defending Freedom of the Press: The Baruch Ivcher Affair* at www.ivcher.com (site now discontinued).

20. The Bareto-La Rosa revelations were also the subject of the cover story, "Suplícios de inteligencia: Agentes SIE Mariella Barreto (descuartizada) y Leonor La Rosa (torturada), *Caretas,* April 10, 1997. As this book went to press, there was renewed controversy in Peru concerning the veracity of La Rosa's allegations of torture. La Rosa received financial compensation for her injuries and an apology from the Peruvian government in 2002. In the same year, the CSJM concluded that two army officials convicted of torture in a hasty trial in 1997 were innocent and ordered their release from prison. La Rosa is now charged in a defamation case brought by Colonel Carlos Edmundo Sánchez Noriega, former head of army intelligence. To date, La Rosa has not retracted her version of events. For a review of the current controversy and defense of his reporting on SIN leaks, see Edmundo Cruz, "Leonor La Rosa sí fue torturada," *La República,* December 9, 2004.

21. *La República,* April 4, 1997.

22. *Resumen Semanal,* April 2–8, 1997.

23. In his appearance before congress, Castillo told legislators, "A criminal should be punished, a torturer should be punished, but every branch has its own powers. Investigate the executive, investigate the congress, but let's fold our arms and leave the judiciary alone. Shoemakers, to your shoes! Each one to their own job!" See *Resumen Semanal,* April 9–15, 1997.

24. The *oficialista* spin on the La Rosa case was painfully reminiscent of the La Cantuta case when it was suggested that the *desaparecidos* might have staged their own kidnapping, an *auto-secuestro.* Shortly thereafter, the absurd suggestion was discredited by the discovery of the bodies.

25. *La República,* April 30, 1997.

26. *La República,* May 9, 1997.

27. For the full text of the document see Comando Conjunto de las Fuerzas Armadas, "Comunicado Oficial Number 002-97 CCFFAA," *El Sol,* May 24, 1997.

28. *Gestión,* May 29, 1997.

29. The cover featured a photograph of Baruch Ivcher with the title, "La Conexión Ecuatoriana: Documentos que acusan," *Sí,* June 2–8, 1997.

30. *Gente,* June 4, 1997.

31. *La República,* June 11, 1997.

32. See the previously cited, "Discurso del presidente," *El Peruano,* June 2, 1997.

33. *Gestión,* July 11, 1997.

34. *El Mañanero,* July 16, 1997.

35. *El Mañanero,* July 11, 1997.

36. For a partial list of the individuals tapped, see "Cinismo oficial," *Caretas,* July 17, 1997.

37. On Chávez's findings, see *Resumen Semanal,* May 27, 1998. For Montesinos's testimony, see Congreso de la República, Primera Legislatura Ordinaria de 2001, December 20, 2001.

38. *La República,* September 20, 1997. For a report on the station takeover see the cover story, "Ivcher: Borrada del Mapa," in *Caretas,* September 18, 1997.

39. For American coverage of the Ivcher case see, Jonathan Friedland, "Peruvians Recoil from Fujimori Despite Peace, Prosperity He Won," *Wall Street Journal,* July 8, 1997; "Eliminating the Critics," *Miami Herald,* July 17, 1997; Calvin Sims, "Crusading TV Station is the City's Daytime Drama," *New York Times,* July 21, 1997.

40. The Helms-Gilman Letter was dated June 17, 1997. The letter was reproduced on "Defending Freedom of the Press: The Baruch Ivcher Affair," http://www.ivcher.com (accessed February 1, 2000; site now discontinued).

41. The University of Lima poll appeared in *La República,* September 20, 1997. The Imasen poll, covering the Lima-Callao metropolitan areas, was cited in *La República,* September 26, 1997.

42. In a conversation with Julio Vera, owner of Andina Televisión, Montesinos joked that Ivcher was in Los Jardines de Paz, a Lima cemetery. For the remarks, see Congreso de la República, Segunda Legislatura Ordinaria de 2000, "Transcripción del video #1197, Reunión Dr.—Borobio—Julio Vera," October 12, 1998. For his dismissal of the U.S. congressional resolutions, see Congreso de la República, Segunda Legislatura Ordinaria de 2000, "Transcripción del video #1753, Reunión Dr.—Eduardo Calmell," October 5, 1999.

43. According to the findings of the Townsend Commission, the commander general of the army, José Villanueva Ruesta, called high-ranking military officials to a meeting in 1999 to discuss military support for the reelection. The meeting included a discussion of media issues. See Congreso de la República, Comisión Investigadora sobre la actuación y el origen, movimiento y destino de los recursos financieros de Vladimiro Montesinos Torres y su evidente relación con el ex Presidente Alberto Fujimori Fujimori, http://www.gwu.edu/~nsarchiv/NSAEBB/NSAEBB72/final.doc (accessed August 1, 2004): 156.

44. *La República,* February 19, 2001; *La República,* July 2, 2002.

45. For the discussion of the loan problem with Montesinos see Congreso de la República, Segunda Legislatura Ordinaria de 2000, "Transcripción de los videos #1349 y 1350, "Reunión Dr.—Crousillat (H)—Gisela," February 26, 1999.

46. Congreso de la República, Segunda Legislatura Ordinaria de 2000, "Transcripción del video #1197, "Reunión Dr.—Borobio—Julio Vera," October 12, 1998.

47. Congreso de la República, Segunda Legislatura Ordinaria de 2000, "Transcripción de los videos #1459 y 1450, Reunión Dr.—Delgado Parker—Joy Way," April 7, 1999.

48. Shutz tried unsuccessfully to get Montesinos to increase the monthly payments to $1.7 million. For the transcript of their meeting see Congreso de la República, Segunda Legislatura Ordinaria de 2000, "Transcripción del audio #1783, Dr.—Shutz," November 10, 1999.

49. Montesinos told Ernesto Shutz and Manuel Delgado Parker of his media-monitoring system in their conversation of August 1999. See Congreso de la República, Segunda Legislatura Ordinaria de 2000, "Transcripción de los videos #1677 y 1679, Reunión Dr. Montesinos—Delgado Parker—Shutz," August 25, 1999.

50. Laura Bozzo's political trajectory included a radical conversion to *Fujimorismo* after the 1995 reelection. Previously, Bozzo had worked as a host on Channel 11, a television station owned by Ricardo Belmont, the Lima mayor who ran against Fujimori in the 1995 election. Bozzo joined station director Guillermo Thorndike in hysterical rants against Fujimori during election-day coverage, in which they accused the government of an electoral fraud. For more on Bozzo's career, see "Bozzo, morbo y votos," *Caretas,* June 10, 1999.

51. Montesinos passed along the idea in a conversation with José Francisco Crousillat López Torres in July 1999. For the transcript, see Congreso de la República, Segunda Legislatura Ordinaria de 2000, "Transcripción del video #1607, Reunión Dr.—Crousillat—Sr. Wo—Sr. Bertini," July 19, 1999.

52. Congreso de la República, Segunda Legislatura Ordinaria de 2001, "Transcripción del video #1792, Reunión de Comandantes Generales de las Fuerzas Armadas, Los Hermanos Winter, Carlos Boloña Behr y Vladimiro Montesinos Torres," November 26, 1999.

53. Congreso de la República, Segunda Legislatura Ordinaria de 2000, "Transcripción del audio #1780, Calmell—Vincente—Grl. Delgado," November 6, 1999. Ulloa denied knowing the source of the stock purchase. Vincente Silva Checca, a media consultant and shareholder in CCN, acted as Montesinos's intermediary in the deal, making the cash payment to Ulloa. See the report, "Ulloa a la carta," *Caretas,* January 25, 2001.

54. The payments are documented in the transcripts of two meetings between Montesinos and Calmell. See Congreso de la República, Segunda Legislatura Ordinaria de 2000, "Transcripción del video #1736, Reunión Dr.—Eduardo Calmell," September 14, 1999; "Transcripción del video #1753, Reunión Dr.—Eduardo Calmell," October 5, 1999.

55. For the *Serie Coleccionable* supplements, see the following editions of *El Chino*: "D'Ornellas: El mas corcho del periodismo," October 13, 1997; "Los enemigos del pueblo: Antipatriotas libran batalla para deestabilizar el Perú," October 9, 1997; "Hidelbrandt: Un chato mental, Cecilia, una diabla," December 13, 1997; "Los Rabiosos: De la prensa antiperuana," March 27, 1998.

56. For the reports by Cruz, see *La República,* April 5–7, 1997. For further coverage see the cover story, "Agente Zanatta: La historia completa," *Caretas,* March 19, 1998.

57. The choice of Claudia Schiffer was probably inspired by Schiffer's brief visit

to Lima in April 1997, which garnered frenzied media coverage. Placing Schiffer in the SIN office was likely thought to be the most extravagant and outrageous story that could be concocted—a "tall" tale indeed.

58. For a review of the state of press freedom in this period and the statement issued by the international mission at the June meeting, see Instituto Prensa y Sociedad, *Perú 1998: Informe Anual sobre Prensa y Democracia* (Lima: InterPrensa, 1999).

59. Congreso de la República de 2001, Primera Legislatura Ordinaria de 2001, December 20, 2001.

60. Testimony by the former editors of *El Chato* and *La Yuca,* along with the estimate on *El Tío* revenues, was reported by Edmundo Cruz in *La República,* May 5, 2001.

61. For a comprehensive analysis of media coverage during the 2000 election campaign, see Jacqueline Fowks, *Suma y resta de la realidad: Medios de comunicación y elecciones generales 2000 en el Perú* (Lima: Fundación Friedrich Ebert, 2000).

62. Montesinos reportedly used Peruvian cooperation as a bargaining chip and threatened to pull out of the joint counternarcotics programs when U.S. officials pressed the government on political matters. See Anthony Faiola and Scott Wilson, "U.S. Took Risks in Aiding Peru's Anti-Drug Patrols," *Washington Post,* April 29, 2001. The U.S. ambassador Dennis Jett noted Montesinos's "flexible" attitude on air operations in 1999; see U.S. Embassy (Lima) Cable, "Support by Peru's National Security Advisor for Landing Rights, Refueling, and Ron for USG Aircraft Operating out of Manta," May 21, 1999, http://peruembassy.gov/wwwsclasse.shtml (accessed August 1, 2004). For an up-to-date analysis of the role of Montesinos and the U.S. drug war, see Washington Office on Latin America, "Drug War Paradoxes: The U.S. Government and Peru's Vladimiro Montesinos," *Drug War Monitor* (July 2004): 1–18.

63. For Montesinos's views on Peru's irrelevance to the United States, see Congreso de la República, Segunda Legislatura Ordinaria de 2000, "Transcripción del video #1753, Reunión Dr.—Eduardo Calmell," October 5, 1999.

Chapter 8: Perú 2000

1. A high-ranking leader of Peru's elite business community assured this author in August 1998 that Fujimori would not seek reelection because of health troubles. The informant said that Vladimiro Montesinos was the source of this information.

2. *Gestión,* July 12, 1999. His remarks echoed those in an earlier interview with a Brazilian newspaper in which he said he had no plans for what to do after his presidency, and that the presidency "fascinated" him. The remarks were reported in *Gestión,* July 7, 1999.

3. Montesinos described the campaign facilities and the visits by officials in testimony to congressional investigators. See the transcript, Congreso de la República, Primera Legislatura Ordinaria de 2001, December 20, 2001.

4. *Gestión,* February 21, 2002.

5. On the evolution of Hermoza's relationships with Fujimori and Montesinos, see "Una historia de encuentros y desencuentros," *Gestión,* August 21, 1999. Hermoza came to resent the president and Montesinos taking all the credit for the successful military operation that rescued the MRTA-held hostages in April 1997. For his version of the events, see Nicolás De Bari Hermoza Ríos, *"Operación Chavin de Huantar: Rescate en la residencia de la Embajada del Japón* (Lima: Talleres Gráficos de Fimart, 1997).

6. Analysts anticipated Montesinos's power grab well in advance. See the cover story, "En 1997: La Promoción Montesinos," *Caretas,* September 5, 1996. For a comprehensive analysis of Montesinos and his relations with the armed forces, see Fernando Rospigliosi, *Montesinos y las Fuerzas Armadas: Cómo controló durante una década las instituciones militares* (Lima: Instituto de Estudios Peruanos, 2000). For a discussion of Montesinos's takeover of the posts in the high command, see *La República,* December 11, 1999.

7. Montesinos described his use of the military in the reelection campaign to congressional investigators. See the transcript, Congreso de la República, Primera Legislatura Ordinaria de 2001, December 20, 2001.

8. The figures are from the Instituto Nacional de Estadísticas e Informática and cited in Julio Carrión, "Peru's Impoverished Voters: The Battleground of the Second Round," *Peru Election 2000,* http://qsilver.queensu.ca/csd/peru2000/trends (accessed April 30, 2000; site now discontinued).

9. Congreso de la República, Primera Legislatura Ordinaria de 2001, December 20, 2001.

10. *Expreso,* October 30, 1999.

11. The Asamblea Metropolitana de Alcaldes issued a statement expressing their concerns that government-appointed governors and lieutenant governors were harassing mayors, especially those affiliated with Somos Perú. See *El Comercio,* September 1, 1999.

12. *La República,* August 27, 1999.

13. "La Planilla Negra," *Caretas,* January 17, 2002.

14. The Asociación Prensa Libre was founded in August 1999 by journalists concerned about government abuses of journalists and political candidates. The founders included Congresswoman Anel Townsend, Mabel Barreto María Elaen Belaúnde, Roxanna Cueva, Iván García, Guillermo González, Luis Ibérico, David Montoya, and Bruno de Olazabal.

15. Congreso de la República, Segunda Legislatura Ordinaria de 2001, "Transcripción de los videos #888 y 889, Montes de Oca—Dr.," May 3, 1998.

16. Montesinos testified that José Alberto Bustamante, the president of the council of ministers and minister of justice, along with C90-NM congressman Jorge Trelles, helped to prepare the documentation. Montesinos claimed that General José Villanueva, General Bello, and Admiral Ibárcena and General Dianderas were also in attendance at the meeting. Congreso de la República, Primera Legislatura Ordinaria de 2001, December 20, 2001.

17. The coverage was published in *El Tío* from May 20 through May 31, 1999.

18. *La Repúdica* circulated on May 31, 1999. The title was an obvious play on *La República* using the word *"repudiar"* (to repudiate). The publication included a death threat aimed at *La República* reporter Edmundo Cruz. The incident was reported in *Caretas,* June 3, 1999. *Repudio* appeared in July. It also mimicked the previous tabloid attacks on Mohme and reporters Edmundo Cruz and Angel Páez.

19. *Caretas,* April 15, 1999. Faisal published a long open letter to Mohme denying that the Web site was a SIN operation. See *Expreso,* May 19, 1999.

20. See the reports in *La República,* April 8, 2002; July 17, 2002; July 18, 2002.

21. For descriptions of the event and the controversy, see *La República,* July 28, 1999; Silvia Rojas, *"¿Bailas conmigo?" La Revista Domingo, La República,* August 1, 1999.

22. *La República,* July 29, 1999. The most dramatic moment in the tense session came when Congresswoman Anel Townsend approached Fujimori and placed an empty pot on the podium to symbolize Peru's continuing poverty under the Fujimori regime. Congressman Carlos Chipocco placed a copy of the charter of the OAS on the podium, a reference to the government's withdrawal from Inter-American Court of Human Rights. C90-NM congresswoman Luz Salgado got up to remove the pot from the podium, and threw the OAS charter to the floor.

23. *La República,* November 23, 1999. Gustavo Mohme, the publisher of *La República,* was one of the architects of the pact. Mohme strongly advocated that the opposition should field a single unity candidate to run against Fujimori, as did former president Fernando Belaúnde.

24. For a discussion of the mobilization of human rights groups, see Coletta A. Youngers and Susan C. Peacock, *Peru's Coordinadora Nacional de Derechos Humanos: A Case Study of Coalition Building* (Washington DC: Washington Office on Latin America, 2002).

25. The project eventually compiled a list of 830 reasons why the 2000 election was fraudulent. For the complete list, see Instituto de Defensa Legal, *Las elecciones Frankenstein: Nacieron con deformidades incurables, se armaron a la mala, con fallas estructurales insalvables y terminaron con cicatrices monstruosas en todo el cuerpo* (Lima: Instituto de Defensa Legal, 2000).

26. *Gestión,* October 4, 1999.

27. For Transparencia's report on the video, see Transparencia, "Resultados de la verificación realizada con motivo de la denuncia publica presentada por el Partido Solidaridad Nacional," Transparencia, http://www.transparencia.org.pe/verden.htm (accessed November 5, 1999; site now discontinued).

28. *La República,* October 3, 1999.

29. *Gestión,* June 5, 1999.

30. *La República,* September 8, 1999.

31. *Gestión,* December 9, 1999.

32. Cantón's findings were reported in *Gestión,* May 7, 1999. For the previously mentioned reports, see Committee to Protect Journalists, *Attacks on the Press in 1998,*

http://www.cpj.org/attacks98/index_attack98.html (accessed May 4, 1999); Freedom House, "Press Freedom Survey 1999," http://www.freedomhouse.org/pdfs99 (accessed on May 30, 1999).

33. *La República,* August 4, 1999. Fujimori dismissed Abrams's remarks, saying that Abrams lacked "moral authority" to make such judgments because of his involvement in the Iran-Contra scandal during the Reagan administration.

34. *La República,* August 6, 1999.

35. *Expreso,* November 10, 1999.

36. *El Sol,* November 11, 1999.

37. *Expreso,* November 13, 1999

38. *El Comercio,* October 13, 1999.

39. The payment figures were taken from testimony provided by former foreign minister Fernando de Trazgenies to the congressional investigative commission chaired by Congresswoman Anel Townsend. See Congreso de la República, Comisión Investigadora sobre la actuación y el origen, movimiento y destino de los recursos financieros de Vladimiro Montesinos Torres y su evidente relación con el ex Presidente Alberto Fujimori Fujimori: http://www.gwu.edu/~nsarchiv/NSAEBB/NSAEBB72/final.doc (accessed August 1, 2004): 251.

40. *Gestión,* November 15, 1999.

41. Coletta Youngers, *Deconstructing Democracy: Peru under Alberto Fujimori* (Washington DC: Washington Office on Latin America, 2000).

42. *Datos Electorales,* December 7, 1999. Transparencia's subsequent studies of television, the tabloid press, and government advertising can be found in their *Datos Electorales* series in 1999 and 2000.

43. *Gestión,* December 15, 1999.

44. *Gestión,* December 3, 1999.

45. *La República,* December 6, 1999.

46. *Expreso,* December 7, 1999.

47. *El Comercio,* December 3, 1999.

48. National Democratic Institute–The Carter Center, "NDI/Carter Center Pre-Election Statement—December 3, 1999," in *Peru Elections 2000: Final Report of the National Democratic Institute/Carter Center Joint Election Monitoring Project,* The Carter Center, http://cartercenter.org/documents/292.pdf (accessed August 1, 2003).

49. *Gestión,* December 8, 1999.

50. The U.S. State Department document is cited in Cynthia McClintock and Fabian Vallas, *The United States and Peru: Cooperation at a Cost* (New York: Routledge, 2003), 147. The statement is dated December 28, 1999.

51. See Congreso de la República, Segunda Legislatura Ordinaria de 2001, "Transcripción del video #1792, Reunión de Comandantes Generales de las Fuerzas Armadas, Los Hermanos Winter, Carlos Boloña Behr y Vladimiro Montesinos Torres," November 26, 1999.

52. Among the Defensoría's major projects was its work in reviewing cases of individuals unjustly imprisoned on terrorism charges. The office also created new pro-

grams on women's issues and the rights of the physically challenged. For an overview of the activities, see Defensoría del Pueblo, *Al Servicio del Pueblo: Primer informe del Defensor del Pueblo ante el Congreso de la República 1996–1998* (Lima: Defensoría del Pueblo, 1998).

53. The Defensoría produced special reports on specific cases of abuse during the campaign that included the harassment of candidates, the government slogan painting campaign, and the use of public resources in the campaign. For the complete findings on the electoral process, see Defensoría del Pueblo, *Elecciones 2000: Informe de la Supervisión de la Defensoría del Pueblo* (Lima: Defensoría del Pueblo, 2000).

54. *Gestión*, January 20, 2000.

55. *La República*, February 20, 2000; February 21, 2000.

56. *La República*, February 22, 2000.

57. Congreso de la República, Primera Legislatura Ordinaria de 2001, December 20, 2001.

58. *El Comercio*, February 29, 2000. For an extensive interview with Rodríguez, see *El Comercio*, March 1, 2000.

59. Martínez identified the chief of the Arequipa office of ONPE as one of the organizers of the forgery operation. In addition, she identified a Vamos Vecino city councilwoman and C90-NM congresswoman María Jesus Espinoza. See *El Comercio*, March 19, 2000.

60. *El Comercio*, March 1, 2000; *La República*, March 2, 2000.

61 *La República*, March 10, 2000.

62. *Expreso*, March 4, 2000.

63. *La República*, March 4, 2000.

64. *El Comercio*, March 14, 2000.

65. *La República*, March 15, 2000.

66. *Gestión*, March 3, 2000.

67. *Expreso*, February 15, 2000; February 20, 2000.

68. *Gestión*, February 15, 2000.

69. *Gestión*, March 9, 2000.

70. *Gestión*, March 8, 2000.

71. See Organización de los Estados Americanos, Misión de Observación Electoral, Elecciones Generales República del Perú Año 2000, Boletín 1 (March 10, 2000); Boletín 2 (March 17, 2000); Boletín 3 (March 23, 2000).

72. Portillo's statements were reported in *Gestión*, March 28, 2000. Stein's response appeared in *El Comercio*, March 30, 2000.

73. *La República*, March 20, 2000. Tudela's comments prompted an acidic reply from NDI official Gerardo Chevalier: "Señor Tudela took off his tie as foreign minister to put on one of an *ayayero*" the colloquial term used by Fujimori that meant "sycophant"; *Expreso*, March 25, 2000.

74. National Democratic Institute–The Carter Center, "NDI/Carter Center Pre-Election Statement—March 24, 2000" in *Peru Elections 2000: Final Report of the National Democratic Institute/Carter Center Joint Election Monitoring Project*, The Carter Center, http://cartercenter.org/documents/292.pdf (accessed August 1, 2003).

75. *Expreso,* March 27, 2000.

76. *Expreso,* March 28, 2000.

77. *Gestión,* March 29, 2000.

78. *Gestión,* March 30, 2000.

79. *Gestión,* March 31, 2000.

80. *Gestión,* March 30, 2000.

81. Julio F. Carrión, "Fujimori at a Standstill, Toledo on the Move," *Peru Election 2000,* http://qsilver.queensu.ca/csd/peru2000/trends/t5.shtml (accessed July 19, 2002; site now discontinued).

82. *La República,* April 5, 2000.

83. For an overview of the reports of abuses during the week leading up to the election, see Catherine M. Conaghan, "The Final Days of Campaign 2000," *Peru Election 2000,* http://qsilver.queensu.ca/csd/peru2000/in-site (accessed April 15, 2000; site now discontinued).

84. Organización de los Estados Americanos, Misión de Observación Electoral, Elecciones Generales República del Perú, Boletín 6 (April 7, 2000).

Chapter 9: Reelection and Resistance

1. Montesinos made the comments in a conversation with Callao mayor Alex Kouri and television station owner José Francisco Crousillat in January 2000. See Congreso de la República, Segunda Legislatura Ordinaria de 2000, "Transcripción del video #1822, Reunión Kouri—Crousillat—Dr.," January 27, 2000.

2. *Liberación,* April 7, 2000.

3. Apoyo and CPI exit polls respectively gave Toledo a 1.6 percentage point lead, showing Toledo with 45.2 percent and 46.2 percent of the vote to 43.6 percent and 44.6 percent of the vote for Fujimori, respectively. The exit poll by Datum gave a bigger margin to Toledo, with his victory at 48.5 percent of the vote to Fujimori's 42.7 percent of the vote.

4. Stein was astonished at the suspension of the vote count. He observed: "In my own experience, I know of no other country in the hemisphere where computer centers close for an entire morning the day after the election. There should have been a second shift prepared so that computing could have gone on uninterrupted until it was finished." *La República,* April 11, 2000.

5. *Gestión,* April 11, 2000.

6. Ibid.

7. The U.S. reactions were reported in *El Comercio,* April 12, 2000.

8. *La República,* April 12, 2000; April 13, 2000.

9. Stein said that individuals involved in the operation, recruited from the Instituto Nacional de Estadística, revealed these facts to him in 2001 when he had returned as the head of the 2001 OAS election mission. See the interview with Stein, "Stein: Sí hubo fraude en el 2000," *La República,* April 7, 2001. To date, Montesinos has refused to admit involvement in vote tampering in 2000. He told investigators that the SIN did

have the country's voter-registration list on a CD, but that the SIN did not have the capability to hack into the ONPE computers. Montesinos did acknowledge actively supervising the reorganization of the software operations of the local affiliate offices (Oficinas Descentralizadas) of ONPE in the week prior to the election to insure that Eduardo Stein would approve the computer system for the first round. See the transcript, Congreso de la República, Primera Legislatura Ordinaria de 2001, December 20, 2001.

10. Gregory D. Schmidt, "Solving a 'Perfect Crime'? Partisan Poll Watchers, Observers and Vote Fraud in Peru's 2000 Presidential Election" (paper delivered at a conference of the LASA-Peru Section/Instituto de Estudios Peruanos, Lima, July 9, 2004). The possible falsification of *actas* was also the subject of investigation by the congressional commission headed by Mauricio Mulder, although no definitive evidence was established. See Congreso de la República, Comisión Investigadora de la Gestión Presidencial de Alberto Fujimori, *Informe Final*, June 15, 2002.

11. Roger W. Cobb and Marc Howard Ross, eds., *Cultural Strategies of Agenda Denial: Avoid, Attack, and Redefinition* (Lawrence, KS: University of Kansas Press, 1997).

12. *Expreso,* April 19, 2000.

13. *Gestión,* April 12, 2000.

14. *La República,* April 19, 2000.

15. *Expreso,* April 29, 2000.

16. *La República,* April 16, 2000.

17. National Democratic Institute–The Carter Center, "Statement of the NDI/Carter Center, May 2000 Pre-Election Delegation to Peru—May 5, 2000" in *Peru Elections 2000: Final Report of the National Democratic Institute/Carter Center Joint Election Monitoring Project,* The Carter Center, http://cartercenter.org/documents/292.pdf (accessed August 1, 2003).

18. *La República,* April 18, 2000.

19. *Gestión,* April 14, 2000; *El Comercio,* April 12 and 13, 2000.

20. *La República,* May 17, 2000.

21. For a discussion of U.S. reaction and the disenchantment with Toledo, see Cynthia McClintock and Fabian Vallas, *The United States and Peru: Cooperation at a Cost* (New York: Routledge, 2002), 150–52.

22. Reuters, "U.S. Urges Free Vote in Peru, Monitoring Situation," *ABC News,* http://abcnews.go.com/wire/World/reuters20000519_2967html (accessed May 19, 2000).

23. Clifford Kraus summarized the concerns: "Should Mr. Toledo and Mr. Fujimori hold firm the Clinton administration and the Organization of American States would be put in the difficult position of having to validate an uncontested re-election victory or reject it because of irregularities. A decision to reject the election could lead the United States Congress and the Organization of American States to apply economic and political sanctions to Peru, which would be damaging not only to the country's weak economy but to its alliance with Washington in the fight against cocaine." See his story, "Challenger Predicts Fraud and Drops from Peru Race," *New York Times,* May 19, 2000.

24. Salazar revealed that JNE members on the videos were Alipio Montes de Oca and Romulo Muñoz. The attack on Salazar was the cover story in *Caretas,* May 26, 2000. For the findings of the congressional investigation into the Salazar affair, see Congreso de la República, Comisión Investigadora sobre la actuación y el origen, movimiento y destino de los recursos financieros de Vladimiro Montesinos Torres y su evidente relación con el ex Presidente Alberto Fujimori Fujimori: http://www.gwu.edu/~nsarchiv/NSAEBB/NSAEBB72/final.doc (accessed August 1, 2004): 184–222.

25. The exception was Compañía Peruana de Investigación, a firm that Montesinos used for polling.

26. *El Comercio,* May 29, 2000.

27. *La República,* May 29, 2000.

28. See, e.g., Fujimori's interview with Spain's *El Mundo* reprinted in *Expreso* on May 28, 2000. Also see his interview with France's *Le Monde* cited in *Gestión,* May 26, 2000.

29. *Expreso,* May 27, 2000.

30. *Gestión,* May 30, 2000.

31. The complete text of the speech was published in *Gestión,* May 30, 2000.

32. McClintock and Vallas, *The United States and Peru,* 152.

33. *La República,* April 7, 2001.

34. Stein later explained that he felt compelled to adopt a narrow, "technical" definition of fraud, one that referred only to an assessment of election-day vote counting, not to the electoral environment as a whole. See "La memoria del observador," *El Comercio,* June 16, 2001.

35. For the text of Resolution 1080, see Organization of American States, "Representative Democracy," AG/RES. 1080 (XXI-0/91), Resolution adopted at the fifth plenary session, held on June 5, 1991, http://www.oas.org/xxxiiga/english/docs_en/Representative_Democracy.htm (accessed January 8, 2005).

36. *Expreso,* June 5, 2000.

37. See Fujimori's interview with Associated Press reporter Monte Hayes reprinted in *El Comercio,* June 8, 2000.

38. The text of de Trazegnies's speech was reproduced in *Expreso,* June 6, 2000.

39. Organization of American States, Inter-American Commission on Human Rights, "Second Report on the Situation of Human Rights in Peru," OEA/SerL/V/II/.106, Doc 59, June 2, 2000.

40. *El Comercio,* June 6, 2000.

41. *El Comercio,* June 7, 2000.

42. *Gestión,* June 7, 2000.

43. *Liberación,* June 9, 2000.

44. No such videotapes were aired. Karp was interviewed on the subject in *Caretas,* April 19, 2000.

45. For his reflections on the *marcha,* see Álvaro Vargas Llosa, *Tiempos de resistencia* (Lima: Promoción Editorial Inca S.A., 2000).

46. The political organizations included Solidaridad Nacional, Frente Nacional de Trabajadores y Campesinos, Partido Aprista Peruano, Partido Unificao Mari-

ateguista, Unión Demócrata Cristiana, Somos Perú, Movimiento por la Democracia, Acción Popular, Unión por el Perú, Perú Posible, Coordinadora Nacional de Democracia y Solidaridad. The trade union organizations included the CGTP. The text of the communiqué appeared in *La República,* June 1, 2000.

47. Olivera put the idea in play even before the second round of the election. He announced that his organization, the Frente Moralizador Independiente (FIM), was prepared to present the measure to congress. See *El Comercio,* May 25, 2000.

48. Analysts can only speculate as to why Montesinos did not arrange sufficient vote tampering to produce a congressional majority. He may have felt constrained by the preelection polls that unanimously predicted that the government would fall short of an absolute majority. Another possibility is that resolving the crisis surrounding the first-round presidential results took priority over the congressional count.

49. For Montesinos's extensive testimony, see Congreso de la República, Subcomisión investigadora de la denuncia constitucional numero 6, Comisión Permanente del Congreso de la República, *Informe Final,* January 14, 2002, Lima.

50. Montesinos described the operations to congressional investigators. Members of his office staff gave similar testimony. See Congreso de la República, Primera Legislatura Ordinaria de 2001, December 20, 2001.

51. *La República,* July 24, 2000.

52. The survey was taken by Imasen in the Lima metropolitan area and published in *La República,* July 23, 2000.

53. Adriana León, "Re-sis-ten-cia Ci-vil," *Domingo, La República,* July 23, 2000.

54. Elizabeth Cavero, "Una radiografía de la oposición surge de las calles," *La Revista Domingo, La República*, October 15, 2000. For further consideration of the new groups in civil society, see Stephanie McNulty, "Cada vez más fuerte: The Role of Civil Society in Peru's Transition" (paper delivered at the Twenty-fourth International Congress of the Latin American Studies Association, Dallas, TX, March 27–29, 2003). The clearinghouse Web site called "Opposition" was located at http://oposición.tripod.com but is no longer active.

55. For Montesinos's instructions to officials regarding plans for the *marcha,* see Congreso de la República, Primera Legislatura Ordinaria de 2001, "Transcripción del audio #353," n.d.

56. *El Comercio,* July 29, 2000.

57. For further description of the events of the day, see Álvaro Vargas Llosa, *Tiempos de Resistencia* (Lima: Peisa, 2000), 11-52; Sebastian Brett, "Peru's Questioned Elections," Human Rights Watch, http://www.hrw.org/campaigns/peru/dispatches.html (accessed September 1, 2000).

58. *El Peruano,* July 30, 2000.

59. For the text of the video, Chacón's testimony, and the opposition reaction, see Congreso de la República, Primera Legislatura Ordinaria de 2000, "Transcripción 4 A Sesión," August 10, 2000, http://www.congreso.gob.pe (accessed September 1, 2000).

60. *Gestión,* August 1, 2000.

61. *Gestión,* August 10, 2000.

62. *Gestión,* February 15, 2001.

63. As videotapes later revealed, Montesinos was already recruiting possible successors to Fujimori. He conferred with economist Carlos Boloña and Callao mayor Alex Kouri.

Chapter 10: Fujimori Falling

1. Declassified CIA documents obtained by the National Security Archive of George Washington University demonstrate the agency's awareness regarding how the reelection drive was taking a toll on democratic institutions. See Central Intelligence Agency, Office of Asian Pacific and Latin American Analysis, *Intelligence Report, Peru: President Manipulating Judiciary*, May 20, 1998; Central Intelligence Agency, Office of Asian Pacific and Latin American Analysis, *Intelligence Report, Peru: Reelection Maneuvers Circumventing Democratic Institutions*, November 12, 1998. In 1999, Freedom House placed Peru in its category of "partly free" countries and characterized its political system as "presidential-authoritarian." See Freedom House, "Peru," *Freedom in the World 1999–2000*, http://www.freedomhouse.org/research/freeworld/2000/countryratings/peru (accessed March 1, 2000).

2. The data is drawn from surveys taken in June and August 2000 by Apoyo. The polls were taken in the Lima metropolitan area.

3. National Democratic Institute–The Carter Center, "Statement of the National Democratic Institute/Carter Center Post-Election Delegation—July 14, 2000," in *Peru Elections 2000: Final Report of the National Democratic Institute/Carter Center Joint Election Monitoring Project,* The Carter Center, http://cartercenter.org/documents/292.pdf (accessed August 1, 2003).

4. Congreso de la República, Segunda Legislatura Ordinaria de 2000, "Transcripción de los videos #1347 y 1348, Reunión Dr.—Crousillat (H)—Gisela," February 26, 1999.

5. For example, *La República* published a special supplement, "Fujimori's Svengali," featuring Gustavo Gorriti's investigative reporting on July 4, 1994. Montesinos was featured in the cover story of *La República*'s Sunday magazine, "Mil mentiras y una verdad," *La Revista Domingo*, December 19, 1999. "El Doctor" was the cover story in *Debate*, November–December 1998. Augusto Zimmerman Zavala published an extensive report *El Espía de Fujimori* (Lima: Imprepsa, July 1997). For biographies of Montesinos, see Sally Bowen and Jane Holligan, *The Imperfect Spy: The Many Lives of Vladimir Montesinos* (London: Latin American Bureau, 2004); Luis Jochamowitz, *Vladimiro: Vida y tiempo de un corruptor* (Lima: Editora El Comercio, 2002).

6. Montesinos discussed his views of how Fujimori's reelection converged with U.S. interests. He reasoned that the United States needed a stable partner in the region to help resolve the problems in Colombia. Referring to the need for long-term cooperation between Peru and the United States, Montesinos remarked: "We're going to get married." See Congreso de la República, Segunda Legislatura Ordinaria de 2000, "Transcripción de los videos #1677 y 1679, Reunión Dr.—Delgado Parker—Shutz," August 25, 1999.

7. Montesinos was skillful in cultivating contacts. According to a U.S. embassy cable in 1976, Montesinos received a recommendation for his travel grant from Yale professor Alfred Stepan, who considered him to be the "most theoretically sophisticated of young military officers in national security doctrine." The cable noted that Montesinos had expressed interest in spending time at Yale and Harvard along with numerous think tanks in the United States. See U.S. Embassy (Lima) Cable, "FY-76 IV Nomination," January 8, 1976, National Security Archive, http://www.gwu.edu/~nsarchiv/NSAEBB/NSAEBB37/19760108.pdf (accessed July 1, 2003).

8. Army Intelligence and Threat Center, Counterintelligence Periodic Summary [Extract], "Who Is Controlling Whom?" October 23, 1990, 3417, National Security Archive, http://www.gwu.edu/~nsarchiv/NSAEBB/BSAEBB37/01-02.htm (accessed June 21, 2003).

9. U.S. Embassy (Lima) Cable, "Retired Peruvian General Requests Asylum in Argentine Embassy," January 5, 1993, National Security Archive, photocopy.

10. The U.S. Department of Defense Joint Intelligence Command declassified an untitled document in the National Security Archive with this information. See the document, Origin Unknown, "Peru: Military Unease Growing," December 23, 1992, National Security Archive, http://www.gwu.edu/~nsarchiv/NSAEBB/NSAEBB37 (accessed June 22, 2003).

11. That was the conclusion of a 1992 U.S. Embassy report. See U.S. Embassy (Lima) Cable, "Montesinos: Rumors and Facts on a Powerful Behind-the-Scenes Player," January 7, 1992, http://peru.usembassy.gov/wwwfe10.pdf (accessed August 6, 2004).

12. For a detailed discussion of the evolution of drug policy during the Fujimori administration and the role that Montesinos played, see Cynthia McClintock and Fabian Vallas, *The United States and Peru: Cooperation at a Cost* (New York: Routledge, 2003), 111–30. Also see Julio Cotler, *Drogas y política en el Perú: La conexión norteamericana* (Lima: Instituto de Estudios Peruanos, 1999), 179–261.

13. International Consortium of Investigative Journalists, "Peru: U.S. Shrugged Off Corruption, Abuse in Service of Drug War," Investigative Report of the Center for Public Integrity, http://www.puglic-i.org/story_05_071201.html (accessed July 15, 2001).

14. U.S. Embassy (Lima) Cable, "The Montesinos Factor," July 22, 1999, National Security Archive, http://www.gwu.edu/~nsarchiv/NSAEBB/NSAEBB72 (accessed June 22, 2003).

15. *Gestión,* August 26, 2000.

16. *La República,* August 22, 2000.

17. *La República,* August 23, 2000; August 26, 2000; *Gestión,* August, 26, 2000.

18. *Gestión,* August 26, 2000.

19. International Consortium, "Peru: U.S. Shrugged Off."

20. Karen DeYoung, "The Doctor Divided U.S. Officials," *Washington Post*, September 22, 2000; Juan O. Tamayo, "Peru's Link to Arms Deal Worried U.S.," *Miami Herald*, September 20, 2000; Sebastian Rotella, "Peru Spy Chief's Fall Reminiscent of Noriega Saga," *Los Angeles Times*, October 1, 2000.

21. McClintock and Vallas, *The United States and Peru*, 153.

22. The surveillance program was one of the areas subsequently investigated by the congressional commission led by Congresswoman Anel Townsend. The final report was made public on June 25, 2002. See Congreso de la República, Comisión Investigadora sobre la actuación y el origen, movimiento y destino de los recursos financieros de Vladimiro Montesinos Torres y su evidente relación con el ex Presidente Alberto Fujimori Fujimori: http://www.gwu.edu/~nsarchiv/NSAEBB/NSAEBB72 /final.doc (accessed August 1, 2004): 467–77.

23. Montesinos later testified that Colonel Huamán supervised more than a hundred employees in the wiretapping operations. Montesinos claimed that Huamán demanded $2 million dollars (USD) in September 2000 to compensate the employees for their many years of service. Montesinos said that Fujimori authorized the payment to Huamán, and that Huamán promised to keep tabs on the voluminous materials acquired in the operations. Montesinos's testimony was cited in a report in *La República*, September 14, 2003.

24. The text of the transcript was published in *La República*, September 15, 2000.

25. "Vergüenza nacional y un farol presidencial," *Caretas*, September 22, 2000.

26. *Caretas* broke the story that Pinchi provided testimony to investigators regarding her role, although publicly Pinchi denied the story. See "La mujer que se tumbó al regimen," *Caretas*, April 24, 2003. As this book went to press, additional information emerged that identified Matilde Pinchi Pinchi as the person who allegedly made the Kouri video available through intermediaries. According to Germán Barrera, the person who passed the video to Luis Ibérico, Pinchi had told her chauffeur that she was tired of the wrongdoing in the SIN, and asked him to make contacts with opposition politicians to leak the video. See the reports by Edmundo Cruz, "La historia secreta del video Kouri-Montesinos," *La República*, January 16, 2005; "Pudo recibir US $6 millones si devolvía los videos al SIN," *La República*, January 17, 2005.

27. Jochamowitz, *Vladimiro*, 221.

28. *La República*, September 15, 2000.

29. Clifford Krauss, "Fujimori's Fall: A Nation's Lion to a Broken Man," *New York Times*, December 3, 2000.

30. For Salas's congressional testimony, see *La República*, November 30, 2000. Salas later wrote a thinly disguised fictional account of his experience as prime minister; see Federico Salas Guevara Schultz, *Incendiando la pradera* (Lima: Editorial Planeta, 2001).

31. *Gestión*, February 20, 2001.

32. Transcripts of the documents prepared for the March coup were turned over to a congressional committee and published in *La República*, October 3, 2001. Carlos Boloña adamantly denied any direct involvement in the plot. Boloña appeared in a video with Montesinos, recorded in 1999, in which they discuss his possible candidacy for the presidency in 2005, but there was no discussion of any contingency plans for a coup.

33. Montesinos conversed with an unidentified individual in June regarding the

contingency plans for a coup. For the transcript of the conversation, see Congreso de la República, Primera Legislatura Ordinaria de 2001, "Transcripción del audio #351-A/351-B," n.d.

34. Prosecutor Nina Rodríguez closed the investigation just eleven days after the Kouri video was broadcast. "El destape de la corrupción," *Gestión,* December 3, 2000. Alberto Kouri later testified that Montesinos summoned him to SIN headquarters after the video surfaced and had him meet with Prosecutor Rodríguez and Supreme Court Justice Alejandro Rodríguez Medrano who assured him that his case would be taken care of. Kouri said that Montesinos supervised Kouri in writing his affidavit. Kouri's testimony is cited in Comisión Investigadora de la influencia irregular ejercida durante el gobierno de Alberto Fujimori Fujimori (1990–2000) sobre el poder judicial, ministerio público y otros poderes e instituciones del estado vinculadas a la administración de justicia, *Informe Preliminar,* December 12, 2001, Lima, 43.

35. Anthony Faiola, "Army Played a 'Key Role' in Departure of Fujimori," *Washington Post,* September 18, 2000; Faiola, "How Fujimori's Power Unraveled," *Washington Post,* September 24, 2000.

36. The transcript of the speech was published in *La República,* September 17, 2000.

37. In an audio recording, Montesinos discussed political strategies for the second round of the election with an unidentified individual. The audio was taped on April 12, 2000. During the conversation, Montesinos mentioned that Fujimori floated the idea of resigning. For the transcript, see Congreso de la República, Primera Legislatura Ordinaria de 2001, "Transcripción del audio B/1-B," n.d.

38. Montesinos later denied that the money was for his personal use. He said that Fujimori told his ministers that it was to go to Montesinos, but Fujimori expected it to be deposited abroad for his own use in his 2006 reelection campaign. In November, Fujimori returned $15 million in cash, but Montesinos claimed that the cash returned did not match the serial numbers and denominations of the original money. See his testimony in Congreso de la República, Segunda Legislatura Ordinaria de 2001, April 25, 2002.

39. The U.S. and OAS decisions to facilitate Montesinos's flight evoked criticism in Peru and abroad. See Andres Oppenheimer, "Global Justice for Peru Exile," *Miami Herald,* September 28, 2000.

40. The photograph, originally published by *El Panama América,* was widely disseminated by the Associated Press and other news agencies. The varying interpretations of each of the elements in the photo were analyzed by Mark Shapiro, "Postcards from the Edge: Applying Kremlinology to Peruvian Spymaster Vladimiro Montesinos," *Harper's,* January 2001, 74–75.

41. Reportedly, General Pace visited separately with the defense minister, General Carlos Bergamino and the armed forces chief, General José Villanueva Ruesta. Pace advised the officials to cooperate with the OAS mission on the transition. See Kevin Hall, "Military in Peru Continues Coup Threat," *Miami Herald,* September 27, 2000.

42. John Lancaster, "Fujimori Makes Surprise Visit to Washington," *Washington Post,* September 29, 2000.

43. Portions of Helms's letter were published in *Gestión,* October 6, 2000.

44. First Lady Keiko Sofia and cabinet president Federico Salas said that the trip had quashed the prospects of a coup; *Gestión,* October 2, 2000.

45. "El poder tras el fono," *Caretas,* October 12, 2000.

46. "Vladimiro Montesinos revela que regresó al Perú porque lo iban a matar," *Radio Programas del Perú Notícias,* October 24, 2000.

47. *Gestión,* October 24, 2000.

48. S.R. 155, 106th Cong. *Congressional Record* (October 24, 2000): S10931-S10932.

49. Huamán was arrested during the search and Fujimori spoke privately with him. See Ana Véliz, "Fujimori sólo buscaba videos y documents que lo comprometían," *La República,* September 5, 2000.

50. "La fuga de Vladimiro," *Caretas,* December 14, 2000; "La aventura del marinero," *Caretas,* December 21, 2000.

51. Organización de Los Estados Americanos, "Tercer Informe Provisional a los Cacilleres de La OEA sobre las actividades de la Mision de Alto Nivel al Perú," November 10, 2000.

52. Fujimori insisted that he knew nothing of the corruption, despite the longstanding questions about Montesinos's income; see "Y la era de inocencia," *Caretas,* November 9, 2000.

53. Susana Higuchi, Fujimori's ex-wife, dismissed the story, noting Fujimori had not yet met Montesinos in the year that Escobar claimed to have made the donation.

54. "Pruebas y trabas," *Caretas,* November 16, 2000.

55. Elizabeth Cavero, "Los auténticos decadents," *La Revista Domingo, La República,* November 26, 2000.

56. Justice Minister José Alberto Bustamante testified that Fujimori took several of Montesinos's suitcases when he fled; see the report in *Radio Programas del Perú Notícias,* February 25, 2001. On Fujimori's flight, see "Mecida y fuga," *Caretas,* November 24, 2000.

57. Commentators immediately saw the parallel; see Rossana Echeandía, "Del bacalao a la gripe asiática," *El Comercio,* November 20, 2000.

58. Historian Nelson Manrique pointed out that the only other president to flee while in office was Mariano Ignacio Prado, who left in 1879 during Peru's war with Chile, ostensibly to search for foreign loans in Ecuador. Several days later, Nicolás de Piérola overthrew the Prado government in the president's absence.

59. "Mensaje a la Nación del Señor Valentín Paniagua Corazo, al asumir su cargo," *La Gaceta,* November 26, 2000.

Chapter 11: Everybody Knew

1. By August 2002, 83 persons were jailed in connection with corruption charges, 72 were under arrest, 892 were under orders to appear in court cases, 110 suspects were being sought, and 7 individuals faced extradition proceedings in other countries.

A total of 1,475 persons were being investigated or tried in the judicial system. The figures are from *El Comercio,* August 27, 2002. For a reflection on the video scandal, see Alberto Fuguet, "This Revolution Is Being Televised," *New York Times Magazine,* February 25, 2001, 34–37.

2. *Gestión,* February 2, 2001. Fujimori's remark is reminiscent of the one made by John Dean during the Watergate scandal when he advised President Nixon that there was a "cancer growing on his presidency."

3. Congreso de la República, Primera Legislatura Ordinaria de 2001, December 20, 2001.

4. The idea of "weird transparency" is taken from the insightful analysis of presidential hypocrisy in the Bush administration; see Mark Crispin Miller, *The Bush Dyslexicon: Observations on a National Disorder* (New York: W. W. Norton, 2002).

5. Fujimori made the admission in 2003, speculating that Montesinos had cooked up the absurd media campaign to sabotage his reelection. See "Chino en Kamiya," *Caretas,* October 24, 2003.

6. Major Santiago Martín Rívas made the observation; see "Confesiones de un sicario," *Caretas,* September 25, 2004.

7. Central Intelligence Agency, Office of Asian Pacific and Latin American Analysis, "Intelligence Report, Peru: Reelection Maneuvers Circumventing Democratic Institutions," November 12, 1998, National Security Archive. For further discussion of the legitimacy issue, see Jane Marcus-Delgado, "El fin de Alberto Fujimori: Un estudio de legitimidad presidencial," in the book by Jane Marcus-Delgado and Martín Tanaka, *Lecciones del final del fujimorismo: La legitimidad presidencial y la acción política* (Lima: Instituto de Estudios Peruanos, 2001), 9–56.

8. For an analysis that focuses on the problematic behavior of parties, see Steve Levitsky and Maxwell Cameron, "Democracy without Parties? Political Parties and Regime Change in Fujimori's Peru," *Latin American Politics and Society* 45, no. 3 (Fall 2003): 1–34; Maxwell A. Cameron, "Endogenous Regime Breakdown: The Vladi-videos and the Fall of Peru's Fujimori" and Kenneth M. Roberts, "Do Parties Matter? Lessons from the Fujimori Experience," both in *The Fujimori Legacy,* ed. Julio Carrión (University Park, PA: Pennsylvania State University Press, forthcoming). For another analysis of the opposition's debilities, see Martín Tanaka, "¿Crónica de una muerte anunciada? Determinismo, voluntarismo, actors y poderes estructurales en el Perú, 1980–2000," in *Lecciones del final del fujimorismo,* 57–112.

9. On NGOs and nonstate diplomacy in the Peruvian transition, see Diego García Sayan, "La tenaza de la democracia y los derechos humanos," *Foreign Affairs En Español* (Fall–Winter 2002), http://www.foreignaffairs-esp.org (accessed September 1, 2003).

10. The subject was the Clinton presidency; see Christopher Hitchens, *No One Left to Lie To: The Values of the Worst Family* (London: Verso, 2000).

11. The notion of "subjective crisis" is taken from Alan Knight, "Historical and Theoretical Considerations," in *Elite Crises and the Origins of Regimes,* ed. Mattei Dogan and John Higley (Oxford: Rowman & Littlefield, 1998), 32. For further analy-

ses of the final crisis, see Carmen Rosa Balbi and David Scott Palmer, "Political Earthquake: The 70 Days that Shook Peru," *LASA Forum* 31, no. 4 (Winter 2001): 7–11; Cameron, "Endogenous Regime Breakdown"; and Carlos Basombrío, "Peru: The Collapse of 'Fujimorismo,'" in *The Crisis of Democratic Governance in the Andes*, ed. Cynthia Arnson (Washington DC: Woodrow Wilson International Center for Scholars, 2001), 11-32.

12. Comisión de La Verdad y Reconciliación, "La década de los noventa y los dos gobiernos de Alberto Fujimori," *Informe Final*, 59, http://www.cverdad.org.pe/final (accessed October 1, 2003). For the latest investigative reporting about conduct of army intelligence during the counterinsurgency war in the 1980s and 1990s, see Ricardo Uceda, *Muerte en el pentagonito: Los cementerios secretos del ejército peruano* (Bogotá: Planeta, 2004). For a history of the conflict, see Steve J. Stern, *Shining and Other Paths: War and Society in Peru, 1980–1995* (Durham, NC: Duke University Press, 1998); Cynthia McClintock, *Revolutionary Movements in Latin America: El Salvador's FMLN and Peru's Shining Path* (Washington DC: United States Institute of Peace, 1998); David Scott Palmer, ed., *The Shining Path of Peru* (New York: St. Martin's Press, 1992).

13. Steve Ellner, "The Contrasting Variants of the Populism of Hugo Chávez and Alberto Fujimori," *Journal of Latin American Studies* 35 (2003): 139–62.

14. For a complete discussion of the evolution of public opinion and how the changing salience of different issues affected support for Fujimori, see Susan C. Stokes, *Mandates and Democracy: Neoliberalism by Surprise in Latin America* (Cambridge: Cambridge University Press, 2001). Mirko Lauer argued that Fujimorismo achieved a "social hegemony" in Peru that lasted until the struggle around the 2000 election. For a panoramic view of the problems affecting Peru in this period, see Francisco Sagasti, Pepi Patrón, Max Hernandez, and Nicolas Lynch, *Democracy and Good Government: Towards Democratic Governance in Peru,* 3d ed. (Lima: Agenda Perú, Peru Monitor, 2001).

15. Frank Bonilla coined the term in his study of Venezuela, *The Failure of Elites* (Cambridge, MA: MIT Press, 1970). Elite failure has been a major theme in recent Social Science Research Council workshops on the crisis in the Andes led by Paul Drake and Eric Hershberg. See Paul W. Drake and Eric Hershberg, "The Crisis of State-Society Relations in the Post-1980s Andes" (paper presented at the Twenty-fourth International Congress of the Latin American Studies Association, Dallas, TX, March 27–29, 2003).

16. Leonardo Avritzer, *Democracy and the Public Space in Latin America* (Princeton, NJ: Princeton University Press, 2002), 63–76.

17. Congreso de la República, Primera Legislatura Ordinaria de 2001, December 20, 2001.

18. Gino Garibotto, reporter for *El Peruano;* personal communication with author at the Conferencia Anual de Ejecutivos, Ica, Peru, December 1, 1994.

19. Abraham F. Lowenthal, "The United States and Latin American Democracy: Learning from History," in *Exporting Democracy: The United States and Latin*

America, ed. Abraham F. Lowenthal (Baltimore: Johns Hopkins University Press, 1991), 383–405.

20. Cynthia McClintock, "Perú: El viejo cuento de la estabilidad," *Foreign Affairs En Español* 1 (Spring 2001): 19–27. For further discussion of U.S. foreign policy, see Coletta Youngers, "Peru: Democracy and Dictatorship," *Foreign Policy in Focus* 5, no. 34 (October 2000), http://www.fpif.org/pdf/vol5/34ifperu.pdf (accessed April 1, 2004).

21. Cynthia McClintock, "The OAS in Peru: Room for Improvement," *Journal of Democracy* 12, no. 4 (2001): 137–40. Also see Andrew F. Cooper and Thomas Legler, "The OAS in Peru: A Model for the Future?" *Journal of Democracy* 12, no. 4 (2001): 123–36.

22. The Peruvians who spearheaded the effort to establish the Inter-American Democratic Charter served in the cabinet of President Valentín Paniagua: Foreign Minister Diego García Sayán, OAS ambassador Manuel Rodríguez, and president of the council of ministers Javier Pérez de Cuéllar.

23. Organization of American States, Unit for the Promotion of Democracy, "Inter-American Democratic Charter," http://www.upd.oas.org (accessed August 1, 2004).

24. Fujimori faces an uphill battle in the effort to salvage his reputation. The U.N. Subcommittee on Human Rights issued a report naming Fujimori as one of the most corrupt living former presidents. He shared the distinction with Serbia's Slobodan Milosevic, Ukraine's Pavel Lazarenko, the Philippines' Joseph Estrada, and Nicaragua's Arnoldo Alemán. The study was based on data from Transparency International. The findings were reported in "Fujimori, Nicaragua's Alemán on World Corruption List," *EFE,* August 5, 2004.

INDEX

manipulation, 161, 273n12; polls, 153; takeover, 152. *See also* Ivcher, Baruch
Freedom Forum, 159
Freedom House, 152, 173, 220
freedom of the press, 23, 36; Bareto-La Rosa case, 148; Fujimori, 140–41; government manipulation, 158–59, 161, 167; hostage crisis, 146; international notice, 173, 177. *See also* media
Frente Democrático (FREDEMO), 45
Frente Democrático Nacional de Mujeres, 214
Frente Independiente Moralizador (FIM), 45, 47, 228, 269n18
Frente Independiente Nacional Perú 2000, 180
Frente Nacional de Trabajadores y Campesinos (FRENATRACA), 45, 47
Freundt, Jaime, 67, 70
Fuerzas Armadas Revolucionarias de Colombia (FARC), 225
Fuj-cuadernos, 92
Fujimori, Keiko Sofia, 2, 229, 231, 233, 237
Fujimori, Rosa, 86, 120
Fujimori, Santiago, 26, 42, 88, 119, 167
Fujimorismo, 4, 134, 158, 186, 252; *Fujimorismo sin Fujimori (Fujimorisimo Lite)*, 95

Gamarra, Enrique, 47
Garciá, Alan, 16–18, 20, 28, 29, 32. *See also* Alianza Revolucionaria Popular Americana (APRA)
García, Carlos, 17, 38
García, Iván, 143
García, José, 127
García Belaúnde, Víctor, 191
García Sayán, Diego, 206
Gavíria, César: democratic reforms, 207–8, 210, 226; elections, 97–99; La Marcha de los Cuatro Suyos, 218; MOE, 183; removal of Montesinos, 233, 237, 239. *See also* Organization of American States (OAS)
Gente, 150
Gestión, 22, 160
Gilman, Benjamin, 152; U.S. House Resolution, 57, 153
Giusti, Carlos, 74, 278n22
Global Televisión, 146

Goldenberg, Efraín, 97
golpe de estado, 27, 33–35, 265n10
Gonzales Reátegui, Tomás, 92
Gorriti, Gustavo, 28–29, 209, 263n14
Governability Pact, 171
Grompone, Romeo, 8
Gros Espiell, Héctor, 37, 38–40, 50
Grupo Colina: amnesty, 147; Barrios Altos case, 105, 107, 246; La Cantuta, 72–73, death squad, 68, 248; Dirección de Inteligencia de Ejército (DINTE), 73; 144; Montesinos, 244
Guerrero, Luis, 166
Gullo, Marcelo, 150
Gutiérrez, Miguel, 146
Guzmán, Abimael, 32, 54, 62. *See* Sendero Luminoso

Habermas, Jürgen, 11–12. *See also* public sphere; wild complex
Hamilton, John: *El Comercio*, 182; Montesinos, 178, 229, 233, 235; Transparencia, 180, 193
Helfer, Gloria, 25, 51, 67, 69
Helms, Jesse, 152, 153, 174, 235; Resolution 209, 174
Hermoza, Carlos, 142
Hermoza Ríos, General Nicolás de Bari: La Cantuta, 67, 68, 70; corruption, 119, 142, 145, 244; coup, 31; hostage crisis, 129; media, 150; retirement, 165. *See also* Grupo Colina
Hernández, Walter, 133, 168
Hidelbrandt, César: 1990 election coverage, 19, 20; harassment, 144, 155, 158; Plan Bermuda, 145, 280n2
Hidelbrandt, Martha: Carter Center-NDI Mission, 184; congressional president, 213, 241; Fujimori, 236; reelection project, 122, 128, 129
Higuchi de Fujimori, Susana, 25; congressional candidate, 194, 228; family corruption, 31, 85–88, 120, 246, 248. *See also Ley Susana*
honor pledge, 212. *See also* Montesinos, Vladimiro
Hora 20, 197, 201, 231
hostage crisis, 125–26, 128–29, 146
Hotel Country Club, 225, 226
Huamán, Colonel Roberto, 227, 238, 295n23, 297n49

Malca, General Víctor, 68
Mansilla, Carlos Augusto, 107
Mantilla, Agustín, 28, 29
Marcenaro, Ricardo, 125, 272n99. See also
   Ley Marcenaro
Marcha de los Cuatro Suyos, La, 209–10,
   211, 214–18, 221–22, 224
Márquez, Ricardo, 193, 234, 241
Martínez, Cecilia, 240
Martínez, Erika, 181
Mauricio, General Carlos, 104, 105
McCaffrey, General Barry, 143, 174, 193
McClintock, Cynthia, 8
Medelius, Oscar, 122, 133, 145, 181
media, 16; Fujimori, 128, 146, 151, 153;
   government harassment, 141–44;
   hostage crisis, 128, 146; independent
   press, 161; manipulation, 140–62,
   282n43; Montesinos, 154, 156–57, 160,
   182; polls, 153; *la prensa secuestrada,*
   168; SIN, 141; spending, 54. *See also*
   Bareto-La Rosa case
Mellet Castillo, General Luis, 104
Menem, Carlos, 5
Merino, Beatriz, 47, 52
Miró Quesada, Alejandro, 182, 248. See
   also *Comerico, El*
Ministerio de la Presidencia, 42, 79, 82,
   230; 2000 election expenditures, 166
Misión de Observación Electoral (MOE),
   182, 184, 188, 191; vote tabulating,
   198–200, 201, 204–5. *See also* Stein,
   Eduardo
Mohme, Gustavo: Faisal, 169; Pérez de
   Cuéllar, 95; Plan Bermuda, 145; referen-
   dum, 63; tabloid attacks, 159 168. See
   also *República, La*
Moncayo, General Francisco, 150, 151
Montes de Oca, Alipio, 167–68, 182, 244
Montesinos, Vladimiro, 222–25; arms
   trafficking, 225–28, 244; betrayal, 229,
   230, 232; La Cantuta, 67, 69, 70, 73;
   corruption, 1, 76, 230–31, 253; *El
   Doctor,* 25; drug trafficking, 44, 149,
   280n5; financial practises, 120, 149,
   223, 239, 296n38; Fujimori, 19–20, 208;
   Fujimori's successor, 219, 232–33; intelligence agency, 13, 86, 143, 165, 227;
   judiciary, 154, 167; loyalty, 57–58, 212;
   military amnesty, 145; narco-trafficking,
   59, 125, 141–43, 147, 223, 243, 246;

political strategy, 146, 154, 166, 189,
   215; reelection project, 117, 124, 178,
   211, 284n1; referendum campaign,
   132–34, 138, 139; SIN, 24, 133, 136,
   217, 280n4; vote tampering, 194,
   292n48. *See also* Servicio de Inteligencia
   Nacional (SIN)
moral incapacity, 31, 211, 240, 241
Moreyra, Manuel, 48, 49, 51–52, 59, 62,
   120
Mosqueira, Edgardo, 167
Movimiento Democrático de Izquierda
   (MDI), 51
Movimiento Libertad (ML), 45, 47, 52
Movimiento Obras, 61, 90. *See also* Bel-
   mont, Ricardo
Movimiento Revolucionario Tupac Amaru
   (MRTA), 125, 146, 174. *See also*
   hostage crisis
Moyano, Martha, 218
Mulder, Mauricio, 124, 136
Municipal Compensation Fund, 80
Muñoz Arce, Romulo, 88, 132, 168, 244
Murgia, José, 60
Murray, Santiago, 85, 89, 93, 99
Murrugarra, Edmundo, 48, 49, 51

Nacional, El, 28
narco-trafficking, 10, 29, 31. *See also*
   Montesinos, Vladimiro
National Democratic Institute (NDI), 177.
   See also Carter Center-National Democratic Institute mission
National Dialogue for Peace and Development, 46–47, 48, 49–50
national security, 4, 28; counterinsurgency,
   71, 75, 105, 119, 161–62, 250–51; intelligence system, 42, 43, 89, 150, 173. *See
   also* counterterrorism
neoliberal economic reforms, 5, 10, 25, 75,
   254–55, 259n8; policies, 118, 251
neopopulism, 5, 163, 251
Noboa, Gustavo, 217
Nueva Mayoría (NM), 52–53, 269n28. *See
   also* Cambio 90-Nueva Mayoría
Nugent, Ricardo: JNE, 84, 92, 97; TC, 126,
   127, 129–30

Obey, David, 72
O'Donnell, Guillermo, 7
Odría, Manuel, 30

United States government, 10, 161, 162, 254; CIA, 224, 233; Congress, 222; Drug Enforcement Administration, 224; Fujimori, 38, 174, 235; Joint Resolution 43, 193; Joint Resolution 609 (House Resolution 57 and Senate Resolution 209), 153; joint resolution proposed by Senator Coverdell, 185; Resolution 155, 237; Senate, 174; State Department, 75, 106, 177, 193, 199–200, 204–6

Universidad Enrique Guzmán y Valle (La Cantuta), 66, 104. *See also* Cantuta case, La

Universidad Nacional Agraria La Molina (Lima), 16–17, 20

Universidad Nacional Mayor de San Marcos, 104

Valenzuela, Cecilia, 71, 155, 158
Vamos Vecino, 166, 181, 240
Vargas, Dennis, 129
Vargas Alzamora, Augusto, 75, 123, 130, 189–90
Vargas Llosa, Álvaro, 210
Vargas Llosa, Mario, 35, 52, 234; presidential bid, 15–18, 45, 90
Vásquez, Absalón, 181, 240
Vásquez, General Elesban Bello, 150, 156
Vecco, Mónica, 71
Vega Alvear, Miguel, 52
Vega Llona, Ricardo, 52
Velasco, General Juan, 21, 30

Velasco Ibarra, José María, 8
Viaña, Fernando, 142, 280n2
Villanueva Ruesta, General José, 207, 238, 244, 285n16
Vladi-polos, 180

War, Rossy, 169–70
war against guerrillas, 23–24, 63, 250
Washington Office on Latin America, 142, 175
Way, Lucan, 9
Web sites: APRODEV, 169; 282n40; Fujimori, 256; Baruch Ivcher, opposition, 215
weird transparency, 245–46, 298n4
wild complex, 12, 141, 221, 247, 249. *See also* Habermas, Jürgen; public sphere
Winter, Mendel, 150, 152, 179, 244
Winter, Samuel, 150, 152, 179, 244

Yoshiyama, Jaime: amnesty law, 105; La Cantuta, 69; CCD president, 56, 79, 259n6; constitutional campaign, 62–64; electoral law, 83–84; failed mayoral bid, 119, 169; and Fujimori, 52, 54, 167; polls, 77; selection of C90-NM congressional list, 100
Youngers, Coletta, 174

Zakaria, Fareed, 6
Zanatta, Luisa, 158–59, 248
Zileri, Enrique, 21, 24, 247. See also *Caretas*